Testimonials or What Others Are Saying about This Book

"This book is deep, sometimes esoteric, yet inspirational and conversational in tone, and peppered with lots of examples that illustrate the author's points. My hunch is you will find the book enriching, and it should be on everyone's Law of Attraction reading list. Go ahead, hitch a ride, and see where this tour de force of a book takes you!" – Michael Losier, Best-Selling Author of *Law of Attraction*

"Not since *The Secret* and *What the Bleep Do We Know!?* have I seen a book that so insightfully connects the dots between the Law of Attraction, science, and spirituality as *Explorer's Guide to the Law of Attraction* does. Jim Alvino takes you on his personal journey and guides you through the maze of how the Law of Attraction works, why it works, and the pragmatics for attracting and creating the life you desire. This book is truly transformational!" – Raymond Aaron, *New York Times* Best-Selling Author

"This book shows that it is the action behind attrACTION that makes your dreams come true." – Greg S. Reid, Best-Selling Author of *Think and Grow Rich Series, Three Feet From Gold*, and *Stickability*

"If you really want to understand and apply the Law of Attraction to your life and business, *Explorer's Guide to the Law of Attraction* is a must read. With topics ranging from quantum physics to karma to setting up a meditation practice, this book excels at taking advanced concepts and presenting them in ways that are cogent and make sense. This is the book you've been waiting for that pulls it all together! – Joe Nunziata, Best-Selling Author of *Karma Buster*

"As an artist and award-winning painter, I can tell you that transforming a blank canvas into a vibrant work of art is a magnificent act of creation. Jim Alvino achieves the same thing in his book on the Law of Attraction. Each chapter displays a colorful palette that at once draws you in, inspires, gives you an experience of the author's personal spiritual journey, and invites you to create your own masterpiece. And like a great work of art, the richness this book will have for you, is for you to determine."– David Lloyd Glover, Internationally Known Award-Winning Artist

Explorer's Guide to the Law of Attraction

How to Tap into the Quantum-Heart
for Happiness and Success

James Alvino

BALBOA.
PRESS
A DIVISION OF HAY HOUSE

Balboa Press books may be ordered through booksellers or by contacting:

Balboa Press
A Division of Hay House
1663 Liberty Drive
Bloomington, IN 47403
www.balboapress.com
1-(877) 407-4847

Printed in the United States of America

ISBN: 978-1-4525-6579-8 (sc)
ISBN: 978-1-4525-6578-1 (hc)
ISBN: 978-1-4525-6577-4 (e)

Library of Congress Control Number: 2012923794

Balboa Press rev. date: 02/08/2013

Contents

List of Illustrations

Explorer's Guide to the

Law of Attraction

How to Tap into the Quantum-Heart for Happiness and Success

James Alvino, PhD

Certified Law of Attraction
Trainer and Facilitator

To my mother and father who always believed in me and taught me to believe in myself.

Foreword

One July about two years ago, I received an e-mail from a guy in Huntington Beach, California, who had just listened to an interview of me and was very excited about the Law of Attraction. "First time it really made sense to me," he said. He wanted to meet with me and talk about how he could integrate the Law of Attraction into his coaching business.

As I was going to be doing a seminar in Las Vegas a few weeks later, I agreed to meet with Jim Alvino over lunch—he offered to buy!—and we spent several hours getting to know each other and exploring whether my certification program was a good match for his business model. I guess you could say we attracted each other.

It turns out it was a great match. Jim is a very creative and flexible thinker. His next step was to become a certified Law of Attraction facilitator with me. I didn't have another program on the calendar in his area for nine months, so he proposed an alternative path whereby I would personally coach him in my model over several months until we both felt comfortable that he had earned the designation of Certified Trainer and Facilitator. He was an ideal client for me.

Jim has distinguished himself as a highly successful Law of Attraction certified trainer who specializes in bringing LOA principles into the corporate world and helps companies of all sizes create a Law of Attraction culture in the workplace. Jim has taken my "how to" method into insurance companies, real estate offices, high-end resorts and hotels, the entertainment industry, and other venues to help with goal setting, increasing sales, and attracting ideal clients and relationships.

When Jim came to me with the idea for his book, tying Law of Attraction to quantum physics, spirituality, and related topics, I told him I thought there was plenty of room for a book like this in the dialogue on Law of Attraction and how pervasive its principles are in creating the life we desire.

Explorer's Guide to the Law of Attraction distills and synthesizes many of the key underlying concepts that explain how the Law of Attraction works. It is the *why* that underlies and informs the *how to*. With a background in philosophy, Jim is a foundational thinker who has a special talent for anchoring his personal experiences to life's universal principles and making his unique journey relevant and applicable to your own.

The reason the Law of Attraction is a *law* is because it applies to everyone, is obedient, and defines and describes how the "vibe world" truly works. Jim's book probes these connections in ways that bring philosophy, science, and spirituality into clear focus for those who are curious and interested in diving beneath the surface with these subjects.

This book is deep, sometimes esoteric, yet inspirational, conversational, and peppered with lots of examples that illustrate his points. I believe you will find the book enriching, and it should definitely be on everyone's Law of Attraction reading list. Go ahead, hitch a ride, and see where this tour de force takes you!

—Michael Losier

Best-selling author of *Law of Attraction: The Science of Attracting More of What You Want and Less of What You Don't*

Preface

It is the ides of January 2012, and I am driving from Huntington Beach, California, to Laguna Woods to pick up my mom and dad for dinner. I am listening to the audio book of *What the Bleep Do We Know!?*, the chapter in which Ramtha is berating one of the creators of the movie by the same title for wanting to engender the same old emotion he has experienced a million times before rather than experience a new emotion outside the confines of his existing paradigms. That's where genius is, Ramtha tells him.

And I am thinking to myself, *When was the last time I had a new emotion? When was the last time I stepped so far out of my comfort zone that it truly was transformational emotionally and spiritually?* Maybe in 1988 with my intense *shaktipat* awakening (chapter 2) or maybe a couple of years later in the No Ego Course, where the *tapasya* (heat) of the humiliating encounter with my own self (small "s") had me trembling (chapter 3). Or maybe it was the first time I experienced the exhilarating rush of finishing the Pike's Peak Ascent (half marathon), having successfully morphed from a sprinter into an endurance athlete, or the time during the Ascent in 2007 when I left body consciousness and entered a euphoric white light.

But what would a new emotion be for me *today*? The truth is, I cannot answer this question because to know, to be able to predict it, would mean I would be coming from the same familiar neuronal-net despite my best attempts at self-deception. When it comes to experiencing a *new* emotion, you cannot plan what it's going to be, what it's going to feel like. You can't *plan* that.

And then it came to me. I was listening to JZ Knight channel Ramtha, and I knew intuitively that I needed to walk the talk, that

I needed to tap into the quantum field, the Akashic Record, and essentially "channel" this book from the Foundation of All Knowledge, from point zero aka the *bindu*, from God's heart, the Quantum-Heart, where all boundaries of the limited mind and perception dissolve—magically, mysteriously, mystically.

Writing has always been organic for me, taking on a life of its own. Sometimes I don't know where it is coming from or where it is going, and oftentimes "I" don't remember what "I" wrote. The conduit is but a vehicle for Truth and its expression. Authorship is secondary.

I have experienced "cosmic consciousness," but only fleetingly, not to the degree that I now must sustain with this intention to create a truly remarkable, astounding book in which you, my reader, will both learn the "how to" as the title promises and experience the depths of new emotion and knowledge at the same time. Here's to a grand, grand adventure!

✦
✦ ✦

I want to thank my mentor Michael Losier for teaching me by example how to apply the Law of Attraction in every area of my life and business. His ongoing coaching and guidance has been nothing less than transformational for me. And a special thank you goes to my extraordinary musician and artist friend Endre Balogh for designing my cover and illustrations and for being a superb sounding board and editor in the process.

—James Alvino, PhD

October 24, 2012

Introduction
From the Perfect Springs the Perfect

Om. That is perfect. This is perfect. From the perfect springs the perfect. If the perfect is taken from the perfect, the perfect remains.

—Mantras of Perfection

It Begins with an Impulse of Intention

Let's set our intentions and desire statements together. You will learn more about desire statements later, but let's jump right in. Here is my intention for this book: *I am in the process of attracting everything I need to do, know, and have to create, manifest, and allow a best-selling, advanced book on the law of attraction and the quantum field.* We'll get to your intention and desire statement in a minute.

But wait. There is a far more significant intention than fame and fortune—two familiar Sirens that have lured and seduced me off course for decades if not lifetimes. And that is to enter and advance the dialogue that we are indeed all one, that science and spirituality are two faces of the same irreducible coin, and that we can access the fundamental nature of reality directly. (However, were this book to become a best seller, I would reach more people with my message! Wouldn't that be having my cake and eating it too?)

What does it mean to be a conduit or a channel? What does this presuppose about reality and the underlying foundation of reality? What does all paranormal psychology and experience presuppose? The answer to all three questions is the same. First, it presupposes connection at the most pervasive level of our being. Second, it presupposes that we are all entangled all at once all the time in a dimension beyond space and time. This dimension is the quantum field, or what I call in this book the *Quantum-Heart*™.

When I studied philosophy many years ago, one of my favorite philosophers was the late-eighteenth century German philosopher Immanuel Kant. He talked a lot about the "conditions of possibility" for a phenomenon or an event to take place. And so I apply the Kantian Question here: What underlying conditions must exist such that we *experience* that we are all connected, that we are all part of the same energy field, that we can transport ourselves to the past and into the future in an instant, faster than the speed of light?

My premise is that the world of the five senses is illusory, that the notion we are independent and separate beings and entities is illusory, and that if we are able to penetrate this veil just a little, we will be able to perceive reality in its truth and in its true manifestation.

I have spoken to hundreds of people from all over the world who long to know if they can really attract and create the life they envision. They want to know how to do it and how it all works. *Explorer's Guide* addresses and answers these questions.

Throughout our journey together, I will from time to time introduce you to my avatar, actually my alter ego, whose name is Sagara. This is my spiritual name, which in Sanskrit means "ocean." Sagara is a spiritual seeker whose destiny is to become spiritually enlightened and fully established in the realization of his own divinity. The tales I will share about him are true, as incredible as some may seem while reading them.

So who is this book for? It is for the magician inside of you, that magnificent magician you knew as a young boy or young girl who was always there, lurking in the background, urging you to let him or her out. Not the phony trickster who entertains you with sleight-of-hand and misdirection, but the real deal, the presence we all sense inside ourselves and of which we are all more or less aware, who indeed has the power to create our life any way we want it to be. *That's* who this book is for. And that, my reader, is *you!*

I want you to read this book with an open mind and an open heart. I want you to read it with the anticipation and expectation that something great is about to happen for you. I want you to know with certainty that if you remain willing and receptive, you will receive all that you need to receive to transform your life. And that's a promise. How do I know? Because while this book is based on and infused with theory, philosophy, methods, and practices, it is, in the final analysis, about *you,* your personal experience, and your divine creation.

New Knowledge Review and Action Steps

So now it is time for you to set your intention, to create your own desire statement just as I did at the beginning of this section. Here is my suggestion for you: *"I am in the process of attracting everything I need to do, know, and have to fully absorb all that I desire and need to absorb from this book."*

Would you like to create your own? Good! Here is a template for doing so, which you will learn more about in the next chapter: "I am in the process of attracting everything I need to do, know, and have to

_____."

Chapter 1
Cracking the Secret Code

*B*efore school would begin and during recess and lunch, Sagara and his friends would play on the "mountains"—mounds of gravel that had been piled at the northern-most boundary of the school grounds that separated the school property from the grove (a thickly wooded area known for its backseat sex) and the local cemetery. There were no Little League fields, goalposts, or concession stands in those days. It was all sandlot. Those were happy days.

Amidst the gravel and clumps of tall, brown weeds that grew in the open field, Sagara and his buddies would search for broken pieces of glass they averred to have magical properties—this one green, this one light amber, this one clear and smooth. "Look," Sagara said as he swooshed his piece of silicon treasure against a clump of weeds. "See the smoke? See the smoke!" And he did see it. It was magic glass that produced magic smoke and Sagara, King of the Mountains, held the power right in the palm of his hand.

Letting Go of What You Don't Have

Some things in life we find. Some things we lose. Some things we give up. And some things we get back. So it is with the power we inherently have and forget. Just like Sagara.

In this chapter, I explain the basic principles of the Law of Attraction as contained in Michael Losier's book *Law of Attraction: The Science of Attracting More of What You Want and Less of What you Don't.* Michael is my LOA mentor. I am a Certified Law of Attraction Trainer and Facilitator with his program, and his method is my starting point in this chapter.

I want to point out something about the subtitle of his book, *The **Science** of Attracting More of What You Want and Less of What You Don't.* This really has two meanings. Michael describes himself as the "how to" guy in the Law of Attraction and tells you how to do it. So science in this context represents a methodology that I call The Losier Method, but it also refers to the quantum physics underpinnings of the Law of Attraction that I will introduce in the next chapter.

Studying the Law of Attraction and becoming a deliberate attractor have been transformational for me. I want to put this in a broader framework of other transformations I have experienced in my life, some of which have been deliberate and some of which have not been deliberate. This will illuminate the distinctions between the conscious mind and the nonconscious mind and between what can be categorized as the four parts of a human being—physical, mental, emotional, and spiritual.

Keep in mind that what I am about to share is *my* experience. You need to reflect on your *own* experience. And you must own it. Also, I want you to understand that the various transformations that have brought me to today, to this moment at the computer keyboard, did not and do not happen in linear fashion. Yes, I can trace the steps consciously from A to Z, but the real work, the transformational work, goes on behind the scenes at the nonconscious levels of our being (see illustration on page 14).

"I Want to be a Philosophy Major"

My *intellectual (mental) transformation* came at college. Prior to that, I had little interest in school. Although I did well enough academically, I lacked passion for most things intellectual (save for maybe public speaking and business law). When I attended Dickinson College, a small liberal arts school in Carlisle, Pennsylvania, all of that changed. I came alive intellectually. Pandora's Box opened, and I tasted worlds theretofore unbeknownst to me.

I had only read Plato's "Allegory of the Cave," but it so excited and inspired me that one day I pranced into the chairman of the philosophy department's office—whom I had never met before—and proclaimed that I wanted to be a philosophy major. Dr. Frederick Ferré said yes. I then went on to graduate with honors in philosophy and received my PhD in philosophy from Boston College with the highest distinction.

Who created this? Who attracted it? I did. This is not the same as taking full or inappropriate credit for the good things that occur in our life (we are responsible for the "bad" things as well); it is acknowledging that we participate fully in whatever is going on. So why not be deliberate about it? My energy created the space for the Law of Attraction to unfold in such a way as to bring me my desire.

When the Disciple Is Ready, the Master Appears

Sometimes we go through periods in our lives that are particularly challenging on multiple levels. I was in such a space about twenty-five years ago where I felt psychologically and emotionally bankrupt. Breakthroughs can emerge out of near or actual breakdowns just as great opportunities can emerge from extreme adversities. It was time for me to bottom out so I could reidentify myself with my Higher Self. Would I have consciously attracted the pain that was to take me to the next level? No. However, I did create the conditions and specifics of my karma that brought about seismic change.

This was my *spiritual transformation*. I met my guru on July 15, 1988, and I have never been the same since. Have I always remained on the straight and narrow? No, I have not. But my profound experiences on the meditation path have put God back in my life

3

and have taught me that God dwells within me as me, and that the heart of God is compassion. This is the Quantum-Heart.

It is not my intention to proselytize or convert you to a particular religious persuasion. However you conceive "God" is your business. If you do not like or use the G-word, that is okay. If you choose to see or not see a divine force underlying all of creation (and creating), this is okay too. But one thing is clear and certain: Scientists have identified an energy substratum that is as real, if not more real, than the world we perceive with our five senses. To become a deliberate attractor, you must find a way to tap into this Quantum-Heart, as it is from *here* that we create our day, our future, and our life.

"I Just Have to Do This!"

I am sitting at the top of Pike's Peak in Manitou Springs, Colorado, groping my way from boulder to boulder with altitude sickness. I am waiting for my wife, Margaret, and sister-in-law to finish the Pike's Peak Ascent, a grueling half marathon in conditions that can range from extreme heat to pellets of sleet (and I have experienced both). And as I watch the runners—actually walkers by this time— make their way the last thirty yards or so to the finish line, tears of admiration well in my eyes, and I am hooked. I am going to do this!

I had always been a sprinter. Bursts of speed, bursts of power. A quarter mile was the farthest I had ever raced, and that had been decades ago. Thus began a *physical transformation* as I successfully morphed into an endurance athlete.

Having been an athlete all of my life, I was no stranger to training regimens. In my mid-twenties, you could find me working out four to five hours a day in Isshinryu karate on my way to a second-degree black belt. I created that, and I created my metamorphosis to a high-altitude trail runner. Not that I did this alone. No one ever does it alone. I credit my wife for pushing me along—a coach, mentor, guide, guardian angel ... presumably like the one that brought me back to body consciousness on one of my Pike's Peak Ascents.

Coming Full Circle

Which brings me to the current culmination of an *emotional transformation* many years in the making (in fact, all transformations have some emotional component), when I was first exposed to the principles of The Losier Method of the Law of Attraction. You see, I had seen the movie *The Secret*, which left me cold. I still have residual images of seemingly instantaneous manifestations that I did not find credible at the time. And conventional affirmations never worked for me.

But Michael's approach made sense, and I decided to embrace it, become certified as a trainer and facilitator, and incorporate it into my success coaching and business consulting. Michael is a brilliant coach and mentor, and it is especially gratifying to know that at some level we *attracted each other* by being in vibrational harmony. Our respective histories on the conscious level are quite diverse, but on the nonconscious level, we are quite "entangled" in the Quantum-Heart and run on parallel tracks.

So what follows is a summary of The Losier Method, as it is the springboard from which I dive into the mysteries of quantum. The goal is to become a Deliberate Attractor, to deliberately, consciously create your day. The goal is to learn how to tap into the Quantum-Heart for happiness and success.

Below, I explain the basics of what the Law of Attraction is, how it works, why you keep getting negative things in your life, how to stop getting negative things, and how to start attracting more positive things deliberately. (For more information on The Losier Method, visit www.lawofattractionbook.com.)

Definition of the Law of Attraction

The law of attraction, traditionally defined, presupposes that we and everything else in the universe are immersed, enmeshed, and entangled in a vast, pervasive energy field. And we attract to ourselves whatever we give our attention, energy, and focus to—positive or negative, wanted or unwanted.

In the world of Newtonian physics—the world of our senses, cause and effect, natural forces, electricity, gravity, and the like—if you dropped a pebble in a pond, the ripples would emanate outward until they dissipated. This is my metaphor for an ever-expanding entropic universe.

In the world of quantum physics, on the other hand, the basis of the Law of Attraction, a better metaphor might be that of a boomerang. Send it off sailing, and it returns home to its place of origin. It is the same with every mood, feeling, or vibration we emanate—it returns to us with exactly the same frequency with which it was sent. A positive vibe engenders more positives; a negative vibe engenders more negatives. And the Law of Attraction is neutral; it just matches vibrations, regardless of frequency. Imagine you are a point of pulsating energy. Your world mirrors your predominant pulsations exactly.

This is a double-edged sword. As a "law," the Law of Attraction is both the sun and the rain; it doesn't discriminate. If we are in its "environment"—and we always are—we will experience our own weather report.

How Does the Law of Attraction Really Work?

It is all about vibes. They are either positive or negative, and you can only have and/or send one vibration at a time.

Every emotion, feeling, and thought has its corresponding frequency that engenders more of itself. Our microcosm is self-spawning. But unlike the conventional understanding of karma where, metaphorically speaking, my ego hits you and your ego hits me back, the Law of Attraction is more subtle and involves deeper, subtler energy levels. Each of us has a kind of *Net Energy Index*™ (our NEI) that reflects our predominant "vibrational charge."

Is Your Glass Half Empty or Half Full?

This makes a big difference. As well known and overused as the riddle of the chicken and the egg, this metaphor speaks volumes about worldview and the conscious as well as unconscious belief systems through which we filter (and create) our experience of reality. If you see the glass half empty, you tend to operate out of lack, fear, pessimism, skepticism, cynicism, defensiveness, contraction, and negativity. Collectively, these personality traits and their underlying beliefs and emotions are called *poverty consciousness*.

Of course, if this is you, you see yourself as objective and realistic. You tend to see those who view the glass half full as naïve, unrealistic, wearing rose-colored glasses, even delusional. As a critic, you may even feel superior to your glass-half-full counterparts because you *know* how people are and how the world works whereas those other poor souls are living in a dream world that doesn't exist. Or so you think.

The opposite cluster of beliefs, personality traits, and emotions is called *abundance consciousness*. Positive thinking, optimism, gratitude, making progress, getting there, people are basically good, opportunity abounds everywhere—you don't understand why others are so negative and always complaining. Neither do I.

Here is what I want you to get: The real significance of the glass-half-empty/half-full metaphor is the *direction* of the water in each glass. The water in the glass half empty continues to go down, continues to evaporate, leaving a parched, dried-out vessel filled with the sediment of regret, recriminations, and I-told-you-so's that reinforce for our thirsty friend just how bankrupt reality is. Of course, what is bankrupt is the paradigm; it cannot lead anywhere else.

The water in the glass half full continues to rise. There is always enough to quench one's thirst, nourishing and replenishing itself until eventually it overflows the brim, and the tipping point is realized in the material world as we attract abundance of all kinds into our life. This is the paradigm of emotional compound interest. In both scenarios—glass half empty, glass half full—we get what we expect. What do you want, and what do you expect? Are they congruent?

Water Naturally Runs Downhill

In Newtonian physics, which governs in the macro-environment perceived by our five senses, water will flow downhill unless it is redirected by a force or conditions strong enough to overcome gravity and/or inertia. It is the same with our emotions and the tendency some people have to love gossip, negativity, criticism, putting other people down, and a host of other emotional addictions that has the perpetrator unwittingly stuck in his or her own mire and, of course, dragging others down. That's the fun part for some or at least what is required for their validation.

Misery loves company. It only takes one bad apple to spoil the barrel. If you allow yourself to get sucked into this energy, even just be around it, it can carry you away in a flashflood of mental, emotional, and spiritual destruction. Remember the glass half empty? There is no quicker way to empty it than to succumb to or participate in negativity, whatever its guise.

Why You Keep Receiving Negative Things in Your Life

I want to share something personal with you. I used to be a cynic and a critic. I washed my mind with gallows humor and felt superior to the rest of the world and too good for the "common" man. I was disinterested in personal development (I had OD'd on formal education, I told myself), embraced negative philosophies, shunned personal responsibility for what I saw as my plight, and generally was on a downward spiral of burn and blame.

Why am I telling you this? To let you know that you can turn your life around in a heartbeat. The Law of Attraction isn't about keeping score, and it doesn't require amends ("Jim, you've been negative for forty years, so now you have to be positive for forty years before I can help you"). No. It is about who you are *now*, what your energy is *now*, what you are vibrating *now*. In fact, *now* is all there is ... but I will save that for a later chapter.

You keep receiving negative things in your life because you persist in giving attention, energy, and focus to what you *don't* want. How does this work?

It All Begins with Language

~~In the beginning was the Word ... oops, wrong sermon ...~~

The words we use—deliberately or not—are very important to the results we get, whether we like them or not. On a sheet of paper, draw four boxes horizontally across the page. From left to right, in the first box, write, *words*, in the second, *thoughts*, in the third, *vibes*, and in the last box, *results*. In The Losier Method, this illustration is used to explain the relationship between language and the life we live. Our words articulate or string together to create our thoughts, each of which emanates a corresponding vibe, which in turn brings about a specific result.

What if we don't like the results we are getting? Well, fortunately, there is a reset button, but first, I want you to commit to eliminating three words from your vocabulary: *don't, not,* and *no*. These are not (I used "not"!) "bad" words, but in the neurolinguistic world, they refer to nothing, drop through an escape hatch in our consciousness when we hear them, and leave us attending to what's left in the sentence that was intended to be negated.

For example, "don't walk" draws our attention to walking. "Don't eat popcorn" focuses our attention on eating popcorn. If I ask you to *not visualize* a pink squirrel, what did you just do? Try Google-ing "no basketball" or "don't search for basketball." At the time of this writing, 826,000,000 results popped up in .21 seconds! *All for basketball.* You get the point.

How to Stop Attracting Negative Things Right Now

The Law of Attraction gives us what we give our attention, energy, and focus to whether we are being deliberate about it or not. This is why someone who is constantly complaining (I don't like *this*, I don't like *that*) gets *more* of this and that. Someone who is inherently positive, thankful, and generous, who carries or exudes a feeling of abundance, tends to receive more of the same. The parable of the talents in the Bible is a good illustration of how abundance accrues to abundance (see p. 87).

The reset button in The Losier Method is a simple question. "So what do I want?" I invite you to notice and feel an immediate vibrational shift when you ask yourself this question. Go ahead, try it. It works! The next time you catch yourself using the words *don't*, *not*, or *no* or complaining about something you have received or that is absent from your experience, ask yourself, "So what *do* I want?"

In short, when the words change, the vibration changes, and when the vibration changes, the results change. You can only have/ send one vibration at a time.

Special social-cybernetic point—when we ask ourselves, "So what do I want?" the answer is typically the opposite of that which we are complaining about. For example, "I don't like being around stupid people." Okay, so what *do* I want? "I want to be around smart people." This is fine as far as it goes.

At the same time, the *act of complaining* itself might also be the "object" to be replaced or eradicated with the reset button. So what do I want (instead of complaining)? I want to [be more accepting, centered, understanding, compassionate ... whatever is appropriate to *you* in the *now*]. We exhibit habitual thought and emotional patterns, which engender more of the same and more attention, energy, and focus to what we do or do not want.

Reframing My Limiting Belief

I have a joint venture partner in the UK who builds affiliate marketing turnkey websites (www.sitegap.com) that I used to resell for him. (In fact, at the time of this writing, he is building one for me for an advanced Law of Attraction training certification program I am developing.) One day a couple of years ago, I was complaining to Paul about something, saying, "Why is everything always harder, costs more, and takes longer than we originally thought it would?" To which he responded, "Jim, I see things just the opposite."

I then reframed my limiting belief this way. "Things are always easier for me, cost less, and take less time than I might have originally anticipated." You see, it is all about attitude! You get what you expect.

Michael Losier's Three-Step Formula for Deliberate Attraction

Remember what I called the Net Energy Index, your NEI? Here is an oversimplified way to look at it. Imagine you have a vibrational thermometer from 0 to 100. Say your "vibrational heat" has registered an average of ninety degrees for one hour. That's pretty hot, you are feeling good and emanating positive heat waves. Somebody comes in and gives you some disturbing news. You cool off, and your temperature drops to fifty degrees for an hour. Overall, your NEI is seventy, you are still emitting positive vibes and there is still abundance in your life, but it is not as free-flowing as it could be.

Before you can fully turn up the heat on your abundance flow, you have to fix the furnace. This is what we just did when we eliminated you-know-what. Now you are ready to apply Michael Losier's three-step formula: 1) identify what you want; 2) give it attention, energy, and focus; 3) allow it to manifest. "Allowing" means the absence of doubt and is the most important step in the formula. "The speed at which the Law of Attraction manifests your desire is in direct proportion to how much you are Allowing" (*Law of Attraction*, p. 77).

You can think of it this way: When you are watching a movie or reading an intriguing piece of fiction, you are *in* the movie, you are *in* the book. The phrase often associated with this is "suspension of disbelief." You *are* Luke Skywalker maneuvering to evade Darth Vader (or maybe you are Darth Vader in pursuit). Now, think of *allowing* as being in a perpetual state of suspended disbelief, where all things are possible and your imagination is as real as anything—because it is essentially creating *everything*.

In the pages ahead, you will learn how you are the writer, producer, director, projector, and screen of the movie of your own life!

If you would you like more information about The Losier Method and how to apply Michael's three-step formula, you are going to have to read his book!

"Whether You Think You Can Or You Think You Can't ..."

"You're right!" says Henry Ford in one of my favorite quotes that sums up the essence of Allowing. It is all about *belief*. Faith. Certainty. Absence of doubt. Does believing make it so one way or the other? What if I believe I can fly or travel to the future? Or simply live the life of my dreams?

What beliefs are running in the background of your psyche like spyware that constitute the paradigms of your world? What assumptions are driving you forward or have you spinning your wheels? What are you telling yourself about your capabilities, your life, your money story, your worthiness, where you belong, what you can achieve, what you are or desire to be? What is propelling you upward or holding or bringing you down?

"Boys, it you want a touchdown you have to think touchdown; if you only think 5 yards, that's all you're going to get." – Joe Pino, Sagara's Jr. High Football Coach

---

If you wish to uncover any self-imposed set of limiting beliefs (and they *all* are), just pick any area of your life you are dissatisfied with or desire to change and ask yourself this question: What am I really telling myself about my ability to

_____?

Asking this question is the first step in cracking the secret code to your transformation. The truth *will* set you free!

What Does Gravity Have to Do With It?

Gravity [gravitation] is a natural phenomenon by which physical bodies appear to attract each other with a force proportional to their mass (according to Wikipedia, December 11, 2012).

Gravitas similarly may be translated as gravity, weight, or as displaying the traits of seriousness, sobriety, solemnness, and the like. Are you an antigravity machine or an automaton conforming to the laws of gravity and plummeting headlong into a predictable destiny?

In the next chapter, we are going to leave the Newtonian universe and dive headlong into the unpredictable world of quantum. Here is a preview of things to come.

Diagram 1
Conscious and Non-Conscious Reality

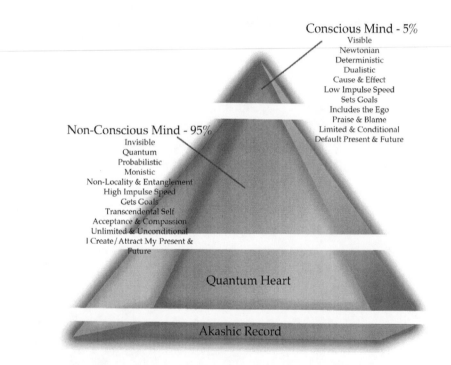

Conscious Mind - 5%
Visible
Newtonian
Deterministic
Dualistic
Cause & Effect
Low Impulse Speed
Sets Goals
Includes the Ego
Praise & Blame
Limited & Conditional
Default Present & Future

Non-Conscious Mind - 95%
Invisible
Quantum
Probabilistic
Monistic
Non-Locality & Entanglement
High Impulse Speed
Gets Goals
Transcendental Self
Acceptance & Compassion
Unlimited & Unconditional
I Create / Attract My Present & Future

Quantum Heart

Akashic Record

New Knowledge Review and Action Steps

1. What is the science underpinning the Law of Attraction?

2. Recall at least one transformation you have had in your life—physical, mental, emotional, or spiritual.

3. List some of the attitudes associated with poverty consciousness.

4. List some of the attitudes associated with abundance consciousness.

5. What is the relationship between words, thoughts, vibes, and results?

6. Why should you eliminate the words *don't, not,* and *no* from your vocabulary?

7. What is the most important step in attracting more of what you want?

8. Right now, I will

_____.

Chapter 2
Which World(s) Do You Live In?

The world of the happy man is different from that of the unhappy man.

—Ludwig Wittgenstein

This book is about tapping into the Quantum-Heart for happiness and success. What are the mechanics of quantum theory? It depends on whom you ask, as there is no consensus whatsoever among quantum physicists as to how this presumed, ultimate substratum of reality actually works. But let's start with what we believe we do know, that is, the universe as presented to (projected by?) our senses.

Just Like Clock Work?

We live in the world of *Newtonian*, or classical, physics, which is presumed to be independent of our consciousness. It is the world of billiard balls, vectors, and forces, such as gravity and electricity; a world of objects large and small with mass and determinable boundaries that can be quantified and measured. This world is deterministic and, generally speaking, can be described and predicted with mathematical precision and certainty. All objects, including humans, are understood and perceived as independent entities that conform to and obey the laws of physics (and other "laws of nature"). In *this* world, the fastest an object can travel is the speed of light.

But wait. Is it really that set and that simple? Not if you live in the world of *quantum* physics, which presumably we all do as well in the sense that *energy* is really the underlying field that nurtures our roots, including the "building blocks" most of us learned about in elementary school (you remember, *atoms*!).

It turns out that atomic and subatomic particles are not so solid after all, that they are indeterminate in their state, mass, velocity, and location, can communicate over vast expanses of the universe instantaneously (the speed of light is a relative slowpoke), and even can be in more than one place at the same time (this is called "nonlocality")—and all of this is *probabilistic*, as there is no certainty about it. So much for Aristotelian logic, which states that a thing cannot be in two different places at the same time in the same way.

Still, here is the real kicker: In quantum theory, the universe is a unified whole in which everything is connected, interrelated, entangled, mutually influential, and interdependent and in which *there is no sharp distinction between subject (us, the observer) and object (the world, the observed). Unlike classical physics, in quantum the observer influences the object observed.*

This is really good news for proponents and practitioners of the Law of Attraction. Not that the state of the universe is an indeterminate and probabilistic mess, you understand, but that *we*, the observers of our inner phenomena (our mental, emotional, and spiritual stirrings) as well as outer phenomena (the world we perceive with our five sense) can alter physical reality with our minds! How do we do this, and how is it even possible?

Let's Get Our Assumptions on the Table

As an astute reader, you will have noticed that I used the word (quantum) *theory* a couple of paragraphs ago, and we all know what that means. Well, actually, *theory* is as good as it gets. Even Newtonian physics is a theoretical model that works quite well in the macrocosmic world of relatively BIG THINGS but fails to account for, explain, or even describe the microcosmic frontier of quantum mechanics. Newtonian physics just doesn't work at the most fundamental substratum of reality.

And as I mentioned earlier, there is no consensus either as to how quantum mechanics definitively works, including the extent to which its principles and mechanisms scale up to the Newtonian world. As early as I can remember in my studies of philosophy, I resonated with what is generically referred to as "philosophical idealism," which means I believe that everything, *everything*, springs from Consciousness. The chair you are sitting in, hard as a rock—Consciousness. The infinite number of grains of beach sand on which you lie to welcome and receive your sunburn—Consciousness. Our magnificent brain, the most powerful supercomputer in the known universe—Consciousness. Some scientists would argue with these assertions (really?!), especially the last one. Some contend instead that consciousness is not the foundation of the brain at all but rather a by-product of brain activity. It is the same old "chicken and the egg" taken to its highest nerd level.

Perhaps the most radical proposition in this entire conversation among physicists is the one that asserts that objects (at the quantum level) do not even exist until they are observed. This "genesis by observation" may be the most significant framework for understanding and exercising the Law of Attraction in its everyday applications.

Among the other interpretations of quantum physics that I subscribe to and other related, associated, or complementary principles, paradigms, or mindsets that I am *aware* I embrace are the following. These are discussed in more detail in later chapters:

1. The principles of quantum physics can be extrapolated to scale up to the Newtonian world. This means *I can alter physical reality* with my mind (through the dynamic of "observation").

2. Our inner world creates our outer world fundamentally, not the other way around (see chapter 4).

3. You *choose* whether you are a victim of your circumstances or are responsible for creating them. Successfully applying the Law of Attraction in your life requires that you take full responsibility for your circumstances whether positive or negative.

4. Poverty consciousness and abundance consciousness are mutually exclusive. You get what you vibrate, you can only emanate one vibration at a time, positive or negative, and you *choose* which one it is.

5. The Law of Attraction is operating all the time whether you are deliberate about it, i.e., *consciously* attracting and creating your reality, or not.

6. At the same time, 95 percent of our consciousness is beneath the surface (see Diagram 1, page 14), running our lives in the background like a computer operating system or GPS, invisible to the conscious mind. *This* at its roots and origin is the Quantum-Heart.

7. We are divine beings. Our creativity mirrors divine creation.

8. And as the subtitle of this book promises, we *can* tap into the Quantum-Heart (in fact, as you will observe, we *are* the Quantum-Heart) and happiness and success *are* attainable, even *guaranteed*.

Expanding Your Paradigms

A paradigm is a set of implicit, taken-for-granted beliefs and assumptions about how the world functions, your place in it, and what is and is not possible for you. (Do you know the difference between something that is *not possible* and something that is *impossible*?) I just gave you a few of my explicit assumptions that bubbled their way to the surface of my consciousness. But what is lurking beneath the waves? The trick to expanding your paradigms is to render the unconscious conscious.

This can happen by design (I can choose to expand my horizons by acquiring new knowledge and/or new experiences beyond my current comfort zone), or it can happen "by accident" (when some experience or viewpoint collides with my current paradigm(s) and seeks to intrude itself into my Matrix-like purview. Think Neo and his first encounter with Morpheus. Which color pill would you take?).

In *The Answer*, John Assaraf talks about our reticular activating system (RAS), the neurological pathway hardwired from our brain and down and along the spinal cord that filters the four billion (yes, *billion*) bits of information per second we are bombarded with in sensory data and whittles it down to the two thousand bits per second our brain actually processes. Our RAS is part of the 95 percent running in the background, and unless we can find a way to reprogram it, we will only let in and "see" what our preprogramming allows us to. So our paradigms have a hardwired, neurological foundation. As you are seeking to become a Deliberate Attractor, you will stretch your RAS to accommodate broader and broader perspectives *as you are doing in reading this book!*

Additionally, the RAS is a system that works on our behalf to deliver what we give our attention, energy, and focus to. But remember, this is a double-edged sword: We attract whatever we give our attention, energy, and focus to, positive or negative. Repeated meditations on "no more debt," for example, may cascade you further down debtor's lane. Fear is one of the fastest ways to precipitate a self-fulfilling prophecy for that unpleasant whatever-it-is you just *knew* was going to happen to you. (Can you recognize the other "error" in this belief system? What is it?)

Here is another example to illustrate my point. If I ask you to not think of a pink elephant, what did you just do? What if I were to ask you to not think of a *scatakioptr*? What now? Hmmm. Would your mind construct *something* to fill the void or just dismiss this nonsense word as a temporary irritation and then move on?

One more mechanism that Assaraf speaks about is our *psycho-cybernetic mechanism*, which works in conjunction with our RAS. Simply put, our PCM is our internal alarm system that alerts us when we are about to step out of our comfort zone or expand our paradigms into a theretofore Unknown Zone. This is a biochemical event that triggers an internal red flag. We can *feel* it, and we have two choices: We can retreat or press forward, much like our "fight or flight" response in the physical world in the face of real or imagined danger. (See chapter 5 for more on biochemical events.)

Quantum Koan: Maybe the Earth Really *Was* Flat

I emphasize *was* to make my "quantum point" in contrast to the myriad of contemporary flat-Earth believers and societies still clinging to ancient and medieval notions that one could actually fall off the earth into oblivion. Absurd? Well, consider this *koan* (*very* loosely translated as "riddle" or paradox): If we assume the quantum "genesis by observation" principle (objects come into existence only when observed), and if we assume that the principles and laws of quantum mechanics scale up to the Newtonian world and apply to BIG THINGS as well as the miniscule and that these principles apply collectively to societies as well as to individuals, prior to *observing* that the earth is round or spherical, the earth must have been flat as it had been universally "observed" as such.

There's more. The earth (indeed the universe) as most of us believe we know it—notwithstanding the diehard flat-Earth advocates—is, therefore, by virtue of our collective observation, being recreated every moment ... right now right now right now and right now!

"God Dwells Within You as You"

Okay, I chose to use the G-word because it is *my* experience, my *experience*, that God dwells within me as me, as the above quote by Swami Muktananda teaches. As far as religious belief goes, prior to the experience I am about to share with you, I was agnostic, at best. But again, my intention is not to proselytize but to lay a foundation for tapping into the Quantum-Heart, which ultimately I came to discover was my own Inner Self. Actually, it would be more accurate to say that I arrived at the insight that my own Inner Self was, in fact, the Quantum-Heart. You will understand why later.

In my collegiate and graduate studies, I always had an affinity for Far Eastern philosophy. The cosmic oneness of it all just resonated with me, although I did not understand it from the inside, that is, *experientially*, until decades later.

In classical Indian metaphysics, there are five powers of God: Creation, Sustenance, Destruction, Concealment, and Grace. These five powers, complex processes really, are in perpetual motion. They are happening all the time and all at once. Imagine you are at a carnival with a cacophony of sights and sounds—colors, music, sentence fragments, screams, you get the picture—and it is all happening *simultaneously*. This is the nature of our reality whether on a small or grand scale.

Imagine, too, that seemingly out of nowhere someone bumps into you and spills his Coke all over you. You are startled at first, but then your eyes meet, and in that fleeting moment, an infinite number of possibilities present themselves (the word is *superposition* in quantum talk). One of them is "observed" (plays itself out), ranging from being really pissed off at the a-hole who soaked you with cola to falling madly in love. The choice that is made "collapses" (more quantum talk) the infinite into the lived moment.

23

James Alvino

A Personal Paradigm-Busting Event

Grace is the fifth power of God. Grace is gratuitous divine intervention, a gift without conditions, expectations, or strings attached. It is always an act of love despite its myriad forms as in the cola example above (the fourth power of God = Concealment), and it is sometimes bestowed by an enlightened being. The guru (principle) is the grace-bestowing power of God in Indian philosophy.

It is July 16, 1988. My alter ego, Sagara, is seated in the second row of a large meditation hall ... but it is best to let him tell the story:

"With my eyes closed, I was unaware that the guru was now moving about us—that is until she or her wand of peacock feathers brushed lightly against me from behind. I was a bit startled and also excited. Our row was next! She entered the row from the aisle softly yet swiftly, first stopping briefly in front of the fellow to my left and then in front of me. I was filled with anticipation, peeking at her feet so close to me, almost touching my left knee as I sat cross-legged on the floor. For a fleeting moment, I had an urge to hug her ankles—a guru's **shakti** *(divine energy) is supposed to flow profusely from his or her feet—but I resisted and closed my eyes again to await whatever was about to happen.*

"What did happen was beyond all expectation. The guru swatted me with her peacock feathers three times on the crown of the head. There was a brief pause between the first and second swats as though she gave me the last two for good measure. I had no consciousness of the guru's movement after that; I assume she proceeded to the next person in my row.

"With these strokes of her magical wand, I immediately felt my body, my whole being inside and out, kind of sink into itself as a wave of **shakti** *from the guru entered me and instantly rippled its way from my head to the floor. Down the* **sushumna nadi**, *the fiber optic-like central meridian that runs along the spinal cord, the divine energy pierced my* **chakras** *(energy centers) like a bolt of lightning.*

"*I felt as though I had collapsed and contracted into a single point, into that presumed state of highly compressed energy just before the Big Bang created the universe, as if such a scientific explanation could ever come close to capturing God's magnificent, primordial act. I remember a slight grunt accompanying an involuntary exhale like the wind had been knocked out of me.*

"(Flashback exactly forty-three years to the day) July 16, 1945, and the first atomic bomb has just been tested at the Trinity Site in New Mexico. The Oscuro Mountains thundered in witness and in awe. The Land of Enchantment has just been shattered from without and accessed from within.

"*My entire body started to quake uncontrollably with tremors called* **kriyas***, which felt like a mild electrical shock. This lasted for maybe thirty seconds. At the same time, I tried to maintain my composure, Lord knows why, and to continue silently repeating the mantra. But the* **kriyas** *overtook me completely, my world was rumbling now, and my voice too became broken and trembling. I could see the shattered syllables of the mantra,* **Om Na-mah Shi-vay-a, Om Na-mah Shi-vay-a***, spilling out of my mouth piece by animated piece until everything wound down to an abrupt and irrevocable halt. (**Om Namah Shivaya** means "I bow to my own Inner Self.")*

"**It was, in the words of Brig. Gen. Thomas Farrell, an 'unprecedented, magnificent, beautiful, stupendous' power that had seared my being 'with the intensity of many times that of the midday sun.'**

"*Then, with a kind of reverse impetus and momentum that was just as inexplicable, my universe expanded again as the floodgates of emotion burst open, and I became like Lakshmi, Goddess of Abundance, showering the field of my existence with torrents of life-bestowing rain. I had never cried like this before—part of me felt an ineffable joy; I was so happy. Part of me felt like I was being cleansed like a man who had just bathed in the pure waters of the Ganges and had been absolved of all his sins of all past lives.*

"*I felt blessed by the guru's grace and generosity, but it was too* much to behold. The thought that I was actually worthy of such bestowals in her eyes precipitated even more cascades of joyful tears."

What Sagara experienced is called *shaktipat*, the descent of grace, the awakening of one's spiritual energy. This transfer of energy from guru to devotee pierced the "knot of the heart," the *anava mala*, one of three taints or impurities that characterize aspects of the "subtle body" in Indian metaphysics. The subtle body is considered the blueprint of the physical body and contains the ego, our conditioning, memories and emotions, dreams, and other psychic functions and phenomena. It is this which leaves the physical body at the appointed time of death.

The *anava mala* is our latent sense of unworthiness, which must be eradicated before we can realize our inherent perfection (or take our business to the next level, for that matter). This is one of the most limiting, debilitating beliefs we can have about ourselves and is the reason the myriads of humanity are stuck in their own *Groundhog Day* movie. It can take lifetimes to clear the screen.

In the Aftermath of My "Trinity Explosion"

If you have ever had your foundations shaken to such a paradigm-busting degree, like standing at the epicenter of a 6.7 magnitude quake in Southern California while being struck by lightning, you can imagine how intense this experience was for me. My neural circuitry had gotten scrambled pretty well. Remember the reticular activating system, the RAS? Mine really got stretched this way and that ... and I also became a believer in the process (a believer in God, in my connection to ultimate Truth, and in my *identity* with the Quantum-Heart. More on this later).

Let's put all this into quantum talk. Quantum events are fundamentally random events, and for some physicists, this even accounts for why we have free will. For example, one never knows where a subatomic particle is going to show up, when it is going to leap, not even when it is going to emerge as a particle per se from its more amorphous energy state that gives birth to it upon observation. Remember, the Newtonian world is deterministic; the quantum world is probabilistic.

As the grace-bestowing power of God, the Guru Principle (GP) is the conduit between the divine soul and the human soul and is the *portal* or *channel* between the quantum world and its Newtonian counterpart and the many, many nested layers of conscious and nonconscious realities in between. Grace is (or appears) random because it originates in the random manifestations of quantum mechanics. Grace is the Quantum X factor. This is why it is so amazing.

So can you *draw* grace to yourself, whether spiritual in nature as in Sagara's case or as other forms of abundance, such as happiness, loving relationships, and money? Unequivocally, the Law of Attraction is based on it. And to become a *deliberate* attractor is to become "be-graced" with and by abundance.

Just as experiments with random number generators (RNGs)— where subjects push a button to generate bits and *intend* that more ones or more zeroes result—have proven that conscious intention can measurably alter statistical outcomes, i.e., register changes to physical reality just as the precursors of thought-manifestation are clear about the power of focus and one-pointedness in materializing an object of desire—*so too does the Law of Attraction reflect a universal rule that we can become deliberate attractors by learning to tap into the Quantum-Heart.*

Creating an Emotional Anchor

In the experience I described as Sagara's, it felt as though my neural circuitry had gotten blasted and rewired, electrical polarities reversed and then reset, and new neuronal networks were created to accommodate an expanded paradigm now encompassing a universe of possibilities theretofore unknown. A new blueprint had been etched into my brain's neuronalnets, precipitating a transformation that you too can undergo with intention, openness, receptivity, and know-how for accessing the ultimate source of your power.

Sagara's cascading tears of joy expressed a *new* emotion for me. Imagine being so joyful that it makes you cry freely, uncontrollably, ecstatically, cathartically in unbridled happiness. I have revisited and relived my spiritual awakening many times over the years, and today this "remembering" serves as an emotional anchor grounded deep in the Quantum-Heart in a presumed dimension of consciousness known as the Akashic Record. This dimension is said to contain all wisdom, knowledge, and information—past, present, and future—and is accessible to everyone. It is the collective memory and DNA of the universe.

Right now, grab a sheet of paper, brainstorm, contemplate, choose, or create anew an emotional anchor, some intense experience you have had in the past and with which you associate great joy, power, triumph, success, love, happiness, or some other recollection of abundance. Maybe your first romantic love, winning a championship athletic contest, making the valedictorian speech at graduation, the thrill of free fall while skydiving, or an encounter with nature's beauty. Are you getting the picture? Anything that resonates with you at a high emotional level.

Bring up the experience, remember the details with as many senses as you can, relive it, remember how you felt as you are learning to tap into and emanate at a highly positive vibrational frequency, which will return to you more of the same.

Karate or Aikido?

In chapter 8, you will learn how to connect your emotional anchor to a new affirmation, declaration, goal, even to a new destiny. You will learn the secrets of neural reconditioning to rewire your brain, forgive your past, break through your karma, and create a new day and new life for yourself.

But before you can do this, you have to get rid of the stranglehold your limited ego has on you with its limiting beliefs and straightjacket-like paradigms that blind you to the richness your life can have in serving others and yourself. You see, it is not the ego that will create your new vision. It cannot, will not. The ego is only interested in maintaining and protecting the same old vision. It is the Transcendental Self (refer back to Diagram 1 on page 14) that does the creating.

I studied and practiced Isshinryu karate for many years as a younger man and earned a second-degree black belt. You can strike or parry, attempt to dominate or neutralize an opponent as one does instead in the art of Aikido. Get ready for an encounter with your ego ... but beware! It is surreptitious and conniving. If you attack it head-on, it will win. In fact, if you attack it at all, you lose! It is a battle that must be fought persistently but gently and obliquely.

New Knowledge Review and Action Steps

1. In Newtonian physics, the world is "out there" and _____ of our consciousness.

2. In quantum physics, the _____ influences the objects observed.

3. I choose whether I am a _____ of my circumstances or am _____ for creating them.

4. Create and describe at least one emotional anchor.

Chapter 3
Kiss Your Old Paradigms Good-bye!

The only difference between the Guru and disciple is that the Guru knows there is no difference.

—Gurumayi Chidvilasananda

The Good News and the Bad News

At the risk of violating somebody's rules or sense of political correctness, men are sometimes heard to say of women, "You can't live with 'em, and you can't live without 'em." The same might be said of the ego. Friend or foe, lover or nemesis, and everything in between, the ego is what we project to ourselves and the outside world as "who we are." It is that which builds fences to separate us from others and maintains the illusion of differentness.

The trouble is, this is *not* who we are, at least not deep down. Our ego is a *construct* based on our conditioning, socialization, upbringing, education, experiences, karma (more on this in the next chapter), and a fair measure of DNA. Even as I write these words, my ego is jockeying for advantage in an effort to make itself look good, to impress the reader. This is my small self, and I can catch him in the act by becoming aware of Awareness, by observing the Witness who is always there in the background (or is it really the foreground?) of my consciousness, present yet detached.

Different philosophical and religious traditions have different names for this, but let's call it the Transcendental Self. And, in truth, I am *that*. But I am getting ahead of myself. Sagara wants to tell you the story of how he came face to face with his ego, Mr. In-Between. As he does, take note of which ego type best describes your own.

There Is *No* Growth in Your Comfort Zone

I have always been one to take my shot. As hockey legend Wayne Gretzky is often quoted as having said, "You miss a hundred percent of the shots you don't take." It is hard to argue with this, so when opportunities present themselves, I am inclined to go for it.

Opportunities in life come from creation, not by chance. You yourself, either now or in the past (including the past of former lives), have created all opportunities that arise in your path. Since you have earned them, use them to the best advantage.

—Paramahansa Yogananda (from *The Law of Success*)

A couple of years after his spiritual awakening, Sagara promoted himself to the front row of the large meditation hall in which the attendees were participating in "The No-Ego Course." This course was designed to allow, even welcome, an assault on one's ego in order to clear a space for the Higher Self to emerge.

Every day for five days straight, we delved into the machinations of the ego, one of four "psychic instruments" in Indian metaphysics. We explored nine impure ego types, nine kinds of divine energy that manifest as diverse personalities. Indeed, identification with the ego personality instead of the Higher Self is one of many links in the chain that binds the soul to the cycle of birth and death, to one's karma. The impure ego must be overcome, and to a large extent this is why one invokes the grace of a guru, as the ego cannot, will not, overcome itself. Its nature is to fight to the death.

A Peek Into Nine Ego Types: Which One or More Are *You*?

Sagara was asked to reflect on the nature of his ego and to describe it, which required taking an honest, nonjudgmental look at himself, as being judgmental is one of the ego's trademarks. Here is what Sagara wrote at the time in a kind of flow of consciousness. He reports with delight that most of these descriptors no longer apply.

"What was my ego type? Was I 'The Critic'—the self-righteous rule follower, the perfectionist always looking for cracks, the angry and harsh self-critic, the moralizer, ignorant of feelings, fearful of making mistakes, who believes that my way is the only right way, and that everyone else is wrong?

"Was I 'The Brown Nose'—the flattering people-pleaser who always needs approval from others; a chameleon without my own center, principles, or values, dependent and manipulative; the flirt who wants to be found attractive, who doesn't know what I really feel or want?

"Was I 'Mr. Wonderful'—the vain and deceitful macho-man; the ultimate can-do guy who believes my achievements will bring status and fame; the workaholic craving success and praise and loathing failure, mired in doer-ship, always performing; one person in private another in public, dissociated from my feelings?

"Was I 'The Sitting Duck'—the internally wounded victim; the hypersensitive creative type whose mantra is 'poor me,' haunted by a constant sense of deprivation and loss; the envious complainer and scorekeeper who withdraws into self-destructiveness, feeling

oppressed and depressed, loathing routine, believing I am special and above it all?

"Was I 'Mr. Ice Cube'—the unenlightened Buddha; Mr. Cool holding life at arms length; the perceptive observer of other people's problems; the lonely, ritualistic minimalist not wanting to get involved, afraid of intimacy, obligations, and commitment; the paranoid who cherishes privacy, is greedy, and stingy, incapable of giving and loving?

"Was I 'The Bleeding Heart'—the vacillating devil's advocate, Mr. Yes, but the suspicious rebel against authority, wanting to be in charge without the responsibility; the procrastinating coward plagued by self-doubt, ambivalent and fearing success; the skeptical champion of the underdog, afraid of my own anger, which I repress?

"Was I 'The Eternal Teenager'—the free-spirited Peter Pan type, craving excitement, whose insatiable appetite and gluttony can never be satisfied; the hedonistic dilettante, unable to commit to anything very long, needing constant distraction, insensitive to others, rationalizing my behavior; a glib and manipulative charlatan and faker?

"Was I 'The Terminator'—the easily bored avenger thriving on confrontation and fighting, needling others; the enforcer of justice, protector of the weak, extremely sensitive to others' negative intentions, never letting down my guard; the high-energy troublemaker who must dominate and call the shots, breaking the rules when it suits me?"

Close But No Cigar

*My God, I am **all** of these things*, I thought, and yet none of them captured me to the point of my being able to say, "Yes, that's me!" At least not yet. There was one ego type to go, and like Pisces, the final manifestation of the Zodiac, it would represent in this taxonomy the last potential incarnation of impure ego types in the cycle of birth and death. Sagara continues:

"One night mid-course, we did a meditation in which we were asked to contemplate whether we were sitting on the fence, whether we really wanted to step into the fire, confront our ego, and engage in the battle that must be fought. And it occurred to me that I was sitting on the fence and had been for a long time in multiple areas of my life. I had been feeling like I had a foot in both worlds—the spiritual and the mundane (I was still thinking as though these two realms were mutually exclusive.)

"On the last night of the course, I heard myself described perfectly. Sitting on the fence, that's me, aka 'Mr. In-Between.' This ego type is the mediator, the politician, unable to make up his mind. Its mottoes are, 'I know what you mean; don't ask me what I think' and 'Scratch my back, and I'll scratch yours.' It checks out to express anger and resentment, disappears, quits, just gives up, and goes through the motions without caring about the results. It's apathetic.

"This ego stalls until it can make up its own mind; it can't say yes and won't say no. It won't be rushed. Neither fishes nor cuts bait. Its chief characteristics are insolence (or was it indolence?) and sloth. It is angry, mad as hell, in fact, and its recalcitrance is its way of getting back at the world with which it has been pissed off for years but won't show it. This is the quintessential passive-aggressive personality.

"The consummate politician, never taking a strong stand for or against anything, as it is not its style to go out on a limb. It doesn't want to hurt another's feelings. It doesn't know what it wants to do. 'Mr. Wet Blanket,' it sabotages enthusiasm by raising questions. It revels in surreptitious power, understanding that its refusal to make decisions is a form of control. It doesn't like authority telling it what to do.

"Sometimes it operates only on automatic, not being present even to its own life. The path of do-nothing-ship. It tends to overdose on food, drugs, or whatever it takes to keep its anger down, the brain drugged, the decision on hold. It likes to keep the atmosphere tranquil and avoids conflict and tension. It never voices its own feelings but puts others' feelings first. Whew! I was busted."

Sagara's Interrogation On the Platform

Throughout the week, people who were well known in the meditation community and across the country were called to step up on a platform at the front of the meditation hall and be grilled by the emcee, who wore a full mask and had an earphone inserted in his left ear. He chided someone for addressing him by name. The general belief was that he was wired directly to the guru at the back of the hall, and that it was she who was asking questions of and making comments to the people on the platform. This was never confirmed.

After Mr. In-Between had been described, the emcee started to ask for three volunteers to come stand on the platform. Before he got the words out of his mouth, I bolted out of my chair; it was as if I had been catapulted out of my seat and to the front. I had been sitting in the first row throughout the course and didn't hesitate at this opportunity one iota. Still, I was very aware that it was grace that had beckoned or compelled me forward. After all, Mr. In-Between would still be sitting there, deciding what to do.

What follows is a pieced-together account of what happened to Sagara on the platform. The experience was so disorienting and traumatizing that I needed to ask two friends from Ann Arbor, who also were in the course, to help me recall it.

"Several of us had rushed up front and were told by the emcee to get on the platform. I stepped to the top and kind of shared the space with someone else. 'Okay, who wants to go first?' I edged my way to the center with just a little more assertiveness than the guy to my left, so I was it.

"The microphone was right in my face and the emcee said, 'It's a good thing you don't have a big nose.' Whammo! Hit me where it hurts even before the interrogation began. I felt my face flush crimson and a rush of heat from my head to my feet. The emcee asked someone to adjust the microphone, but I did it myself—raising it, I think. He referred to it again, saying that I would have to see someone

named Frank if it were not adjusted, which I didn't understand at all. Apparently, I was slouching to reach the microphone, and Frank was a chiropractor in the hall.

"The emcee asked me my name and I answered Jim. 'Jeem?' he asked. And I repeated Jim, thinking he hadn't heard me, not realizing he was just toying with me, trying to push my buttons, and was succeeding. This went on a couple more times until I got smart. But he didn't stop. 'Jeem, Jimbo, Jimmy-boy,' he said over and over in a kind of mock Southern accent until he was finished having fun with it. Public ridicule and humiliation, two of my deepest fears (at the time).

"'Okay, tell us about your ego.' It is full of conflicts and ambivalences. 'It?' It, me, I? (I was going to explain how I was trying to differentiate It from my Self, but I sensed I couldn't pull this off.) My ego is out of control, controlling me. (I felt my face quivering; I was fully exposed.) 'What do you mean?' I just witness it playing all these roles (I had my new relationship in mind), and I don't know how to control it. Fatal mistake!

"'YOU CAN'T CONTROL YOUR EGO!' the emcee shouted at me, and it brought roars from the hall. Several times, I focused on friends laughing at me as my legs began to shake; heat rose from my shirt collar and sweat drenched my palms and armpits. I was trying to stay detached, but I was barely holding myself together.

"'Are you boring?' Yes. 'Are you lazy?' Yes. 'This guy's the Boss of Nothing. He's constantly taking vacations from a job he doesn't even have.' (I didn't understand this. A friend explained later that it referred to the characteristic of just going through the motions as though I was not there.)

"'Okay you're done. Step down.' (I started to step down.) 'No, get back up.' (I started to step up.) This went on at least two more times to the roars of the hall, as it was the perfect caricature of the indecisiveness of Mr. In-Between.

"'What do you want people out there to think about you?' I am *really indifferent about it (perfect!). 'You're indifferent?' Yes, in many ways I really don't care what they think about me.*

"'How would you like to be remembered by this group?' As someone who risked going up there. 'Oh, you're a real sport. Yeah, a real sport. What a sport.' He said this again and again.

"'What do you want on your tombstone?' I was ready for this one because all week others on the platform had been asked this, but it didn't quite come out as I had rehearsed. 'He didn't come back!' This time the hall applauded, knowing exactly what I meant. Take that! You've had your fun, now it's my turn! 'Yeah, well, the way things look, you'll be back. Okay, step down. You're done. What a sport. Yeah, what a sport.'"

The Debriefing

Could there be a more graphic demonstration of my ego type? In less than ten minutes, I had to face and acknowledge either verbally or behaviorally several of my most persistent demons at that stage of my spiritual journey: self-consciousness about the size of my nose; my poor posture; the distaste and discomfort of being ridiculed and laughed at publicly; the belief that I was boring and lazy; my indecisiveness and indifference; the expectation of public acknowledgment; and having to swallow being summarily dismissed as someone who thinks he does others a favor by putting himself on the line. Wow!

It was exhausting yet invigorating. Once I recovered and debriefed with my friends over dinner, I felt revived. I realized that I had received an amazing gift of grace. But I think it took me several years to really comprehend the degree to which I allowed my ego to be exposed and trampled on. Remember, the ego in its array of veils is *not* the highest Self you are capable of, it is *not* the Quantum-Heart, and, in fact, will do everything in its power to block you from tapping into it.

And Now It's *Your* Turn

Go back and reread the descriptions of the nine impure ego types and decide which best characterizes you. (If you are Mr. In-Between, don't take all day!) Use the table below first to rate each type on a scale of one to nine with one being a low match and nine being a high match; second, rank-order the nine types from "most like me" to "least like me" also on a scale of one to ten. Example illustrated.

Impure Ego Type	Match on Scale 1-9	Most to Least Like Me
The Critic		Mr. In-Between
The Brown Nose	1	
Mr. Wonderful		
The Sitting Duck		
Mr. Ice Cube		
The Bleeding Heart		
The Eternal Teenager		
The Terminator		
Mr. In-Between	9	The Brown Nose

"You Can't See the Picture When You're In the Frame"

This statement by well-known inspirational speaker Les Brown is a great rationale for why you need a success coach, and I have used it often in presenting my coaching and Law of Attraction seminars to individuals as well as companies.

It is also a less obvious framework for understanding how our ego, personality, and belief systems (our paradigms) preframe everything we experience. So without a little ego-busting—actually, without a considerable amount of ego-busting—expanding our reticular activating system (RAS), attaining a higher state of consciousness required for tapping into the Quantum-Heart, and having an experience or emotion that is *truly new* are not likely to happen easily, if at all. It would be like expecting a left-handed person to suddenly become right-handed or ambidextrous. This tendency is too hardwired to reverse overnight. But it *is* possible.

The Cemetery Is Filled with Indispensable People

I would like you to take a leap of faith with me. I am going to ask you to step *way* out of your comfort zone and imagine your own death. Not the death of the divine and eternal soul that lives on and on, but the demise of the ego-construct or personality you have come to believe is really you. The man or woman who sees him- or herself first of all as a man or a woman who possesses limitations, flaws, talents, idiosyncrasies, stress, maybe even hopelessness. You are going to kill off this person symbolically.

Recently in meditation, I visualized myself laid out at a grand old age, content, smiling, fulfilled at having come to Earth and discovering my calling and passion. Whatever challenges and struggles I encountered while here were all resolved now. There remained a golden glow of peace and joy. I marveled at this scene in my mind's eye. After all was said and done, it turned out that it really was perfect, and I surrendered ultimately to peace and joy.

I want you to imagine that you are standing at the back of a group of friends and family members who are dressed in black. They are looking at a photo of you in an open casket mourning your passing. The perspective shifts, you are in the photo now, gazing out at those who are still encumbered by their shrouds of limiting ego whereas you are released and no longer bound. You feel compassion for the lives they chose, some knowingly, most not, and you sense the mysterious, pervasive oneness that calls us and binds us all together.

You see your epitaph now, and it reads

_____.

Step Into the Sacrificial Fire

Figuratively, of course! You are going to take each personality trait you identified with above—there may be several from each ego type—and one by one, release it by offering it to the sacrificial fire. This is a ritual, which serves the purpose of infusing an act with conscious intention and meaning. Fire purifies by transforming whatever it touches and returns to the Quantum-Heart that which has emerged first as a thought and then an ego-construct, person, or object.

I have performed this ritual many times, giving over my personality traits, attachments, aversions, tendencies, compulsions, and addictions to the purifying fire.

I want you to witness how much lighter you feel in having unburdened yourself of the weight of your ego, how much freer you are to choose your state of mind, your purview of the world, and what you accept as your vision, potential, and reality. I invite you to sense how much easier it is to access a deeper, quieter dimension of consciousness that you recognize in your heart as foundational and primordial, the alchemy from which all creativity springs. This place is indeed magical, and it is your source of love, power, and wisdom.

The "I AM" Meditation

Now it is time for contemplation and meditation. Sit either on the floor or in a chair in a comfortable, upright position. The most important thing is to keep your back straight. You may place your palms on your knees or thighs either with palms up or down. Close your eyes. I want you to visualize yourself in one of your many routine roles—for example, son, daughter, parent, spouse, company president, employee, bank teller, or teacher. Choose a role you "wear" most every day, and notice what it feels like.

Repeat to yourself several times, "I am a _____"
(e.g., mother, father, teacher, etc.). Is there any stress that shows
up in your mind? Where do you feel it in your body? Can you sense
yourself contract and become smaller under the pressures or
expectations of this role? Are overwhelming feelings associated with
aspects of this role? Are there any negative emotions that come up
for you in this role?

If you answered yes to one or more of these questions, know
that this is the typical experience for the vast majority of the billions
of people alive today. In fact, we tend to take these stresses for
granted as part of the human condition.

But there is also a divine aspect to the human condition that we
can recognize and access by focusing our attention away from our
ego, our small self, our problems, emotions, and stresses by getting
clear about who we are and what we want to become. (Remember
"So what *do* I want?" from chapter 1?)

When we peel away all the layers of our multiple role-identities,
when we let go of all the expectations and related negativity we
carry around and project to the world, when we allow ourselves to
become centered on our incoming and outgoing breath, we are left
with an insight, an intuition, with the recognition of "I AM" as an
abiding presence, indeed power, in which we know with certainty
that all things are possible. Feel what *that* feels like!

This is the Quantum-Heart from which we create our day, life,
future, and destiny. This is the state from which springs the truth of
the declaration, "My inner world creates my outer world," which I will
explore with you in the next chapter. (For more detailed meditation
instructions, see chapter 8.)

New Knowledge Review and Action Steps

1. From the nine ego types described, which best describes
   your own?

2. Were you uncomfortable visualizing your own death?

3. There is no _____ in your comfort zone.

4. Rethink and rewrite your epitaph _____
   _____
   _____.

5. Create your own ritual with conscious intention and meaning.

Chapter 4
My Inner World Creates
My Outer World

The title of this chapter is either very obvious to you, maybe even taken for granted as a fact of existence, or it is one of the most radical concepts you may ever encounter. If obvious and taken for granted, you recognize how your inner life of thoughts and emotions create your outer life. But if you are not yet on the same page, you may be in for one wild ride!

Most of the credit for introducing the notion that our attitude and how we think can materialize wealth and other desires seems to go to Napoleon Hill, author of *Think and Grow Rich* (1937). And putting aside the ancient scriptures of several spiritual traditions, where this principle was first espoused, there actually were several early twentieth-century predecessors to Mr. Hill. James Allen in *As a Man Thinketh*, Wallace Wattles in *The Science of Getting Rich*, and Charles Haanel in *The Master Key System* all advanced the now popular idea, "Your inner world creates your outer world."

In other words, we create our own karma. This is a popularized and an overused word. What is karma really?

A Primer on Karma

Most people understand karma in Newtonian terms, that is, in terms of simple, mechanistic cause and effect. Do something "bad" (for instance, hit someone), pay for it in a similar way (someone hits me back); do something "good," get rewarded later. ("Later" in each case can also be immediate as when we commit a random act of kindness and feel satisfaction in the act itself.) Thinking of karma as simple cause and effect, however, also binds us to traditional moral polarities like good and evil, reward and punishment, deserve and payback, and the like. Karma is not so simple and not so Newtonian.

There are actually three kinds of karma: 1) the present destiny of this life, what we are *living* now; 2) our future destiny *being created* by us now; and 3) destiny *created in the past* and waiting to be fulfilled in the future.

Imagine an expert archer who shoots an arrow, and while it is still in flight, he notches up another one. He has no control over the arrow once in flight, which represents the unexpected, unanticipated, and unpredictable events throughout our present destiny. (Sounding a little "quantum" to you?) This is the first kind of karma.

The archer does have initial control over the arrow that is in his bow ready to aim and shoot. This is the second kind of karma, the karma that results from what we consciously plan and do. There is a target envisioned, which sets the energy in motion with intention and focus. Once in flight …

The third kind of karma is represented by the arrows remaining in the archer's quiver. These represent the accumulated karmas from the past that must be experienced in the future, unless there is an *intervention* either by divine grace and/or by learning to tap into the Quantum-Heart to rewire our neuronal networks. The paradox of the archer is that by becoming a Deliberate Attractor, we can reduce the quantum randomness of the arrows we *choose* to shoot, thereby *creating the karma we desire.*

"If a Tree Falls in a Forest …

"And there is no one there to hear it, does it make a sound?" In classical physics, the answer would have to be yes as there is assumed an objective reality "out there" independent of our consciousness. So *we* do not have to be there in order for it to make a sound. (In a strict sense, there may only be vibrational disturbances, but we can also *infer* that the birds hear the tree fall, the animals hear it, and the rest of nature hears it.)

But we now know that this paradigm is flawed. The observer (that's us or our consciousness), the observed (what is assumed to be "out there"), and the process of observation (the act of observing) are all part of an interrelated and intertwined whole.

In chapter 2, I listed philosophical idealism as one of my key assumptions, namely that *everything* is Consciousness, including the keyboard I am typing on and the computer monitor I am staring at and the book you are reading. You can think of it this way: Just as a spider spins its own web out of itself and then lives in its own creation, so do we.

Or think of sitting in a movie theater, watching the movie of your life unfold in front of your eyes. You are the observer of your life even as you are living it. Consciousness is the projector, the movie with all its characters and plots, and the screen upon which the movie is projected.

From the One to the Many

In the history of western philosophy, the seventeenth century philosopher Leibniz was first to ask explicitly, "Why is there something rather than nothing?" With answers ranging from the Big Bang to creationism to evolution, the "why and how" questions have driven civilization to its multitude of glories as well as horrors.

How the One (a pure state of unity, or Oneness, before "creation") becomes the observed and experienced, the Many (the world of people, places and things as we know it) is at Ground Zero of philosophic, scientific, and religious inquiry of all traditions.

One superb explanation of the manifestation of reality in the Indian tradition—which by now you realize I'm partial to—is that of *Kashmir Shaivism* (hereafter mostly referred to as KS). This is a non-dual, or *monistic*, philosophy (i.e., everything is *one* reality or God, also called the Self or Transcendental Self) that dates back thousands of years in northern India, although it was first articulated in writing sometime in the ninth century. The word *Shaivism* derives from Shiva, the Supreme Lord in this philosophy, and Kashmir is the place where the sutras, or short aphorisms, were revealed. The Shiva Sutras form the basis of KS.

Why am I introducing you to this rather esoteric philosophy? First, to help you step outside the traditional Judeo-Christian paradigm; second, because of its congruence with several key quantum principles; and third, because I have had a *direct experience* of this, in which Sagara has an "encounter of the unusual" on a bridge overlooking a lake.

An Introduction to Kashmir Shaivism states,

> Kashmir Shaivism describes one's own true nature,
> the nature of the world around him, and God. So the
> aim of this system is to help the individual achieve
> Self-realization. According to Shaivite thought, Self-
> realization is the recognition of one's own true nature
> by removal of the veil of ignorance. This recognition
> is the awareness that one is united with God and
> everything in the universe.

NOTE: In the description below, the following terms can be used interchangeably: *Shiva, Shakti, God, Self, Transcendental Self, Divine Consciousness, Supreme Being, Lord, Witness, Observer.*

Some Basic Principles

Again, KS is a monistic, or non-dual, system that answers some very existential questions, such as Who am I? Why am I here?

What is God? How does God become the individual? It is a mystical system whose essence is captured in the very first sutra, "The Self is Consciousness." God and humankind are not separate beings who live in separate worlds, one above, one below; they are united in the heart, as one, even if this truth has been forgotten or goes unrecognized.

This is the exact opposite of most traditional Western religions where God and man are fundamentally separate, existing in different realms and in a relationship of estrangement. God alone is the creator, man is the created, and never the twain shall meet ... at least not on the same level or with the same parity.

Although KS is a monistic philosophy, i.e., everything is *one*, call it Shiva, God, or the Self, dual aspects operate. For example, the world of ceaseless and dynamic change is empirically if not ultimately real, and at the same time, the basis of the empirical world is transcendent Consciousness (with a capital *C*, another name for God), which is more static and permanent in nature as the Witness of everything that exists.

This has a quantum feel to it. The world of Newtonian physics we live in, with its own set of laws governing reality and how "super-sized" objects within it behave, is real enough. But it is a macro-world that is not *ultimately* real. Beneath this macrocosm is a substratum of reality—call it energy, God, Consciousness—which is the foundation of everything that exists, including living things and inanimate objects as well.

This implies that the empirical world of our senses is really an illusion (*maya* is the common Indian term), as it is not ultimate reality (if by "ultimate" is meant the most fundamental, irreducible layer of existence we can penetrate and know). The model of the atom and electrons, which were considered the building blocks of reality until quantum theory came along to supplement this view, is just such an example of a foundation presumed to be true about reality as perceived by our five senses.

The Cosmic Dance

Imagine you are at a grand masquerade ball and have become separated from the person you came with. One of you remains put, observing and witnessing everything that is going on, aware of the Grand Play and all the players in it; the other one of you is on the move, creating this, causing that, rapidly changing costumes between scenes, until eventually you recognize each other and become reunited. As Jerry McGuire says to his wife in the movie by the same name, "You complete me."

In KS, God's static nature is called Shiva, and His dynamic nature is known as Shakti. They complete each other, as they are two sides of a single coin. They are one and inseparable, much like gold and its luster or fire and its heat. This philosophy teaches that the Inner Self, God, and world exist as an essential *identity*. When looking at a tree, for example, God is not merely *in* the tree; the tree *is* God *as* the tree. This also applies to human beings.

The once-secret mantra of KS, *hamsa*, which means "I am That" and which is said to repeat itself spontaneously with each breath, establishes this fundamental identity: I am that Consciousness; I am that eternal, infinite, pure Awareness of Being, which is God. (See chapter 8 for use of mantra in meditation.)

Why We Are Able to Create Our World

Swami Muktananda, who popularized this philosophy in the West through his lectures and books, became well known for his teaching "God dwells within you as you." Let's translate this into quantum talk: *I am the Quantum-Heart*. To tap into the Quantum-Heart, as the subtitle of this book promises, means being able to access the deepest aspects of your very own divine nature. It is from *this* space that our inner world creates our outer world, which we attract to ourselves and which reflects the predominant vibrational frequency we are emanating. Divinity gets to create, and we are divine beings.

At the same time, speaking in terms of an inner world and outer world betrays dualistic thinking when, in fact, the underlying substratum of reality is a unified, monistic vibrational field. This is why a philosophy like KS is so compelling as a spiritual framework although it is not the only one by any means. (I leave it to you to discover or create your own.)

It's All Just for Fun

According to this philosophy, the entire universe is a product of God's freedom, the dynamic and joyful expression of the energetic power of Consciousness. For no other reason than creative, energetic enjoyment, God, or the Transcendental Self, projects and unfolds the world out of Himself and projects it onto His own screen. (Remember there are not two beings, just two aspects of the same single Being, static and active.)

The world is a reflection of the Self, and everything in it, including human beings, contains the same Self and mirrors the divine's creative agency. *The key principle is this: The effect cannot be different from the cause, which means what God creates out of Himself must also be God. From the perfect springs the perfect.*

With the primordial sound of "Om" (call this the spiritual equivalent of the Big Bang), the universe is created and sustained according to thirty-six levels of manifestation. It is a great game of hide-and-seek in which the Self conceals Herself in Her creations. Self-realization means living in the awareness that the Seeker and the Sought are one and the same. Imagine a game of "come out, come out wherever you are," and it is *you* whom you see emerging from the bushes.

The Levels of Creation

The universe is born out of a divine impulse, a flutter within pure

Consciousness that wills and propels a pouring forth out of Itself, much like a spider spins its web from part of its own substance. This sets in motion a multiplicity of events culminating in the complex of reality as we know and experience it.

The first five levels of creation are considered to be "pure." One eternal Supreme Reality, undivided, infinite, omniscient, omnipotent, and all-pervasive. These qualities are more or less the same as those used to describe the supreme deity of many Western philosophic-religious traditions.

The Self's omnipotence reflects our own primary powers back to us: awareness and illumination; independent bliss and contentment; will, resolve, and decision making; knowledge and intelligence; and, of course, action. Or to paraphrase Jim Rohn, wisdom without action is useless. (See chapter 9.)

It's All Just an Illusion

In descending from the heights of pure and unlimited Consciousness, a world of illusion is created to veil this divine play. Duality appears even though reality forever remains only One. *Maya* (this illusion) is the limiting principle that reduces the qualities and powers of Universal Consciousness and produces the limited experience of the individual. You can call this Divine Contraction.

In the remaining "lower" levels of creation, in a kind of free fall from the realms of subtle energy to more dense and sloth-like dimensions, subject and object split up, making it look as though there is an "in here" of the mind and an "out there" of the world. Space and time are born.

And so is the ego. Remember chapter 3? Les Brown has an acronym for ego—"Edging God Out." In the process of creation, God edges Himself out first, and then we do the rest.

Nature manifests with qualities all Her own, some bright, some dark. Personality, cognition, intellect, the categories of perception and understanding, intuition, our inherent tendencies and abilities, the senses and their corresponding objects—everything all in its turn as layer after layer of the Self's creation is born, dies, and is born again.

The Birth of "Me" Consciousness

In chapter 5, I talk about attachments, aversions, addictions, compulsions, and wrong identification. Wrong identification is the same as "me consciousness." Instead of identifying with the Divine Self (the one with the big *S*), which we *are*, according to the KS philosophy, we identify with the little self. I am a man, a woman, a teacher, a coach, and so forth—each with its baggage of attributes, beliefs, experiences, conditioning, and stresses that keep us stuck in our limited view of our world and ourselves.

And what about the mind? That which thinks, imagines, doubts, worries, and so forth. It is the nature of the mind to be active, restless, and full of kinetic energy (pay attention to your own inner chitchat as an example of this). The mind is the origin of all kinds of desires, including our wildest dreams. It is also the source of negativity, uncertainty, and other limiting beliefs and tendencies, all of which maintain our inertia and serve as obstacles to our attaining happiness and success.

The Double-Edged Sword

A double-edged sword cuts both ways. In the act of creation and manifestation, God, Shiva, the Self, Consciousness, _____ (whoever or whatever, fill in the blank with your own name for this) remains pure and "above it all." God is transcendent; He transcends His creation. At the same time, God is *in* His creation, so He is immanent as well.

When the Self contracts to become the individual, it is like steam condensing to become water and then ice. In the process of contracting, Consciousness, by its own free will and for the sake of the game, takes on three major impurities. These impurities delude the Self into ignorance, into forgetting its true nature, and become major impediments to Self-realization and recognizing and using one's inherent powers.

On page 26, I introduced the concept of one's sense of being imperfect and unworthy. As a success coach and business consultant having coached or interacted with hundreds of students and clients from around the world, *I can tell you unequivocally that feelings of unworthiness and not being deserving are at the root of failure for many otherwise potentially successful entrepreneurs.*

This deep-rooted notion of unworthiness combined with feeling different and cut off from everyone and everything else in creation, as well as the ego's pride or shame associated with so-called "good and bad" actions, plague the human condition and is expressed in unique and sometimes destructive ways.

On the Bridge Overlooking Lake Nityananda

Sagara is standing on the wooden bridge overlooking Lake Nityananda at Shree Muktananda Ashram in South Fallsburg, New York. It is about 9:15 a.m. in late August 1996, with the promise of fall already teasing his nostrils. He is watching some guy in a motor boat about fifty yards away scare several dozen geese in Sagara's direction toward one corner of the lake.

The geese fly toward him in formation just above the water's surface. They seem to cover a lot of distance quickly before dropping their landing gear and in a swish coming to an abrupt halt in their new location. Sagara chuckles to himself, thinking the geese looked like animated cartoon characters all braking on the water in unison to a skidding finale. Almost tottering, and then repose.

Sagara is very engrossed in the moment and remembers reading how the Transcendental Self is revealed in the wake of a flock of birds going over. In the stillness, silence, and emptiness left by their passing is the Witness, the Observer, ubiquitous and omnipresent.

Sagara senses a flutter in his consciousness and turns slowly to the left to observe his guru coming down the path toward him, leading an entourage of her devotees challenged to keep up as if they were goslings scurrying after their mother.

He does a double take as this completely catches him off guard. For an instant, Sagara is not sure he recognized her at all. In the act of observing, he experienced a kind of perceptual unity between observer and observed, two elements of the same event, locked in each other's visual field. Then Sagara feels his jaw drop at once in disbelief and recognition of whom he is gazing upon.

In that moment of recognition, their unity shatters into the illusion of subject and object, into I and Thou. Language, too, arises from this dichotomy, as Sagara hears himself say, "Good morning" and then regrets having broken the stillness. Does he think he is worthy of addressing the guru so casually?

But he also realizes instantly what just happened, how in those few moments he experienced all of creation in a kind of condensed, time-lapse photography. How gazing at his guru first without an awareness of differentness or separateness represented the unity within Divine Consciousness before She contracts to unfold and manifest all the levels of creation. How in his moment of recognizing Her per se, how that One, that unity, split and became two and then an infinite multiplicity giving birth to ego and me-consciousness, speech, all behind a veil of maya and separateness. And then "forgetfulness" that there ever was a One as God hides Herself in Her creation, concealment being one of Her five powers.

And then with the same flutter, she passes him, and Sagara watches as his guru and her flock disappear along the wooded path. He is left once again witnessing a seemingly empty horizon but one pregnant with abundance and possibility. And it is as if this "encounter of the unusual" had never happened. Sagara needs no further "proof," though, of the truth of Kashmir Shaivism for him; in his mind and heart, he had just lived it.

It would be about fifteen years before Sagara would realize how he had *created* the experience on the bridge, how he had *attracted* it to himself. At the time, though, this was quite beyond the purview of his world, his understanding, and his acceptance of whom he was and the divine magic he held. But he would eventually get it.

Ramtha, Create Your Day!

One of the most mind-boggling, contemporary movies and books on the relationship between the Law of Attraction and quantum physics is *What the Bleep Do We know!?* (2004). This movie explains many of the relevant concepts that underpin the tenets of this book as well as provides the scientific validation of how and why the Law of Attraction is even possible.

And within *What the Bleep*, a magnificent teaching by Ramtha (aka JZ Knight) on "creating your day" ties it all together with the pragmatics to apply each morning to expand your paradigms and transform the boundaries of whom you think you are into what you desire to become. (See chapter 6 for a summary of these instructions.) As I am using these terms, you may think of *attract* and *create* pretty much as synonymous and interchangeable as they imply each other.

Why Our Thoughts Matter

There was the thought of this book, and now you are reading this book. Our day is filled with innumerable examples of how our thoughts manifest reality, not in theory but literally *in and as reality*. Take a few moments *right now*—your power is in the *now*—to reflect on how you either have manifested or intend to manifest your thoughts in reality *today.* Can you think of five examples?

1. _____

2. _____

3. _____

4. _____

5. _____

Does size matter? Does it matter how large or small your examples are? This may or may not surprise you, but *yes*, it matters! Small thoughts manifest a small reality. Grandiose thoughts manifest the probability of a grand reality.

But in either case, large or small, our thoughts become first the blueprint and then the foundation and architecture of our lives. Our thoughts structure our reality neurologically into "belief systems"—thoughts that we have over and over again until they are biochemically hardwired into our brain and psyche.

So we compose our day first through thinking. As we observe our thoughts, they mold our reality. Our reality takes the shape of our thoughts. We create this reality; we attract it to ourselves. This is rooted in brain chemistry and quantum mechanics where objects come into existence with and through observation. Reality responds accordingly. The Quantum-Heart obeys our thoughts because we *are* it, and it is how we create. This is why the Law of Attraction is called a *law*. It obeys the science of quantum physics.

Victim or Victor?

One of the assumptions I listed on pages 19-20, was that we are *responsible* for creating, i.e., *attracting*, the circumstances of our life. Now you know how this is done. Everything we think, believe, and accept will manifest. The issue is not whether this is true, but whether we are aware of everything going on beneath the surface in our nonconscious mind—that 95 percent of our cognition (see Diagram 1 on page 14) of which we are mostly oblivious. The trick is how to tap into *that*.

We are powerful, magical beings. We take a thought, a no-thing, and out of nothing we create dreams as well as nightmares, the good and the bad in karmic terms, but really just the electrical polarities rooted in the subatomic vibrational world that returns to us a panorama matching our specific frequency resonance. And we *choose* what we resonate. (As Michael Losier puts it, "The only thing we have control over is our vibration.") The Quantum-Heart is a magical field, and it is the essence of our being.

There are no boundaries whatsoever except those we impose on ourselves, no ceiling to our earning potential except that which we acknowledge and accept, no limit to our greatness or to our freedom except that which we fear.

Circumstances don't just happen to us passively. We create them. Now is the time to take the hill and destroy the victim within yourself! You champion your own life, you choose your own colors, and you ride on your own crusade however you conceive it and wherever in the universe it takes you. As the popular Chilean writer Isabelle Allende says, "You are the storyteller of your own life, and you can create your own legend, or not."

So create your own legend!

New Knowledge Review and Action Steps

1. What are the three kinds of karma?

    a. _____

    b. _____

    c. _____

2. If a tree falls in the forest and no one is there to hear it, does it make a sound? Explain your view on this.

   _____

   _____

   _____

3. List as many words as you can think of that were used or might be used interchangeably in this chapter for "Supreme Reality." Here are a few hints: G_____, S_____, C_____, TS_____, QH _____, GP _____. Create your own word _____.

4. On a scale of 1–10, rate your *belief* that "I create my day."

   _____

5. On a scale of 1–10, rate your *ability* to "create your day."

   _____

6. In each case above, what would it take to make it a 10?

   _____

   _____

Chapter 5
Bound, Tortured, and Killed by What Is Not Happening

In chapter 1, I summarized The Losier Method for attracting more of what you want in your life and business and less of what you don't want. Before you can open the floodgates of abundance and start attracting more of what you want, you must first cease, or at least reduce, attracting what you do *not* want. Unless you do, you will continue to neutralize your positive intentions and vibrations.

Do you remember the three words you are striving to eliminate from your vocabulary? Of course you do: *don't*, *not*, and *no*.

In this chapter, I will explain how limiting beliefs and emotional addictions form the two other "compass points" of what I call the *Law of Attraction Perfect Storm*™—that black hole that renders your capacity to employ the Law of Attraction essentially null and void. Negative language of all kinds, limiting beliefs and paradigms, and emotional addictions are like kryptonite to Superman. Whereas once able to "leap tall buildings in a single bound," you are now reduced to taking the stairs.

Diagram 2
Law Of Attraction Perfect Storm™

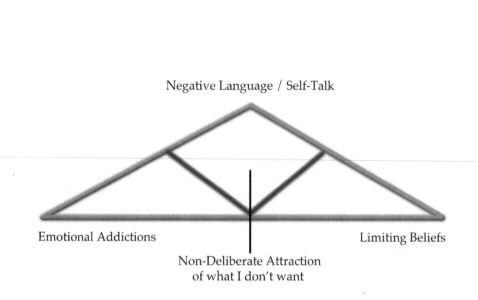

Negative Language / Self-Talk

Emotional Addictions

Limiting Beliefs

Non-Deliberate Attraction
of what I don't want

What Is *Not* Happening Has No Solution

What is not happening are all the fabrications of the mind—positive and negative—that configure and determine whom we think we are, what we think we are capable of achieving, and ultimately what we believe is within our power to attain as a human being, more precisely as _____ (insert your name here). After all, we do create all these things ourselves. We get what we believe and accept as our reality and our potential.

When I was a schoolboy, I vividly remember my teachers telling my parents on more than one occasion that "Jimmy is not working up to his potential." This may or may not have been the case. What is important, though, is that I internalized this judgment. While it initially was an external judgment, it became a limiting belief I accepted about myself and pretty much lived until I discovered philosophy in college and became excited and passionate about intellectual pursuits.

A limiting belief is a thought you have over and over again about yourself, others, or the world—consciously or nonconsciously, true or false—until it becomes so ingrained that it defines your persona, energy, life, and destiny. It becomes part of your story, part of the tapestry you weave about yourself and hang before the world to see. In my case, what began as an external judgment and then became internalized as a limiting belief morphed first into a career helping gifted children fulfill *their* potential and eventually into what I now describe as my calling to coach and mentor others. The irony abounds!

Limiting beliefs are like chimera. They seem to be there but have no substance, they feel heavy but have no weight, turn quickly to catch them in the act ... and they are gone. You seem to need eyes in the back of your head, but what you are trying to glimpse has already prescribed the rules of engagement, and the house always wins.

A paradigm is a set of beliefs, values, assumptions, a taken-for-granted worldview through which we create our life. Think about it. However you "see" reality will be the filter through which your reality is constructed or created. How else could it be? For example, if you see rich people as greedy or evil and do not wish to become this yourself, you may likely have a challenging time obtaining and/ or keeping money. Your money story, running in the background like a computer's operating system, will impose all sorts of parameters, restrictions, or ceilings to insure that you get exactly what you believe. This is why it is so important to shatter or at least become aware of your paradigms. What are they? Where do they come from? How do you expand or replace them?

One of the benefits I derived from studying philosophy for as long as I did in college and graduate school was that I learned to deconstruct assumptions, to question *everything*. I became the Socratic torpedo fish, looking to dismantle everything I could and looking for the contradictions and absurdities in all belief systems so I could dismiss them and move on.

When nothing is sacrosanct, you sometimes end up staring into an abyss. But on the other side of this no-thing is what I came to understand and experience as the true foundation of my being. Or to paraphrase the existential philosophers, "You are freer than you might be comfortable knowing."

What *Is* Happening Has the Solution Contained Within Itself

Let's say that every now and then, roughly between 4:00 and 4:30 a.m., you hear a rustling in the trees outside your open bedroom window. It startles you out of your sleep, and for a few moments, you imagine there is someone out there who could harm you. What to do? You don't know what it is, but you're afraid. You could take an extreme approach and push your alarm system's panic button or call the police. However, by the time they would arrive, they would find no evidence of someone lurking in the trees ... because it was not a person at all, just an animal in the night.

There is *no* (Newtonian world) solution to the imaginary person who is a threat to your being; he or she does not exist "out there." This is *not* what is happening. What *is* happening has multiple solutions, one of which might be to close the bedroom window so you do not hear the sound of the trees rustling. Another might be to seek therapy for your phobias.

Déjà Vu All Over Again!

It is a similar case with our endogenous (produced from within), biochemical addictions that can trap us in a reality like Bill Murray in the movie *Groundhog Day*—reliving, make that *recreating*, over and over again the same inescapable nightmare.

Several years ago, one of my first mindset coaches told me I was "addicted to disappointment." At the time, I had no idea what he was talking about and became rather defensive over this assessment. Years later, though, I recognized my pattern. Every time I was about to break through to the next level with my business, I would find a way to self-sabotage and stay stuck so I could remain disappointed and hold onto the identity of "little Jimmy" not working up to his potential. Wow! This was a transformational insight for me.

I want you to grasp this: A vibe is a mood or a feeling, remember? When do we have a mood or feeling? *All the time*. Positive vibes/moods/feelings = positive results; negative vibes/moods/feelings = negative results. Now, with every emotion (i.e., mood or feeling), the hypothalamus in our brain releases a corresponding neuropeptide that attaches itself to our cell membranes. In her book by the same title, Dr. Candace Pert calls these "molecules of emotion."

Addicted to Our Own Juice

And here is the kicker. Just as we can develop a tolerance and addiction to exogenous chemicals (ingested drugs, for example), so too can we build up tolerance and become addicted to the biochemicals produced within. In other words, with the repetition of the same emotion(s), our body's opiate receptors begin to expect and crave the corresponding peptides. This is the addiction.

As an example, take a person who is perpetually angry. Do you know anyone like this? Always ticked off about something, chip on his shoulder, looking for a fight, ready to pounce, come on—bring it on! This becomes his modus operandi in the world, and with each expression of anger (positive or negative vibration?), he attracts more of the same. The "job description" of the Law of Attraction is to "match vibrations." Like begets like.

At the same time, there is a biochemical event going on that adds the neurophysiological and emotional variables to the equation. You might think of this as "The Recipe of Attraction"—a quantity of this, a pinch of that. In response to the growing tolerance to our internally produced chemicals, the brain and reticular activating system begin to seek out situations, circumstances, and conditions that feed the addiction.

Why else do you think our angry soul seems always to find himself in some kind of fight? These do not just happen to him. He is not a victim; he creates his reality. The same phenomenon was operative with my "addiction to disappointment." Moreover, it was not my small self ("little jimmy"), my ego, or my personality that created this reality. I would never have deliberately created failure. Staying stuck was a product of the stories running beneath the surface in my nonconscious mind that we now know steers the ship.

If It's Not One Thing, It's Another

There is a scene in *Godfather III* in which Michael Corleone, who is trying to go legitimate, exclaims, "Every time I try to get out, they pull me back in!" (And then he has a heart attack.) It is similar with our emotions. Conscious will alone is not sufficient to break the stranglehold of our emotions or emotional history because they are hardwired, biochemically, into our brains. So what is wrong with this?

First, what is right with this: Our emotions, through their biochemical reactions, set and reinforce into our long-term memory experiences that help us learn, avoid harm, create meaning, and evolve as soulful/mindful beings. Emotions are good for us as a species in guiding us to seek pleasure and avoid pain. But just like chocolate (one of my addictions), too much of a good thing can have diminishing returns.

"When we continuously reexperience the same emotions and

never build on these," says Dr. Joe Dispenza in *What the Bleep...,* "we are caught in the same pattern of stimulus response." This means we cannot expand or experience anything new outside of our (emotional) box. The choice we have—once we become aware that it is a *choice*—is to either default to our biochemical processes, our uninspired genetic destiny, or to deal with our emotional tendencies head-on and transform them into new knowledge.

If you are interested in releasing an emotional addiction, Dr. Dispenza offers an effective strategy. Pick one limitation or propensity that you know about yourself and consciously and deliberately act to alter it. You will gain something called wisdom. Maybe easier said than done. As Jeff Olson states in *The Slight Edge,* "Simple to do, simple not to do." But worth the effort. How else would you expect to change?

Sagara is on autopilot, driving to Starbucks to buy his usual quad-shot of espresso and four-hundred-calorie chocolate brownie. Every day. His only variation is the time of day he might go to fetch his treat. Now that's being flexible! What task might he suspend to "take a break"? How might he justify anew his procrastination in getting to that pile of papers that he was scheduled to tackle today?

So he is about to turn onto the street that would lead to his destination when it hits him—he is observing this habit, this pattern, and it makes no sense. And in a moment of deliberate pattern-interrupt, he aborts his routine, reverses direction, and never purchases that brownie again.

The Solution Contained Within Itself

The only way to experience something truly new is to overcome the emotional addictions and energetic blocks that prevent new experience. As we are divine beings, we are meant to create and enjoy prosperity and abundance, to dream new dreams and experience new realities. But we cannot do this under the influence of any kind of addiction. We have to own up to our emotional states and transform our addictions into wisdom.

My friend Joe Nunziata in his book *Karma Buster* has a very simple prescription for dealing with old emotions that have us stuck. "Do the opposite." Once my pattern became evident to me, I did the opposite. I went "cold turkey" on the chocolate brownie, and that is all it took.

Nerve cells that habitually fire together wire together. Repetition is a major way we learn things. Habitually thinking *anything* burns a pathway in our brains that is sometimes challenging—but never impossible—to undo. Nerve cells that cease firing together eventually disassociate from each other (like two lovers who break up), and this is how we are able to break a habit neurologically. Breaking my brownie habit might be a silly example, but a profound protocol is contained within it, which I call *The Emotional Circuit Breaker™*:

1. Awareness: Become Aware

2. Understanding: Recognize the Dynamics

3. Action: Do the Opposite

4. Ownership: Retire the Emotion/Behavior to Wisdom

5. Reset Button: So What Do I (Really) Want?

6. Reactivate Button: So What Am I *Doing* About It?

7. Replacement: Substitute Emotion/Behavior with Positive Intention/Action

Quantum-Heart Contemplation Technique™

Contemplation can be a useful technique to "Become Aware" of habitual patterns or emotional addictions that have us stuck. These 5 steps can help you bring to the surface and identify them.

1. *Take an honest and courageous look* at your issue(s), which may manifest as some form of anguish or depression. You must first acknowledge your uneasiness or fear and be willing to face the source of it.

2. *Focus* (in your meditative state, see p. 41)—Allow yourself to become attentive, open and receptive—letting the real issue(s) bubble forth and reveal themselves.

3. *Inquire*—Bring your conscious mind into the process to ask specific questions about your feelings and fears: "What is this really about?" "What is the worst of this?"

4. *Tap into the Quantum-Heart*—Turn the issue over to grace, to the Transcendental Self; ask for clarity and resolution. The answer comes in the space of silence and stillness. (It may or may not appear in a given period of meditation, but it will come eventually.)

5. *Put the answer into practice*—Action is always the ultimate outcome of inner resolution. What can I do about this issue/answer that came up? Use the Reset Button and Reactivate Button to map out your plan.

Journey Back Into the Light

In the "Allegory of the Cave" from Plato's *Republic*—the first piece of Western philosophical literature I ever read—prisoners sit chained in a cave, unable to turn their heads, and stare only at shadows cast by a fire behind them. They cannot see the source or cause of the shadows and know this as their only reality. One of the prisoners gets free and makes his way out of the cave and into the sunlight, which initially blinds him until his eyes adjust.

The allegory is a metaphor on several levels—the stages of knowledge from ignorance to insight, the evolution of perception from illusion to reality, and the transformation of one's being from bondage to freedom. Each of these metamorphoses associated with the prisoner's ascent represents a quantum leap along the journey of self-discovery.

✦ ✦ ✦

I want you to close your eyes and visualize that it is you who has been imprisoned in the cave your entire life. I want you to imagine diving deep within yourself until you reach a tiny treasure chest waiting to be opened. You open it. Inside is a talisman that will set you free. What does it look like? You grasp it and explode upward and out of your chains! And you realize there never were any shackles except those you custom-fit for yourself.

The light is brilliant. It is momentarily blinding as it infuses you with all the knowledge, history, and manifestation of the universe. You realize you are one with the light. And you see your life passing in front of your eyes—not in the moment before your death but in the moment of your birth when it is all given and then forgotten. How you disacknowledged your divinity and disempowered yourself, how you chose abdication and accepted your life sentence. And now you are free!

Take one new action today in celebration of your creative freedom.

New Knowledge Review and Action Steps

1. What are the three compass points of the Law of Attraction Perfect Storm?

a. _____

b. _____

c. _____

2. A neuropeptide is an e_____
   biochemical manufactured by the hypothalamus in the

   _____.

3. Name and explain the six steps of *The Emotional Circuit Breaker*™ for overcoming an emotional addiction or habit?

   a. A _____

   b. U _____

   c. A _____

   d. O _____

   e. R _____

   f. R _____

   g. R _____

4. Apply the six steps to your own emotional addiction(s) or habit(s).

5. What are the 5 steps of the *Quantum-Heart Contemplation Technique*™? Use the technique and journal your experience.

Chapter 6
From Deliberate Attractor to Master Creator

In chapter 4, I talked about how our inner world creates our outer world, and that our thoughts, positive or negative, are what manifest our reality. This is a law, perhaps the *supreme* law, of the universe. The choices we make create our life, our reality, and our future. Therefore, shouldn't we be more vigilant about our thoughts and choices? How can we make better, more deliberate, choices?

The Observer and the Observed

In asking the above question, there are a myriad of answers (possibilities in "superposition," in quantum talk) from which to select. If you are lazy or indifferent and simply shrug off the question, you will only get the default answer, which is rooted in your hardwired habitual behaviors. No answer is an answer in the same way that no decision is a decision.

Or look at it this way. Say you are with someone at a restaurant, looking at a menu. All of the possible dishes from which to choose are there on the page in front of you; they exist as multiple possibilities until you select one. But for reasons of dementia or distraction or any other set of mental impediments, your dinner partner is unable to observe his options and focus long enough to make a decision.

If left to his own devices, his dinner would not come into existence, and he would probably go hungry.

Among the numerous interpretations of quantum theory is one that states that objects do not come into existence until observed. Herein lies a great alchemy, a power even greater than that released in splitting the atom, for it is our means of regaining the capacity to wield true magic—to create something concrete out of no-thing from the *Thought-Prints*™ of our mind.

A question creates a void that must be filled. Ask yourself this question: How might I receive the greatest comprehension and usefulness from the book I am currently reading?

I Am a Master Magician

One of my thirty-two personal declarations (see chapter 7) is, "I am a Master Magician." I am in the process of attracting everything I need to do, know, and have to *regain* my status as Master Magician. You see, I lost or abdicated my power somewhere between childhood and adulthood, just as you might have. I gave up the notion of being Peter Pan and Superman and being invisible and being able to know what someone was going to say before they said it so I could assume my "rightful place" in the world. This was nondeliberate.

What about you? What have you sacrificed? Or, as we are speaking about observation, upon what have you turned a blind eye?

In accepting the myth perpetuated by mainstream science that there is an objective reality "out there" independent of our consciousness, and that this reality is capable of being measured without our affecting it in any way, we give up the primacy of *subjectivity* in our experience. We say, in essence, our consciousness doesn't matter in constructing reality, as reality is already sitting there waiting to be discovered and measured.

SPURIOUS NEWS FLASH (Reported by Irreverent News Agency based on a true story in the *The New York Times* on the day of this writing, July 5, 2012)

"Physicists Find Elusive Particle Seen as Key to Universe"— *GENEVA—Okay, fire up the Large Haldron Collider, a gigantic particle accelerator, and then collide the hell out of protons. Amidst the debris is something called the Higgs Boson (named after physicist Peter Higgs), a fleeting, subatomic particle believed to give all other such particles their mass. A massive champagne celebration ensued as scientists congratulated themselves on busting the Higgs Boson out of its hiding place so they could now begin searching for the particle that gives Higgs its mass.*

Said a spokesperson, quoting the late logician Ludwig Wittgenstein from Tractatus Logico-Philosophicus, *"The whole modern conception of the world is founded on the illusion that the so-called laws of nature are the explanations of natural phenomena."*

Call It a Feedback Loop

I am catching snippets of the Michigan-Notre Dame football game (my wife is as "Go Blue" as they come), and I see one of the tight ends, just seconds before the snap, stand up from his stance and motion with his arms for the fans to make some noise, which they dutifully oblige. I find this irritating because I believe the players are supposed to be focused on the *game*, not the fans. It is also interesting because of the interaction between the observers and the observed. In fact, such interaction has become *part of* the game.

(Is this an implicit acceptance of quantum entanglement with each other?)

Remember, the observer affects the observed in the quantum realm, the vibrational world, and does so too in our Newtonian world, although this is not as obvious or as universally acknowledged, particularly among mainstream scientists. Now back to our football game. The players encourage and invoke the fans to increase their energy output, which in turn provokes the players to increase theirs. This feedback loop ultimately affects both the measured (progress on the field) as well as the measurement itself (moving the chains one way or the other).

To become a Master Magician, we must first acknowledge that observation unequivocally affects the observed; in fact, it largely *creates* the observed from an indeterminate pool of possibilities. The "halo effect" in education is another example of this. Students who are observed and expected to do well, most often do. Students branded as inferior either academically or behaviorally typically perform in keeping with their observed expectations. The results (creations) are two sides of the same coin and are mutually reinforcing. This is the feedback loop.

---

*You **cannot disprove** the hypothetical proposition that objects are engendered with and through observation. Genesis by observership cannot be disproved in the same way that you **cannot prove** the existence of objects in a dark room until a light is cast on them or they are perceived in some other manner.*—Sagara

---

Returning to the Source

So you see how observation has a direct impact on the observer's world, including the subjects in that world, e.g., football players or students, who are simultaneously creating their *own* observations that are manifesting reality. It is an extremely complex, layered scenario.

Nonetheless, to become a Master Magician, we must become a Master Observer. We must regain the Power of Observation that we lost as we grew out of childhood. Says Dr. Joe Dispenza, again in *What the Bleep…*, "We should be willing to sit down every day and take a piece of our day and set it aside and begin to observe, to design a new possible future for ourselves, and if we do it properly and we observe it properly, we should have opportunities begin to show up in our lives."

Our default reality, upon losing the focus and power of our observations, will become habitual stimulus-response behavior, the same old same old, nondeliberate "choices" governed by a restrained reticular activating system (RAS, read page 21 again) and stultified paradigms with little or no chance of expanding and regaining your magical powers. So what *do* you want? What do you *choose*?

Thought-Prints Are the Blueprints of Our Destiny

Let's recap. Your thoughts manifest your reality through their corresponding vibrations. Everything in your life is frequency specific. You get what you vibrate. Each thought, conscious or not, represents a choice that collapses an infinite array of potential outcomes with the actual one you experience. In this sense, as the ancient Greek philosopher Aristotle noted, potential is always greater than actuality. And that is good news because it means you are not locked into your current or future life unless you choose to be.

Just as an architect creates a set of plans out of his mind, out of no-thing, which then become the blueprint for a great edifice, so too do our Thought-Prints pattern the constructs of our life. We begin to compose our day from the moment we awake, and what we observe and how we feel about the day will largely filter or color, pixel by pixel, what we accept, expect, encounter, and experience. This is how it works. If there is no "out there" out there in the Newtonian sense, neither is our existence already set in stone. It is like clay, and we shape it to our imagination.

How to Create Your Day

I promised I would summarize Ramtha's instructions for creating your day. As with all the principles and techniques I teach, everything contained in these pages are methods I consistently use to tap into the Quantum-Heart. Each morning, just as I awake, I begin my day first by "remembering" *what I desire to become*, not who I am, as this will restrict me to my current identity and what I can accept and believe is possible for myself. Empower yourself each morning; give yourself permission to create a magnificent day and a new you.

Where does this creating and creation come from, and what makes it possible? I have made a strong case in this book that we *are* the Quantum-Heart—that we are the *observer* at the quantum level—from which spring the manifestations of our Thought-Prints.

Revisit Diagram 1 on page 14. At the base of the triangle of the 95 percent designated as "nonconscious" lies the Quantum-Heart. As we awake each morning and gradually become cemented to our conscious mind and identity, illustrated at the top of the pyramid, it is like a deep sea diver returning to the surface, back to the world with which he is most familiar.

But the Law of Attraction is spawned in quantum mechanics. The reason we attract whatever we give our attention, energy, and focus to is because it is *here*, in the cauldron of ephemeral thinking, in the recesses of our consciousness, that we are the Master Magician capable of creating/attracting what we desire to bring into existence. This is how it works.

Hope Springs Eternal

I feel, sense, and perceive that we are in a Great Age, where the best is always in front of us, where we can live out our dreams, where believing makes it so, I am Man of La Mancha, crazy to the rest of the world, and yet ...

Allowing—the absence of disbelief—is the most important step in Michael Losier's three-step Law of Attraction formula. Remember, the Law of Attraction will manifest for you only to the degree that you *believe* it will. I am making two points here. First, to manifest the object of your desire statement, you must allow it; you must believe it will manifest. This is how our Thought-Prints draw, attract (i.e., *create* out of no-thing), our reality to us. But second, you must believe this is how the universe works, and that you are capable of making this law work for *you*.

It is a subtle distinction, but I have found, for example, that in bringing Law of Attraction training into corporate settings (I am known as the "Corporate Law-of-Attraction Guy"), the nut to crack is converting the doubters into believers. It is epidemic that many people, corporate or otherwise, simply cannot accept their power to manifest. With some, it is case by case. "I could never manifest *that*." You're right, I tell them. How could they with that belief? With others, the no-can-do mindset is even more pervasive.

An Invitation to Open Your Mind

In the DVD *Create Your Day*, Ramtha asks us to consider whether our acceptance is greater than our doubts because we can only get what we can accept, what is within the parameters of our acceptance about ourselves and our reality. If you accept the Newtonian universe as your only reality, for example, you accept a world of mechanistic predictability. So how can there ever be hope in that to express the freedom essential to manifest your desires and design your life?

Hope, Ramtha says, is a personal thing, but it means giving ourselves permission to think outside the box, outside whatever confines us to our smallness like ants mindlessly and dutifully scurrying around on behalf of their community. (My example, not Ramtha's, and as Jim Rohn used to point out, there is something to be said for the "ants philosophy" of persistence in the face of whatever obstacles are in their way!)

Hope is the calling deep within ourselves that defies confinement, the salvation and journey out of the dark "menagerie of predictability" and into the light of a better day. It is the bubbling upward out of the Quantum-Heart the recognition that through deliberate choice, intention, focus and action, we can create anything we desire.

If belief is the engine of attraction and creation, education is the engine of hope. As Joe Dispenza continues, "You have to have knowledge that allows you to dream great dreams. You have to have the willingness and the passion to step outside the boundaries of your own comfort zone and your own need for conformity ..." And action is the purpose of knowledge. (See chapter 9.)

The Recipe for Transformation

You know that place between sleep and awake, the place where you can still remember dreaming? That's where I'll always love you. That's where I'll be waiting. —J. M. Barrie, *Peter Pan*

In chapter 8, I present several meditation, contemplation, and visualization techniques I personally use to tap into the Quantum-Heart. What follows is a distilled version of *Create Your Day*, which I employ every single morning before I get out of bed. (To obtain a copy of this DVD, go to www.ramtha.com.)

I orient very quickly upon awaking. My wife and I are up and about between 4:00–4:30 a.m. daily, and I typically have a very small window before I greet the world as Jim Alvino. It is within this window that I go beyond *who* Jim Alvino is to *what* Jim Alvino can become. What do *you* desire to become? Remember *that* first.

Before I bond with my usual identity, before I "remember" who I am, as Ramtha puts it, before all my neuronal networks fire up and activate *me*, I reprogram myself with several affirmations designed to cultivate an openness to expanding my horizons this day. I invite opportunity into my world, I invite in the unknown, I invite in the astounding, and my reticular activating system accommodates me.

Today *I know extraordinary people.* **Today** *I have an encounter of the unusual.* **Today** *I know wealth greater than I have ever known it before.* I repeat the entire sequence three times, hanging on each word, being fully present with them, *feeling* the intention with intensity ... and then allowing the affirmations to settle like nutrients seeping into the soil of a magnificent wish-fulfilling tree.

When I get out of bed, head to the bathroom, and stare at myself in the mirror, is it the same Jim Alvino? Unequivocally *not*. I have become a slightly different person. Do I really *believe* this? Absolutely! Because in the quantum world, where my consciousness and Thought-Prints are rooted, *believing makes it so*. The effects are cumulative and unmistakable. Day by day, until whom you recognize in the mirror is no longer whom you are but what you wanted to become.

Sagara is at the John Wayne Airport in Orange County, California, waiting to board a plane to Dallas. He remembers that he has forgotten to bring a book to read on the flight, so he goes into CNN Newsstand to find a piece of nonfiction or personal development he can sink his teeth into for a few hours. Nothing jumps out at him. Oh, well.

On his way out, he spots some Godiva dark chocolate he can sink his teeth into instead and stands at the cash register, preparing to pay. He is aware of a woman and her young child, about seven or eight years old, approaching another cash register just a few feet to his right. As he is standing there, his eyes are drawn down to the bottom shelf of the counter as if his head were on hinges to where he sees a magazine entitled The Brain. *Oh great, Sagara thinks,* as he has been reading about the brain for his new book, Explorer's Guide to the Law of Attraction.

Sagara picks up the magazine and notes the price, $9.95. "Wow! That's expensive for a magazine!" he says aloud to his captive audience of store clerk, mother, and daughter. The woman at the adjacent cash register says something to Sagara to which he replies, "Perhaps I will make a million dollars with this." To which she replies, "In that case, it would be an investment."

Sagara is blown away by this comment—not for himself or for the woman's message, which he knew all too well, but for the young girl who has just received an invaluable lesson on the distinction between cost and investment. Sagara would tell this story at a training several days later as an example of an "encounter of the unusual" and will continue to tell this story forever. Wisdom never dies.

The Doppelganger Effect

I'm in CNN Newsstand with my daughter buying some Oriental Mix before our flight to Denver. A guy comes in looking at the books at the back of the store but settles for some candy or gum by the cash register to our left. As we are approaching the other register, he picks up a magazine, looks at the price and exclaims, "Wow! $9.95! That's expensive!" As he is looking to engage, I say to him, "Well, that depends" to which he replies, "Perhaps I will make a million dollars with this." "In that case, it would be an investment," I say to him. He smiles, looks at my daughter, and leaves.

Life is full of unusual encounters. If that man hadn't come in and stepped up to the cash register at just the right moment, and if we hadn't been there at the very same time, my daughter Rachel would not have overheard this conversation, which I would reinforce later. How serendipitous!

SPECIAL REQUEST: If you are that woman with the child with whom I had an "encounter of the unusual," in May 2012, please contact me so I may send you a signed copy of my book.

You Might Say I'm a Dreamer

I remember doing a lot of daydreaming as a child. I couldn't tell you about what, just that I had a rich fantasy life and a strong desire to be free—I can recall that much—from confines of all sorts, most significantly *school*. With rare exception, I remember elementary school and high school as the straightjacket of my life. But I did conform, became obedient, and then rebellious.

Life is wondrous and mysterious to a child, magical. Anything and everything is possible because a child has not yet been conditioned and socialized to surrender his or her uniqueness to normative values and is not yet programmed with the prevailing social, political, academic, scientific, and religious paradigms of our age. Knowledge can bind us or set us free to marvel again at the mystical nature of reality—not how it exists but *that* it exists.

> *You might say I'm a dreamer*
>
> *But I'm not the only one*
>
> *I hope someday you'll join us*
>
> *And the world will live as one.*
>
> — John Lennon, from "Imagine"

New Knowledge Review and Action Steps

1. Our conscious mind is our observer as the nonconscious mind cannot observe anything. T or F _____.

2. The Law of Attraction is spawned in the _____ _____.

3. Allowing is the absence of _____.

4. What are Thought-Prints? _____.

5. Belief is to _____ as education is to _____.

6. Memorize the three daily affirmations you will say upon awaking from this day forward.

7. Recount a personal "encounter of the unusual."

   _____

   _____

   _____

   _____

Chapter 7
Now Repeat After Me

I concluded the last chapter with three powerful affirmations that have the capacity to transform your life if repeated with understanding, intention, belief, the right state of consciousness, and at the right time of day. Timing really is everything as they say.

Probably many of you have had the experience that your affirmations are not quite working for you. Maybe every day for the last ten years you have been standing in front of a mirror proclaiming, "I am a multimillionaire, I am a multimillionaire," and you are not quite there yet. Understatement? Often our affirmations over-promise and under-deliver. Why is this so?

Let's look at this. "I am a multimillionaire" would pass the muster of the AP (that's the "Affirmation Police"). It is short and sweet, present tense, positive, and about me. So what is wrong with it? Nothing ... unless you are like a million other people staring in the mirror and this little voice inside your head keeps harassing you, "No, you're not, no, you're not. Who do you think you're kidding? Get real! Go get a job," and a myriad of other snide retorts that your self-talk saboteur has in his chamber.

You know that the affirmation is not (yet) true, which makes it a false statement, a lie, that offends our inner sensibility and produces a negative vibration that crashes the whole system. I just love the advice proffered by many multi-level marketing gurus to "fake it until you make it." What does this make you? Hint: A FAKE! Positive or negative vibration?

The Correction

Michael Losier in *Law of Attraction* offers a "correction" to the affirmation mishap if you find that your affirmations do not always work for you. (If they are working for you, fine, jump to the next section.) There are two requirements: 1) The affirmation must be *true* for you; and 2) the actual statement is relatively unimportant but how you *feel* about it is crucial. You can repeat "I am a multimillionaire" until you are blue in the face, but if your feeling about this belies your words—in short, if you do not *believe* it—you will never manifest your desire.

The correction is a statement that *declares* you are in the process of manifesting your desire. It is a template, really, that reflects the action, knowledge, and possession of everything you will need to attract and manifest whatever it is you want. There are several variations of this; here is the one I use: "*I am in the process of attracting everything I need to do, know, and have to attract, manifest, and allow my ideal _____ (fill in the blank)."*

The beauty of this is, by virtue of *declaring* that I am in the process, I *am* in the process, which makes the statement *true*, which sends off a positive vibration, which enhances the quantum probability (remember the Net Energy Index from p. 6) of the Law of Attraction unfolding and orchestrating to fulfill my wish. We all have a magic lamp with its resident genie deep inside ourselves.

Why I Prefer Declarations

Each morning after my daily meditation, I repeat two sets of declarations. The first set is "Declarations of the Millionaire Mind" from T. Harv Eker's book, *Secrets of the Millionaire Mind*. The second set is my own customized list of expansive identities that represent how I see myself *right now*. They are, therefore, *observations* more than wanna-be's, reminders of my greatness and the sources of my greatness.

As descriptors and characteristics, they paint a self-portrait as though looking in a mirror that reflects back what I believe and project about myself. **As *observations* founded in the Quantum-Heart, they bring into existence more of the very traits being observed in the same way that observing and celebrating success attract even more success.** Have you ever wondered why it seems "the rich get richer"?

In the parable of the talents, Jesus tells the story of a wealthy man who, before leaving on a trip, gives each of his three servants a different number of talents. (In those days a talent was a form of money.) The first servant received five, the second two, and the third one. He wanted to see what they would do with the money.

Upon returning, the wealthy man learned that the first servant, the one with the most talents, had doubled his money, as did the second servant who had the second most talents. However, the servant with the least number of talents had buried his so as not to lose it. The man scorned the third servant, took his talent from him, and gave it to the servant who had doubled his money to ten.

Following are my thirty-two *Personal Declarations of Greatness™*. I invite you to adapt or adopt whichever one(s) you like to suit your actual or desirable self-image. We create our persona in the same way we weave the tapestry of a memoir. Our imagination is the loom, and our Thought-Prints are the thread and pattern of our creation. Some of the following declarations will be obvious in their intent, others more idiosyncratic to me, but all have a universal kernel of truth from which to draw your own sustenance.

Thirty-Two Personal Declarations of Greatness

1. I Live in God's Heart/I live in the Quantum-Heart

2. I Am My Fullest Potential/My Best Self

3. I Am a Master Deliberate Attractor/Master Allower

4. I Am a Master Magician

5. I Am a Master Creator

6. I Am a Master Connector

7. I Am an International Best-Selling Author

8. I Am a Sales Champion

9. I Am a Master Persuader

10. I Am Becoming Whom I Want to Attract

11. I Expect to Have It All/I Deserve to Have It All

12. I Am Rewriting My Money Story

13. I Am the Personification of Abundance

14. I Am a Money Attractor

15. I Am a Master of Accountability

16. I Monetize My Niche

17. I Pursue My Passion for Profit

18. I Am Transforming My Future/My Vision IS My Future

19. I Am My Own Champion

20. I Am My Own Hero

21. I Expect a Miracle Today/I Am My Own Miracle

22. I Inspire Myself and Others to Greatness

23. I Am a Tremendous Coach and Mentor

24. I Am a Fantastic Writer, Speaker, Presenter, and Motivator

25. I Have Game/I Am In the Game

26. I Play the Game at Level 10

27. I Commit to Personal Development

28. I Am a Winner

29. I Stay One-Pointed on My Declarations and Desire Statements until They Manifest

30. I Am ENOUGH!

31. I Am the Quantum-Heart/I Am That

32. I Am a Brilliant and Wealthy Entrepreneur: Infinite Abundance, Creativity, and Intelligence Flow through Me.

33. **BONUS DECLARATION—I am in the process of attracting everything I need to do, know, and have to put the Law of Attraction into conscious, deliberate use in my life.**

Now create five declarations of your own to add to this list. Remember, it is the feeling and vibration that you emanate that are most important in this process.

1. _____

2. _____

3. _____

4. _____

5. _____

How Long Does It Take?

Conventional wisdom (if this is not an oxymoron) has always held that it takes between twenty-one and thirty days to make a significant change in behavior to break a habit, cultivate a new one, or alter your thinking or mindset. This is simply untrue. It can happen in a heartbeat as it did for Sagara in the moment of his spiritual awakening or when I went cold turkey on my brownie addiction.

It can happen in an "aha" experience, in an insight or intuition, in a revelation. Even faster than the speed of light. It takes a full eight minutes for sunlight to traverse ninety-three million miles to reach the earth, which is an eternity in quantum time.

Albert Einstein believed that nothing could travel faster than the speed of light. This may be true in our Newtonian world, which still forms the backdrop for e = mc². But quantum physics defies this formula because objects can appear in more than one location *simultaneously* (this is called "nonlocality") and can communicate *instantaneously* over vast expanses of the cosmos. Keep in mind my assertion that we live in both worlds, and that the principles of quantum scale up to the Newtonian universe.

In other words, *any* change involving the mind—thinking, consciousness, intention, even breaking emotional addictions—*can* happen with the snap of a finger, but I am not claiming that it always will happen that quickly. The twenty-one to thirty-day plan is an old-school model of linear time that might apply to the physical universe and even to the time required to hardwire a new neural pathway, but definitely not to our inner world of cognition, which is the entangled and collective dimension of the Quantum-Heart.

If You Can Think It, You Can...

Most of my adult life, I have been fond of saying, "If you can think it, you can *do* it." Oh, that is so Newtonian! I realize now, "If you can think it, you can *go* there!" Think about it. What else is imagination, visualization, and meditation (see chapter 8) than a form of time travel into the future or past? *This* is the real significance of visualizing the future. You must first *travel there* in the mind's eye before you can see it with your physical eyes, before you can manifest and materialize it as concrete reality.

A skeptic might say, "I'll believe it when I see it," but for one who understands the connection between belief and attraction/manifestation, the motto is just the opposite. "I'll see it when I believe it." This is the meaning of *allowing*.

Can We Change the Past?

In the movie *Back to the Future*, the main character, Marty McFy, travels back in time to 1955 from 1985, which alters the past he travels to as well as how the future unfolds for himself, his family, and their other relationships. When Marty returns to 1985 (his "future" relative to the past he was stuck in), he awakens to find that his *present* life has undergone a complete makeover as well.

We, in fact, do the same thing all the time ... in the time tunnel of our mind's eye. History is replete with radically different accounts of the same event depending on perception and point of view. The 2012 election of the United States president, for example, was a very different experience and outcome for a Democrat than it was for a Republican.

Most of us believe we cannot go back and alter the event itself (e.g., that one candidate won and the other lost). However, the *significance* of the past *for me* comes out of the future. If I were to have changed party affiliation after the election, this would be tantamount to changing my past … and therefore my present and future.

"Time travel" in this sense is such a common experience that we take it for granted, and it goes unnoticed and unrecognized for what it really is. Try this exercise. Sit down and make up a grocery list. Which store are you going to? On which aisles are the products you intend to buy? For which dish tonight? Do the kids need cereal? Where is it in the store? How will you get there? What will the traffic be like, and how long will it take you? What size lines do you expect at the cash register? (We get what we expect, you know.)

The Three Laws of Performance

When I coach on the topics of branding and marketing, I show my clients how their business brand reflects their personal brand, and how their personal brand reflects, to a large degree, their personal story. It was no accident that "little jimmy," who was judged in the past by his teachers as not working up to his potential, found himself on (i.e., attracted and created) a career path to help others fulfill *their* potential.

It was no accident either that the growth of my business was stymied for a while as a result of my a) nonconscious identity with underachievement as a young student, which became my personal "brand," and b) its accompanying emotional addiction to disappointment.

Just as your personal brand and business brand are intimately commingled or entangled, so too are your personal future and business future. And the tricky part, according to Steve Zaffron and Dave Logan in *The Three Laws of Performance*, is that in the absence of awareness and intervention, *the future is already written*. Of course, I am not going to leave you there. You can rewrite your future with what they call *future-based language*.

How to Reengineer Your Future

Future-based language transforms how situations occur to us, but to rewrite or reengineer your future—in other words, to take charge of your default future and redirect it—a few positive affirmations are neither adequate nor sufficient. To reengineer your future, you must to a certain extent become a revisionist historian and recreate your past as well. *Recreate* it, not *deny* it. The meaning of the past comes out of the future, not vice versa (more on this later).

Let's say you have experienced a personal bankruptcy—an event generally regarded as a financial disaster. But from a Quantum-Heart or transcendental point of view, this event does not have "bad" connotations; it is merely the Law of Attraction and Law of Observation unfolding and orchestrating to bring about a state of affairs that matches your predominant, underlying beliefs and Net Energy Index (and their associated behaviors).

Future-based language, also called *generative* language, means reframing or regenerating the event and its significance: I can *choose* to see this as a failure, as negative and shameful, as a blight on my record, as fear-inducing ... or as the best thing that has ever happened to me as a cornucopia of lessons and opportunities I would never have received otherwise. The most significant person to forgive the debt is you!

If, on the other hand, you do nothing to alter how situations *occur* to you or how you *observe* them, you will live out your default future based on the same old expectations, hopes, fears, and predictions—all rooted in your default past. And the stronger you resist it, the more it will persist. As leadership guru John Maxwell puts it, the more we replay yesterday, the further away from today's opportunities we get. Is there a past dogging you that you can transform into a blessing with future-based language?

What Is Your Money Story?

Happiness and success (two primary destinations of the *Explorer's* roadmap) can be measured in many ways. Money is a big one. In fact, if you are an entrepreneur or business owner, you may even be measuring your success by the size of your bank account.

A couple of years ago at a seminar I was attending, I started a conversation with a young man who was videotaping the event for a college project. He explained to me that he was an entrepreneur, and that a nine-to-five job was not his idea of a suitable career path for himself. Still, he admitted, he would have to devise a way to generate income to pay his bills and live the lifestyle he desired. And then he dropped this emotionally charged bombshell: "Money is my enemy."

By now you understand that we get more of what we give our attention, energy, and focus to, and that the language we use frames and filters (via our RAS) what we observe, attract, create, and experience. This young man was in for a rough ride. Are you able to identify his possible emotional addictions? Do you share any of these or others related to your *feelings* when it comes to money? Remember, the quantum world, that spawning ground of the Law of Attraction, responds to the "vibes" we send out, positive or negative, conscious or not.

The reason our emotional and behavioral relationship with money, i.e., our current money story, is so important is that it can largely dictate success or failure, as well as the extent to which the challenges we invariably encounter in life may knock us out of the game.

The Secret Language of Money

In *The Secret Language of Money*, David Krueger goes even further when he says our money story is really about everything—day by day, thought by thought, dollar by dollar—and that it becomes our life story. Our unique money story is running in the background like spyware on our computer, although we are not usually conscious of what "viruses" it is keeping out or letting through.

So it is critical to get a grip on your *feelings and thoughts* about money, what you do with it and for it, and what experiences are shaping and reinforcing your beliefs about money. Figure out where your ideas and beliefs about money come from. Maybe you can even track an earlier time in your life when you made a conscious decision about money and determine whether your current patterns and Thought-Prints are congruent with your goals and worth keeping, or whether they should be tossed out and rewritten.

For example, I can vividly remember as a young boy being denied a toy gun that I wanted and sulking about it. Was I being bad, selfish, or ill-mannered in asking for it? In college, I expressly threw my lot in with the poor and held the mistaken philosophy—I repeat, *mistaken* philosophy—that poverty was on a higher spiritual plane than wealth. Such a money story had been among those operative in my nonconscious mind for several decades, and it would take some undoing.

It would be twenty years after graduating from college before I would read an account by a spiritual Master who was being challenged by one if his devotees for the opulence evident at the Master's ashram when so much poverty existed elsewhere in the world. The Master replied simply, "What makes you think God prefers poverty to wealth?" Thus began the rewriting of my money story.

What Are *Your* Roots?

Go ahead now and examine the roots of your money story, and identify and uproot any weeds that might be strangling your garden from bearing its abundant fruit. What experiences, beliefs, conditioning, and values have been defining your relationship to money? Can you uncover a time or incident when you made a decision to *be* a certain way in the world—in essence, when you gave yourself *your own life sentence*?

Give this serious attention if you wish to become fully cognizant of how your money story is playing itself out as your life story and if you desire to become free from your self-imposed shackles. Remember, awareness is the first prerequisite of change.

_____

_____

_____

Krueger is also an MD, and he stresses the value of visualization. The repeated act of visualization causes actual physical changes to occur in the brain, as the process etches the vision into our neural networks and pathways, and eventually, our imagination becomes our reality. So what have *you* been imagining lately? Is it time to change your inner movie? "God eschews poverty," says Wallace Wattles in *The Science of Getting Rich*. He wants us to be rich. Go for it!

♦
♦ ♦

Now! Create your day. Create your week, your month, your year, your future. This is the true foundation of goal setting, and in working with companies and their executive and sales teams, this is where I start. Remember, we may *set* our goals with the conscious mind (top 5 percent of the pyramid on page 14), but we *get* our goals deep beneath the surface by accessing the Quantum-Heart. Recognize that we do this anyway but most of the time nondeliberately.

Is your life on autopilot, which may mean defaulting to patterns of emotional addiction, including self-sabotage and a predetermined future based on a thwarted sense of the past? Or are you taking deliberate, regenerative action founded on deliberate intention/attraction/creation?

Toward a Feeling of Abundance

Imagine a world where you are steeped in prosperity of all kinds—love, relationships, joy, wealth, creativity, charity, service, peace, and tranquility. You get to decide what this means for you. The list you just read reflects some of my values and desires. I push the proverbial envelope when it comes to abundance consciousness. My glass is neither half full nor half empty but overflowing with possibility and opportunity.

Each of us has had our ups and downs in life and business, and we can take some solace and advice from Rocky Balboa, in the movie by the same title: "It's not how hard you hit, but how hard you can get hit and keep movin' forward ... That's how winning is done." And, adds the great Les Brown, in a recent seminar I attended, "It's not over until you WIN!"

Ours is truly a remarkable journey that typically is witnessed as such only when looking in the rearview mirror and standing in the purview of how one's life is currently unfolding. We are fundamentally future-oriented beings, whether we are positive or negative, yet we find ourselves with a history that has brought us to this very moment. "I am as having been," Martin Heidegger proclaims in *Being and Time*, the book on which I wrote my doctoral dissertation.

Without getting into details that would glaze your eyes over, several of my conclusions anticipated my later interest in quantum: 1) that there is a fourth dimension of time, namely *simultaneity*; and 2) that "we-consciousness" (aka quantum *entanglement*) is a fundamental part of "I-consciousness."

Moreover, Heidegger's signature notion of *dasein* (a German word which means "being there" and loosely translates into "human consciousness") represents a "clearing in the forest," or illumination of that which exists.

Taking a quantum leap in interpretation, *dasein* might be considered the "observer" that brings objects into existence. The parallel is too compelling to ignore—observer, observed, and the process of observation in quantum talk correspond roughly to illuminator, illuminated, and the process of illumination. The significance of this is that we, you and I, are the *source* of what exists for us in reality as well as the meaning it has for us. The creative light shines outward from within.

Releasing Your Grip On the Past ... and Vice Versa

There are things from our past, including residual connections to and interactions with others, from which we need to extricate ourselves in order to move forward. We hold on. In 1989, after nearly ten years as president of a publishing company, we shut our doors, and I went into a psychological tailspin. I had so identified with my position and status that when the end came, I felt like Robert Duvall in the movie *Network*—"a man without a corporation."

I took home relics from our office, including a four-by-four-foot sign that was attached to the front of the building. I negotiated for pieces of art that had hung in my office so I could feel like I was still there. I fantasized about continuing the company on my own, but it was all for naught. I hate to disappoint you, Les, but sometimes things are over, and it turns out you *haven't* won. I harbored a lot of anger, resentment, guilt, and shame. And a lot of forgiveness had to take place before I could move on.

Forgiveness is a key element in letting go of and getting beyond the paradigms that keep us stuck. It means to absolve, to clear the screen, to bring closure and start afresh. And forgiveness is critical for spiritual growth, as it signifies rising above blame, having compassion for another's issues, and accepting our participation in creating the situation that has us hurting or that we may still be stewing over.

Without forgiveness, something negative binds us to the past as a referent that colors our present and future. Unlike the rosy eyeglasses of the perennial optimist, an unwillingness or inability to forgive is akin to the dark sunglasses of an addict. Biochemical and emotional addiction chains us to a repeating stimulus-response pattern, and we perpetuate more of the same.

Several years ago, I was in a business partnership that eventually dissolved with my business partner owing me a little over five hundred dollars. Repeated attempts to collect my money yielded nothing but promises. I was angry and held onto it for several years. Then recently, I decided to let it go. I called my friend three times and left three voicemails. The first one invited him to let bygones be bygones; the second and third calls offered him a look at an opportunity that might have produced millions of dollars. He did not return any of my calls, and the window of opportunity is now closed. But I forgave him, and I am free.

Who Is Deserving of Your Forgiveness?

In my ongoing spiritual memoir, *The Story of Sagara*, I write about my childhood, of course, and the various experiences, good and bad, that shaped my life. I am blessed and grateful for the love, caring, and sacrifices my parents made in wanting to give me the best life they could. At the same time, I am aware that they are probably holding onto some pain and guilt for the conflicts and crises that arose in our family as these things do in most families to lesser or greater degrees.

And so I hereby affirm my forgiveness of my father and mother for any wrongdoing, real or imagined, that were committed out of anger or out of love during any period of my life. I at once absolve you from whatever sins, real or imagined, that bind you to a sense of blame or guilt for anything that has taken place or will take place in my life. So be it decreed and enacted from this day forward.

Who in your life is deserving of your forgiveness so you can release your grip on the past and continue to create your destiny unfettered by it? This is how *we can change the future*—by reappropriating our past! At the same time, as the existential philosophers have said, meaning comes out of the future. In a sense, then, we can alter the

significance of our past through that which has not yet happened!
Go ahead, commit your act of forgiveness *now*.

_____

_____

Have You Forgiven *Yourself*?

As I was writing the previous section, I realized that the most
important person to forgive is oneself. Many of us carry around
some degree of guilt from our past for either a) doing what we
believe we should not have done or b) not doing what we believe we
should have done. The problem with guilt, according to relationship
coach Dr. Mamiko Odegard, author of *Daily Affirmations for Love*, is
that it is toxic and prevents us from tapping into the wellspring of
our creative potency. Guilt is like a dark, negative shroud that saps
our Net Energy Index.

Making a bad choice or committing a bad action does not make
us a bad person, Dr. Odegard advises. Instead of choosing guilt and
self-recrimination, we can choose to forgive ourselves. At its roots, a
feeling of guilt engenders a sense of unworthiness as a human being,
which in turn raises doubt as to what we deserve to receive in life.
Allowing—the third step in the formula of The Losier Method—is the
absence of doubt, and it is the most important step in manifesting
what you want. Do you see how guilt can prevent you from attracting
your desires?

How to Expunge Your Guilt

We can expunge our guilt and shame and any number of other
debilitating emotions or psychological states through a process called
"tracking" developed by Dr. Vernon Woolf, creator of holodynamics.
Holodynamics takes a quantum physics approach to understanding

how consciousness and life unfold. (For more information on holodynamics and tracking, go to www.holodynamics.com.)

The root of the word *holodynamics* is *holodyne*, which refers to information systems stored at the micro-level of our cells. "Tracking" refers to a process of exploring, identifying, connecting with, and transforming mutant information systems so they no longer have a negative impact. You might think of this as cleaning out the cobwebs in the recesses of your room or closet. While you may ignore them, they continue to collect dust and pollute your air. The good news is, anyone can do self-tracking.

Template of the Tracking Process

A few years ago, I learned how to do tracking from one of Dr. Woolf's certified trainers and have applied this process numerous times on and with other coaches. Here is an abbreviated self-tracking process, which you can use to expunge and transform whatever guilt you might be feeling. You may follow and apply this sequence on yourself with any emotional challenge:

Where in your body?

1. Identify where in your body you are feeling the guilt (or other emotion). Do you feel it in your throat, heart, solar plexus, stomach? Where?

2. What do you notice about this feeling? If it had a color, what would it be? How about shape and texture? Is it heavy as a stone, light as a feather, or somewhere in between? Is it large or small? What is the image you are getting?

Surround the image with love

3. In your mind's eye, surround the image with as much love and appreciation as you can muster. It is there to help you. *It wants to help you*, but it doesn't know how.

4. Ask the image, "What are you doing to me?" Then "listen" for the response that bubbles up from your nonconscious mind. (The following "dialogue" with the image is an example to illustrate the rest of the process. The image's responses are in all caps.)

    "What are you doing to me?" I AM REVEALING YOUR SHAME. When you make me feel shame, what do you get? I GET TO KEEP YOU IN YOUR BOX. When you get to keep me in my box, what do you get?

    SAFETY, SECURITY. What do you get with safety and security? I DON'T HAVE TO FACE MY UNWORTHINESS. What does that get you? I CAN STAY WHERE I AM. And what does that get you? I DON'T HAVE TO EVOLVE.

5. (Again, surround the image with as much love and appreciation as you can.) Ask the image, "What do you *really* want?" ACCEPTANCE. What else? LOVE. What else? HAPPINESS. Is there anything else? (Continue the questioning until there is nothing else that the image wants.)

Transform the image

6. Ask the image to *create a new image* that would represent what happiness would look like. SUBTLE BALL OF WHITE LIGHT. Is there anything else? NO. (If YES, if the new image morphs or if another image emerges, combine the two.) Tune into this new image. Can you see it, feel it?

7. Ask the new image if it is willing to help the old image transform into happiness. YES. Surround the old image with more love and appreciation. Introduce the old image to the new one, and ask the old image if it is ready to grow up and become happiness. YES. (If NO, ask the old image, "What else do you want?" and continue the process.) Assimilate the old image into the new one.

8. See, feel, and experience the white light radiating throughout your entire body. Journal your experience of the process.

The Boy Who Would Never Grow Up

As a young boy, I was rather fond of *Peter Pan* by J. M. Barrie. In fact, I *was* Peter Pan as I was so many other childhood heroes, donning their cloaks and personas and becoming greater than my small self. I *could* fly to Never Never Land, my true abode, where a youthful spirit ruled and triumphed and where I found solace and magic in the mystery of life. The fireflies where I grew up, each with its unique code and sequence of flashes beaming in search of its identical mate, were like Tinkerbell spreading enchanted dust over me. It was magical!

Belief can be expressed so powerfully in a child because he or she has not yet grown up and out of that sense of wonder and connection to all things both animate and inanimate. Disbelief has not yet set in. Or as Mr. Barrie put it in his story, "The moment you doubt whether you can fly, you cease forever to be able to do it."

Just as every thought or emotion releases its corresponding neuropeptide and frequency specific vibration, so too does every belief, whether it is positive or negative, expansive or limiting. But if we can become addicted to limiting beliefs that keep us in our box, we can also become addicted to expansive beliefs that propel us out. And if this *is* an addiction, I will drink its elixir all day long. Remember, belief is the engine of attraction and the definition of allowing, which is the most important variable in the Law of Attraction/creation equation.

"How do you measure your progress? If you measure it only by tangible results and outcomes, you may push away that which you seek or desire. Pushing and driving often meet with resistance that thwarts your progress. Over-aggressiveness sometimes compensates for and masks an underlying fear that you might not really attain your goal or even be capable of attaining it. And if the worry is what you concentrate on, if this is your true mindset, you're on a sure path to failure. If, on the other hand, you measure your progress by your emotional state—and maintain high vibrational ground, a 'lightness of being' and happiness first—then you will eventually see evidence of the results you are seeking. This is 'allowing,' surrendering to the Quantum-Heart."—Sagara

---

New Knowledge Review and Action Steps

1. What is the "correction" if your affirmations are not working for you?

   _____

   _____

2. What is the shortest period required to break a habit or emotional addiction?

   a. _____ 3 days

   b. _____ 2 weeks

   c. _____ 14–30 days

   d. _____ a heartbeat

3. Explain why forgiveness is important.

    _____

    _____

4. _____ Limiting beliefs as well as expansive beliefs are accompanied by a release of neuropeptides into your body. T or F?

Chapter 8
The New Alchemist's Handbook

*S*agara is seated not six feet from his guru. Her diminutive frame, draped in golden vestments, rests imperiously on a large chair at the front of the meditation hall reserved only for the Master. The chant is "Jaya Jaya Shiva Shambo," honoring the Supreme Being in its dual aspects. It is among his and her favorite chants.

And then, as the chant is building toward its culmination, the drum, rocking with an explosive tekka, or pattern, as they repeat the lines, "Shiva Shambo! Shiva Shambo!" over and over in crescendo as is customary at the peak of the rhythm, the guru and her devotee sway back and forth in unison, moving as one body, mirror images of each other. The distinction is now blurring between guru and devotee in Sagara's unconscious abandonment of self-consciousness, swept and carried away as he is by the sacred Ganges that has flowed over its fertile banks, purifying and nourishing everything that it touches.

Now, at the very same time, they connect and communicate with an amazing LOOK! One body, one head, one voice, one energy, Isshinryu! Two as One: Shiva and Shakti, a single look into that single reflection, rocking head and body in symmetrical motion, an identical, simultaneous, emphatic NOD—BOOM! YES!—perfectly in sync with the accelerated drumbeats and turnarounds between verses, all of which now meld into pure, divine, sonic vibration. It is, indeed, the Big Bang all over again!

✦
✦ ✦

To Abide in the Quantum-Heart

It has come down to this. The Quantum-Heart is the divine heart from which all creativity springs. As the fundamental, unifying energy field, it already dwells within us and pervades who we are. But in order to deliberately create and attract the life of our dreams, the life we desire or envision, we must dwell intentionally and *deliberately* within the Quantum-Heart. Consciousness, or Awareness, is the portal between the quantum world and the world of ordinary perception and experience.

To abide in the Quantum-Heart is to become aware of Awareness and to stay centered in the omnipresence of its gaze. —Sagara

---

Awareness is the conduit for manifesting our reality. Our Thought-Prints structure the dimensions of our existence in the same way that a set of architectural plans specify the dimensions of a grand edifice. Remember our friend the archer from chapter 4? Observing and manifesting a Thought-Print is like shooting an arrow and watching it fly all the way to its target. En route along its particular trajectory it picks up or attracts the circumstances and conditions that are frequency-specific *to the archer* and to his or her focused intention.

This is *how* "you get what you vibrate" and *why* it is always a "perfect match." But understand this: The Law of Attraction usually operates *nondeliberately* for most people, in much the same way as our breathing takes place involuntarily and unconsciously. It is similar with what I designate as the *Quantum Law of Observation™*. It is in the act of *observing* our thoughts that brings them to manifestation and fruition. If we observe them halfheartedly, which seems to be the norm for most people, or focus on fear or lack, we will receive halfhearted or undesirable results.

The *Quantum Law of Observation states, "We create whatever we observe."* **The Law of Attraction and the Law of Observation are two sides of the same coin.**

Meditation Unlocks the Quantum-Heart

On average, we breathe in and out about 21,600 times in a twenty-four-hour period! What a pity to do so entirely unconsciously when our breath can be a vehicle to deeper levels of awareness, which are the true spawning grounds of our creative impulses. You must penetrate the veil of the nine ego types (see chapter 3), each with its limiting beliefs, characteristics, and perspectives, to arrive at "I AM." This is the Quantum-Heart, and meditation is the key to unlocking it.

I have been on an ancient meditation path for roughly twenty-five years. When Sagara received spiritual awakening in 1988, the act of initiation "pierced the knot of the heart." He dove deeply into the Quantum-Heart, which unleashed at once an unprecedented catharsis and ineffable joy. It was like cleaning house on the first full day of spring. To *abide* in the Quantum-Heart, to *become established* in the Quantum-Heart, became a goal worthy of devoting a lifetime to its fulfillment.

Set Up a Daily Meditation Practice

The ultimate *purpose of meditation* is to have a vision of the divine within (God, Life Force, Universal Energy, Great Spirit, Love, Transcendental Self, etc.), which is achieved by tapping into the Quantum-Heart and recognizing "I AM That."

The *object of meditation* is our very own Self, our Awareness, the Inner Witness, the Observer, the Quantum-Heart. As Swami Muktananda used to instruct, "Meditate on the One who's meditating on you."

Joe Nunziata, author of *Karma Buster*, stresses that in order to make progress, especially emotional progress, "you have to do the work." There is no free lunch. It is the same with meditation. While there are high-tech options available—one of which I personally use to supplement "the work"—I do not believe that shortcuts can replace the consistent discipline of a daily meditation practice and achieve the same results. I guess that dates me.

But I am also in good company. Physicist and author Amit Goswami, speaking on the necessity of meditation in *What the Bleep...*, states,

> It became clear that the place from where I choose to create my own reality, that place of consciousness, is a very special non-ordinary state of being ... It's from this non-ordinary state that I choose ... We have to meditate and reach non-ordinary states of consciousness before we become the creator of our own reality.

This is the highest outcome. At the same time, there are numerous side benefits to meditation, including increased levels of serotonin in the brain, with enhanced feelings of well-being and tranquility; reduced agitation and anxiety; greater capacity to handle whatever comes up in our lives with ease, confidence, dignity, and compassion; enhanced creativity, energy, purpose, and love; and greater capacity to tap into and fulfill our true potential.

How to Meditate

Environment, Time of Day, Length of Meditation

- Pick a quiet place, the *same place every day* if possible, preferably dedicated to meditation and nothing else; no lights, no media, no distractions; this is *your* time with your

Self. Early in the morning is best, but any time during the day or night will do if early in the morning is a challenge.

- Meditate at the *same time every day* if possible, and gradually extend the length for as long as feasible within your daily schedule or routine. You may set a gentle timer (chimes, soft music). Start out with 10–15 minutes or 20–25 minutes.

- *Twice a day is ideal*—upon awaking and just before bed—but be compassionate toward yourself if you are unable to get in two sessions or if you occasionally miss a day. Just start again "tomorrow."

Posture, Breathing, and Mantra Repetition

- *Sit in a comfortable, upright position* with your eyes closed, and your hands resting palms down on your thighs or knees. It is okay to sit cross-legged on the floor or in a chair. The most important thing is to keep your back straight.

- *Take several deep "yogic breaths"*—fill the lower lungs first, expand the diaphragm, and then fill the upper chest. Exhale in the same order: bottom, middle, upper. Allow your breathing to return to normal.

- From this state, just *begin to focus on your breathing* as it moves in and out. Breathe through your nose, and "watch your breath" as it arcs its way in and down and then up and out. Gently notice where the in-breath rests before flowing out again ... and where the out-breath rests before flowing in again.

- You may simply *watch your breath or repeat a mantra,* such as *Om Namah Shivaya,* which means "I bow to my own Inner Divinity." (A mantra is a series of syllables or sounds that vibrate at the frequency of Divine Consciousness.) You will repeat your mantra silently once on the in-breath and once on the out-breath.

- *If unwanted thoughts arise, don't fight with them*, just watch them go by as clouds pass in the sky, and gently bring yourself back to your breathing and mantra repetition. Regardless of how you are feeling on any given day (i.e., whether you believe it is a good or poor meditation for whatever reason), *stay seated for the period of time you have allotted*, and then gently bring yourself back to normal awareness.

- This is a good time to *repeat any affirmations or declarations* you are working on, as your mind is very receptive during and immediately following meditation. You may also incorporate the visualizations on pages 113-121 into your meditations. You may wish to keep a journal or note pad handy to jot down any insights, directives, actions, etc. that might arise for you.

Like Begets Like

By this chapter in the book, you should be well versed in such principles as: we get what we vibrate, our outer world is a mirror image of our inner world, a feeling of abundance attracts even more, and love begets love just as fear begets only more fear.

"Remembering the Self" in meditation (however you name "the Self" or describe it) is an act of devotion and gratitude. I want you to remember that *you and I* are extraordinary manifestations of the divine, *we* are extraordinarily blessed to have evolved to the present moment of Awareness, *our future* is greater than anything in our past, and *we* are intimately connected, entangled, and bonded in the Quantum-Heart.

For More Information

For more information on meditation, yoga practices, and related topics, see my sister website, www.TheYogaAdvisory.com. I have found the high-tech set of Holosync CDs from Centerpointe Research Institute to be very effective, although I do not subscribe to the claims that "the lazy man's way to meditate" can or should replace traditional meditation. I use Holosync in the evening before bed. You may check this out at www.MeditateWithHolosync.com.

My friend and meditation expert Sally Kempton, aka Swami Durgananda, has a book entitled *Meditation for the Love of It: Enjoying Your Own Deepest Experience* with an accompanying CD, Beginning Meditation. Sally is an extraordinary human being and teacher, and I highly endorse her resources.

---

*"We don't **have** Consciousness, we **are** Consciousness. If we say we have Consciousness, who is the 'we' that possesses it?"*—Sagara

---

Guided Journeys to the Quantum-Heart

We hear a lot about the power and necessity of visualizing our goals and desires to bring them to fruition. And it is one essential way to execute step two in The Losier Method—giving our desire statements attention, energy, and focus. (See chapter 1.) How is it possible to attain a goal or desire through visualization (i.e., to manifest your reality through observation)? How does this work?

It is based on neuroscience. According to Joe Dispenza, in *Evolve Your Brain: The Science of Changing Your Mind,* the brain neither distinguishes between what it sees in its environment and what it imagines, nor does it apparently know the difference between an action performed and the same action imagined or visualized.

Many years ago (several decades actually), I trained for racquetball by using an early adaptation of high-tech visualization by racquetball champion Dave Peck. Over and over again, I performed the same motions I was viewing on video accompanied by a patterned audio in sync with the visuals. (I viewed it in a mirror because I am left-handed.) To my pleasant discovery on the court, I observed myself applying the exact same motions in my game as I had practiced in my living room. Today, use of visualization techniques in athletics is commonplace.

Dr. Dispenza asserts that the brain does not know the difference between what is taking place within itself and what is taking place outside itself; hence, a visualization is as good as—let's say it has the same potency as—its corresponding "reality," whether in the present or as a visualized, anticipated future. This is good news for goal-setters everywhere and for others who have always believed in the principle that "thinking makes it so."

Visualization Number 1: Journey to the Inner Sanctum as Recorded by Sagara

Sit in your meditative position, and take a few deep yogic breaths. Let your breathing return to normal.

I want you to imagine that you are standing before a large, exquisite door that you are about to open. Visualize what it looks like in as much detail as you can. Is it plain, or is it ornate? What color is it? What is it made of? How heavy is it? This is the door to the Quantum-Heart, to your own Inner Sanctum. Only you can open this door and step inside.

As you open the door, you release any fears, concerns, worries, or anxieties you have been carrying or holding onto. They are fleeting past you now as the door opens wide. As you step across the threshold, you feel a lightness of being and a soft breeze pass over the crown of your head. It is welcoming and inviting, and you realize you are floating toward the center of a large, bright blue ball surrounded by a golden light.

You float closer and closer to the center of the blue ball, and it begins to envelop you. You let it. It is comforting, peaceful, alive, and pulsating throughout you. The ancient Upanishads describe a deep, fourth state of consciousness called *turiya*, in which one sees the "Blue Pearl" surrounded by a golden halo. This is the Quantum-Heart. The Supreme Lord (however you wish to describe or name Him/Her) lives within the Blue Pearl enveloped by yellow radiance.

Stay for as long as you like. When your visit is over, you begin to float back toward the open door of your Inner Sanctum, and the Blue Pearl begins to recede back into itself. You will meet each other in meditation again. Gradually bring your awareness back to your place of meditation, open your eyes, and return to normal awareness. Journal your experience.

Visualization Number 2: The Column of Fire Experience as Guided by the Master

Sit in your meditative position, and take a few deep yogic breaths. Let your breathing return to normal.

Imagine a ring or column of fire in and around yourself that extends upward to protect you from all external forces or distractions. There is an energy center at the base of your spine called a *chakra*. Imagine this column rising from that chakra upward through six other chakras of energy and out through the energy center at the crown of your head. Become aware of the Observer, the Witness, who is "meditating on you."

Visualize how the column extends infinitely into the universe. The fire is purifying. Give any negativity you might feel over to the fire. If you feel any physical discomfort in your meditative position (legs, knees, or back, for example), see it and feel it dissipate as fiery blue offshoots from the column of fire. (It is natural to feel heat in one or more of your chakras.)

Feel the alchemy in the fire as it transforms everything it touches, leaving a pure and blank canvas upon which to paint a new masterpiece of your life. Choose one of your key affirmations or declarations, and repeat it with presence, reverence, gratitude, and certainty three times. (Remember, *allowing*, which is the absence of doubt, is the most important element.) Observe your affirmation(s), see them manifesting, feel the abundance you are creating in your life.

Gradually bring your awareness back to your place of meditation, open your eyes, and return to normal awareness. Journal your experience.

Visualization Number 3: The Blue Energy Waterfall Experience as Guided by the Master

Sit in your meditative position, and take a few deep yogic breaths. Let your breathing return to normal.

Visualize yourself in a lush tropical environment or in one of your favorite natural places. What sounds do you hear, what smells enter your nostrils that awaken and enliven your senses? You feel peaceful, tranquil, at one with your surroundings. You belong there. And you realize that the boundaries between "inside" and "outside," between "you" and "other," have dissolved.

You feel a cool mist across your face and realize you are sitting under a waterfall of brilliant blue energy. It is magnificent. You are immersed in streams of soothing blue energy, gently pulsating and rippling, permeating every cell of your body, every atom, every particle, and all the space in between.

You see yourself floating now in an ocean of brilliant blue energy and understand "I AM That." Your Consciousness is the Consciousness of All, and you are connected to everything in the universe. The energy extends infinitely in all directions ... as above so below, as within so without. This is your true abode, and it is from *this* place that you create and attract your life ... just as you want it.

In the peace and stillness of this recognition, choose one of your key affirmations or declarations, and repeat it with presence, reverence, gratitude, and certainty three times. (Remember, *allowing*, the absence of doubt, is the most important element.) Observe your affirmation(s), see them manifesting, feel the abundance you are creating in your life.

Gradually bring your awareness back to your place of meditation, open your eyes, and return to normal awareness. Journal your experience.

Visualization Number 4: The Chakra-Piercing Breathing Experience as Guided by Sagara

Sit in your meditative position, and take a few deep yogic breaths. Let your breathing return to normal.

Imagine that there is a golden thread, a golden filament, extending from the crown of your head to the base of your spine. It is radiant and pulsating with a subtle yellow glow.

As you slowly inhale, visualize your breath traveling along the golden filament and piercing each of the seven chakras, or energy centers, starting at the crown of the head and then the Third Eye (middle of your forehead between the eyebrows), throat, heart, solar plexus, sexual region, and, finally, the base of the spine. As the breath travels down the golden filament and pierces each chakra, the subtle yellow glow pulsates a little brighter.

Hold the breath for a moment or two, and focus on the space at the base of your spine just before your breath reverses and you begin to exhale. It is a vast and expansive space. Just as an ocean wave on the shoreline rolls in up to its apex, pauses briefly, and then begins to recede again, so too is the movement of your own breath.

[At the "pause," in the space where the breath dissolves, whether at the end of an inhale or exhale, resides the Inner Self or Quantum-Heart. *This* is the non-ordinary state from which we attract, create, and manifest our reality. It is from within this state that your affirmations and declarations should be installed, and like seeds, they will eventually but inevitably be harvested as the conditions and circumstances of your life.]

Now exhale. As you do, your breath again pierces each chakra, this time upward along the golden filament until it reaches the crown of the head where it dissolves in the space of stillness, which is your very own Inner Self or Quantum-Heart. Linger there in your true abode and become comfortable tapping into your divine source of creativity. Repeat the process of inhaling and exhaling like this for twenty minutes.

Gradually bring your awareness back to your place of meditation, open your eyes, and return to normal awareness. Journal your experience.

Visualization Number 5: Neural Reprogramming with Your Emotional Anchor

In chapter 2, I introduced the notion of creating an emotional anchor, which is an intense, positive event or experience so memorable and hardwired in your brain that you can return to it at will and relive it anew (see page 27). John Assaraf in *The Answer* explains how we can piggyback a new affirmation or declaration on an already existing neural pathway. He calls this "neural linking," whereby the new affirmation "hitches a ride" on a road already well known and traversed.

From within your meditative state, recall your emotional anchor event in as much detail as you can *recreate* (your brain doesn't know the difference between an actual memory and a fresh visualization), and evoke all the emotion you can associate with the event. Next, pronounce your new declaration three times or more while in the visualization and biochemical flow of the neural linking process. For example: "I am a brilliant and wealthy entrepreneur. Infinite abundance, creativity and intelligence flow through me."

Sagara's spiritual awakening, the chant with his guru, and his experience of the Blue Pearl are all powerful examples of emotional anchors that cascade neuropeptides into the body to reinforce our hitchhiking affirmation.

Observe the authors of *What the Bleep...,*

> Passion, divine love, feeling oneness with everything, bliss, and mystical experiences are all emotions—they generate those neuropeptides that flood the body and alter consciousness itself. A profound realization ... can so significantly rewire the brain that when people come back from it, they are different, and this world is never the same.

Choose your emotional anchor, sit in meditation, "relive" the anchor event, repeat your affirmation with deep feeling, and observe your affirmation in its trajectory to fruition. Repeat this process as often as you like. Journal your experience.

(NOTE: You can also create your own "mind movie," incorporating your emotional anchor, photos, music, declarations, "mindset reminders" on pages 128-129, etc. by using a sophisticated software package designed to help you reinforce who and what you desire to become, achieve, or acquire. You may check it out here: www.VisualizeWithMindMovies.com.)

Visualization Number 6: You Already *Are* What You Desire to Become

For much of my prior career, I had been a recognized expert and outspoken proponent for gifted education. One of my pet peeves is still the concept of academic "overachievement." Children are given an aptitude test of some kind, and then their achievement is measured against the test results. If you perform better academically than the test predicts, one is said to be "overachieving." The discrepancy between a low IQ and high performance would be an example of this.

There are several problems with this construct, but only one interests me here: It is *impossible* to "out-achieve" yourself. Or, as the Beatles sang in "All You Need Is Love," "Nothing you can do that can't be done." No matter where you are in your life compared to anybody's standard of potential but your own, you *can* achieve what you desire to become if it exists as a Thought-Print in your mind. Conversely, you cannot possibly achieve what does not first exist as a Thought-Print. How could you? It would be beyond your purview and acceptance of reality.

Anything you desire to become already exists inside you as a possibility. In fact, there are many possibilities in quantum superposition (infinite possibilities existing simultaneously). We "collapse" or observe one of these possibilities into a probability and then into existence.

If you desire to be a world-renowned author and speaker, for example, through intention, focus ("observation" in quantum talk), and appropriate action (see chapter 9), you can become this. If the thought is observed consistently and powerfully enough, its manifestation is virtually inevitable. Are there some inherent limitations to this? Sure. Someone born with severe cerebral palsy is not likely to become an NFL linebacker ... but it is *you* who gets to acknowledge and decide your boundaries of possibility.

Sit in your meditative position, and take a few deep yogic breaths. Let your breathing return to normal.

Imagine that your Future You is sitting right across from you. Who are you? What have you become? What does he or she look like? A little older and wiser? What are you wearing? What are the badges of your success? You have discovered your mission, your calling. What is it? Imagine the love, admiration, and respect you are receiving from your family, peers, and clients. What does this feel like? Life has never been better than it is right now. This is who you are, what you were destined to become, and it has always been so.

It is time to let go of the Old You. It has been holding you back out of fear and uncertainty. All doubt is gone now. Both of you stand facing each other, walk toward each other, and merge. You feel the power of what you have become, your posture is certain and confident, you have grown into your True Self, and you have left the vestiges of your former, limited identity as a snake sheds its skin. You are renewed, fresh, and alive, and it has always been so.

*SAMPLE VISION (replace with your own): You are sitting in a large conference center or stadium among ten thousand people listening to someone on stage who sounds and looks remarkably like you. You realize it **is** you. You are being paid fifty thousand dollars for a ninety-minute talk. You are wearing a black, custom-tailored suit, white shirt with monogrammed cuffs, and a power red tie.*

You are the purveyor of hope. You are inspiring your audience to take responsibility for their lives and empowering them to create and attract what they want out of life. They are pumped up and cheering, and you are teaching them how to do it and why it all works.

They gather for an autographed copy of your book. They are joining your Inner Sanctum membership community in throngs, you are being invited to other countries to conduct your Advanced Law of Attraction Certification Program, and it is standing room only wherever you go.

Observe the thought of this taking place, see it materializing, feel the excitement, and map out the action steps that will take you back to your future.

(NOTE: CDs of the meditation instructions and visualizations in this chapter are available. Go to www.ExplorersGuideToTheLawOfAttraction. com for information on how you may purchase them.)

New Knowledge Review and Action Steps

1. Thought-Prints structure the dimensions of our
    _____ in the same way as a set of
    architectural plans specify the dimensions of a
    _____.

2. The Quantum Law of Observation states: _____
    _____.

3. What are three important elements in setting up a
    meditation practice?

    a. _____

    b. _____

    c. _____

4. Identify three emotional anchors you can use in neural
    reprogramming:

    a. _____

    b. _____

    c. _____

5. What is neural linking?
    _____

6. *Allowing* is the absence of
    _____

Chapter 9
Power Is Knowledge in Action

There is a myth or distortion circulating in some professional circles—perhaps perpetuated by the movie *The Secret* even as it opened the eyes of many viewers to alternative ways of contemplating the universe—that the Law of Attraction is about *attracting* and then *waiting* for something to happen (which of course never does without *action*). This is a straw man, a misrepresentation of what the Law of Attraction is and how and why it works.

To attract, you must *act*. Attracting is about *acting* in appropriate and timely ways to bring about a desired outcome. Early in this book, I spoke of our having a foot in two camps: quantum and Newtonian. If the quantum world is the invisible substratum of energy from which manifestation ultimately takes shape and bubbles forth, the Newtonian world, as its visible counterpart, is the stage where actors and their actions draw out the manifestations of their Thought-Prints.

Let's revisit the stem of the desire statement template: "I am in the process of attracting everything I need to *do, know, and have* ..." ACTION, KNOWLEDGE, and POSSESSION *in that order* are the necessary ingredients for manifesting the outcome you desire. Sitting back and waiting for gifts to drop out of the sky is not part of the equation!

To put it another way, action is what brings attraction to fruition. I call this principle *Attraction Endorsed by Action*™.

Diagram 3
Attraction Endorsed By Action™

Attraction
Attention
Energy
Focus

Right Action

Allowing
Absence of doubt

Manifestation

How Do You Get There From Here?

Two words. If action is the catalyst for configuring and attracting the reality you desire, *new knowledge* is the fuel that stokes the fire. Joe Dispenza reinforces this in his book, *Evolve the Brain,* when he states that it is new knowledge at the basis of expanding one's possibilities, experience and dreams. To grow we need to get out of our comfort zone, break the mold, and take action toward becoming our own hero.

Your challenge is to take the first step, to heed the call from deep within the Quantum-Heart, which "knows" you may be living a *Matrix*-like existence of uneasy self-deception like Neo in the movie.

You can *choose* to stay comfortable and have an ordinary life, or you can step out of the norm, expand your knowledge base and neural networks, seek and embrace the extraordinary, and create an extraordinary, adventurous life.

Either way, though, from the point of view of the Transcendental Self (aka the Quantum-Heart), it is really all the same—*you* decide—but why not play your role on life's stage with gusto? Why not strive to cut through the myriad of distraction, seduction, superficiality, and falsehood that we are inundated with daily, find and step into your soul's true desire, and create your reality according to *your* will and terms?

The Great Paradox

When I was a student of existential philosophy, I confronted both intellectually and viscerally the dilemmas that define and haunt the human condition. One of the key underlying tenets of existentialism is that we are "thrown" into the world without our choice, but we are still responsible for playing the hand we are dealt. In short, banish victim mentality; we are empowered and expected to create our life and the meaning life has for us. (Philosophies and religions that embrace reincarnation would likely contest that we are "thrown into the world without our choice," but that's a different book.)

The French novelist and philosopher Albert Camus described the human condition as absurd: We are given no choice (about our birth) yet compelled to choose (how we define our life). We must create personal meaning out of the meaningless. Our roles in life are fleeting and transitory, but we strive to imbue them with passion nonetheless. For Camus, an actor best embodied these behaviors and best exemplified how to "be in the world."

An actor lives many lives through his roles. He demonstrates how our inner life is expressed as our outer life. Freedom of thought and action is paramount to an actor's craft, and he knows intimately the power of projecting self-image and attitude in attracting, creating, and manifesting his desired lifestyle.

My "quantum point" is this: We are all actors on multiple planes of existence. We step in and out of various roles all the time. We conceive, attract, and create these roles, and then we adorn ourselves with the costumes to play our parts. We choose, decide, and actualize our own self-fulfilling prophesies in life. Whether we are conscious and reflective about this or not, whether we are deliberate about this or not, it is how the universe works.

(NOTE: if you are an actor, musician, athlete, author, or other accomplished person of fame or notoriety, please visit www.CelebrityLawOfAttractionCoach.com for information on how I can help you manifest even more of the happiness and success you desire.)

+ +
+ +

It is the last weekend in May, 1992, in Milwaukee. Sagara was watching closely as the Master came into the meditation hall, sat in her chair, and began chanting the mantra. The lights were on her dimly. As he watched her, he noticed that her form kept changing: She morphed into old men and women with white hair, soldiers with hats and uniforms and epaulets on their sleeves; she took the form of other gurus. The forms were changing so rapidly that Sagara couldn't identify them all.

If he focused, really concentrated hard, he could bring the Master's form back into focus temporarily, but it was just as easy and actually more comfortable to let the stream of images continue.

At first he thought it was just an optical illusion as he realized he hadn't been wearing his glasses. But when he put them on, the same phenomena continued... only a little clearer this time! From deep within the Quantum-Heart came this recognition: "The Master doesn't have a singular identity; she is really everybody." And he felt intuitively that he was witnessing the formless manifest into an infinite array of forms, just as Krishna revealed Himself to Arjuna on the battlefield... in The Bhagavad Gita.

Summary of the Quantum-Heart Method

We have covered a lot of ground together. It is time to pull the method out of the madness with a systematic and daily prescription for tapping into the Quantum-Heart and creating the happiness and success you deserve.

The *Quantum-Heart Method*™ consists of four "faces" as illustrated in Diagram 4 below: 1) Mindset Reminders; 2) Right Preparation; 3) Daily Executables; and 4) Available Modalities (systems and tools introduced or covered in this book). Following are examples of each of the four faces. There may be some overlap, and there may be several items under one "face" that could have easily gone under another. Reminders, preparations, and daily actions are intended to be *ongoing*. Perform them in any order that makes sense or works for you.

Diagram 4
Four Faces Of the Quantum - Heart Method™

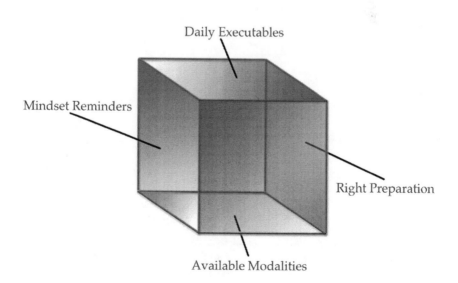

Daily Executables

Mindset Reminders

Right Preparation

Available Modalities

Face 1: Mindset Reminders

- See yourself as divine.

- Remember your greatness and the mystery and majesty of your existence.

- Strive to abide in the Quantum-Heart.

- Set a daily intention to grow in ways known and unknown.

- Remember that your inner world creates your outer world; it's a perfect match.

- Choose happiness and success.

- Recognize and accept that you are responsible for everything in your life.

- Trust your intuition and your own experience. If it feels right, it is. If it doesn't, it's not.

- Cultivate an open heart and open mind.

- Become aware of and eliminate knee-jerk reactions based on your internal alarm system, limiting beliefs, and emotional addictions.

- Commit to looking for opportunities to step out of your comfort zone.

- Remember you will see it when you believe it, not the other way around.

- Acknowledge that you are the personification of abundance; your cup is overflowing with possibility and opportunity.

- Embrace the attitude that anything is possible, that you can do and accomplish anything. The only ceilings that exist for you are those you impose on yourself.

- Ask yourself frequently, "So what do I want?"

- And the follow-up question, "So what am I *doing* about it?"

- Remember your inherent worthiness. You are enough!

- Take action. Attraction is endorsed by action!

Face 2: Right Preparation

- Learn and practice the three-step formula of The Losier Method.

- Commit to exploring the nonconscious mind and bringing to your conscious mind any "stories" and/or limiting beliefs that may be running in the background, keeping you stuck.

- Identify and examine the roots and conditioning surrounding your money story.

- Examine when, how, and why you decided to be who you are.

- Determine what elements and/or experiences of the past you must let go of in order to grow.

- Make a list of everyone you must forgive in order to move on. Forgive them.

- Identity and overcome your ego type. Strive to abide in the Quantum-Heart.

- Decide what you want to be and what you desire to achieve.

- Observe the thought of what you want to be all the way to its future manifestation.

- Review the declarations on pages 88-89 and/or create several of your own.

- Learn and review the information asked at the end of each chapter of this book.

- Commit to perpetual acquisition of new knowledge.

- Identify or create one or more emotional anchors for neural linking and neural reprogramming.

- Try the various visualizations in chapter 8; pick your favorite or create your own for meditation.

- Prepare a regular place for meditation; commit to daily meditation.

Face 3: Daily Executables

- Review and execute the Mindset Reminders and Right Preparation.

- Set up and commit to a daily meditation practice, morning and evening.

- Each day, every day, "create your day" (Ramtha's three affirmations).

- Create a daily intention for what you will manifest and achieve today.

- Observe, celebrate, and journal your successes.

- Observe, celebrate, and share your feelings and evidence of abundance.

- Schedule time for personal development and acquiring new knowledge.

- Enjoy your day; enjoy your life!

Face 4: Available Modalities (described in this book)

- The Four Faces of the Quantum-Heart Method™

- The Emotional Circuit Breaker™

- Quantum-Heart Contemplation Technique™

- Meditation instructions with six guided journeys/visualizations

- The Impure Ego Table

- The Losier Method

- Ramtha, *Create Your Day*

- Holosync

- Holodynamics

- Mind Movies

- Neural linking/Neural Reprogramming

✦
✦ ✦

Sagara had returned from South Fallsburg on Sunday and was scheduled to play racquetball with John that next Tuesday. They had been partners for a couple of years, and John held a slight edge in skill and victories, but they were both closely matched and very competitive. Sagara had never enjoyed a game in all his life as much as he did that Tuesday in July.

Bham! The blue ball careened off the side wall with perfect force, velocity, and precision. Ah, the beautiful laws of physics and math—the vectors and fractals sending the pliant sphere this way and that. Bham! Sagara smacked the perfect return and grinned at the back-and-forth of it all as John and he hustled with joy to keep the momentum going.

The ball was the **nila bindu** now, the "blue pearl," the point said to be the size of a sesame seed and dwelling in the chakra at the crown of the head. It was God Himself, the creator of this Newtonian universe in which He was bouncing around and all other universes, seen and unseen.

Bham! He expanded from the face of Sagara's racquet and would return to it again and again as if contracting to His point of origin. Sagara thought, isn't this twenty-by-forty-foot court, including the pungent aroma of perspiration clinging to the wooden floor, a microcosm of the vast space that contains the world and all the heavens?

Isn't it, too, the divine will contracted and objectified? Isn't our play as perfect an example as any of the "play of Consciousness," a perfect reflection of God's sport, His revealed yet secret answer to Leibnitz's question (see p. 47)? This is why there is something rather than nothing—the love of the game!

Epilogue
Beyond Quantum Physics to the New Science

It really is not new at all. Nor would most people—including most scientists—probably call it a science in the conventional meaning of the word. In this book, I have talked about magic, I have presented some rather esoteric philosophy, I have shared Sagara's mystical experiences, and I have urged you to expand your thinking and your feeling (your "vibe world") in a variety of ways. Where do we go from here? Where *is* here?

The truth is, *you cannot get here from over there!* Imagine you have gone into a jewelry store to purchase a string of pearls. The jeweler brings out a tray of pearls loosely scattered all over the place and asks you how you like the necklace. How would you answer? The pearls are not yet strung, the necklace has not yet been created, and it is unlikely to manifest before your very eyes.

In the same way, if we start with a conception of ourselves, our reality, and others as independent, discrete, and isolated objects and beings, which is the Newtonian model, there is no way to explain or account for the connections we experience, the psychic and energetic intimacies we share, or the universal knowledge and principles we live by. In fact, we cannot even prove that each other exists. This has been a major problem in Western philosophy. We cannot get to authentic unity or togetherness ("here") if we start with disunity and separateness ("over there").

But if we begin with the pearls already strung—as Krishna instructs Arjuna in *The Bhagavad Gita*, "Everything in the universe is strung on Brahman [Consciousness, the Self] like jewels on the thread of a necklace"—then the challenge of discovering the unified field is eliminated. We start with our sameness, with what we have in common, with an underlying substratum of energy that binds us all together at the hip like the thread in a pearl necklace, if I may mix my metaphors. The Quantum-Heart is this thread.

The Limitations of Language

Using the "wrong" language (e.g., don't, not, and no) gives attention, energy, and focus to what we desire to avoid. But using *any* language carries inherent limitations for getting at the heart of experiences, phenomena, and realities that are cosmic or mystical in nature or those beyond the boundaries of subject and object (observer and observed).

Why? Because every idea or concept, to the extent that it is capable of being articulated in language, is inherently dualistic as it bifurcates reality and perception into subject and object, I and other. There is no getting around this. Newtonian physics and the classical scientific method are based on this distinction. And this paradigm cannot be penetrated by anything *within* the paradigm itself, in the same way that the ego cannot and will not overcome *itself*.

And so the language of the sacred and the mystical is a profound silence, as words at best can only speak indirectly of these things and at worst destroy the very experience we seek to capture and hold onto. Yet this is not an empty silence but the abundant silence of meditation, the pregnant stillness of the Quantum-Heart, which gives birth to the life we envision, create, and attract.

Beyond quantum physics is Quantum Mystiphysics. This is the "new science" yet to be fully delineated as a set of precepts for understanding the relationship between Consciousness, our experience of reality, and the world we create. It is a mystical science to the extent that our power and capability to attract and manifest our desires derive directly out of the Quantum-Heart, which is our very own Inner Self. This science is rooted in the supreme no-thing that spawns both the Law of Attraction and Law of Observation.

I hold this to be the direction of the evolution of Consciousness: the progressive and reflective Awareness of the unity and oneness that binds us all. *We* are the elusive unified field.

You can join my membership community, The Innermost Sanctum, at www.QuantumMystiphysics.com. I look forward to continuing our conversation!

New Knowledge Review and Action Steps

1. What are three necessary ingredients for manifesting the outcome you desire?

    a. _____

    b. _____

    c. _____

2. What are the three elements of *Attraction Endorsed by Action*™?

    a. _____

    b. _____

    c. _____

3. Give three reasons or examples of why an actor exemplifies the Law of Attraction in action:

    a. _____

    b. _____

c. _____

4. List the four faces of the *Quantum-Heart Method*™.

   a. _____

   b. _____

   c. _____

   d. _____

5. What we cannot speak about we must pass over in

   _____.

Sagara awakens to find himself being ferried across a river to its opposite bank. The ferryman is hooded with his back to Sagara. Sagara remembers the journey of Hesse's Siddhartha and the unspoken, unwritten truth that the ferryman was his guru, as only the guru can take one across the ocean of worldliness. The ferryman turns toward Sagara, who recognizes the ferryman as himself. They speak to each other, "The river doesn't become less as it empties into the ocean. It becomes the ocean." And then the ferryman is gone. Only Sagarananda remains, and he remembers, there only ever was One.

The End

Selected Bibliography

Aaron, Raymond. *Double Your Income Doing What You Love.* New Jersey: Wiley & Sons, 2008.

Abraham, Jay. *Getting Everything You Can Out of All You've Got.* New York: St. Martin's Griffin, 2001.

Allen, James. *As a Man Thinketh.* New York: Tribeca Books, 2012.

Arntz, William, Betsy Chasse, and Mark Vicente. *What the Bleep Do We Know!?* Florida: Health Communications, 2005.

Assaraf, John and Murray Smith, *The Answer.* New York: Simon & Schuster, 2008.

Byrne, Rhonda. *The Secret.* Bel Air: Atria Books/Beyond Words, 2006.

Canfield, Jack. *The Success Principles.* New York: HarperCollins, 2005.

Clason, George S. *The Richest Man in Babylon.* Seattle: CreateSpace, 2011.

Dispenza, Joe. *Evolve Your Brain: The Science of Changing Your Mind.* Deerfield Beach: Health Communications, 2007.

Eker, T. Harv. *Secrets of the Millionaire Mind.* New York: Collins, 2005.

Fisher, Ken. *The Ten Roads to Riches*. Hoboken: John Wiley & Sons, 2009.

Foxx, JT. *Advanced Wealth Strategies*. Florida: Top One Coaching, 2011.

Gillette, Richard. *Change Your Mind, Change Your World*. New York: Simon & Schuster, 1992.

Gladwell, Malcolm. *Outliers*. New York: Little/Brown, 2008.

Goswami, Amit. *Physics of the Soul: The Quantum Book of Living, Dying, Reincarnation and Immortality*. Newburyport: Hampton Roads Publishing, 2001.

Goswami, Amit. *The Self-Aware Universe: How Consciousness Creates the Material World*. New York: Tarcher, 1995.

Goswami, Amit. *The Visionary Window: A Quantum Physicist's Guide to Enlightenment*. Wheaton: Quest Books, 2012.

Haanel, Charles. *The Master Key System*. New York: SoHo Books, 2012.

Heidegger, Martin. *Being and Time*. New York: Harper & Row, 1962.

Hesse, Herman. *Siddhartha*. Mineola: Dover Publications, 1998.

Hill, Napoleon. *Think and Grow Rich*. Seattle: CreateSpace, 2012.

Kempton, Sally. *Meditation for the Love of It: Enjoying Your Own Deepest Experience*. Louisville: Sounds True, 2010.

Kiyosaki, Robert. *Rich Dad's CASHFLOW Quadrant: Rich Dad's Guide to Financial Freedom*. Scottsdale: Plata Publishing, 2011.

Kiyosaki, Robert. *Rich Dad, Poor Dad*. New York: Business Plus, 1997.

Krueger, David and David Mann. *The Secret Language of Money: How to Make Smarter Financial Decisions and Live a Richer Life.* New York: McGraw-Hill, 2009.

Langemeier, Loral. *Put More Cash in Your Pocket.* New York: HarperBusiness, 2009.

Langemeier, Loral. *YES! Energy.* Carlsbad: Hay House, 2012.

Losier, Michael. *Law of Attraction.* New York: Hachette, 2003.

Losier, Michael. *Law of Connection.* New York: Hachette, 2009.

Muktananda, Swami Paramahansa. *The Philosophy of Kashmir Shaivism.* New York: SYDA Foundation, 1978.

Muktananda, Swami Paramahansa. *I Am That.* New York: SYDA Foundation, 1975.

Nightingale, Earl. *The Strangest Secret.* Naperville: Simple Truths, 2005.

Nunziata, Joe. *Karma Buster.* Irvine: Top Notch Training, 2011.

Odegard, Mamiko. *Daily Affirmations for Love.* Gilbert: Sortis, 2011.

Olson, Jeff. *The Slight Edge.* Dallas: VideoPlus, 2005.

Pert, Candace. *Molecules of Emotion: The Science Behind Mind-Body Medicine.* New York: Simon & Schuster, 1999.

Qubein, Nido. *Seven Choices for Success and Significance.* Naperville: Simple Truths, 2011.

Reid, Greg S. *Three Feet from Gold: Turn Your Obstacles into Opportunities.* New York: Sterling, 2011.

Radin, Dean. *Entangled Minds: Extrasensory Experiences in a Quantum Reality.* New York: Paraview Pocket Books, 2006.

Rohn, Jim. *The Five Major Pieces to the Life Puzzle.* Southlake: Dickenson Press, 1991.

Ruiz, Don Miguel. *The Four Agreements*. San Rafael: Amber-Allen, 1997.

Sarrucco, Shamayah and Eric Lofholm. *Step into Your Vision*. Florida: Komera Press, 2012.

Talbot, Michael. *Mysticism and the New Physics*. New York: Penguin Books, 1993.

The Bhagavad Gita. Translated by Eknath Easwaran. Tomales: Nilgiri Press, 2007.

Trump, Donald J. and Robert Kiyosaki. *Why We Want You to Be Rich*. New York: Rich Press, 2006.

Wattles, Wallace. *The Science of Getting Rich*. New York: SoHo Books, 2012.

Wittgenstein, Ludwig. *Tractatus Logico-Philosophicus.* London: Ruoutledte & Kegan Paul, 1961.

Yogananda, Swami Paramahansa. *The Law of Success*. Los Angeles: Self-Realization Fellowship, 1998.

Zaffron, Steve and Dave Logan. *The Three Laws of Performance*. New York: Jossey-Bass, 2011.

About the Author

James Alvino is founder and president of Monetize Your Niche®, Inc., a business consulting firm dedicated to "helping entrepreneurs pursue their passion for profit." He is a celebrated business success coach and certified Law of Attraction trainer and facilitator. Jim is known as "The Corporate Law of Attraction Guy" for his success in helping companies of all sizes get into action and create an LOA culture in the workplace. In this capacity he has worked with insurance  companies, real estate offices, high-end resorts and hotels, the entertainment industry and other venues to help with goal setting, increasing sales, and attracting ideal clients and relationships.

Currently as one of the premier business coaches affiliated with Top One Coaching and the JT Foxx Organization, Jim has dozens of clients all over the world ranging from start-ups to well established companies. His coaching expertise includes strategic planning, motivational speaking, creative problem solving, Law of Attraction, and developing a winning mindset for success.

Jim has a Ph.D. in philosophy from Boston College, has been practicing meditation for 25 years, has been a certified meditation instructor, and has written two books for Little/Brown on parenting gifted children. He is an award-winning educational journalist and a contributing author to the best-selling book, *Step into Your Vision* (2012). It was during his graduate studies that he was first introduced to the principles of quantum physics and other underpinnings of the Law of Attraction, which he has incorporated into his life and business ever since.

During a long and successful career in upper management, Jim had run a publishing company and had been the top executive for several national organizations, including a foundation started by actor Hugh O'Brian. He brings all of his acquired knowledge, expertise and wisdom to bear in his own company and coaching practice. Jim is committed to personal development, transformation, and stepping out of his comfort zone in order to grow.

Jim and his wife Margaret live in Huntington Beach, California, where you might spot them training for high-altitude endurance races, or running on the beach with their lab Koda.

12557696R00099

Made in the USA
San Bernardino, CA
19 June 2014

KANT

The Arguments of
the Philosophers

EDITOR: TED HONDERICH
Reader in Philosophy, University College, London

The group of books of which this is one will include
an essentially analytic and critical account of each of the
considerable number of the great and the influential
philosophers. Each book will provide an ordered
exposition and an examination of the contentions and
doctrines of the philosopher in question. The group of
books taken together will comprise a contemporary
assessment and history of the entire course of
philosophical thought.

Already published in the series

KANT

The Arguments of
the Philosophers

Ralph C. S. Walker

Magdalen College, Oxford

Routledge & Kegan Paul
London, Boston, Melbourne and Henley

First published in 1978
by Routledge & Kegan Paul Ltd
39 Store Street
London WC1E 7DD
9 Park Street Boston Mass. 02108 USA,
296 Beaconsfield Parade,
Middle Park, Melbourne,
3206, Australia and
Broadway House
Newtown Road
Henley-on-Thames
Oxon RG9 1EN
Set in Monotype Garamond by
HBM Typesetting Ltd, Chorley, Lancs
and printed in Great Britain by
Unwin Brothers Ltd
The Gresham Press
Old Woking, Surrey
A member of the Staples Printing Group
Reprinted and First
published as a paperback
in 1982

British Library Cataloguing in Publication Data

Walker, Ralph Charles Sutherland

Kant. – (The arguments of the philosophers).
1. Kant, Immanuel
I. Title   II. Series
193   B2798   78-40585

ISBN 0 7100 8994 5 (c)
     0 7100 0009 x (p)

Contents

CONTENTS

Figures

Preface

Any list of the great philosophers has to include Kant. His influence on philosophical thinking in the nineteenth and twentieth centuries has been immense, and his work remains of the most immediate contemporary relevance. For he faces up to the most fundamental problem that confronts philosophers, and tackles it in a more illuminating way than anyone else has done before or since. This is the problem which scepticism raises: how can one ever establish that one belief is better justified than another? What beliefs is it rational to hold? How, indeed, is knowledge possible at all? Some philosophers, in our day as in Kant's, prefer to ignore these questions, and to pretend that no such problem exists; but those who have seriously tried to answer them have nearly always done so by developing, or amending, ideas which are due to Kant.

He produced not one solution to the problem but two, though he saw them as closely intertwined. One of them involves the metaphysics of transcendental idealism; the other makes use of transcendental arguments, but does not depend on such apparently extravagant theories. Ultimately neither is completely successful, but they are none the less worthy of a careful examination, for each does achieve something. And their failures and their limitations can only be instructive to anyone who may hope to get further than Kant did in resolving the problem of knowledge.

In what follows the name of Strawson will appear from time to time. Strawson's work is of great value in its own right, and his interpretative reconstruction of Kant has become accepted as orthodox by surprisingly many people, especially in England. But the principal reason for considering him here is that he can be taken as the representative of a long tradition of Kantian criticism, as common in Germany as in Great Britain and going back to Kant's own time. This tradition dispenses with the contrast between the transcendental ideality of the world we know and the reality of things as they are in themselves; but I believe, and shall try to show, that it has been misguided in its underestimate of transcendental idealism and equally misguided in its overestimate of what can be achieved without it. Transcendental idealism will not solve every problem, and is not without difficulties of its own, but the alternative of relying on transcendental arguments turns out to be much more disappointing than its proponents expect; not because there is anything wrong with the method, but because of the difficulty of finding satisfactory arguments of that kind which lead to interesting conclusions.

Anyone who tries to write a book on Kant faces a fourfold task. Almost any philosophical writer will want both to be comprehensible to the general or undergraduate reader who is not already familiar with the subject, and at the same time to say something that is not without interest for professionals working in the field. But in discussing the views of a philosopher like Kant there is also the difficulty of deciding what weight to give to historical considerations, and to what extent historical accuracy may be abandoned for the sake of dealing with arguments whose ascription to Kant is highly dubious. I have tried above all to be intelligible, and to be historically accurate while subordinating the discussion of historical points to an overriding philosophical purpose; and where it is necessary to examine an argument which cannot safely be ascribed to Kant I have endeavoured to make this clear. But in a work of this kind it is not possible fully to defend all of the historical contentions as thoroughly as historians of ideas would expect; the less so since, in keeping with the aim of this series, I have attempted to say something – though not always much – about all of Kant's main philosophical preoccupations. This I have tried to do in such a way as to make clear to the reader what I see as the principal merits and difficulties in Kant's views, but at the same time I have tried to make everything subservient (as it was for Kant himself) to the central issues of transcendental idealism and transcendental arguments. As a result, in many cases I have been able to do little more than touch on matters which deserve a fuller discussion than I could give them here. But if I have said enough to encourage a few readers to pursue them further then I shall have achieved my objective.

My thanks are due to the editor and publishers of *Open Mind* for allowing me to reproduce material from my article 'The Categorical Imperative: Form and Content' (*Open Mind* 1.4 (1976), pp. 13–19). They are due also, and in large measure, to the many people who have read or have listened to drafts of sections of this book; including my undergraduate pupils, who have often provided valuable criticisms. But I am specially grateful to Dr J. D. Kenyon, Mr D. Bostock and Mr M. J. Woods for their useful comments and objections, by which I have done my best to profit.

Dr Kenyon, in particular, read the entire manuscript and made a very large number of extremely helpful suggestions, practically all of which I have followed. And finally I owe a great debt to Merton College, Oxford, for giving me the opportunity to work on Kant as a Junior Research Fellow; and above all to my former supervisor, Mr H. H. Cox, without whose guidance and encouragement I should never have persevered in seeking a path through the labyrinths of Kantian thought.

References and Abbreviations

The definitive edition of the works of Kant is the one published by the *Königlich Preussische Akademie der Wissenschaften* and its successors, beginning in 1902 but not yet complete. Where possible references to Kant's works are made to this edition (abbreviated 'Ak.' in the text and notes), except in the case of the *Critique of Pure Reason*. Many English translations carry the *Akademie* edition's page references in their margins, but where they do not and where it would facilitate matters I have tried to include page references also to the translations. These are indicated by the names of their translators or editors, and publication details may be found in the bibliography.

The volumes of the *Akademie* edition which contain Kant's correspondence exist in two versions, the second being more complete than the first; references are to the second version, but I have included the paging of the first in brackets. Thus 'Ak. XI: 255 (243)' would refer to p. 255 of the second version of vol. XI, p. 243 of the first version.

The *Vorlesung über Ethik* and the *Duisburg'sche Nachlass* are cited in the editions by Menzer and Haering respectively, for which see the bibliography. For the *Critique of Pure Reason* I have followed the convenient and customary method of referring to the pages of the first (1781) and second (1787) editions, known as 'A' and 'B'. In the case of the *Grundlegung (Foundations of the Metaphysics of Morals)* the practice seems to be developing of making references to the second (1786) edition, the page-numbering of which is given by Paton in the margins of his translation; so I have done this as well as giving references to the *Akademie* edition.

In quoting Kant I have used translations where they are available, and where there are several I have used the first one listed in the bibliography unless otherwise stated. In a number of cases I have amended the translations; where the alterations are of major significance I have indicated this.

Other abbreviations used in the text and notes are:

KdpV   *Kritik der praktischen Vernunft* (*Critique of Practical Reason*).

KdrV   *Kritik der reinen Vernunft* (*Critique of Pure Reason*).

KdU   *Kritik der Urtheilskraft* (*Critique of Judgment*).

MAdN   *Metaphysische Anfangsgründe der Naturwissenschaft* (*Metaphysical Foundations of Natural Science*).

MdS   *Metaphysik der Sitten* (*Metaphysics of Morals*).

MdS R   *Metaphysik der Sitten, Rechtslehre* (*Theory of Right*).

MdS T   *Metaphysik der Sitten, Tugendlehre* (*Theory of Virtue*).

Refl.   *Reflexion* (the *Reflexionen* are notes of Kant's, collected in vols XIV–XIX of the *Akademie* edition).

I

How is Synthetic A Priori
Knowledge Possible ?

Kant did not originally intend to write a Critique of the Pure Reason. His first published works were on questions in physics – on the concept of force, on the nature of fire, on planetary motion, and so forth; though even in those days he studied physics more as a philosopher than as a scientist, for his underlying concern was to discover how far physics rested upon metaphysical foundations and what these metaphysical foundations were. Some form of the Principle of Sufficient Reason, according to which there is an explanation for everything that happens, seemed to be a presupposition of science, and the physical concepts of force, matter, and space appeared to be topics on which metaphysics also had something to say. But as time went on he became more and more uncertain about the character and status of metaphysical claims in general; so that he found himself diverted from the provision of metaphysical underpinnings for physics to the antecedent question of the legitimacy of metaphysics itself. Philosophers put forward conflicting assertions, often with equal plausibility and equal show of rational argumentation behind them; no satisfactory method existed for determining where the truth lay. So before anything else could be done it seemed to Kant essential to put metaphysics itself on a secure foundation – to show how, or to what extent, genuine metaphysics is possible. And that is the task of the *Critique of Pure Reason*.

Similarly when he first turned his attention to morals his principal interest was in the metaphysical assumptions on which he took morality to rest. These concerned the character of man as an agent who is at once both rational and subject to non-rational desires, and who is, above all, free: free in a sense which seemed liable to conflict with the demands of the Principle of Sufficient Reason, according to which every act and every choice must be antecedently determined. But his project of writing a book on the metaphysical foundations of morality had to be deferred, just as the book on the metaphysical foundations of physics was deferred, until pure reason had been critically examined. And because he came to think that metaphysical claims in the service of ethics have a different status and a different justification from those the interest of which is purely factual, this critical examination could not be completed in the first *Critique*: a critique of pure *practical* reason was required as well. In fact the *Metaphysics of Morals*, first promised by Kant at the end of 1765,[1] appeared only in 1797, as his last major work; the *Metaphysical Foundations of Natural Science* came out in 1786, five years after the *Critique of Pure Reason* was published.

When Kant was a young man the great figure dominating German philosophy was Christian Wolff; when he started to do philosophy he set out along broadly Wolffian lines and against a background of Wolffian assumptions. Behind Wolff stood the rather more shadowy figure of Leibniz – shadowy because much of his most important work had never been published. Wolff claimed to have developed his views largely independently of Leibniz, but it is hard to believe there was not a closer connection than he was prepared to admit, for much of what Wolff gives us is a cruder and less subtle, but also much more systematically set out, treatment of characteristically Leibnizian theses. Wolff had a passion for system, as a guarantee of proper order and completeness, which Kant was to inherit. He also had a facility for writing (voluminously) in a straightforward and readily comprehensible way, both in Latin and in German; this unfortunately Kant did not inherit, though he did take over much of the German philosophical vocabulary which Wolff had for the first time forged.

The positions of Leibniz and Wolff were sufficiently close for Kant and his contemporaries often to bracket them together, and even to speak of the Leibniz–Wolffian philosophy. All the same, Wolff was not a slavish follower of Leibniz. For example, he regarded the material world as built up not out of Leibniz's spiritual monads but out of physical point-particles. And these physical substances could act on one another directly; whereas for Leibniz no two substances can genuinely interact, the appearance of interaction being the result of a pre-established harmony between them, Wolff only requires the harmony to explain the apparent interaction of mind and body – the action of body on body being perfectly genuine. Leibniz's logical reflections, which Russell and Couturat argued (and in my view justly) to lie at the centre of his conception of substance,[2] were at that time unpublished and unknown, and there is nothing in Wolff parallel to them. Indeed, he entirely lacked Leibniz's logical sophistication. Had it been otherwise he could not have produced his most distinctive amendment of Leibniz, his deduction of the Principle of Sufficient Reason from the Principle of Contradiction. The deduction goes as follows:

Let us suppose that A exists without some sufficient reason why it should rather be than not be. It follows that nothing is to be postulated (*nihil ponendum est*) from which it can be understood why A exists. So it is held that A exists because nothing is taken to exist. But since this is absurd, nothing is without a sufficient reason, or in other words, if something is taken to exist, some other thing must also be admitted from which it can be understood why it exists. (*Ontologia* §70.)

Like Leibniz,[3] Wolff distinguished between necessary and contingent truths, holding that necessary truths are 'founded on' the Principle of Contradiction, contingent ones on the Principle of Sufficient Reason. The Principle of Contradiction is formulated in various ways, e.g. as 'It cannot come about that the same thing both is and is not at the same time' or as 'If A is B, it is false that the same A is not B',[4] but clearly the aim is to include as necessary all those propositions which we, following Kant, should be inclined to call analytic, as well as metaphysical claims like the Principle of Sufficient Reason itself which Wolff thought he could establish in the same logical way. Such truths can be known a priori, without appeal to experience; contingent truths on the other hand must be discovered empirically, for although there is a reason for everything that happens the chain of reasons goes back endlessly and is ultimately grounded in the choice of the Creator.

Wolff's Principle of Sufficient Reason clearly committed him to a form of determinism, which many of his contemporaries regarded as unacceptable in the extreme. Leibniz had been driven in the same direction by the same pressure and had tried desperately (in the *Theodicy* and elsewhere) to resist the conclusion, but without noticeable success. Many philosophers therefore opposed Leibniz and Wolff on this, arguing in defence of a kind of human freedom irreconcilable with determinism; but much the most significant and incisive of these opponents was C. A. Crusius. Crusius did not reject the Principle of Sufficient Reason entirely – he accepted a modified version of it which was supposed to leave a proper place for freedom.[5] But he also, and for our purposes more importantly, pointed out the flaw in Wolff's supposed derivation of the Principle of Sufficient Reason,[6] and showed in general that Wolff had tried to get far too much out of the Principle of Contradiction. Wolff had wanted it to be the sole ultimate and self-evident principle of reason; Crusius saw that it was by no means sufficient to yield the metaphysical claims Wolff needed to make, and had to be supplemented by other principles equally ultimate and equally self-evident. Crusius' achievement was, in effect (and still rather obscurely), to distinguish within the class of necessary truths those Kant would call analytic from those which while not analytic were still necessary. Truths of the former class held, he thought, in virtue of the Principle of Contradiction; he did not recognize, any more than Wolff did, that not all logical laws could be reduced to this. But truths of the latter class included all those substantive, non-logical claims on which metaphysicians continually relied, and which could not be derived from logical laws.

The admission of non-logical first principles naturally faced Crusius with the question what grounds we can have for accepting such principles as true. Here he relied in the first instance on intuition, enunciating the general rule 'Whatever can only be thought as true is true, and whatever can only be thought as false is false.' Wolff himself had defended the acceptance of the Principle of Contradiction on similar lines: 'We find the nature of our mind to be such that while it judges that something is, it cannot simultaneously judge that it is not.'[7] If the objection is pressed that what we can or cannot think is purely a matter of human psychology, Crusius falls back on the answer of Descartes: that God, who is no deceiver, guarantees the truth of that which we cannot think to be false, and the falsehood of that which we cannot think to be true. It is God's benevolence that secures the correspondence between how we think and the way the world is.[8]

It was Crusius, not Hume, who woke Kant from his dogmatic slumbers. For Crusius had asked a fundamental question, the question Kant was later to put as 'How is synthetic a priori knowledge possible?' And he had returned an answer which seemed to Kant utterly unsatisfactory. Among the metaphysical assertions which Crusius confidently made were such claims as that the world has a purpose, and that every existent thing – including God – is in space, claims which Kant considered far from self-evident and which conflicted with counter-claims that appeared equally obvious to other metaphysicians. Crusius' psychological test of truth left things far too subjective and provided no way of resolving disagreements or antinomies. And the appeal to a non-deceiving God was circular, as Arnauld and many others had pointed out against Descartes, for whatever arguments one uses to establish the existence of such a God must ultimately rest on the acceptance of certain principles as self-evidently correct – the very thing one is trying to justify. So in writing to Marcus Herz Kant could sum up his rejection of Crusius thus:

> *Crusius* accepted certain innate rules of judgment and certain
> concepts, as planted by God in the human soul so as to harmonize
> with things. . . . But in determining the origin and validity of our
> knowledge, however, the *deus ex machina* is the most absurd
> argument one could choose. Apart from the vicious circle in the
> series of inferences from what we know, the argument has the
> further disadvantage of countenancing every whim and pious or

4

speculative figment of the imagination. (To Herz, 21 Feb. 1772, Ak. X: 131 (126).)

A few years earlier, with even less sympathy, he had described Crusius' metaphysical system as 'produced by Crusius out of nothing, by means of a few magical sayings about the thinkable and the unthinkable.'[9]

His own initial reaction was to regard Wolff as fundamentally right in holding the necessary truths of metaphysics to be analytic. In the *Nova Dilucidatio* (1755) he attempted to derive a version of the Principle of Sufficient Reason from a logical principle called the Principle of Identity, which he took to be prior to the Principle of Contradiction. His arguments, however, are on a par with Wolff's; and as time went on he became more and more convinced by Crusius that no such derivation could ever succeed. On the other hand, in view of the untenability of Crusius' own position, it was very hard to see how the substantive claims of metaphysicians could possible be vindicated. The existence of antinomies particularly disturbed him (as it did others at the time); in a number of cases it seemed possible to find equally convincing arguments both for a proposition and for its contradictory. It appeared that human reason naturally led itself into contradictions, and thinking of this period afterwards he wrote:

> I tried very seriously to prove propositions and their opposites, not
> to erect a sceptical doctrine, but because I suspected there was an
> illusion of the understanding, in which it was stuck. (Reflexion 5037.)

It is not perhaps surprising, however, that for a time he should have embraced the sceptical alternative, and rejected metaphysics wholesale. This was his position when he wrote *Dreams of a Spirit-Seer* (1766), in which the speculations of Wolff and Crusius are treated as on a par with the spiritualist imaginings of Swedenborg. The illusions of spirit-seers are said to arise from their transposing into the world what is really no more than the product of their own disordered fantasy; in the same way metaphysicians read into the nature of things the principles they find attractive, and mistake a fiction for reality. Not that such speculations are meaningless; we cannot even be sure that they are only fictions, for the position is rather that in these areas we can know nothing. 'The rule of our reason concerns only comparison in respect to *identity* and *contra-diction*',[10] i.e. it only provides us with analytic truths, and otherwise we must rely upon experience; where experience cannot guide us knowledge is not available. Fortunately, such knowledge is also unnecessary for the practical purposes of life.

There is much that is valuable in *Dreams of a Spirit-Seer*, and that points ahead to the critical philosophy Kant had not yet evolved. At the end of it he makes, but does not develop, the suggestion that although a theoretical belief in the soul's immortality will not provide a satisfactory basis for a good life we may perhaps be able 'to base the expectation of a future world upon the sentiment of a good soul'[11] – which looks forward to the Postulates of Pure Practical Reason as well as to the view that an action based on the agent's interest cannot have moral worth. The earlier part of the book contains a tentative description of the immaterial or spirit-world, governed by moral laws, which might be supposed to exist alongside the material world in such a way that we were members of both; which prefigures much in Kant's later thought about the noumenal self. Indeed, the spirit-world is thought of as genuinely real in a way the material world is not: the material world is a 'systematic appearance', a coherent representation which spirits share and which has no reality independent of them.[12] This, together with the fact that he describes rationalist metaphysicians as reading into the world their own ways of thinking, points ahead towards the transcendental idealism which he was to adopt in earnest in three or four years' time.

His dismissal at this stage of synthetic a priori metaphysics may recall the empiricism of Berkeley and Hume. But there is no need, I think, to postulate any significant influence of theirs upon Kant's views about metaphysics. He had certainly read Hume's *Enquiries* by 1762, but there is no evidence that he took Hume's doubts seriously or even gave them much thought, except in so far as he had discovered the same difficulties for himself. When he discusses metaphysics in the 1760's he sees it through the eyes of Crusius and his other German contemporaries, and sets out the problem in their terms; he became concerned about causality, for example, through considering the inadequacy of Crusius' conception of a *Realgrund*, and he never expressed the matter in a Humean way before 1781. Both before and after the *Dreams of a Spirit-Seer* his thoughts about necessary truth develop perfectly naturally and comprehensibly without requiring us to postulate empiricist influences, and it is particularly perverse to suppose (as some have done) that a reading of Hume somehow enabled him to *resolve* his difficulty about the synthetic a priori. It is true that in the *Prolegomena* (1783) he ascribed to Hume his awakening from dogmatism,[13] but this may be no more than a rhetorical device in a book written to present the *Critique* as an answer to Hume. Even there the question is approached in a manner rather different from Hume's. For Hume the problem about cause was in large part the problem of induction, but induction was never a major preoccupation of Kant's – if it had been he might have been less completely satisfied with his transcendental idealism, as we shall see in the final chapter. Instead he poses the question almost as Crusius might have done: how can the a priori concept of cause be guaranteed to apply to the objects of experience?

His rejection of substantive metaphysics did not last long. Even at his most sceptical Kant declared himself in love with metaphysics and strongly tempted to believe its unprovable claims (or some of them at any rate).[14] I suspect – though this is no more than a speculation – that what made him abandon the position of *Dreams of a Spirit-Seer* was the discovery that such scepticism would have to extend to geometry as well; a discipline it appeared to him absurd to call in doubt. He makes no attack on mathematics in 1766, and at that time would presumably have agreed with Hume that mathematical propositions, like the truths of logic, just express 'relations of ideas'; certainly this seems to me the position he adopts in his Prize Essay of 1763, though the matter is not entirely beyond dispute.[15] But in 1768 he wrote an essay entitled 'Concerning the Ultimate Foundation of the Differentiation of Regions in Space', in which he thought more deeply about space and geometry than he had ever done before. The conclusion he came to was that space is a *thing*. Previously he had been inclined to the relational view of space defended by Leibniz against Clarke and the Newtonians, according to which space is a system of relations between objects: the objects being identifiable on the basis of their internal qualities alone, prior to and independently of their spatial properties. And on this view there is nothing more to be said about space than can be said by describing these interrelations. The alternative Newtonian position which Kant now came to adopt was that space should be recognized as having properties of its own, independently of and prior to the objects which fill it. His reason for changing his mind was that he thought Leibniz's relational theory incapable of handling the distinction between incongruent counterparts, a claim we shall have to examine in chapter IV. But the conclusion that space is a thing in its own right, with intrinsic qualities of its own, made him sharply aware that geometrical propositions could not be dismissed as unproblematic. Geometry (in the opinion of Kant and his contemporaries) is a body of a priori truths about space, but if space is a thing in the world independent of us how can we have a priori knowledge about it? Geometrical truths cannot be analytic if they describe the nature of a real external entity.

As a matter of fact Kant might have seen that even on a relational account the same problem arises, for geometry will still purport to give us a priori knowledge of something external to us: namely, the ways in which objects can be related to one another. He did not see this, however, partly perhaps because he had not yet clearly formulated the distinction between analytic and synthetic judgments, and no doubt the problem is highlighted much more dramatically if space is actually an independent substance. At the end of the 1768 essay he points out the connection with the problem over the fundamental principles of metaphysics: 'this difficulty shows up everywhere, if one still wants to philosophize over the first data of our knowledge'.[16]

It was natural for Kant to consider time as closely parallel to space, and to come to the view that it also was more than a system of relations.

7

He did not yet think of arithmetic as being about time in quite the way geometry was about space, but he was sure all the same that we do know things about time a priori. The first major step towards the critical philosophy was taken when, in his *Inaugural Dissertation* of 1770, he was able to give an account of how such a priori knowledge of space and time was possible: instead of being independent of us, space and time are forms imposed by our minds upon their experience. Only if we ourselves read them into the world, he concluded, can we be assured – independently of all experience – that our beliefs about them correspond to the way things are. This of course does not involve a return to thinking of them as systems of relations; they have features no relational analysis can allow for, as the example of incongruent counterparts is intended to show. The change between 1768 and 1770 lies not in a denial that space and time are things, but in a rejection of their independence from us: they are there because we put them there.

'The year 69 gave me great light', Kant wrote later, and it is hard to resist the view that this great light was the discovery of the thesis that space and time are forms that we impose.[17] In a way the move was fairly natural for him, if one remembers how he expressed his scepticism in 1766: metaphysicians and spirit-seers read into the world the fictions that their minds create. That we had no reason to suppose these to be anything more than fictions was borne out by the lack of general agreement about them.[18] But over geometry and arithmetic and the character of space and time in general there is no lack of agreement. Nor could there be; for space and time are the forms under which we sense objects, and we could not be aware of the sensible world at all except through them. So although they are not in the fullest sense real they are not simply fictions either: space and time can be called 'most veridical' (*verissimum*) and so can the sensible world, the world of things as they appear in space and time (phenomena). For something to be the case in the sensible world is just for it to appear so to everyone under the appropriate conditions, and this universal agreement allows us to speak of phenomena as being in a sense objective (though Kant does not actually apply this word to them until later).[19]

In the *Inaugural Dissertation* it is only space and time that are held to be mind-imposed. On metaphysics Kant does not repeat the scepticism of 1766, but he has nothing positive to offer. Somehow, reason must succeed in producing substantive principles on which metaphysics can rest, and he seems vaguely to think that it will do all right if it avoids making a number of mistakes (like confusing the sensible world with the underlying noumenal reality) which he carefully warns against. His important letter to Marcus Herz of 21 February 1772 shows him wrestling with the problem of justifying these metaphysical claims and unable to resolve it. What he eventually came to see was that the solution provided by the *Inaugural Dissertation* for space and time, and so for mathematics, could be generalized: the idea of the mind imposing forms upon its world could be used to explain synthetic a priori knowledge in metaphysics as well.

Of course, not all the metaphysicians' claims to a priori knowledge could be justified in this way. In imposing its forms – space, time, and the concepts Kant calls categories – the mind constructs the world as we know it, the world of our shared experience. What we contribute to this construction can give us a priori knowledge only about the world we construct, and not about things as they really are in themselves, noumena. Metaphysical claims that outrun the limits of possible experience and so go beyond anything that the mind can impose lack justification and must be dismissed as illegitimate; as in *Dreams of a Spirit-Seer*, Kant considers not that they are unintelligible but that they concern matters about which we can find out nothing, either empirically or by a priori argument.

But in order to carry through this generalization of his solution Kant has to face more firmly up to his own earlier scepticism than he had needed to do in the *Inaugural Dissertation*. Despite their mind-dependent status, a kind of objectivity could be conceded relatively easily to space and time in view of the general agreement as to the spatio-temporal character of experience and as to the mathematics that (allegedly) depends on them. But Kant now holds that we also order our experience by means of certain a priori concepts, the categories, and the question must again arise whether if we read these concepts in we may not be reading in mere fictions of our imagination, like Swedenborg and his friends. This time the suggestion is less easily rebutted by appeal to universal agreement. The synthetic a priori truths which are supposed to emerge (like 'every event has a cause') are by no means uncontentious, and it is not at all so obvious that Kant's twelve categories play the important part in our experience that he assigns to them.

So a further argument is required; and it is found by developing a point already made about space and time in 1770. Kant had then observed that except through them we cannot be aware of objects of sense-experience, so that they are 'conditions of all appearances and of empirical judgments'.[20] If it can be shown in a similar way that the categories are 'a priori conditions of the possibility of experience' (A 94/B 126) then we no longer have to look to universal agreement to guarantee that they apply and are not fictitious: for we can now prove that there can be no experience without them. Such a proof, a demonstration that the categories must apply if experience is to be possible, would be a transcendental deduction of the categories. 'Deduction', because it establishes the legitimacy of these concepts, and the word is applied by lawyers to a vindication of title. 'Transcendental', because it has to do with conditions for the possibility of experience – or know-ledge: for Kant 'conditions for experience' and 'conditions for know-ledge' come to much the same, because by 'knowledge' he means the synthetic knowledge we could not have without experience and by 'experience' he means a self-conscious awareness which involves at least some knowledge.[21] In the *Critique of Pure Reason* Kant provides the categories with their transcendental deduction; and he also provides separate transcendental arguments for each of the synthetic a priori principles which he considers to hold within the world of appearances in virtue of the fact that we impose space, time and the categories upon it.

We shall be looking fairly closely at what transcendental arguments are and what they can prove. For the moment we can simply notice that (although the matter is not undisputed) their general form appears to be something like this:

We have experience (or, knowledge).
If there is experience (or, knowledge), p must be true.
Therefore, p.

Though there is one important qualification to be made, namely that it is sometimes built into the first premise that our knowledge or experi-ence is of some particular kind – e.g. spatio-temporal experience. Arguments of this form are evidently valid; but it is unfortunate Kant does not say more than he does about the status of the premises. All that he makes really clear is that the second premise must be a priori. We are not concerned with the conditions that may be empirically required for experience; if, for example, organisms of the required complexity can only exist at temperatures below $1000°C$, this is beside the point.[22]

It is a little surprising that Kant should give this function to the word 'transcendental'. There is nothing in its etymology or its traditional usage by philosophers which would appear to suggest a connection with the a priori conditions for the possibility of experience. It was applied by mediaeval philosophers to those terms (notably 'one', 'true', and 'good') which may be predicated of anything whatsoever regardless of what Aristotelian category it belongs to, and by Kant's predecessors in Germany to the most general predicates of things. The connection, I think, is to be found in Wolff, who provides us with an argument Kant would have called transcendental and presents it as a point about what he calls transcendental truth. The argument is in support of the Principle of Sufficient Reason; as we have seen he did try to derive this principle from the Principle of Contradiction, but he also argued quite separately that unless it were true there would be no distinction between dreaming and reality. In that case there would be no facts to be known and conse-quently no knowledge; so that the Principle of Sufficient Reason is a condition for the possibility of knowledge. This may not be a particularly plausible contention, though as we shall see in due course Kant took up the same idea and reworked it into his proof of the Second Analogy. But in setting out the argument Wolff uses 'transcendental truth' as a synonym for reality, and he claims to have shown that the principle is *constitutive* of transcendental truth, just as Kant's transcendental arguments are supposed to establish that the categories, etc., are constitutive of the objective world of appearances. Kant himself sometimes equates reality with transcendental truth, and the usage is not as odd as it may sound, for the old transcendental term 'true' applied not to propositions but to things (of whatever category) and was in effect equivalent to 'real'.[23]

The idea that transcendental arguments always show something to be constitutive of reality, or reality as we know it, needs to be treated with some caution. What they establish is that unless certain things were the case experience, or knowledge, would not be possible, but this does not by itself guarantee that such conditions are constitutive in any sense stronger than that. In particular, it is not necessary that the conditions be imposed by the mind itself in constructing our experience. Kant thought that they must be: on his view transcendental arguments show us what it is that the mind contributes to the world of appearances, and they guarantee its objectivity. We can now see, however, why he should have thought this, and overlooked the possibility that the relevant conditions might happen to obtain in the world quite independently of us. On his view synthetic a priori knowledge was possible only because and in so far as the mind imposed its own forms upon the world; transcendental arguments were brought on only after this conclusion had been reached and in order to play an ancillary role. He failed to notice that they provided him with an alternative solution to the problem about synthetic a priori judgments. For we can be sure of the truth of such judgments if their truth is required for experience to be possible, even though we have not ourselves constructed the world of appearances in such a way as to make them true.

Thus in a way Kant gives us two distinct solutions to the problem, though he did not think of them as separate or even as separable. One is the transcendental idealist solution, according to which we read such truths into the phenomenal world, and the other is the solution Strawson and others consider more 'austere' and respectable,[24] whereby we can discover certain substantive claims to be true by using transcendental arguments. And these solutions are separable. For it is not (or not obviously) indispensable to the transcendental idealist solution that it should be transcendental arguments that guarantee the objectivity of the mind-imposed elements; in the case of space and time the transcendental argument appeared unnecessary because it seemed enough that we had universal agreement. And it is by no means inherent in the character of transcendental arguments that their conclusions should concern what forms the mind imposes. They establish only that certain things must obtain, if we are to have experience, and their obtaining may be in no way due to us: it may just be a fortunate fact about the world, a *sine qua non* of our existence as knowing subjects.

Kant has been much criticized since his own day for not seeing this point, and in recent years most trenchantly by Strawson. It cannot be denied that such criticism is just; even though we may find in the long run that its effects are less far-reaching than such critics have normally supposed. His confusion on the point leads as we shall see to severe difficulties within Kant's system, especially over noumena and over the self. His own theory requires the existence of a subject which is spontaneously active in synthesis, and requires it as a condition for the possibility of experience; yet it also excludes this very claim as illegitimate because there is no way in which its truth can be imposed by the knowing mind. The mind cannot read itself and its own spontaneity into the world of appearances.

Such difficulties as this are not the only ones which arise from the fact that the *Critique of Pure Reason* developed out of the *Inaugural Dissertation*, though perhaps they are the most serious. As we shall see, he never fully succeeded in integrating the *Dissertation*'s theory about space and time into the broader theory of the *Critique*; traces of the earlier and more limited view remain, particularly in the Transcendental Aesthetic, but also in his later recensions of the same material. Not surprisingly, perhaps, in view of its complexity, after 1780 he never seems to have thought his entire system through again from scratch; he changed his view about a great many subsidiary points, but he did not rethink the basic framework. Had he done so he might have cut free of the *Inaugural Dissertation* and become clearer on many matters. Perhaps he would have seen that transcendental arguments have their own contribution to make, independently of transcendental idealism. But it would be wrong to think that this could or should in any way have undermined his faith in transcendental idealism. Transcendental idealism does not rest on any confusion about the role and function of transcendental arguments. It was put forward on its own merits in 1770, before Kant took transcendental arguments particularly seriously; and it can stand on its own feet.

Strawson is only one of a long line of writers on Kant who have seen his transcendental idealism as an unfortunate aberration, a regrettable lapse into the kind of speculation which he himself shows to be groundless. The sympathetic commentator, on their view, should avert his eyes from this embarrassing sight, and seek to reinterpret as much of the *Critique* as possible without it; salvaging the transcendental arguments, but abandoning the contrast between noumena and phenomena and the conception of nature as made by the knowing mind. This has a certain earthy appeal. But I shall argue that it is almost exactly the wrong course to adopt; for although transcendental arguments are by no means useless, Kant and his successors have had altogether too much faith in what can be achieved by them, and it is that side of the critical philosophy which (with regret) we must largely cut away. Transcendental idealism, on the other hand, when properly considered is not so absurd a doctrine as its detractors suggest, and something very like it is forced on us when we reflect upon our knowledge of the world.

II

Transcendental Arguments

If they can be made to work transcendental arguments are a particularly satisfactory way of replying to sceptics. As Strawson has pointed out they offer us the prospect of showing the sceptic that he is undercutting his own position. If the sceptic doubts whether p, and the truth of p can be shown by a transcendental argument to be required for any intelligible thought to be possible, then he is faced with an awkward dilemma: either his doubt must be ill-founded, and p is true after all, or else there is no such thing as intelligible thought and his own doubt cannot be formulated intelligibly. If he were to suggest that not-p the meaningfulness of this suggestion would entail its falsity: there would be no possibility that he had uttered something intelligible and true. 'Thus his doubts are unreal, not simply because they are logically irresoluble doubts, but because they amount to the rejection of the whole conceptual scheme within which alone such doubts make sense.'[1] Indeed, they amount to the rejection of any conceptual scheme whatever.

Kant does not talk of conceptual schemes or of conditions for intelligible thought; he talks of conditions of the possibility of knowledge, or of experience. But it amounts to the same thing. By 'experience' he means a self-conscious awareness which involves thought and a capacity to make judgments; by 'knowledge' he means the sort of knowledge that can be expressed in judgments, the sort of knowledge a self-conscious subject has about his experience. And no one could think or talk intelligibly, as a purposive user of language, unless he could understand what he was doing; which would require him to have knowledge and experience.

He never makes clear the status of this very general claim that we have knowledge or experience (or intelligible thought). Presumably he would regard it as synthetic a priori. It is in rather a special position, for it is too basic to be an ordinary empirical statement and yet it is not analytic. But since he holds that transcendental arguments with this premise have synthetic a priori conclusions we can reasonably assign it that status, if only because it can be looked on as the degenerate case of a conclusion derived from itself.

Unfortunately, though, it is not from this uncontentious premise that many of the most promising transcendental arguments start. They start instead from the more specific assumption that we have experience or knowledge of a certain kind. The more narrowly specified this kind is, the less valuable the argument will be against the sceptic, for it will be open to him simply to deny that we do have experience or knowledge of that kind. By this denial he no longer condemns himself to unintelligibility, for what is required for a particular kind of experience may not be necessary for intelligible thought in general. The argument will now be of use only against a sceptic who accepts the premise to start with; which does not of course mean that there is no place to be found for such an argument. When Kant gives us what he calls the transcendental expositions of the concepts of space and time he relies upon our conceding that we do possess synthetic a priori knowledge about space and time, and argues from there to his conclusion that space and time are a priori intuitions. The concession is one he thinks he can expect from every reasonable person; though all the same he is prepared to dispense with it and argue for his conclusion without it. In general the *Critique of Pure Reason* is designed to avoid relying on concessions of this sort, but in the *Prolegomena* he is more concerned with making the structure of his argument clear and draws on them heavily for that purpose.[2]

Actually even in the *Critique* the main transcendental arguments require a somewhat stronger premise than just that we have knowledge or experience. For the transcendental deduction of the categories the premise is that we have sensible experience – unlike God, whose experience is intellectual. (This means that he is never affected by objects external to himself and creates things just by thinking of them: see further below, pp. 30, 43.) For the Analytic of Principles the premise is that we have spatio-temporal (or at any rate temporal) experience; alternative forms of sensible intuition would be possible, but space and time are the forms of ours. Since this does not mean that we have experience of things external to us in space and time, but only that our experience is spatio-temporally arrayed, this premise still has the merit of being very evident; to raise sceptical doubts about it would not be very interesting. In this it differs from the claim that we have (in geometry) synthetic a priori knowledge about space, which is obviously a much more arguable matter even if many of Kant's contemporaries would not have wished to dispute it. And it is still in Kant's view an a priori premise: we do not learn empirically that our experience is spatio-temporal in character, for the spatio-temporal ordering is something we ourselves contribute to experience and impose upon the world.

More recent transcendental arguments are often concerned not with the conditions for experience in general, nor with the conditions for spatio-temporal experience, but with the conditions for the sort of experience that we in fact have, or can have, given our conceptual scheme. Such arguments cannot be very satisfactory until it is made clear what 'our conceptual scheme' is intended to cover. It sounds as though it simply means the set of concepts we possess, but it is commonly taken to include also the system of beliefs or assumptions we employ them in, or at any rate the most basic and general of these beliefs. No clear criterion is usually offered for distinguishing such fundamental beliefs from the others, though it would be widely agreed that the belief in material objects would count whereas the belief that white heather is lucky would not. Still, there is no denying that the investigation of the properties and interrelations of our most fundamental concepts and beliefs is an important study; and it can be called the delineation of our conceptual scheme.

But we must be careful to distinguish two quite different enquiries, either of which might be intended by someone who spoke of looking for 'the conditions required by our conceptual scheme'. One of them examines what is needed for us to have these concepts and beliefs at all; the other investigates what must be the case if the beliefs are to be true and the concepts to have instances in the real world. They are not always sufficiently distinguished, but neither of them has the anti-sceptical value that Kant's transcendental arguments are intended to have. For in each case the sceptic who does not like the conclusions can reject the premise. It is true that in the first case this seems rather a heroic line, for he will then be denying that we have the concepts or beliefs that we think we have; but in fact sceptics have frequently been prepared to do just this, maintaining in a Hume-like way that we do not have any coherent concept for the words 'material object' to stand for, or that the sentence 'Causes necessitate their effects' is literally meaningless and cannot serve to express a belief. We cannot accuse such a sceptic of undermining the intelligibility of his own utterances, for he is not calling in question the conditions on which all intelligible discourse rests, but only refusing to accept that we really have the concepts or beliefs his opponent alleges we do. Even less can we make this accusation against the sceptic in the second case, where he accepts that we have the concepts and beliefs but just denies that they are instantiated or true. The worst he has to fear is that people will distrust him as a dangerous revolutionary who questions the basic tenets of their faith; or, perhaps, that he may find some practical difficulty in communicating with the rest of us.

It may well be (indeed, it almost certainly is) that our ordinary ways of thinking and talking involve a reliance on such assumptions as, for example, that there are material objects, and *a fortiori* that we have a perfectly viable concept of a material object. In that case the sceptic who doubts or denies these assumptions runs the risk of cutting himself off from being generally understood; not because the assumptions are indispensable for all intelligible discourse (that would need quite another argument) but just because without relying on them he will be unable to think or talk as the rest of us normally do. He is what Strawson calls a revisionary metaphysician, proposing an alternative conceptual scheme. But we must not exaggerate his difficulties. If he considers that most of us are talking nonsense anyway he will not feel left out but will regard himself as having the task of teaching us to talk sense. If he considers that we are not talking nonsense but are taking for granted things that are untrue, then it will be open to him to speak as though he thought they were true, if that makes it easier for him to state his case for doubting them – rather as one may pretend the circle can be squared in order to show by *reductio ad absurdum* that it cannot.

The objection is sometimes raised that it makes no sense to talk like this about alternative conceptual schemes. Our present conceptual scheme is the only one we can envisage. We are, as it were, trapped inside it; we can never get outside to ask whether others might be worse or better. All we can do is to examine it from the inside, seeing how the various concepts function and which beliefs rest upon which. It would follow that to ask Kant's sort of question about what is required for *any possible* conceptual scheme – or for any possible sensible experience, whether like ours or not – is quite hopeless. For it supposes that we can get outside our own conceptual scheme so as to compare it with whatever others there may be, and to discover what features they all have in common.

But this is mistaken. Without throwing off our conceptual scheme we can perfectly well imagine what alternatives would be like; in chapter III, for example, I shall try to describe how experience might be for someone who lived in a timeless world, and his conceptual scheme could hardly be the same as ours. And when we are asked about the conditions for any possible experience we are not being asked to abandon our conceptual scheme, but to examine it in order to see which of its features can intelligibly be thought away. Some features of my experience seem more contingent than others and can more easily be imagined away, while there are others so fundamental that without them nothing could count as experience (or knowledge, or thought) at all. Though we must be duly cautious in claiming to imagine experience radically different from our own, for what we think is a coherent alternative may always turn out on further investigation not really to be one. Some feature we at first think dispensable may later be shown to be necessary for anything that is to count as experience. There is no way of establishing the coherence of an alternative directly except by producing it; in general all we can say is that we know of no reason to suppose it is not coherent.

Transcendental arguments are concerned with the conditions under which experience, or experience of a given sort, is possible.

> I call transcendental all knowledge which has to do not so much with objects as with how we know objects, in so far as this may be possible a priori. (B 25.)[3]

But the conditions under which something is possible are its necessary conditions, its sufficient conditions being rather the conditions that make it actual; so Kant is saying that transcendental arguments deal with the a priori necessary conditions for knowledge (or, equivalently, experience). That they should deal with necessary rather than sufficient conditions is reasonable; it would be tedious to examine possible sufficient conditions for experience unless they or a disjunction of them were also necessary, and it would not achieve the desired result. The objective is to establish that something must be the case because it is a condition of our having experience. But from the fact that the truth of p would be a *sufficient* condition for our having experience (of kind K), together with the fact that we do have experience (of kind K), nothing yet follows as to the truth of p. It is only if p is a *necessary* condition that we are entitled to affirm it. To put it schematically, 'e and if e then p, so p' is valid; 'e and if p then e, so p' is not.

In saying that the conditions which transcendental arguments deal with are a priori Kant is excluding conditions which are required for experience only as a matter of empirical fact. No one, for example, can experience anything if he is at the bottom of the sea without equipment, but it is a contingent truth that we do not find such an environment congenial. It is not a matter for philosophers, and if Kant allowed his transcendental arguments to turn on such a posteriori considerations he could hardly hope that their conclusions would be a priori. But if the conditions are not empirical we must ask what sort of conditions they are. We have already found reason to ascribe to Kant the view that his first premise – the one which says we have experience, or spatio-temporal experience – is synthetic a priori, but what of the assertion that p is a necessary condition for such experience? Is it synthetic a priori too, or it is analytic?

I think it can only be analytic. I am not completely confident that Kant recognized this, for he says even less about the subject than he does about the status of the first premise, and it may be that he never clearly asked himself whether it was analytic or not. But so far as one can infer a view from the few things he does say, it is that it is analytic.[4]

This certainly ought to be his position. The principal task he wants to use transcendental arguments for is to show how synthetic a priori judgments are possible; to vindicate the synthetic a priori against the sceptic who denies that there is any place for it. They can hardly achieve this if they themselves turn upon synthetic a priori propositions the sceptic would be unwilling to concede. The first premise should be one he can hardly deny, so it does not matter if we have to call it synthetic a priori for want of any better classification. But the second premise, the claim that p is necessary for experience (of kind K), he will certainly deny if he gets the chance. And since the only necessary conditions he is prepared to recognize are either analytically or empirically necessary, p must be one or the other if we are to convince him. But empirical considerations have been ruled out of account, so if the second premise is to be effective it can only be analytic.

If we consider what Kant himself says about synthetic a priori judgments we can see that his account of them does not fit the second premise of a transcendental argument. A judgment is synthetic if the predicate adds something not already given by the concept of the subject, or (more generally) if the truth-value of the judgment is not determinable by means of the law of non-contradiction. Such judgments require us to go beyond the interrelations of the concepts: there must be a third thing besides the concepts of the subject and the predicate, to provide the connection between them. In the case of theoretical, or speculative, judgments this third thing can only be intuition – the immediate awareness of things.[5] Synthetic judgments may go beyond concepts by being concerned either with the contents of our spatio-temporal intuitions, or with the formal features of these intuitions; in the former case they are empirical, in the latter a priori. And Kant considers that there are just two ways in which legitimate judgments of this latter sort can occur. Either the concepts must be constructed in pure intuition, as he says mathematical concepts are, or else it must be possible to show that the truth of the judgment is required if experience (and therefore intuition) is to be possible.[6] So the conclusions of Kant's transcendental arguments come out synthetic a priori, as we should expect; but assertions to the effect that these conclusions must hold for experience to be possible must have some other status.

When he himself actually presents transcendental arguments, like the transcendental deduction of the categories, it appears that the steps in these arguments are supposed to consist of analytic propositions, propositions in which the concept of possible experience is analysed. In presenting the Deduction in B Kant does not seek to disguise – on the contrary, he emphasizes – that the principle of the necessary unity of apperception is an analytic proposition. In effect it says that synthesis of the manifold is required for self-conscious experience; and it is on this avowedly analytic proposition, which he goes so far as to call 'the highest principle in the whole of human knowledge', that the argument of the transcendental deduction is supposed to rest.[7] Moreover at about the same time as he wrote B he also wrote in the *Metaphysical Foundations of Natural Science* that the Deduction is really very straightforward,

> since it can be carried out almost in a single step from the precisely specified definition of a *judgment* in general (as an action through which given representations first become knowledge of an object). (Ak. IV: 475 n.)

Kant does admit various different types of definition, but this is clearly a 'nominal' definition which simply analyses the concept concerned and makes no latent synthetic claim.[8] So again the argument must be regarded as going by analytic steps.

Only at one point does he seem at all explicit about this, and that is in a note in the *Nachlass*. In *Reflexion* 6386 he says 'Transcendental propositions a priori are altogether analytic' – though there is perhaps some room for dispute as to what he means by 'transcendental propositions' in this context. Adickes claims that the term is not intended to cover the sort of thing we have been talking about, but only propositions about the three scholastic 'transcendentals' *one*, *true*, and *good*.[9] At B 113 Kant says that metaphysicians have produced a collection of uninteresting tautologies about unity, truth, and goodness, and Adickes suggests that it is these he is referring to here. It is true that the *Reflexion* does go on to discuss these three concepts. But it treats them not as a source of metaphysical superficialities, but as providing conditions which must hold if experience is to be possible; so it looks as if it must be propositions about such conditions that Kant is holding to be analytic, despite Adickes' effort to maintain the contrary. Indeed, Kant also says in B (in the same passage) that properly understood these three concepts can be equated with the three categories of quantity: unity, plurality, totality. It was an early hope of his, which he eventually abandoned only after a great deal of wasted effort, that the three traditional transcendentals could be shown to be as it were super-categories – the most fundamental of the a priori concepts we must possess in order to have experience; most fundamental in the sense that the twelve categories of his table of categories could all somehow be derived from them.

But the strongest ground for taking the second premise to be analytic remains the difficulty of seeing how it can be anything else. All the same, writers on Kant have frequently denied that it is analytic, and recently T. E. Wilkerson has attempted to provide an alternative account of it.[10] Wilkerson disagrees radically with the analysis I have been giving, whereby the form of a transcendental argument is roughly

We have experience (of kind K)
It is analytic that the truth of p is a necessary condition for
  experience (of kind K)
Therefore, p.

On his view it should be more like this:

We have experience (of kind K)
It is synthetic but a priori that the truth of p is sufficient, *ceteris paribus*, for our having experience (of kind K)
Therefore, p.

The point of the *'ceteris paribus'* is to reflect the fact that in general a variety of background conditions will have to obtain as well as the condition he has in mind. Sometimes he speaks of p as being 'materially' sufficient, *ceteris paribus*, for experience of the relevant kind, and this hints at the sort of relationship he takes the second premise to express. The idea is that to say p is materially sufficient for experience of kind K is to say that if p is true then materials are available within experience which can satisfactorily explain how we acquire the concepts we need in order to be aware of that experience. For example, p is materially sufficient for experience of external objects if in virtue of the truth of p we find ourselves able to acquire the concept of an external object. But by what right does Wilkerson suppose that I can only acquire this concept under particular specifiable conditions (p)? It is very hard to see any *a priori* reason why I should not simply possess it or any other concept, regardless of what the world around me was like and regardless of the content of my experience. I could always possess them innately, even if there was nothing I could apply them to. How concepts are in fact acquired is a matter for genetic psychology, which can tell us only about empirical conditions; if the second premise is to be drawn from there it will have to be a posteriori after all. This conclusion Wilkerson sees he must accept, but it is something of a disadvantage for his interpretation.

Moreover no analysis can hope to get very far if it makes the second premise a statement of sufficient, rather than necessary, conditions. For the argument-form then becomes evidently invalid; it proceeds by affirming the consequent. Recognizing this awkward fact Wilkerson makes a concession in the direction of turning the premise back into a statement of necessary conditions by adding to it the qualification 'and we are incapable, given our conceptual resources, of thinking of any *other* conditions which would be materially sufficient'.[11] But this will hardly do. That we cannot think of them does not show that there may not be such conditions, as indeed he admits. More importantly, it may be such alternative conditions on which we ourselves rely; for it may be that we are not capable of grasping the conditions upon which our own experience depends. Nor is this particularly unlikely.

There are two main reasons why people have wanted to deny that transcendental arguments proceed by analytic steps, as I have been arguing they do. In the first place it is felt that if they did they would be essentially trivial: their conclusions would have to be covertly built into the conception of experience (or knowledge, etc.) from which they start. But this is rather harsh. It is not in general impossible to produce important and interesting analyses of concepts; what is covertly contained may be well hidden and may be worth bringing to light. And the concept of experience is not so straightforward and uncomplicated as to be not worth analysing.

In the second place it is suspected that most of the actual transcendental arguments Kant and others have presented would turn out to be unsound if construed in this analytic way. For they assert that p is required for experience when it is not an *analytically* necessary condition, so that the assertion can only be salvaged by construing it as having some mysterious non-analytic status. But should we try to salvage it? Not only can no account be given of this alternative status, it is fairly clear in most cases that if the assertion is not analytically true it is simply not true at all. It has to be admitted that many transcendental arguments do turn out to be unsound, but there is nothing surprising in that; philosophers commonly do produce unsound arguments, and Kant is no exception, as a glance at his non-transcendental arguments will speedily confirm. We ought to recognize the fact, and not seek to disguise it by enveloping the argument-form in mystery.

Perhaps the most serious objection that can be made to transcendental arguments is that in practice they do not get us very far; the few valid ones that have been produced do not establish the sort of conclusions we should like to arrive at. If this is true it is important, for *prima facie* the method looks very promising. There are many claims which we should like to see justified but cannot justify empirically in any immediate way, including the things that traditionally worry sceptics. Transcendental arguments offer us a chance of justifying them, for though they proceed by analysing concepts they offer more than most conceptual analyses can. They do not simply exhibit conceptual interrelations, but show that experience itself would not be possible unless certain things were the case.

We cannot draw boundary-lines in advance to what transcendental arguments can hope to achieve. One cannot tell how much the analysis of the concept of experience, and related concepts, will reveal, and at no stage can one be sure one has considered all the arguments there are to be found. Most of the ones we shall be examining do fail to establish their conclusions; either they are invalid altogether, or what they show is very much less than has been alleged. But that does not mean there may not be others waiting to be discovered, capable of doing the job more adequately. This possibility can never be discounted, though in some cases one may feel after a bit that it is not very likely.

But even where they establish lesser conclusions than their proponents claim, these lesser conclusions may be well worth having. This is the case with a transcendental argument for which Kant himself did not see the need, but to which I intend to devote the rest of this chapter: the transcendental justification of the laws of logic.

2 Logical laws

Kant's problem was about synthetic a priori knowledge. He found no parallel difficulty over our knowledge of analytic truths: for analytic judgments can tell us nothing new about the world, and serve only to clarify the concepts we already possess. He therefore sees no need to justify them in the *Critique of Pure Reason*. But in a much earlier work, *The Only Possible Basis for a Proof of the Existence of God* (1763), he does briefly provide an argument of the transcendental form in defence of not contradicting oneself:

> If I now reflect for a moment as to why that which contradicts itself should be altogether nothing and impossible, I notice that through it the Principle of Contradiction, the last logical ground of everything thinkable, is destroyed, and that therefore all possibility vanishes, and nothing remains over to be thought. (Ak. II: 82.)

He finds analytic judgments unproblematic because they are only 'explicative': they

> add nothing through the predicate to the concept of the subject, but merely break it up into those constituent concepts that have all along been thought in it, although confusedly. (A 7/B 11.)

He is not suggesting here that in thinking the subject concept one is somehow automatically conscious of the predicate concept as well; it is not by introspection that one determines whether a judgment is analytic, but by examining the logical relationship between the concepts. This is made quite clear in the *Logik*, where he defines analytic propositions as 'those whose certainty depends on *identity* of the concepts (of the predicate with the notion of the subject)'[12] – making clear at the same time that examples of the form 'All A's that are B are B' are meant to be covered as well as 'All A's are A'. The restriction to subject-predicate judgments is also inessential; Kant tends to think of all judgments as ultimately having that form, and would certainly admit as analytic judgments which we would normally regard as having some other structure. Thus he characterizes analytic judgments best when he calls them those 'whose truth can always be adequately known in accordance with the Principle of Contradiction' (A 151/B 190) – or, more generally, in accordance with the laws of logic, though for Kant these all derive from the Principle of Contradiction.

The familiar modern account of an analytic statement, as one reducible by means of definitions to a substitution-instance of a logical law,[13] is therefore a clarification of Kant's and not a departure from it. And it has the advantage of making clear that the truth of an analytic judgment like 'All bachelors are unmarried' depends on two factors: the meanings of the words 'bachelor' and 'unmarried' on the one hand, and on the other the laws of logic. We cannot consider here the problem of what makes two expressions synonymous.[14] Our present concern is with the second question: how can we be so confident that the principles we call logical laws are really true?

Those who regard these principles as essentially trivial are inclined to say that they are made true by the meanings of the logical words. 'Not both p and not-p' is determined as true by the meanings of 'not' and 'and'; to doubt its truth is to show a lack of grasp of these meanings. Now there are a number of points to be made about this suggestion, but it is sufficient to raise one: supposing we granted all that is alleged about 'not' and 'and', what would guarantee that these were satisfactory concepts to employ? Within a formal calculus, certainly, we can arbitrarily stipulate the rules governing the elementary symbols and thereby determine which strings of symbols are to count as theorems, but when we do this we should not pretend that the calculus is assured of any particular application to the world. The logical words of ordinary language are designed for the purpose of describing and arguing about the world; we must make sure they are suitable for that purpose, and cannot just stipulate for them whatever rules we like. As Prior pointed out,[15] it would hardly do to introduce a word 'tonk', governed by the principles that whatever statements p and q may be, 'p' entails 'p tonk q' and 'p tonk q' entails 'q'. For then (since entailment is transitive) any statement would entail any other. So it is not enough to say that the truth of 'Not both p and not-p' is fixed by the meanings of 'not' and 'and'; we need some further assurance that the concepts of negation and conjunction, as determined by these meaning-rules, are satisfactory for the purposes of ordinary talk.

Kant's transcendental argument can be seen as offering this further assurance. But it is not adequate just to say that without the Principle of Contradiction 'all possibility vanishes, and nothing remains over to be thought'; the argument needs to be elaborated. Fortunately it can be; it is put thus by D. Mitchell in his *Introduction to Logic*:[16]

> To affirm '*p*' is to exclude the negation of '*p*'. . . . If we did not implicitly exclude when we affirmed, every statement that we made would be compatible with the affirmation of any other proposition whatever; while . . . were it not the case that, whenever a proposition was true, its negation necessarily was false, there would be no point in making statements at all.

Any sort of experience or knowledge, we can add, requires the making of statements at least in thought; it requires that we judge things to be so and not otherwise, and hence requires us to have a concept of negation for which the law 'Not both *p* and not-*p*' must hold. Indeed, someone who failed to recognize the general exclusiveness of '*p*' and 'not-*p*' could not be called intelligent in any way; intelligent behaviour, like thinking and language-use, is purposive and goal-directed, and no one can direct himself upon a goal without distinguishing it from what is not his goal.

Nevertheless I think Kant and Mitchell are claiming too much. Could we not come across someone who accepted that our fundamental logical laws held in most cases, but denied them over a restricted range? He might, for example, admit that the Principle of Contradiction held except with regard to pillar-boxes. In general he would recognize that a statement excludes its negation, but statements about pillar-boxes would be an exception. In his view the sentence 'This pillar-box is red and also not-red (all over)' could express a truth, as could 'There both is and is not a pillar-box here.' His familiarity with the language, and with concepts of negation and conjunction which are at least very similar to ours, would be quite sufficiently attested from other, pillar-box-free, contexts; there could be no question of refusing to admit he could think and talk intelligently. No doubt we should be puzzled as to why he should say these things about pillar-boxes, and in the conservative spirit of charity so strongly recommended by Quine[17] we might seek to interpret his words in such a way as to remove the appearance of contradiction: suggesting perhaps that his 'not' should be translated not as a negative but as the affirmative 'definitely' when it occurs in statements about pillar-boxes. Such Quinean charity may however be misplaced. And we can imagine him making it very clear to us that it would be; discussing with us the Principle of Contradiction, appreciating the need to admit its general validity, remarking the peculiarity of exceptional cases. In fact this example is not much removed from reality, as those acquainted with the amateurs of Zen will recognize.

It is important, however, that he should accept that the Principle holds in most cases. Otherwise he really could not be called a purposive agent, capable of following linguistic rules and of making judgments about his experience. So the transcendental argument does show something, though rather less than its proponents claimed – a common state of affairs. Of course, in a sense the argument is circular, for any defence of the basic laws of logic must already rely on them; but the circularity is harmless, because the argument brings out how the Principle of Contradiction is constitutive of our conception of significant thought. And if a sceptic were to reply that this is only a point about *our* conception of significant thought, or *our* conception of experience, and that perhaps we ought to have alternative conceptions of these things instead, we can dismiss him, for ours are the only conceptions (and he shares them). They cannot be amended by dropping out this feature of conformity to logical law, for it if were dropped out nothing at all would remain.

It may be that not all of our logical laws are equally essential; it is often held, for example, that it may be possible to dispense with the law of the excluded middle ('Either p or not-p'). Similarly, though we have in effect seen that any being who can make judgments must employ something like our concept of negation, it may be possible to do without some of our other logical concepts. Kant gives us a list of twelve fundamental logical concepts, and claims it is complete; it plays a very central part in his system, and it would obviously be of value for him if these twelve, and only these, could be shown to be indispensable.

But it would take us too long to investigate these matters properly. Klaus Reich has attempted (after a fashion) to vindicate Kant's claim,[18] and Mitchell and others have gone part of the way by arguing the need for disjunction, quantifiers, etc.[19] Naturally it is easier to show the need for some concepts than it is for others. It can plausibly be argued, for instance, that some grasp of the hypothetical form (governed by such rules as *modus ponens*) is required for intentional, rule-governed activity, since the agent must be capable of understanding that if he does such-and-such he will achieve his end. It is harder to establish that he needs the ideas of possibility and necessity, in view of the attack Quine and others have mounted on these concepts (at any rate as they are ordinarily understood). Kant himself considered that the antecedent and consequent of a hypothetical judgment must be thought as possible, since they are not asserted as true,[20] but this is a mistake since we can entertain suppositions we know to be logically impossible and indeed show them to be so by *reductio ad absurdum*: 'If there were a highest integer, then. . . .'

It is worth noticing, however, that Kant's table of logical concepts (which he calls functions of thought in judgment) is not so arbitrary and artificial as is sometimes made out. The judgments Kant calls 'infinite' are those which contain negated predicates – 'The soul is not-mortal'

as opposed to 'It is not the case that the soul is mortal' – and although it may be wrong to regard predicate negation as ultimately distinct from propositional negation it is not obviously so.[21] Nor need one blame Kant too severely for failing to recognize that the concepts of necessity and possibility, and the universal and existential quantifiers, are inter-definable given negation. 'If . . . then' and 'or' are not interdefinable, unless one is prepared to settle for a truth-functional account of 'if'; and the admission of singular judgments as a form distinct from universal and particular ones reflects Kant's recognition of the qualitative differ-ence between singular and general terms. (On this he differed from Leibniz and Wolff, for whom all singular terms could in principle be replaced by predicative expressions.) It is not to be denied that Kant is unduly carried away, here as elsewhere, by the lure of the architectonic; the neatly systematic appearance of his four triads undoubtedly makes him too little cautious as to what he includes and excludes. But the table he presents us with is not a bad one all the same, and it would not be unreasonable to hope for transcendental arguments to show that con-cepts much like these are essential to all judgment and hence to all experience.

Kant does not provide such arguments, however; the transcendental arguments of the *Critique of Pure Reason* are concerned not with 'the formal conditions of all thought in general' but with the more specific conditions under which we can have synthetic knowledge, or knowledge of the objects of experience.[22] The next few chapters will be devoted to examining these conditions as Kant understands them, and the argu-ments that he and others have offered with regard to them.

III

Space and Time as A Priori

1   The metaphysical expositions

It is reasonable to start with space and time, since that is where Kant started himself. As we have seen already in the *Inaugural Dissertation* of 1770 he held that space and time were pure intuitions, not abstracted from experience but imposed by the mind in ordering what is given to the senses. And much of the argument he then gave in support of this claim reappears, slightly elaborated, in the Transcendental Aesthetic of the *Critique of Pure Reason*.

A pure intuition is one that is altogether a priori, and by 'a priori' Kant says he means 'independent of experience and even of all impressions of the senses' (B 2). Often he interprets this independence genetically: a concept, an intuition, or a piece of knowledge is said to be empirical if it is acquired from experience, a priori if not. Fortunately he does not stick to this consistently – fortunately, because purely genetic considerations are unlikely to have much philosophical interest. Most of my knowledge of arithmetic was gained by listening to teachers, some of it by induction from experience with marbles; but how it was acquired seems unimportant. What matters – as Kant sometimes sees – is how it can be verified. This gives us a different, and much more satisfactory, way of distinguishing the a priori from the empirical: a priori knowledge can be established without appeal to experience, whereas empirical knowledge cannot. By this criterion my knowledge of mathematics is all a priori, however I learned it, and if someone were born with a capacity to recite the dates of the kings of Israel his knowledge would be empirical despite not being derived from experience. In the same way empirical concepts are not those that happen to be acquired from experience, but those for which experience alone can tell us whether they apply.

28

The metaphysical expositions of space and of time consist of two pairs of arguments, of which the first pair is devoted to showing that space and time are a priori and the second to showing that they are intuitions. I shall defer consideration of the second pair until the next chapter. The first pair suffers rather from Kant's tendency to interpret 'a priori' genetically, but the arguments are not much good in any case.

He starts by claiming that it would be impossible to acquire any notion of space by abstraction from experience, because if we are to represent objects as spatially located 'the representation of space must already be presupposed' (A 23/B 38); and similarly with time (A 30/B 46). This is hardly convincing. Obviously we cannot think of objects as spatio-temporally located without having the ideas of space and time; but we may still have acquired these ideas by observing objects which now, after having performed the abstraction, we can think of as located spatio-temporally. In just the same way one cannot think of an object as red without having the idea of redness; but redness is Kant's paradigm of an empirical concept, acquired by abstraction from the observation of things which once we have the concept we can describe as instances of redness. So the argument fails even to show that space and time are a priori in the genetic sense.

Aware perhaps that it is not very adequate he supplements it with a second argument. This second argument is new in the *Critique* – the first one was repeated from the *Inaugural Dissertation*[1] – and is to the effect that although we can think of space and time as empty of objects 'we can never represent to ourselves the absence of space', or of time either. It is difficult to see this as more than a psychological remark, though Kant draws from it the conclusion that space and time are necessary a priori representations underlying all our experience. In fact it is both false and irrelevant. If it were true it could only be a contingent truth about us, and would no more prove that space and time were a priori than my inability to imagine a chiliagon shows the impossibility of any such figure. But it is false, because we can quite well imagine worlds which are not spatial; and I shall argue shortly that we can even imagine atemporal experience, though I admit this is more difficult.

In these arguments Kant is trying to attack Leibniz's view of space, as a system of relations between objects which can themselves be identified independently of their spatial positions. On this view spatial relations would be just like any other kind of relation which we can discover to hold between things. But Kant feels that Leibniz has gone badly wrong by ignoring the vital role of spatio-temporal position in our identification of objects. He points out elsewhere that Leibniz's theory gives a quite wrong account of how we individuate things: it 'offends powerfully against reason, since it is impossible to conceive why the fact that there is a drop of water at one place should prevent one

from coming across another exactly similar drop at a different place'.[2]
Here he is right; it cannot be denied that space and time do play a very
special role for us, and that in identifying objects they have an importance unlike that of any other properties or relations. But it has not been
shown that this justifies him in calling them a priori.

2 · Experience without space

Some people would argue that spatial and temporal order are required
for there to be any experience at all, and this would be a reason to regard
them as a priori. Kant could not take this line, however. He considers it
a possibility that there might be beings whose experience was neither
spatially nor temporally ordered.[3] We impose the forms of space and
time upon our intuition, and that is why they are a priori for us, but
beings of another kind might impose alternative forms instead. For
them these other forms would serve the function that space and time do
for us, in ordering the data which were given to them in sense. Kant
even thinks there is a kind of experience possible for which there are no
such forms at all and no sensory data either: such is the experience of
God, whose intuition is said to be intellectual, not sensible, and for
whom there is no difference between perceiving a thing and thinking it.
He says very little about this mysterious idea, but apparently takes the
view that, for God, to think an object is to create it.[4] So there can never
be any problem of match between God's thought and what it is a
thought of – God can never be wrong; which is enough to raise a considerable doubt as to whether such a God can intelligibly be said to
think or to know anything at all.

It is not so clear that Kant is wrong to allow the possibility of forms
of intuition different from our own. That he is wrong is argued by
Strawson, among others. Strawson claims that the idea of a non-temporal
experience is incoherent, and also that space, or something very like it,
is required if we are to have room to apply the concept of an objective
particular. In his view no experience would be possible unless we could
apply this concept; a point we shall return to in chapter VIII but can for
the moment accept.

His argument for space, or for a close analogue, is that seeing the
world as objective entails recognizing the possibility of different experiential routes through it. In calling a particular objective one must
recognize that it can exist when one is not perceiving it. And to recognize that, he thinks, is to recognize that things can be somewhere else
than where one is oneself.[5] But why? I do not perceive the bacteria that
are no doubt on this page, but not because they are somewhere else
than in my visual field. Again, if I am looking at a dim light my vision
of it may be obscured by a bright flash, though the dim light is still there

in the same place. Or if the objective particular were a buzzing sound, it could be drowned out by a louder grating sound.

In *Individuals* Strawson says that our only reason for thinking loud sounds can obscure softer ones is that we know this to happen in our own spatial world, where we can have independent evidence that the softer sounds go on – 'the visible but inaudible scrapings of the street violinist as the street band marches by';[6] but this is unpersuasive. One might as well argue that we should only believe in the continued existence of the unperceived tree in the quad if we can obtain independent evidence of its present state (by radar pictures, perhaps). In fact we say that the tree continues to exist simply because whenever anyone is in the right situation he does perceive it, and this leads us to believe that at any time if there were anyone in the right situation then he would perceive it. Exactly the same goes for sounds and for bright and dim lights: if whenever the louder or brighter one is absent the softer or dimmer one can be perceived, this leads one to hold that at any time the softer sounds would be audible if the louder ones ceased, the dimmer lights would be visible if the brighter ones were extinguished. Difference of place does not come into it. Like all good hypotheses the supposition of unperceived existence is introduced to effect an economy in the description of our experience; and this is achieved just as well in these latter cases as in the case of the tree.

Strawson does not think that all experience must actually be spatial, only that it must exhibit an order similar to that of space. Just how similar he does not fully explain, but he explores the possibility of a purely auditory world, in which particular things are arranged not in space but in positions along an auditory dimension.[7] The particulars are themselves sounds or patterns of sounds; the auditory dimension is provided by a continuous and recognizable master-sound of varying pitch, and what gives position to the sound-particulars is that one hears them in association with a particular pitch of the master-sound. One can alter one's own position on the master-sound by coming to hear it at a different pitch, though as Strawson conceives the case whenever one moves from one pitch to another one has to go through all the intermediate pitches. In this auditory world, then, one may find that a certain pattern of sounds is invariably to be heard in conjunction with middle C – whenever one visits middle C one hears that pattern; whereas another quite different pattern is to be heard by going to top E. In such circumstances Strawson considers one would be inclined to think of these patterns as continuing to exist at their appropriate pitches on the master-sound, even when no one is there to perceive them, for it would be natural to suppose that if anyone were at middle C he would hear the customarily associated sound-pattern. Such grounds for the continued existence of sound-patterns would be analogous to our

reasons for thinking that the tree goes on existing when no one perceives it. Furthermore, Strawson could allow that these patterns do not
have to remain fixed in their positions on the master-sound, provided
their movement is fairly regular and continuous. The grounds for
identifying a sound-pattern as numerically the same object which was at
middle C, even though it is now at top E, will be of the same kind as
our present grounds for identifying an object which has moved while
we were not watching it. We do not rely just on similarities between the
object before the move and the object after the move, but on experientially gained knowledge of past cases of a comparable kind – including
cases where we have watched objects make similar moves, or (in the
auditory world) have moved along the master-sound with them. On
this basis we construct a theory of how objects move, which we can
draw on to support the hypothesis of continued existence; and to
support the claim that if anyone had moved from middle C to top E at
the appropriate speed he would have been able to follow this sound-
pattern along its path.

The auditory world is not exactly spatial, but those features of space
which Strawson considers essential are preserved. In fact Bennett points
out that for this purpose we do not require quite as much as Strawson
gives us; in particular we can dispense with the master-sound.[8] The
inhabitants of Strawson's world use the master-sound to determine
position because it is always available and because one's movement
along it is gradual and not discontinuous, so that its pitches come in a
fixed and regular order. But in a fairly stable world without a master-
sound we could rely on the sound-patterns themselves to give us this
order. One might hear seven sound-patterns at once or close together,
so that they defined a region in which one was and out of which one
could move – perhaps by coming to hear some of the seven more and
more faintly, others more and more distinctly and accompanied by new
sounds as well. Alternatively one might hear each sound-pattern by
itself, but always preceded or followed by the same neighbours. In this
world again we can complicate the picture to allow for the possibility
of objects moving, provided movements do not happen too rapidly or
too discontinuously, if we suppose that a sound-pattern need not always be preceded or followed by the same neighbours: it can change its
neighbours gradually without preventing us from reidentifying it as the
same auditory particular. The grounds for the reidentification, and for
the correlative hypothesis that if anyone had been rightly placed he
would have been able to observe the object continuously, are essentially
the same as before.

Bennett maintains that in such a world the auditory dimension would
still be significantly analogous to space, and he also believes that only in
a broadly 'spatial' world can concepts of objects be successfully applied.

But the analogy with our own space has become a bit distant. Our space is three-dimensional, but there is only one auditory dimension; and there is no reason why it should be continuous or even dense. Positions on it may be immediately adjacent to one another, without there always being some third position in between them.[9] Moreover any other dimension would do as well as the auditory one: in principle it would be just as satisfactory to have a temperature dimension, on which the percipients could move about from one degree of warmth to another, though the resulting world-picture is certainly much more difficult to imagine. And since a dimension, properly understood, is no more than an ordered set of properties that objects can have, any alternative set of properties would serve equally well, however unlike it was to the dimensions we are accustomed to describing as such. A percipient could even be faced with several, or many, such systems at once; there is no reason why he should have to be able to integrate all the objects he perceives into a single system (cf. the possibility of ex-periencing two spaces, to be discussed in the next chapter). What does seem essential is that movement – whether of objects or of percipients – should quite often be gradual, for otherwise we should be unable to distinguish persisting objects from qualitatively similar ones in new circumstances, or indeed to recognize the dimension as an ordering along which things can move at all. Experience would just be chaotic. But even this requirement is not absolute; the movement need not always be gradual. Once we have built up our picture of a relatively stable objective world we can tolerate a certain amount of discontinuous change, just as in the actual world the occasional instantaneous switch of position would not make us lose our grip on objectivity concepts (e.g. if I were suddenly to find myself in Baghdad).

If we are to find it useful to apply the concept of an objective particu-lar which is reidentifiable over time, we need to have a certain sort of regularity in our experience, allowing for a pattern of more or less gradual change. But to be more precise than this – to try to specify how much patterning, what sort of order – would be an unprofitable business, for to such questions there are no clear answers to be had. The hypo-thesis that something has continued to exist while unperceived must be supported inductively, by evidence taken to warrant counterfactuals to the effect that if . . ., then it would have been perceived. This evidence must be provided by the observation of regularities, but one cannot say exactly how much regularity would be required. Of course claims about unperceived existents could be made without any evidence whatever (and they might happen to be right), but the present question is rather what would make them rational or give a point to them: and that will depend on what one's standards for rationality or pointfulness are. Considerations of simplicity, neatness and convenience in the light of an overall theory or preconceptions about the shape of a satisfactory explanation are all relevant to determining whether such a hypothesis is acceptable; and much will depend also on the nature of the regularity. For beings like ourselves the sorts of regularity the spatial dimensions allow, and which lead us to think of objects as existing elsewhere when we are not perceiving them, are particularly easy and natural; alternative regularities are the more difficult to see as regularities of the relevant kind the more dissimilar they are to these spatial ones. For percipients radically different from ourselves quite other dimensional orderings, and hence other sorts of regularity, might be far more natural than space, and might make the hypothesis of unperceived particulars useful for them in circumstances very remote from those in which we employ it.

3 Experience without time

The analogy with space can be extremely weak, therefore; so weak that it is misleading to insist upon it. If we are to have grounds to apply the concept of an object our experience must be ordered, but it does not have to be spatially ordered. Now if non-spatial forms of experience are possible might not non-temporal forms be possible as well? Certainly it is more difficult to imagine what they could be like, and Bennett, for example, says that the suggestion is 'one which we do not understand: we cannot see what it comes to, or see how to fill in any details'.[10] But I think that with a little effort we can imagine it, and I want to do what I can to defend the idea that experience does not have to be temporal – unless, of course, it is just uninterestingly built into the meaning of our word 'experience' that it must be, in which case what matters is whether some coherent concept can be found which covers the rest of what we consider essential to experience but allows for alternatives to the time-order. I must emphasize that I do not claim to prove that the kinds of example I shall put forward really are logically possible, for to show that something is logically possible you have to show that it contains no inconsistencies hidden away, and it is in the nature of inconsistencies to lurk. All I maintain is that a number of arguments which purport to show that atemporal experience is inconceivable actually fail to do so; and I see no particular reason to suppose new arguments will uncover more genuine inconsistencies for us. But it is then admittedly open to anyone to find such an argument, and to show that there really is something wrong with the idea of timeless experience.

It is easiest to start by considering a percipient whose thoughts change as ours do, and who can apply concepts of temporal succession to his inner life, but who inhabits an altogether static and changeless world. If he is himself unable to move about, so that his perceptions of what is external to him never change, it would at first seem dubious

34

whether he can find grounds for thinking he is aware of an objective world at all. He cannot go from place to place and meet the old familiar scene when he returns again to where he was before; so he seems to lack that coherent patterning of perceptions which could provide a basis for thinking of objects as continuing to exist independently of his awareness of them. So it would seem that only a temporal world can give us reason to apply the concept of an object; as was, indeed, already implied when we spoke of objects as reidentifiable particulars, as items which go on existing when unperceived.

However, this does not conclude the matter. For space and time are in many ways closely similar, and if we allow that our percipient's experience is spatial we can exploit the analogy and make space play the part of a surrogate for time. If this can be done successfully he will be able to think of objects as existing not when, but where, unperceived. But an object which exists not when, but where, unperceived is still quite properly called an object, for its existence is in just the same way independent of the percipient's awareness of it. And it still raises problems of reidentification, just as the temporally extended objects of our world do; only reidentification over a spatial, not a temporal, gap.

Let us imagine, then, a spatially extended, static world, which exhibits a fair degree of regularity. For example, at regular apparent distances there is a big red square, flanked by little yellow triangles on each side. There is also a thick purple bar running like a meridian across the whole of what one can see. Each square is accompanied by four triangles except in one case, where the bottom side of the square comes close to the purple bar, and on that side there is no yellow triangle. In another case there is not a red square where we should expect one, but a red rectangle touching the purple bar; it again has triangles on three sides, but no triangle on the side contiguous with the bar. Would it not be reasonable to hypothesize that the purple bar is covering up the missing triangle in the first case, and in the second case the third triangle and the missing part of the square? And could one not imagine a third instance, in which it would be reasonable to say that two patches of red flanking the bar were parts of the same square, the rest of it being hidden by the bar? To say this would be to reidentify the square over a spatial gap, as we reidentify objects over temporal gaps. And in each of these cases we should be supposing that things exist even though they are not being perceived. Where we have a square that is partially visible, we can say that a spatial part of it is perceived while another spatial part is unperceived, just as we can say of my desk that various temporal parts of it are perceived while other temporal parts are unperceived. In other words, on this reasonable hypothesis the square continues to exist where unperceived, just as the desk continues to exist when unperceived.

It is, of course, no more than a hypothesis; we cannot verify that it is correct. We cannot, without introducing change into the world, go and lift up the bar to see if the yellow triangles are underneath. But the analogy with my desk remains; in our own world there is no way of verifying that my desk is still in my room when nobody is perceiving it there. In the case of the desk we can say that at all times when someone is in my room (with the lights on, etc.) they see a desk there, and we consider that this warrants us in saying that if someone were there now they would see it. But for the case we are now imagining the analogue is: at all places where the purple bar is not present one can see the squares and their accompanying triangles, and this (I suggest) warrants saying that if the purple bar were not there one would see other squares and triangles, and other parts of those one now sees incompletely. In each instance the hypothesis of unperceived existence goes beyond all the evidence that is received – at any time or at any place; but it is justified by its convenient and economical explanation of the phenomena. The cases thus appear precisely analogous.

Well, perhaps not altogether analogous yet, because the situation in our own world is very much more complicated than that in the static world as we have imagined it so far. The complication can only consist in there being a lot more evidence of fundamentally the same sort, but the hypothesis of unperceived existents no doubt becomes more natural as the situation becomes more involved. To maintain the analogy, then, we ought to make our imaginary static world more complicated. We can suppose that there is a green bar which crosses the visual field diagonally, and that there is a break in this bar just where it comes into contact with the purple bar and nowhere else; at several points where we would expect red squares or yellow triangles to be, and where the bar also is, we can see nothing or only parts of such shapes, as before with the purple bar. It seems reasonable to describe this situation by saying that the green bar is hidden by the purple bar, and itself obscures red squares and yellow triangles, or parts of them. Furthermore, we can suppose that over this whole picture there is superimposed a network of regularly-spaced equal-sized little spots, which are roughly orange, and that even the purple and green bars are not visible where there is a spot (as we might say) covering a part of them; but moreover, although the colours of these spots are not affected by the bars or the red squares, perhaps whenever we see a spot where we should otherwise have expected a yellow triangle to be, we find it is much lighter in colour than usual. Now if there is such a light-coloured spot as it were super-imposed on the purple bar, but in a place where but for the bar we should have expected a yellow triangle, does its light colour not lend some support to the theory that the yellow triangle is still there, under-neath the bar, affecting the colour of the spot?

So it does not seem to me at all impossible to imagine what experience might be like for someone conscious only of an unchanging world, and unable to change his viewpoint on it. In particular he could apply the concept of an object, something capable of existing unperceived, on grounds analogous to those we use, provided that his experience was sufficiently regular and complex. He would think of objects differently from us, in that the part which time plays for us would be taken by space, but his objects are still particulars and not general things like mathematical entities; for they are instantiated in space, and the spatial matrix is used in identifying and reidentifying them. Though incidentally it is not essential to the case that the ordering be spatial. Any alternative to space, like a Strawsonian auditory dimension, would do equally well, provided that items could exhibit the same sort of regularity with respect to it; though of course it would make the case a great deal harder to imagine.[11]

Now what happens if we take a further step, and suppose that our percipient is not even aware of any succession in his own thoughts? One way to do this is by imagining a totally changeless world in which not even his states of consciousness can alter; a less extreme suggestion would be that his mental states might succeed one another in time, but without his being aware of any change, either in his thoughts or in the outside world. In this second case there will be a lot he does not know about himself; he will not be able to appreciate how his present thought may be based upon past ones which led up to it, or how it may in turn contribute to some further conclusion he may ultimately reach. This limitation of self-consciousness seems a considerable drawback, though otherwise I think the suggestion is coherent enough; but since the difficulties which can be raised in connection with it are difficulties also for the more ambitious idea of a completely changeless world, and since I think that the more ambitious suggestion is coherent too, I shall not examine the less extreme alternative any further. For if experience is possible in a world altogether without change, it is possible also for a percipient whose mental states change without his being aware of it.

Experience in an entirely changeless world is not indeed easy to imagine, and one may feel inclined to dismiss the idea out of hand. But the fact that something is hard to imagine does not make it conceptually incoherent. And at least no new difficulty seems to arise over the concept of an object. So far as his experience of the external world goes our present percipient is no worse off than the observer we considered before, from whom he differs only in that his thoughts are not successive. He can be aware, all at once, of the sort of ordered world of spatial particulars we have been imagining. It is perfectly true that he will not be able to consider and weigh up the evidence, and then gradually to formulate a theory about the independent existence of squares, triangles, etc.; for all this would take time. But that does not seem to matter very much. We do take time to evolve and test theories, but it is not that which makes them worth while as theories; a theory formed instantaneously is just as good if it is equally supported by the available evidence. And here the evidence available is the same as it was before.

The uneasiness which one feels over the present suggestion arises less over the application of particular concepts than over concept-application in general. As has often been pointed out, concept-application, and hence any form of intelligent thought, requires the ability to follow rules. For this it seems necessary that one be able to recognize on occasion that one has broken the rule, and failed to apply the concept correctly; and that one be able to put this right. But such an ability to recognize and to correct mistakes appears essentially to involve time. For surely one must first make the mistaken application of the rule; then detect the error; then put it right; and no pair of actions performed simultaneously could possibly be construed as the making, and the correcting, of a mistake. What indeed would lead one to single out one of these rather than the other as the correction?

One answer to this would be again to use space (or some other dimension) to make good the lack of a time-dimension. We should have to introduce something corresponding to the asymmetry between earlier and later, but we could try to do that by providing our percipient with analogues of memory and intention. We could suppose, for example, that his body was extended over a considerable distance in one direction, and that each spatial point in it was associated with a set of thoughts in such a way that these thoughts incorporated a great deal of information about the other points to the left but very little about points to the right; and furthermore, that we could explain thoughts, or states of affairs in the external world, as being the results of thoughts (which we could call decisions) occurring further to the left in the percipient's body, but not conversely. Although all his thoughts occur at the same time his analogue of what we call the unity of consciousness will be the unity of his thoughts at a place; and we can think of him as living along a spatial dimension, from left to right.[12]

But some people would say that this just reintroduces time in a new guise. Time, they would argue, is whatever dimension one lives along; we live in the direction of the increase of entropy, but this is a contingent fact and it does not define what time is. We might have lived along a spatial dimension instead, as our imaginary percipient does; and then that would have been time for us, as it is for him. So his experience is not timeless after all; it just contains no development in the order of the increase of entropy.

To consider this properly would take us far afield. But we need not delay over it, for we can defend the coherence of timeless experience by a yet more radical course. Without some alternative dimension to take the place of the time-order we are used to we shall have to admit that our percipient cannot recognize his mistakes and put them right. But if we think again about what is required for concept-application, it is not so clear after all that he has to be able to correct mistakes. Is it not enough if it is true of him that he would have judged differently if the evidence before him had been different? When I correct a mistake I have made, there is a stage at which I recognize some feature of the situation, which can broadly be called a piece of evidence, which previously I had ignored; and to be able to correct a mistake is to be able to take such evidence into account. The percipient we are now imagining is not able to go through the process of making the mistake, acquiring the further evidence, and making the correction, for that would take time; nevertheless it can be true of him that if he had had such further evidence, he would have judged differently. He cannot acquire better evidence than he has before him, but he could have had better evidence, and he would have judged differently if so. This seems enough to let us describe him as applying concepts in a rule-governed sort of way.

It may be objected that it is entirely gratuitous to hold that such counterfactual conditionals are true of the percipient. On what grounds can we assert that he would have judged differently? To this question, however, I think we can give an answer. The general treatment of counterfactuals in a timeless world has already been indicated in dealing with the concept of an unperceived existent; there we used a non-temporal regularity to warrant us in saying that if the purple bar had not been there, other squares and triangles would have been visible. And similarly in the present case. There can be good grounds for saying that if the evidence had been different, he would have judged differently, on the basis of the relationships which generally hold between his judgment of a particular circumstance and the evidence available from his point of view. If he makes a great many judgments about the different features of his environment, we may expect that there will be cases in which the evidence actually available to him is closely similar to the evidence that would have been available in the counterfactual case. We can see how he adjudges it, and use this to justify a claim about how he would have assessed the hypothetical situation. We cannot, of course, actualize the very situation which is envisaged by the counterfactual conditional: we cannot bring it about that he actually has this evidence in this instance. We can only consider relevantly similar states of affairs. But that is just to say that the counterfactual is, after all, a counterfactual; the direct verification of a counterfactual is no more possible in our own world. We can only collect enough analogous cases to give us confidence that if the antecedent had been true, the consequent would have been.

This invites, perhaps, the reply that there is a considerable difference between saying that someone can do something and saying that he would have done it, if the circumstances had been different. In our world there is a sense in which one can take steps to check, and if necessary to correct, a belief. It is not just that if the evidence had been different one would have judged differently, though that is true and relevant; it is also that one could do something about getting further evidence, even if one never does. The possibility is in some way open to one, though one may never avail oneself of it. This seems to be a feature which cannot be replicated in the timeless world.

Now to the extent to which the possibility is thought of as lying in the future, of course we cannot accommodate it in the timeless world. But it is by no means clearly essential for concept-application that it should be thought of in that way. What we mean by saying that someone can do a thing, even if he never does it, is apparently (and roughly) that it depends on his will whether he does it. Presumably, therefore, what is essential is the possibility that his will should be efficacious; and perhaps also, that his will should not itself be determined by factors outside itself. But the idea of the will as efficacious, and as not determined by external factors, can be carried over quite successfully into the timeless world. For although the timeless subject cannot make any future decisions or perform any future actions, the world may still depend in various ways upon his will, in that if he had willed otherwise things would have been different. And his choice to will in one way rather than another may be free, in that there are no true counterfactuals to the effect that if the world had been otherwise he would have willed differently. The basis for supposing such counterfactuals true or false will be the same as before. And it is not improper to talk about will and action here; for what distinguishes agency is its purposiveness, and we can find grounds for ascribing purpose to a timeless percipient. In effect we have done it already. To say that someone acts with a purpose is to say something about what he would do, or would have done, under other circumstances; roughly, that though in fact this was the particular action he did perform, he would have performed whatever alternative act had seemed to him a better means of achieving this goal. Such a counterfactual may be true of an inhabitant of a timeless world, and justified by a consideration of more or less parallel cases. The ascription of purposive agency, as well as the ascription of causal responsibility, is part of the explanatory theory one builds up to account for the phenomena, and it would play the same role in the imaginary timeless world as it does for us. The concepts of purpose and will form part of the theory and are as legitimate as the theory itself.

The grounds for ascribing to our timeless subject such complex concepts as these can be improved by imagining that the timeless world has not just one inhabitant but several – an addition which might be considered advantageous on its own account. The more subjects there are around, the more cases there will be of judgments being made in the face of such-and-such evidence, and the more instances there will be of desires and their concomitant circumstances; and that will make it easier to justify the complex counterfactuals we are interested in, and the explanatory theory to which they belong.

The social life of these timeless beings would, it is true, be a trifle limited; limited in particular by the fact that they could not converse or argue with one another, for these things take time. They could, however, at least be aware of each other's existence. It is even perhaps conceivable that they might have a sort of language (of rather limited usefulness) – though of course they could never have learned it. One can imagine that their bodies are like white rectangular slabs upon which words are written; words which would not have been written had they not intended to induce propositional attitudes in one another by means of recognition of intention. Each is aware of various slabs sprinkled about the place, and each can see such a slab, or part of it, at the origin of his own point of view, and perspectivally distorted by this in the way our own bodies are. Each knows, of course, what is written on his slab, and knows that the words there express what to him appear the most interesting truths. He can read what is written on at least some of the other slabs, but does not consider all of what they say to be equally interesting or even true. The various propositions on one's own slab may describe the world as one sees it, and perhaps add a few mathematical or logical remarks; those written on other slabs will sometimes include mathematical proofs which one believes to contain an error, and they will describe the world from the point of view of the relevant slab – sometimes, therefore, getting things wrong through the omission of features not visible from that point of view. It may be, also, that certain slabs generally contain more mistakes than others; some, perhaps, are just bad at arithmetic, and keep on making arithmetical mistakes of an elementary kind, whereas more intelligent (or more numerate) slabs do not.

This may perhaps be going a little far. And one must obviously admit that life would be very strange, and very limited, in a timeless world. There would be none of the pleasure of putting right someone who has made a mistake one recognizes as such; nor would there be the more dubious, or Platonic, pleasure of being put right oneself. Life would not be exciting; but at least it would not be boring either. For us pleasure resides very largely in getting things done, not in having done them, and none of this would be available in our imaginary world. Aristotle thought that such an existence would be fun all the same; this may be doubted, but at least one could entertain a great variety of thoughts and a great complexity of mathematical argumentation, so long as one did it all at once. And tastes, after all, do vary.

IV

Space and Time as Intuitions

The first two arguments of the metaphysical expositions of space and of time attempted, not very successfully, to show that space and time are a priori. The second pair tries to show that they are intuitions – by which Kant means, particulars of which we are immediately aware. Here he is again attacking Leibniz, for whom space is not a substance but a set of relations between objects, and all truths about space are really truths about how things are related. The relations themselves are, of course, spatial relations like 'x is between y and z' or 'x is n times as long as y',[1] but the character of space is entirely determined by whatever physical limitations there may be on the way objects can relate to one another. Kant feels that this is backwards: space is more than just a system of relations, and the intrinsic character of space itself not only restricts how objects can move but is also responsible for certain of the non-relational properties which they have and by which they can be identified.

The metaphysical expositions are called expositions of the concepts of space and time, and since Kant contrasts intuitions with concepts this has caused some confusion. It need not really have done. Space and time themselves are intuitions, and therefore particulars, and Kant denies they can be analysed predicatively in terms of relations between objects. But we can use concepts to think or talk about particulars, though concepts are essentially predicative and encapsulate information about the objects to which they apply. Even proper names are concepts, according to Kant (though demonstratives are not); so that when we say 'Caius is mortal' the individual concept of Caius will be analysable into a set of predicates whereby we can identify the man.[2] But this is not, obviously, to say that Caius is himself a predicate or a property. In just the same way the fact that we can use the concept of space to talk about that unique thing, space, does not turn space itself into a concept.

In view of some recent misunderstandings it is perhaps worth emphasizing that by calling something an intuition Kant does not simply mean that it is a particular, an individual thing. In its primary sense intuition is the immediate awareness of particulars;[3] by transference the word becomes applied to the particulars we are immediately aware of. The exact meaning of 'immediately aware' is not fully elucidated, and there are problems with it rather analogous to the problems over Russell's notion of acquaintance.[4] But Kant makes it clear that we can both think and talk about objects which are not given to us in intuition and which are consequently not 'intuitions'.[5] The only text which strongly suggests that all our ideas of particular things should be accounted intuitions is the one in the *Logik* in which he says

> An intuition is a *singular* representation (*repraesentat. singularis*), a concept a *general* representation (*repraesentat. per notas communes*) or a *reflective* representation (*repraesentat. discursiva*). (*Logik*, sect. 1.)

But elsewhere in the *Logik* the requirement of immediate awareness is clearly present,[6] and it is a work in which one must be particularly careful about taking passages out of context – it was, after all, compiled not by Kant himself but by Jäsche, from a lot of Kant's scribbled notes. It is not of course necessary (except for finite beings like ourselves) that the immediate awareness should involve the senses, for Kant thinks that God's intuition is intellectual and not sensible at all. This does not mean God is not immediately aware of things – on the contrary, he is immediately aware of everything – but only that for God there is no distinction between immediate awareness and discursive thought.

The arguments of the metaphysical expositions are again thoroughly inadequate; indeed they are hardly arguments at all. As with the earlier pair of arguments the first is borrowed from the *Inaugural Dissertation*[7] and the second is added in the *Critique of Pure Reason* to bolster it up. The first claims – without further defence – that we can only imagine ('represent to ourselves') one single space and one single time; when we speak of different spaces or times we really mean different parts of the unique space and time, which must be thought of as totalities and not as constructions out of their parts. The second argument just supplements this by stating that space and time are given as infinite, and have parts (as things do) not instances (like concepts). This is all supposed to refute Leibniz, and to establish that space and time are things, not systems of relations between objects.

That we cannot imagine more than one space or time is not obvious; there may be some incoherence in the suggestion that there might be more, but it is not evident where it lies. I shall return to this below; but if Kant were right it would not help him against Leibniz. Space might be unique and yet analysable as a system of relations, it would just be the only such system (and the same applies to time). Equally our space and our time might be particular things, resistant to Leibnizian analysis, even though there were other spaces and times to be found – other entities of the same kinds. Kant is confusing particularity with uniqueness.

Similarly with the contention that space and time are given as infinite wholes, except that it is less clear what it means. By calling them given he cannot wish to imply that our representations of space and time come from outside us; that would contradict his transcendental idealism, according to which they are forms we ourselves impose on our experience. He means only that they are objects of immediate awareness: we are directly aware of them as frameworks in which objects and events can be located, but they are frameworks unlimited in extent, even though we can neither perceive nor imagine an infinite series of objects or events arrayed in them. Again this is not obviously correct, and again Leibniz could admit the claim, for they might be infinite but still susceptible of analysis as infinite systems of relations between previously given items. It would also seem quite possible to accept Kant's own view of them as particulars without accepting the difficult doctrine that they are given as totalities, regarding them instead as constructed out of smaller and more convenient-sized bits (themselves, of course, also particulars). Indeed he appears to put forward such a view himself in the *Metaphysical Foundations of Natural Science*, where he says that absolute space as a whole is only an 'idea of reason' representing the limit of the series of larger and larger finite relative spaces.[8]

These feeble arguments do not give us Kant's real reason for holding that space and time are intuitions. That is to be found in his argument from incongruent counterparts, which he formulated first in 1768 and repeated two years later in the *Inaugural Dissertation*. Its omission from the *Critique* is unfortunate and rather puzzling. His statements of it elsewhere suggest that he may have been rather confused on the subject, but he had certainly not come to regard the argument as invalid: he includes it in the *Prolegomena* and refers to it as sound in the *Metaphysical Foundations of Natural Science*, both of which were written subsequently. It directly concerns only space and not time, and he does not try to construct an analogue for time; but he seems to think time is so closely similar to space that if space is an intuition time must be too.

2   Incongruent counterparts

Kant maintains that a right- and a left-hand glove are enough to shatter Leibniz's theory of space. For there is a difference between them that the relational theory can never capture. The difference in orientation, in handedness, cannot be reduced to any difference in the relations between things or between the parts of things; the two gloves share all their relational properties and all their non-spatial properties as well, yet they are quite clearly and obviously different. We can see the difference between them, but we cannot specify what it amounts to in any way that would be acceptable to Leibniz. There must be more to space, therefore, than Leibniz will allow.

The argument is a little hard to assess, and Kant himself seems uncertain just how much it shows. The reason is partly that there are two arguments here, not one. The first makes a perfectly good and straightforward point against Leibniz, though not against everyone who has held that space is no more than a system of relations. According to Leibniz objects must be identifiable independently of their spatial (and temporal) relations: we first identify the objects and then observe the relationships that hold between them. Now Strawson, for instance, differs from him on this, agreeing indeed that to determine spatial relationships we must rely on the identification of things, but holding also that the identification of things depends upon knowledge of their spatial relationships – the two come together and the dependence is mutual.[9] Against Leibniz, though not against Strawson, Kant can offer his gloves. For we find no difficulty in telling the gloves apart, though what distinguishes them is their orientation in space and not any feature which can be identified before spatial relations are discovered. The case of the incongruent counterparts is one in which it is strikingly clear that we distinguish the objects by means of a spatial property, though other examples can be used to make the same point, and we have already seen Kant elsewhere citing two drops of water for the same purpose: they can be qualitatively indistinguishable, but we individuate them without difficulty through their different positions. The advantage of the more complicated example of incongruent counterparts is perhaps that it helps circumvent a reply which Leibniz would make. For he argues that there must always be some hidden internal difference between the drops if we are to be capable of distinguishing them, a difference we may not be consciously aware of but which subconsciously we must apprehend. This contention was made more plausible by the microscope, which revealed endless minute differences between water-drops; and Leibniz took great pride in his triumph over M. d'Alvanslebe, a Hanoverian courtier who offered to find him two qualitatively indistinguishable leaves, and spent a morning vainly trying to do so.[10] But with the two gloves, or a single glove and its mirror image, it seems particularly obvious that the salient feature which differentiates them for us is their orientation in space, not any qualitative distinction consciously or subconsciously perceived.

This first point is a valid objection to Leibniz, though not to Strawson, because Strawson does not hold that things can be identified on the basis of their non-spatial (and non-temporal) properties alone. But Kant also has a second and more far-reaching point to make. For just as the difference between the gloves is patently a spatial one, so it seems equally evident to him that it is not a difference in spatial *relations* : it is internal to the gloves, and they therefore have spatial properties not susceptible of any relational analysis. They differ in absolute orientation.

An obvious counter to this is to point out that any two actual gloves clearly will differ in their external relations to other objects. The internal relations of their parts will be the same, but if they lie side by side face down on my dressing table the thumb of one will be closer to certain objects (my hairbrush, or the Eiffel Tower) than are its fingers, while for the other the reverse will be true. So long as there is some asymmetry in the arrangement of objects in the universe, there will be differences of this sort to appeal to.

Kant would reply that it is not this asymmetry in external relations which we rely on in telling the gloves apart. We can see a difference just by looking at them, without taking external relations into account. This would be parallel to his earlier reply to Leibniz on the d'Alvanslebe question, for there also he was concerned less to deny that there might be hidden qualitative differences between the two drops or leaves than to dismiss the point as irrelevant, since it is not these differences that we go on in making the distinction. But he can strengthen his case by asking us to consider a more impoverished universe than our own, in which there exist only the two gloves side by side. Everything is then symmetrical about a plane mid-way between the gloves, one side being as it were a mirror image of the other. The gloves do not differ in respect of the external or internal relations of their parts, yet they remain distinct and the difference in handedness remains. Leibniz must say that this could not be so; there could not be two gloves any longer, but one glove only, and that neither left- nor right-handed – for these terms become meaningful only when there are other objects to relate to. But this is unconvincing, for the situation envisaged is easy to imagine; one needs some better reason to dismiss it as incoherent than the dogmatic commitment to an analysis of space which has that consequence.

Kant himself does not consider a universe of two gloves symmetrically arranged, but in his original paper of 1768 he does raise the possibility that there might have existed only a hand and nothing more:[11]

Let it be imagined that the first created thing were a human hand, then it must necessarily be either a right hand or a left hand. In order to produce the one a different action of the creative cause is

necessary from that by means of which its counterpart could
be produced.

This does seem plausible; the difference between a right and a left hand
is such that one can hardly imagine a hand neutral as to which it is. In a
similar way one can say of our own (presumably) asymmetrical universe
that there might have existed in its stead a counterpart, exactly similar
save for being orientated the other way, as its mirror image would be.
But I think these examples carry less conviction than does the case of the
two-glove universe; it is easier to suspect an incoherence. Remnant has
recently taken Leibniz's side here, objecting that 'in a universe which
contained nothing but a single hand, it would not just be empirically
undecidable whether that hand were left or right; it would be strictly
indeterminate.'[12] But Kant would say that Remnant had followed Leibniz
in failing to see that there is an irreducibly ostensive element in the
meanings of 'left' and 'right'. A left-handed and a right-handed glove
look different regardless of their relations to other things, and a left-
handed and a right-handed universe would look different too.

Someone might reply that in imagining these situations one cheats
by surreptitiously introducing a relation to one's own asymmetrical
body. It is true that I first learnt the words 'left' and 'right' by reference
to my body, and there may still be circumstances in which I appeal to it
to remind myself which is called 'left' and which is called 'right'. But the
difference between the gloves is immediately obvious without reference
to my body or to anything else; I should perceive it in just the same way
if my body were itself symmetrical about the plane that forms the axis
of symmetry between the gloves.

A more satisfactory manoeuvre for Leibniz would be to accept all this,
but to say it does not show space is more than a set of spatial relations.
What it shows is that among the spatial relations we must include
orientational ones, which are not reducible to any other sort: relations
like 'x is to the left of y as seen from z' (assuming, of course, that the
hypothetical observer is standing on his feet not his head, but that is a
detail). Leibniz himself would not have been very happy with this for
metaphysical reasons which are not relevant here,[13] but the move appears
open to those who do not have his metaphysical preoccupations. One
could then distinguish between the gloves: from a point on the plane
of symmetry between the gloves and palmwards of them, in glove A the
thumb is to the left of the fingers and in glove B the fingers are to the
left of the thumb.

The natural reaction to this suggestion seems to be that it is over-
simple: one cannot treat relations like 'x is to the left of y as seen from z'
as unanalysable, and as soon as one tries to provide an analysis one has to
appeal to features of space which cannot be regarded as mere relationships

between objects. But it is not very clear why one should not treat such relations as unanalysable. The only attempt I know to argue that they cannot be handled in that way is due to Nerlich.[14]

Nerlich points out that amongst the topological spaces we can imagine there are some which are orientable, but also some which are non-orientable. An orientable space is one within which counterparts like the gloves can never be made congruent with one another by any combination of translations and rotations. To take a two-dimensional example, he considers a pair of 'knees' cut out of paper, as in Figure 1.

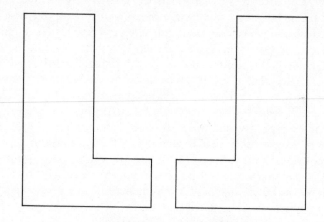

Figure 1.   Nerlich's knees

Confined in their movement to the surface of a table these knees are incongruent counterparts, and they show that the two-dimensional space of that surface is orientable. (Of course they can be made congruent by turning one of them over, but then one has to lift it off the table top.) But one can also imagine a two-dimensional space in which it is possible to move one knee round until it becomes congruent with the other; the surface of a Möbius band constitutes such a space, as would the surface of a Klein bottle (see Figures 2 and 3).[15] Philosophy offers few chances for experiments, but it is entertaining to make a Möbius band of sticky paper and cut holes in it for knees, to investigate these possibilities. Non-orientable spaces are equally possible in three dimensions, and similar things can be done in them with gloves, but unfortunately they are not so easily modelled.

The possibility of moving a right-handed knee or glove around in a non-orientable space until it becomes congruent with a left-handed one means that we can hardly claim its right-handedness is intrinsic to it; for it depends on how we move it. And it also seems to depend upon how we move. If Alice follows a glove round a non-orientable, three

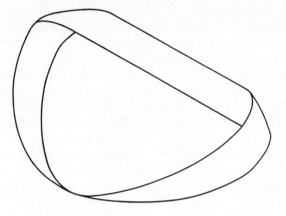

Figure 2. Möbius band

dimensional space and comes back to where she started – or if a two-dimensional Alice follows a knee round a Möbius band – it will look the same to her all the way, and when she gets back again it will still look to her as it did before she started out. Only everything else in that region will now appear to her right-left reversed; the exactly similar glove she left behind will have apparently changed its handedness; she will seem to have come back to a mirror image of the place she started from. To those at home she will appear to have undergone mirror-image reversal and to use 'right/left' vocabulary in a switched way; she will hold her fork with her right hand, her knife with her left, and so on.

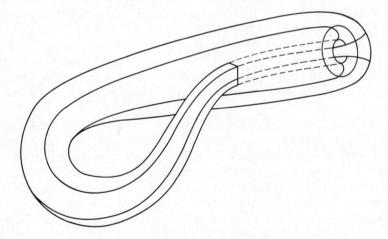

Figure 3. Klein bottle

49

The stay-at-homes will naturally say that Alice has got 'right' and 'left' mixed up. But their only support is in numbers. If half of them had travelled round too there would be no settling who was right; if, from the same position, one group said that A was to the left of B, then the other group would say that B was to the left of A. How things look to you at home will depend on how many times you have travelled round the space. So it cannot be that 'x is to the left of y as seen from z' is an unanalysable relation; and this is Nerlich's conclusion. There could be an objective answer to the question whether A was to the left of B if they were to define 'to the left of' in terms of asymmetrical fixed objects in the neighbourhood, but then this is not what 'to the left of' means.

Nevertheless there is something that Alice and the stay-at-homes can agree upon without appeal to the asymmetrical objects, namely that there is a difference between the two gloves – and a difference in handed-ness. All they cannot decide on is which to call the right-hand glove, but this does not really matter very much. They agree that the adventure-some glove used to have the same handedness as its twin that stayed behind, and now no longer does. 'x is to the left of y as seen from z' will not do as an unanalysable spatial relation, but perhaps 'as seen from z, x lies to y in the same orientation as v lies to w' will. There is no dispute between Alice and the rest as to which gloves are similarly handed; the only dispute is over which orientation to call right and which to call left.

This has to be complicated slightly, for Alice might see stretched out before her a whole series of gloves going all the way round the (finite) space and back to where she is standing. Then she would see herself in the distance, right-left reversed, with the gloves beside her there looking reversed correspondingly. (Assuming, of course, that in this strange world the light rays follow geodesics.) The unanalysable relation therefore does not hold between the gloves, but only between them as they appear from a given position at such-and-such a distance and in such-and-such a direction. So it is a slightly complex relation to admit as primitive, but if one is willing to then we must conclude that one can handle the difference between the gloves within a Leibnizian theory of space.

But if (like the historical Leibniz) one is unwilling to treat orientational relations as primitive one will then have to take Kant's argument seriously. He is not quite right, though, when he says that to distinguish the counterparts we must refer to 'space in general as a unity'.[16] All that is necessary is that we should be able to refer directly to spatial points – points which cannot be adequately characterized in terms of the (non-orientational) relations that hold between objects. Once we can do this we can distinguish between the two gloves, using demonstratively specified points to play the part of the hairbrush or the Eiffel Tower:

the thumb of one glove is closer to here than its fingers are, whereas for the other it is not so. Some other point may have the same relationship to the second glove, but even if the gloves are symmetrically arranged and alone in the universe that point is not this one. Leibniz thinks we can use a demonstrative only when it could be replaced, at least in principle, by some purely descriptive expression capable of individuating the item referred to, but in this case that is not possible. Kant, and common sense, see Leibniz as making a gratuitous stipulation, and recognize that we can pick out places and times directly, regardless of whether they differ from one another in any way expressible without a demonstrative.

It is this ability to make direct and irreducible reference to spatial points which is crucial for Kant's position. And it is plausible to hold that he is right about it, though the idea of direct reference does suggest a second way of avoiding the thrust of the argument from incongruent counterparts. For one could admit such reference not to points in space but to parts of objects – the fingers of the gloves, for example – and one would again be able to distinguish the left-handed from the right-handed glove, in a similar way. Kant, however, overlooks this quite attractive possibility, and concludes that we must be directly aware of space as a framework of demonstrable points; which is what he means by calling it an intuition. In the same way he thinks time is a framework of demonstrable moments, and though he has no parallel argument for this it is very natural to hold that we can make direct reference to the present moment. When he calls space and time 'forms' of intuition his point is still essentially the same: when we perceive objects we perceive them as laid out in space, and the spatio-temporal framework provides us with the matrix for identifying them.

He does also go further, though. He takes the additional step of claiming that we are directly aware of certain properties the spatial framework has, and to a lesser extent certain properties of time as well. We know space to be unlimited in extent (an 'infinite given magnitude') although the objects we experience cover only a limited area, and we know its geometry to be Euclidean. It is therefore, amongst other things, an orientable, three-dimensional space. These extra features of space are supposed to reveal themselves in our inability to imagine it in any other way. But nothing in the argument from incongruent counterparts entitles him to these further claims – not even to the claim that space is orientable. For we can distinguish between the orientations of the gloves even in a space which is not orientable, just as we can distinguish between the paper knees lying on the table. We just cannot use our terms 'left' and 'right' to mark the distinction without getting into the difficulties that faced Alice and her friends, since things can change their handedness by moving around.

3 Absolute space

Both Nerlich and at one stage Kant use the argument from incongruent counterparts to draw conclusions about absolute space. Nerlich thinks it shows that space is a 'primitive absolute entity',[17] because he believes that in calling gloves right- and left-handed we are saying something not just about the gloves but about the character of space. And so we are, if we use the words 'right' and 'left' and do not simply restrict ourselves to noticing the orientational difference: we are saying that we live in an orientable space, for in a non-orientable space these words could not usefully be applied. It may actually be that we are wrong about this, as we have (apparently) turned out to be wrong in thinking space was Euclidean; physicists may find that if gloves are moved far enough they come back with their handedness reversed. But what matters to Nerlich is that either way it is a fact about space whether it is orientable or not.

It is more difficult to see why Nerlich thinks it is a fact relationalists cannot deal with. In their view to say that space has a certain character is only to say that certain motions are physically possible, and if God wanted to alter its topology he would simply have to change the laws about how objects can move – and not to interfere with mysterious invisible scaffolding. Nerlich says he does not see how to construe the modality here, and points out that neither logical possibility nor mere conceivability will do; no doubt physical possibility will not quite do either, for as he says there is a variety of reasons why it may be physically impossible to move objects.[18] But we are dealing here in an idealized physical possibility, which has to be idealized because topological laws are not the only laws which govern the motions of bodies. Nor is this peculiar in the slightest bit. Whenever a scientific law allows that something is possible, 'possible' has to be taken in this idealized way: for what is really being said is that some state of affairs is not ruled out by the law in question. There may be others to rule it out, and very likely there will be.

Kant never thought that facts of this sort proved space was absolute. He would have regarded the question whether space is orientable as something of a red herring. But in his 1768 essay he did present his argument from incongruent counterparts as showing that space must be absolute, not for any reason so sophisticated as Nerlich's, but because he thought it refuted Leibniz's relational theory by pointing out the difference that remains between the two gloves as I see them before me, whether space is orientable or not. The only two theories on the market were Leibniz's and that of Newton and Clarke, whereby space was a fixed immovable container with respect to which bodies are either absolutely in motion or absolutely at rest; he assumed that the refutation of Leibniz would leave Newton holding the field. And certainly Newton can accommodate incongruent counterparts quite easily, by their differ-ent relations to absolute space. Even if they bear the same relations to all other objects, the two gloves must differ in their relations to space itself or to the points in space. Whenever we choose some point asymmetrically related to them the difference between them will show up in relation to it.

But in the *Metaphysical Foundations of Natural Science*, which appeared in 1786, we find him attacking Newton's conception of space, though he is still committed to the argument from incongruent counterparts. He now sees that it proves less than he had thought. It proves (if Kant is right) that we must be able to pick out points demonstratively, even though there may be no way of characterizing them differently in terms of the spatial relations between objects. But this does not show that space provides a fixed reference-system that decides what is absolutely in motion and what is absolutely at rest, and by 1786 he is clear that it does not. For absolute space, he says, is not an object of possible experi-ence; by which he means that we are never aware of a fixed Newtonian reference-frame, but only of different systems of bodies which we can observe to be in motion or at rest relative to one another. When two systems are in motion relative to one another it is often useful to regard one as at rest and ascribe the motion to the other, but how we do this is in general a matter of convenience. It is usually convenient to take the wider and more inclusive system as being at rest, and this way of think-ing leads naturally to the idea of an all-inclusive framework like Newton's container which is at rest absolutely. But this idea is only an idea; we can have no experience of any such frame of reference, nor are we entitled to assume that there is such a thing. We intuit space only as a system of demonstrable points, not as a fixed immovable container. The ability to point to a place as 'here' does not carry with it any capacity for telling whether the place one indicates a moment later is the same one again, and consequently provides no help in determining which objects have moved and which have remained absolutely at rest. We can be aware of space as a locating matrix in which positions may be indicated by pure demonstration, without there being any fixed and static frame by reference to which the motions of bodies can be assessed.[19]

Newton allows that we cannot perceive absolute space, but suggests that we can distinguish absolute from relative motion all the same. For there may be theoretical reasons for thinking that certain bodies are influenced by particular forces, and this would give us a ground for saying that these bodies are in real (absolute) motion, but that bodies whose apparent motion cannot be explained by the action of forces on them are only in motion relative to others. More specifically, in the case of circular motion the absolute character of the motion can be shown by the centrifugal effect: the effect whereby the water in a revolving bucket tends towards the edges of the bucket and away from its centre, so that a concave depression is produced in the water's surface. This phenomenon shows the motion of the water to be absolute and not just relative; it is actually most pronounced when the water is rotating at the same speed as the bucket and is therefore at rest relative to it. The effect is produced by the tendency of each drop of water to continue travelling in a straight line in accordance with the law of inertia, and thus to fly off at a tangent if it were not inhibited by the sides of the bucket.[20]

Kant admits these considerations, but says that they only enable us to tell real from apparent motions, not absolute from relative ones.[21] This at first sounds mysterious, since for Newton real and absolute motion are the same thing, and it is hard to be sure either what Kant is saying or that his position is consistent. But I think what he means is that while such arguments do establish something they do not show as much as Newton wants. They do give us a reason for saying that the bucket is revolving, and not that it remains still while the rest of the universe circles round in the opposite direction, for in the latter case the observable effects would be different. But it is only with rotational and non-uniform motions that they help us in this way, and that is not enough. If Newton is right about absolute space it must be possible to ask not only whether the universe as a whole is revolving but also whether it is in constant rectilinear motion: is the entire universe moving steadily along in a straight line at 10 m.p.h.? And to questions of this sort Kant thinks there can be no answer. No evidence whatsoever could enable one to determine whether the universe was at rest in absolute space or moving along steadily in a straight line; and therefore the Newtonian conception of absolute space must be rejected, as a hypothesis no possible experience could ever establish. Absolute space can be no more than an idea.

But there is a confusion here. Kant is quite right to observe that Newton has given us no empirical tests for determining whether the whole universe is in constant rectilinear motion or not; indeed within Newton's own general theory such tests are not to be expected, since it is a feature of that system that the laws of mechanics are the same in relation to all frames of reference which are in constant rectilinear motion relative to one another. But Newton's theory may be false, or it may require supplementation by laws of another kind which do not remain invariant in this way. There is no reason in principle why it should not be possible to find that one reference frame yields simpler laws than any other, and this would be good grounds for regarding that frame as absolutely at rest. (Not conclusive grounds, of course, but then we never have those in science.) The fact that we have not found such a thing tells against the hypothesis that space is a fixed, absolute container, but it does not show that the hypothesis is empirically unverifiable. On the contrary, it would have been verified if the experimental evidence had not led us to Newton's laws but instead confirmed Aristotle's, or if we had discovered forces that acted in detectably different ways on bodies in rectilinear motion and on bodies at rest.

4 Spaces and times

We have seen, then, what Kant means by calling space and time intuitions, and how his argument from incongruent counterparts supports him against Leibniz without committing him to Newton's strong conception of absolute space. The remaining issue for this chapter concerns whether it is necessary that our lives should be confined to one unique space and one unique time, as Kant affirms without argument, or whether a coherent experience would be possible which spanned several different spaces or time-orders. Space is easier to deal with than time; and in fact it does not seem difficult to imagine someone living his life in two unconnected spaces. Quinton has shown how this might happen, by developing a myth in which after a normal day in England one goes to sleep and finds oneself waking up in a hut on the shore of a tropical lake. There one lives out a day filled with the activities appropriate to such surroundings, and on falling asleep at once wakes up again in England. If this happens quite regularly, so that twelve hours of English experiences are followed by twelve hours' worth of tropical ones and then by English ones again; if from day to day one's English experiences have their customary coherence with one another, and one's tropical ones likewise; and if furthermore one can appeal in each world to the testimony of others to confirm in the usual way the veridicality of one's perceptions; then it is hard indeed to resist the conclusion that one inhabits two different but equally real worlds. If it happened to an isolated individual he might be tempted while in the one world to look upon the other as a dream; but we can easily suppose that the two-world experience is common or even shared by everyone, so that in England we can talk with one another about what we have been up to in the tropics and there we can discuss the goings-on in England.[22]

The two worlds will occupy two spaces only if there is in principle no way of travelling through space from one to the other; only if no line, however long, can be projected from the one to the other. But it is quite conceivable that this is so, and that the only way to get from England to the lakeside is by falling asleep, not by bus or train or spaceship. It is conceivable also that we should have good reason for believing it so, if for example (as Swinburne suggests[23]) the laws of nature operated very differently in the two places, or if the geometry of lakeside space were unlike that which characterizes our space here. And if we change the example, replacing the lakeside world with a Strawsonian sound-world set out in auditory space, the distinctness of the spaces becomes even more evident.

It may be objected that there is a latent incoherence in Quinton's story, because the conditions for personal identity are not preserved through these transfers from space to space. But there is no reason why they should not be. I can retain the same character, and essentially the same set of memory-beliefs, whichever world I am in; my body at the lakeside and my body in England may be as similar as you like (or as the laws of nature will permit). They may even be the same body; for we can suppose that it is not just my consciousness, but my body and all, that is suddenly transferred from England to the lakeside and back again. This would of course violate the principle that spatio-temporal continuity is a condition of the identity of bodies, for there is a spatial discontinuity at each transfer, but that principle was never more than a crude dogma at the best of times. One can insist upon it as a stipulation, but it runs clean contrary to our ordinary habits of thought to suppose that if Magdalen tower were moved discontinuously one millimetre to the east, or went out of existence to be replaced half a second later by a tower exactly similar in every detail, we should no longer have the same original tower we started with.

More interestingly contentious is the suggestion that experience might cover two unrelated times. This need not be the case in Quinton's example; there might be no difficulty in placing the events of the two worlds in a single time-series. In the most straightforward version, events would go on continuously in both worlds whether we were there to witness them or not, and one hour of lakeside time would be equivalent to one hour of English. We would be able to synchronize the clocks, and could travel between the worlds at will by falling asleep. In order to see what was going on at the lakeside now one would just have to go to sleep, and it might be important to do this by 10 p.m. so as not to miss the great feast they are going to have there. The events of the two worlds belong in a universal, public time-order; at 10 p.m. a given individual is either here or at the lakeside, and if he is here he experiences whatever is going on here, while if he is there he can join in the feast.

Swinburne, however, has provided a myth according to which we could have reason to suppose there were two distinct time-series; though more recently he has changed his mind and argued that it does not establish this after all.[24] The suggestion was that there might be two public, objective time-orders, and not that there could be any duality in the subjective order in which one individual's experiences come: my experiences themselves constitute a single series, but they inform me of an objective world whose events succeed one another in a time-order which is objective and shared, and Swinburne canvasses the possibility that they might inform me of more than one such time-order. His story is about two rival tribes, the Okku and the Bokku, which occupy the same territory; to stop them fighting, a magician brings about the following strange state of affairs. As the Okku see it, the Bokku simply disappear and they have the country to themselves for twenty years; after which the Bokku suddenly reappear in their midst. For the Bokku, on the other hand, it is the Okku who disappear, and the separation lasts for thirty of their years, so that after they have come together the tribes do not even agree on how long it is since the magician waved his wand. During the period of separation each tribe believes itself to have lived on in the same place, surrounded by the same objects as before; it is just that the other tribe disappears and later reappears again. Some care is needed in the account of what happens when they do reappear to one another, for it would seem that the Okku might have cut down a tree which the Bokku had left standing, or moved a great rock which the Bokku had left untouched; and a tree which neither tribe disturbed may be presumed to have acquired twenty new rings with the Okku, thirty with the Bokku. Swinburne proposes that at the reunion a sort of compromise is effected: where Okku-land and Bokku-land have become different, the reunited state of affairs combines roughly half of the features familiar to the Okku with half of the features familiar to the Bokku.[25] To minimize the oddity of this Swinburne can stipulate – for it is, after all, his example — that the reunion could not have taken place had not the differences between Okku-land and Bokku-land been very slight.

His own reason for deciding that the example does not show a plurality of times to be possible is that if that were the way to describe the situation, we should be able to say that a given material object exists in both times during the period of separation. And if a material object can do this, surely a conscious being ought to be able to. But no conscious being could exist in two distinct time-series at once; he would have to unite the events of both in a single order in his consciousness, which would provide a way of setting up simultaneity-relations between the series and hence of amalgamating them into one.[26]

This is not much of an objection. Our normal assumptions about identity are not designed for situations like these; it seems rather arbitrary whether we say that the same rock exists in both time-orders, or that it undergoes a sort of amoeba-like split (only in time, not in space) and then fuses together again. With a person perhaps the second alternative is the more natural, since Swinburne is certainly right to say that one could not have an integrated consciousness of both worlds together. We may suppose that the magician who lives with the Okku and the magician who lives with the Bokku both think of themselves as the magician who caused the split, and both have all the memory-beliefs appropriate to him, but neither can communicate with the other in any way; and that after the reunion there is again only one magician, who thinks of both their sets of experiences as having been his own.

Swinburne would say that if the two worlds do not contain the same objects we ought to think of them as in different spaces.[27] Maybe so; but they are in different times as well. He seems to think that the two-times hypothesis and the two-spaces hypothesis exclude one another, because in different spaces there may be different laws of nature, and processes may happen at different rates; so that the apparent time-discrepancy (the Okku's twenty years against the Bokku's thirty) can be explained in that way without supposing any difference in time itself. But this overlooks the essential point, which is that during the separation there is no way of setting up temporal relations between events of the two series. It is easy to see that this is the crucial factor, by reflecting that however we construe the example, even if we insist that only one space is involved, the case for two times collapses completely if the Okku and the Bokku can communicate with one another (perhaps by putting messages under a sacred stone) and synchronize their times in that way. In the total absence of any method of determining, even in theory, what temporal relations a given Okku-event has to a given Bokku-event, we cannot place them in a unified time-order, and there is no ground for denying that they belong to two distinct and separate series.

If we go back to Quinton's story of the lakeside, and abandon the conditions which allowed us to set up objective time relations between the two worlds there, we get a similar result. It might be, for example, that two people who fell asleep at the same time in England woke up at quite different lakeside times; when A goes to the lakeside he might live through events which were a day or even a century later, by lakeside reckoning, than the events B lives through there. This is perfectly compatible with A's experiences forming a single series subjectively for A, and B's doing the same for B, but it destroys the possibility of a public, objective time-ordering that covers the events of both spaces, though the series of lakeside events may still be objective by itself and so may the series of events in England. The present example has a feature Swinburne's did not have, and which some would take to cast doubt on its coherence, for it would appear that A and B might compare notes on their lakeside lives while they were both in England; so that A could receive from B information about lakeside episodes he had not yet experienced. Perhaps A could even find out about his own actions there, and the disastrous consequences they will lead to – consequences B has already witnessed, but which A will meet with only on future visits to the lakeside. I do not think there is any incoherence in this, or in the stories about time-travel to which it bears a close analogy, though they may require us to give up a conception of free will we should never have adopted in the first place. In fact the apparent difficulties can be avoided if the cases that would cause trouble simply do not occur.[28] In returning to the lakeside, for instance, one might always forget just those things that one had learned in England about lakeside life, while retaining the rest of one's memories perfectly clearly; and (to take a well-known example) if A happened to be B's father, who had begotten him at the lakeside at a time which in A's own history had not yet arrived, then B's efforts to assassinate him whilst in England might be unfailingly thwarted by circumstance. (Alternatively, assassination in England might not mean that one died at the lakeside too, but only that one's nights there would thenceforth be dreamless.)

This raises issues that we cannot properly investigate here, and for those who find such fancies uncongenial the case for two times can rest on more straightforward examples like Swinburne's. But for those who are prepared to venture further into the regions of speculation it is worth noticing that God might experience a plurality of time-orders even if we could not. Aquinas, in a famous figure, described God as seeing the whole of our time at once stretched out before him as a man might see a road from a high hill: the past and the future are present to him together.[29] From his point of view the world is an unchanging four-dimensional array, though one of the dimensions is what we call time. But there is no reason why his thoughts should not succeed one another in a time-dimension entirely distinct from ours, and which can metaphorically be said to be at right-angles to it. The whole course of our history is before him at one of his moments, but just as St Thomas' climber might by walking along his hill come to see another road, so as God's time passes he may find or make new worlds, each with its own complete history which he can likewise grasp as a simultaneous whole. There may be endlessly many worlds, each with its own time-order distinct from ours (for there is no conceivable way of establishing simultaneity relations between them) but as it were parallel to it. And not only may there be infinitely many such first-order time-series, the same applies at the second and at every higher order as well. For behind God there may lie another being who sees God as God sees us, and behind him another, and so on for ever.

I should say again that I am not claiming that these things are real possibilities; only that they do not seem to be excluded by the arguments commonly brought against them. But in any case it is time to leave the higher reaches of theology, and return to the solider ground of mathematics; for we must consider Kant's final and most important arguments for his claim that space and time are a priori intuitions – the arguments from geometry and arithmetic.

Geometry and Arithmetic

If the recognition of the possibility of non-Euclidean geometries means the admission that such alternative systems are perfectly consistent, then Kant must be numbered among those who recognize non-Euclidean geometries. For he holds that the truths of geometry are (though a priori) synthetic, and he points out that there would be no contradiction in the idea of a figure bounded only by two straight lines, 'since the concepts of two straight lines and of their coming together contain no negation of a figure' (A 220/B 268). It is of course a feature of certain non-Euclidean geometries that they admit figures bounded only by two straight lines.

But he would have refused to call such systems geometries, on the grounds that geometry is not an abstract calculus but a body of synthetic truths about space: and space is Euclidean. Geometers do not proceed by analysing their concepts, for they would not get much out of them if they did; they have to take into account the nature of space as well, and only so do they succeed in producing interesting mathematical truths. Yet the truths they discover are a priori, or so Kant thinks, so that geometry is a system of synthetic a priori truths. This gives him another argument to show that space is an a priori intuition, which he calls the transcendental exposition of the concept of space. Only if space is a priori can geometrical truths be a priori; only if space is an intuition can they be synthetic, and not simply the product of conceptual analysis.[1]

To argue on this basis that space must be an intuition is merely a confusion. Even if it is not a particular but a system of relations between objects sheer conceptual analysis cannot determine what its properties are, for sheer conceptual analysis cannot tell us what system of relations obtains in the world. It can tell us that if there are relations of a certain kind then certain consequences follow, as it can tell us that if there are bachelors then there are men. But it cannot tell us that there are any bachelors, or how objects are related, or even whether there are any objects at all. Kant's muddle over this makes him place more emphasis than he needs to on the thesis that space and time are intuitions; he can preserve the synthetic status of mathematics without it. The confusion is really a survival from the *Inaugural Dissertation*, for of course by the time of the first *Critique* (1781) he had come to hold that the mind imposes concepts upon the world as well as intuitions, and that by imposing concepts it provides itself with knowledge which is synthetic a priori and not merely analytic; synthetic just because it concerns not the analysis of these concepts but the fact that they apply to the world. If he had fully thought his views through again after 1781 he might have come to see that it is not of great importance to his general theory to maintain the difference in status between space and time on the one hand and the categories on the other, however interesting the point about incongruent counterparts may be in its own right. It has been suggested that late in life, under the influence of J. S. Beck, he moved in this direction and came to hold that the imposition of space, time, and the categories were all different applications of the same mental function of synthesis;[2] and though the evidence for this seems to me extremely dubious it would be a natural and in many ways attractive simplification of his theory.

It is perfectly reasonable to view geometry as a body of truths about space; less easy to accept that so viewed it can be a priori. Nowadays we often think of a geometry as an abstract formal calculus, which can be given a physical application by deciding on physical interpretations for its primitive terms – co-ordinative definitions, as Reichenbach called them.[3] But certain physical interpretations are overwhelmingly normal and natural for us. We take 'straight line', for instance, to mean the shortest distance between two points, as measured by stretched strings or light-rays or whatever we think most suitable. It then seems to be a purely empirical question whether, under this normal and natural interpretation of its terms, Euclidean geometry gives a correct description of our space; an empirical question which now, indeed, would generally be answered in the negative. It is true that the space we live in is not very strongly non-Euclidean, which is to say that it is not obvious from our immediate surroundings that (for example) two equally straight lines can be drawn between the same two points. But it might have been obvious, and one can even visualize what it would be like to live in a world in which it was obvious,[4] though in order to do this it is important to remember that these equally straight lines – geodesics – need not look the same under these circumstances as straight lines do to us. What makes them geodesics is not how they look, but the fact that there are no shorter paths between their termini.

61

This last point is significant. Although he does not make it very clear, Kant's main concern in the transcendental exposition is not really with physical space but with space as we can experience and imagine it, especially visually. And one may well feel that although it is an empirical matter what physical space is like it is nevertheless true a priori that we can never visualize two lines which join the same two points and both look as we expect straight lines to look. One at least of them, one feels, would simply have to look curved. Is there anything in this?

The co-ordinative definitions which are relevant now are no longer physical, as 'shortest distance between two points' was, but phenomenal. A straight line is something which looks like this:

And a plausible reply to Kant is that the appearance of a difficulty here is due to the vagueness of 'like this'. It may be that we would refuse to count two lines as both looking 'like this' if they connected the same two points, and in that case the Kantian claim is a priori all right but also analytic. For it is then built into the co-ordinative definitions that the points and lines we are talking about must be Euclidean (or at least that they must not be noticeably non-Euclidean, since the minuscule differences between Euclidean and slightly non-Euclidean lines are not detectable visually and do not affect our visual imagination). It is a contingent matter that we can set up these co-ordinative definitions satisfactorily, for it is presumably possible that there should have been nothing within our experience or even within the range of our visual imagination which fulfilled the Euclidean conditions; but once the definitions are set up no further appeal to experience is needed to determine the truths of visual geometry. This appears to be Strawson's solution, though he expresses it somewhat obscurely by saying that under this interpretation of their terms the propositions of Euclidean geometry are 'phenomenally analytic'.[5] Alternatively, we might interpret 'like this' in a different way, so as not to build in Euclidean requirements; but in that case it ought to be an empirical question whether the lines and points we can visualize satisfy Euclidean (or roughly Euclidean) requirements. The position should be just as it was with the ordinary physical interpretation of geometry: once we have provided our co-ordinative definitions Euclidean geometry becomes an empirical theory which may or may not be correct.

This is, as I say, a plausible reply to Kant. It is not easy to be fully convinced that it is right. For I think one is still inclined to feel that it is a non-empirical truth that we cannot imagine two lines that are equally straight under the phenomenal interpretation, joining the same two points; and that this is not simply a matter of any stipulations we have built into 'like this'. It is true that it is hard to see how such a thing can be a priori, or more than a psychological fact about us (as with Kant's claim that we can never represent to ourselves the absence of space); it does not appear to be transcendentally necessary, since alternative spaces seem coherently describable and since we failed to establish any transcendental need for experience to be spatial at all. On the other hand I am certain that I shall never be able to imagine two such lines, and it is difficult to accept that this certainty can merely be due to the limitations of my experience up to now. Unlike the Indian's inability to imagine ice, there seems to be something necessary about it.[6]

The case is rather similar to that of the red and green surface. It does not appear to be an empirical truth that no surface can be red and green all over at the same time. Yet it also does not seem to be analytic. It is not reducible by means of definitions to a substitution-instance of a law of logic, because neither 'red' nor 'green' seems to be definable at all, and if they are at least 'not green' is no part of the definition of 'red'. We learn colour words by being shown things of the appropriate colour, making comparisons, and recognizing from these how to deal with new examples. Of course we are also shown negative instances: something green may be produced to show me what the word 'red' does not cover. But it does not have to be. It might be that the only negative instances I was given in learning 'red' were of white things, brown things, and blue things; and the same in learning 'green'; it would still, I think, be obvious to me that nothing can be red and green all over. This can be confirmed by reflection on Hume's missing colour shade.[7] A colour one has never seen cannot have been amongst the negative instances one met with in learning 'red', yet no surface can be red all over and also have this unknown colour at the same time. (And this is not just in virtue of the meaning of 'colour': it was not essential to my learning of 'red' and 'green' that I should learn the word 'colour' as well.)

The proposition that there cannot be two phenomenal straight lines between the same two points has very much the same status. 'Red' and 'green' are introduced ostensively, and the classes so determined turn out to be mutually exclusive, not because this was built into the words but because of a truth about colours; a truth which may only be a well-confirmed induction, but does feel like something more. In the same way the ostension which gives the phenomenal meanings of 'straight line', 'point', etc., determines a class of entities which satisfy Euclidean axioms not because it is built into the meanings of the terms that they should but because of a truth, which does not seem merely empirical, about visual space.

The figures thus determined are two-dimensional only. Complications arise as soon as we try to introduce a third dimension of visual depth, complications which have encouraged philosophers since

Berkeley to think of what is phenomenally given as being essentially two-dimensional, and to regard our perception of depth as a matter of interpretation that has to be learned. Some of Escher's best known drawings, for example, appear to represent objects which could not exist in three-dimensional Euclidean space, and analogous physical models can be constructed which from certain angles give us inconsistent clues as to depth, or at least clues inconsistent with our ordinary assumptions about space.[8] These things exist, so they can clearly be visualized, but the trouble arises only with the third dimension and because of the degree of interpretation which depth perception requires. The two-dimensional space of what is or can be imagined as visually given is still Euclidean, though this conception of what is visually given is not without its difficulties; and that it must be Euclidean seems intuitively to be a priori. But then perhaps one's intuitions about what is a priori are never very reliable.

If it is a priori, or if the red/green example is for that matter, then I do not know how to handle it; and neither does Kant. It will not do to say these things are mind-imposed, for if they were it could only be through our having determined not to classify two lines as straight if they joined the same points, or a surface as green if it were also red. This is just the solution that we felt before was inadequate, according to which the relevant claims are true in virtue of what we have built into the meaning of the words. And they can hardly be transcendentally necessary, so that neither of Kant's proposed accounts of synthetic a priori knowledge will apply.

He of course wants to claim much more than that the geometry of two-dimensional visual space is necessarily Euclidean. He wants to say the same about physical space, and in this he is quite clearly wrong. But he does not simply confuse visual space with the space in which physical objects are located, as Strawson alleges.[9] The transcendental exposition of space is properly concerned only with phenomenal space, the space of pure intuition, which Kant thinks of as primarily visual. He does not make this clear at the time, but later on in the Analytic of Principles he recognizes he has yet to show that physical space must be Euclidean as well, and provides a further argument to prove it.

This is the argument of the section entitled 'Axioms of Intuition', which has to do with the application of both (Euclidean) geometry and arithmetic to the objects of experience. There is not really a parallel problem about arithmetic, but Kant supposes it to bear the same relation to time that geometry bears to space. In each case, therefore, what he takes to need proof is that the physical world we know through empirical intuition must be subject to the same mathematics as governs our pure intuition of phenomenal space or time. The proof is straightforward, and consists in observing that the pure intuitions of space and time are also the forms of empirical intuition. The space and time we are aware of in pure intuition are the same as the space and time we impose on the world in ordering the relationships between the things we experience. As Kant puts it, 'Empirical intuition is possible only by means of the pure intuition of space and of time. What geometry asserts of pure intuition is therefore undeniably valid of empirical intuition.' (A 165/B 206.) So Euclidean geometry applies, of necessity, to physical space.

The argument contains a serious flaw, of course. In applying geometry to phenomenal space a purely phenomenal interpretation was given to its terms; to talk about the geometry of physical space we need a quite different set of co-ordinative definitions. Once that is recognized Kant's argument collapses. It may be true that physical space is in some sense a construction out of phenomenal space, but however thoroughly Euclidean phenomenal space may be, nothing follows about the geometry of physical space, just because the co-ordinative definitions are different. Kant's mistake is to think that when we have given a phenomenal meaning to geometrical terms we have interpreted them once and for all, and not to see that they must be reinterpreted before we can apply them to the objective world of physical objects.

This helps us to understand what he means when he says that geometry proceeds by constructing its concepts in the pure intuition of space. Because we give a phenomenal interpretation to geometrical terms we know how to construct instances of straight lines, points, etc. in the imagination; and since geometrical propositions are about space, the way to determine whether they are true will be to appeal to the space of our visual imagination by making the appropriate mental constructions. We discover, for instance, that Euclid's axiom of parallels is true by finding that through a given point we can envisage only one straight line parallel to a given line. It is less clear how we are supposed to handle theorems about million-sided figures or about the infinite divisibility of lines, for such things cannot be adequately represented in intuition; but Kant's view may be that certain steps in the proofs are to be verified intuitively and that their conclusions ought then to follow by purely deductive moves.[10]

2 *Arithmetic*

In a parallel fashion arithmetic is said to construct its concepts in the pure intuition of time, but Kant tells us a good deal less about how arithmetical construction works. He does speak of using fingers, or alternatively rows of dots, to provide an intuitive representation for numbers like 7 and 5, but the intuition here would seem to be spatial rather than temporal; though this may only be for illustrative purposes, since he thinks that space provides us with a natural model for time and is easier to think and talk about.[11] He also points out that we cannot expect intuition to provide us with satisfactory representations of the larger numbers.[12] But again no doubt we can rely partly on deduction for the appropriate theorems, and can use intuition to tell us that if a given construction is possible then another construction is possible too: to any number, for example, one can always add 1, for to any agglomeration of dots one can add another dot. This is also how algebra works; assuming that the variables represent constructible numbers, the constants denote operations which can be performed on them intuitively. It is wrong to suppose, as people sometimes have, that with algebra the only intuition Kant thinks he can appeal to is that of the written or imagined symbolism – in that case all thought would involve 'construction in intuition', for all thought uses symbols. In algebra as in the rest of mathematics it is not the symbols themselves but 'the concepts attached to the symbols' which are 'presented in intuition'; the operations which must somehow be represented intuitively are addition, division, etc., and not the drawing of lines or + signs between symbols.[13]

There is a certain amount of obscurity in this account of arithmetic and algebra, but the chief difficulty is to see what numbers and numerical operations have to do with the intuition of time. Kant says that if we are to count things 'they must be so given to us that we can grasp their intuition successively',[14] but it would seem fairly obvious that counting does not necessarily have to take time. One can be simultaneously aware of several spots, and aware of them as several, e.g. as four individual dots. If there were a percipient with the sort of timeless experience we have discussed, he could be aware that he saw four dots, and that this was the same as seeing two dots and two dots. Kant seems to be taking a rather accidental feature of our experience – that we normally take time to count things – and reading a great deal too much into it.

The suggestion that arithmetic has something to do with time was taken up more recently by Brouwer.[15] Like Kant, he considered that time is required for the construction of the numbers: our a priori intuition of temporal succession provides us with the idea of 'two-oneness', the idea of one thing following another, and this we can apply repeatedly in order to generate the number series. As a psychological theory in the Lockean mould about the source of the concept of number this is perhaps not wildly implausible, though it is not wildly plausible either. But as a philosophical theory about the nature of number it is by no means clear what is to be said in its defence, and Brouwer himself said practically nothing. It is, of course, perfectly respectable to hold the view that mathematical entities are in some sense constructions due to the human mind, but apart from Brouwer most of the 'intuitionists' who take this position would not insist that temporal notions played any

66

particular part in the constructing. The derivation of numerical succession from temporal succession seems little better than a pun.

The case for saying that geometry is a body of synthetic truths about space (or about our intuition of space) was graphically supported by the development of alternative geometries; one could then point to the logical possibility that space should have been different, and describable by some such alternative system. If arithmetic were parallel one ought to be able to find consistent alternative arithmetics, and if it is the character of time that makes our arithmetic true one would expect these alternative arithmetics to be applicable in worlds whose time-orders were somehow different from ours. But the possibilities for an alternative arithmetic are severely limited, and the task of conceiving one is quite different from that of describing a different time-order.

What could a different time-order be like? For one thing we normally think of time as continuous, just as we think of space as continuous, but perhaps it might have been discontinuous instead. Possibly it might have been dense, every time-interval being infinitely divisible by smaller and smaller rational fractions, but allowing no further divisions to correspond to those fractions which cannot be expressed rationally (like $1/\pi$). Or it might even perhaps have been granular, every finite period of time being built up of a finite number of indivisible temporal atoms. Some physicists, indeed, believe that time is actually like this, and call the atoms chronons; it does not affect their arithmetic, and evidently there is no reason why it should. Differences of this sort are quite irrelevant to arithmetic – even to the arithmetic of real numbers, which would just not apply in the same way to time but would retain its role unchanged elsewhere.

Another possibility (which I touched on at the end of the last chapter) is that time might be multi-dimensional. This has nothing to do with arithmetic either, though perhaps geometry might find a new application.

Again, it may (or may not) make sense to suppose time might be topologically different: that it might be cyclical, for instance, or contain loops. It is not important to investigate here whether these are coherent possibilities; it is enough that they also have no relevance to arithmetic. It is true that if time were cyclical then by going on counting – or constructing the number-series – for long enough we should get back to where we started. But this would be due to the time we took over it, and it would not mean that the number-series was itself cyclical. Even in such a world one would still count pebbles or shoes in just the way we now do, and the fact that by continuing the series '1, 2, 3, . . .' one found oneself eventually saying '1' again would not show that there were positive integers lower than 1. If one took away pebbles from a pile one would not find that one had two, then one, then none, then twenty-nine million.

Differences like these in the time-order do not affect our arithmetic, and one may wonder whether there are any alternatives to it at all. If we look on it as a formal system it can be characterized by Peano's postulates, and it is true that by denying one or more of these postulates we could produce a different and equally consistent formal system, which might have applications in our world or in some other. For instance, one of the postulates (in a common formulation) says that o is not the successor of any number, and if we abandoned this and made o the successor of 29,000,000 we should have a model for the cyclical time-series just mentioned. But one is not much inclined to call this system an arithmetic, or to see it as a possible competitor with our own.

This might be because we were unwilling to call any system an arithmetic unless it gave us the truths about the numbers. If you interpreted this formal system as making claims about these entities you would have to admit that its claims were false, for zero is not the successor of twenty-nine million. If there is a unique set of truths about the numbers then on this view there could be no alternative arithmetics. But this is perhaps not a very interesting stipulation as to how the word 'arithmetic' should be used, since if there remains a logical possibility that the truths about the numbers might have been different it seems rather arbitrary to refuse that title to the systems that might have fitted them.

In any case there is a more important consideration. If the numbers can be said to exist at all they do not exist in isolation from our practice of counting things. It is not a contingent matter that we use numbers for counting; arithmetic is designed to be used for counting things, so that no formal system can be called an arithmetic unless it can serve this purpose. And as we have noticed a system which makes o the successor of 29,000,000 is simply no good for dealing with pebbles.

Now this effectively rules out alternatives to the elementary arithmetic of relatively small numbers, which we actually do use for counting. But arithmetic allows itself to ramify far beyond the part we put to such direct and immediate use, and as the ramifications develop divergent possibilities do seem to open up. A system in which $7 + 5 = 13$ would not do (unless of course it were only notationally different from ours, and the numeral '13' designated the number twelve) because one cannot count seven things and then five more things and get a total of thirteen except by counting them incorrectly. But a system which differed from ours over the transfinite, or over the very high reaches of the finite, might do perfectly well. One which took us up to 10^{79} in the ordinary way, but then went back to 10^{78}, $10^{78} + 1$, $10^{78} + 2$, etc., would require us to say some very curious things about these large numbers, but this would not matter because we never have to deal with that many items. The same applies to a strict finitist system in which 10^{79} has no successor because the series of natural numbers comes to an end at that point.[16]

But what is the status of the claim I have made about counting seven things and five things together? Is it an empirical truth? If so it ought to allow of alternatives too; and it has sometimes been held to be empirical, most notably by Mill.[17] But Mill makes a mistake which is rather commonly made by those who adopt this position: he takes counting, adding, and so forth to be physical operations. Thus he says that when we say 'Three is two and one' we are claiming 'that collections of objects exist, which while they impress the senses thus, $^{o}_{o}{}^{o}$, may be separated into two parts, thus, ^{oo} ^{o}.'[18] But actually it has nothing to do with this physical fact, and would be equally true in a world in which combining objects into heaps or separating them out from heaps did affect the number of objects involved. It would still be true if whenever I tried to count a group of objects some demon made an extra one appear; even if he were powerful enough to produce this effect not only with physical things but with objects in my imagination.

A similar mistake is made by Gasking, who imagines that there might be people who counted and measured just as we do but who operated perfectly satisfactorily with an arithmetic in which $3 \times 4 = 24$. If they discovered that to tile a room three yards by four yards with tiles one yard square they needed only twelve tiles, not twenty-four, then according to Gasking they could retain their arithmetic but hold that the tiles had expanded when they were brought into the room. On the other hand if it were found that twenty-four tiles were needed this would not show that their arithmetic was right and ours wrong, for we could say that the tiles had contracted rather than give our arithmetic up. Gasking's view is that it is arbitrary what arithmetic we adopt, in that we can make any alternative correspond with our techniques of counting and measuring through appropriate adjustments to our physics.[19]

Gasking assimilates arithmetic too closely to geometry. One cannot apply a geometrical calculus to space directly, without making physical assumptions about how such things as measuring rods behave (assumptions which we often build into our co-ordinative definitions). Hence with a particular set of data to describe it is possible to alter these physical assumptions in such a way as to make a different geometry appropriate (though perhaps at a cost in convenience and simplicity of theory). But given that arithmetic is to be used for counting, and that counting is to be done as we now do it, there is no such latitude in the application of arithmetic, and no room for a parallel dependence upon physical assumptions. Multiplication, as Castañeda points out against Gasking, is not limited to the tiling of floors. Tiling a floor is a physical operation, so we can understand changes in physics affecting the outcome; but what if we try to count three piles of four books each – without moving anything? It will not help to suggest that when we count them a demon alters the number of the books, for if he brings it about that there are more or less than twelve there can no longer be three piles of four. And if no such change occurs, the only way we can get any other result is by doing something different from (correct) counting. We would get twenty-four if we counted each book twice, for example, but that is not a very interesting point.[20]

The reason for this is that elementary truths about counting are logical truths. Statements like 'Two things together with another distinct thing make three things' are expressible as theorems of the first-order predicate calculus:

$$(\exists x)(\exists y)\{Fx \ \& \ Fy \ \& \ x \neq y \ \& \ (z)(Fz \rightarrow (x = z) \vee (y = z))\} \ \&$$
$$(\exists w)\{Gw \ \& \ (z)(Gz \rightarrow (w = z)) \ \& \ (x)(Gx \rightarrow -Fx)\} \rightarrow$$
$$[(x)(Fx \vee Gx \equiv Hx) \rightarrow (\exists x)(\exists y)(\exists w)\{Hx \ \& \ Hy \ \& \ Hw \ \& \ x \neq y \ \& \ x \neq w \ \&$$
$$y \neq w \ \& \ (z)(Hz \rightarrow (z = x) \vee (z = y) \vee (z = w))\}]$$

This is not to say that the corresponding arithmetical statements – '$2 + 1 = 3$' in the present case – are logical truths, for it is a highly controversial matter how arithmetical statements are to be analysed. It must be possible to use them in connection with counting things, but it does not follow that statements about counting in any sense give their meaning. Clearly, though, no system could be adequate as an arithmetic unless it contained '$2 + 1 = 3$'. On the other hand, because we do not need to deal with such a lot of things, a system which did not contain '$(10^{79} + 1) + 2 = (10^{79} + 3)$' might be quite satisfactory, even though its predicate calculus analogue (somewhat too lengthy to formulate here) is a logical law.

In fact, even if we could accept that such statements of predicate logic actually gave the meaning of the corresponding arithmetical statements, the possibility of alternative arithmetics would still open up in the higher reaches. For the logical statements in question are hypotheticals with existential quantifiers in their antecedents; the one above says that if there are two F's and a G distinct from them, then there are three things which are either-F-or-G. If there were only two things in the world altogether the antecedent of this would be false; the whole hypothetical would remain true, of course, but then any other hypothetical with the same antecedent would be true equally. For notoriously, in an extensional logic every conditional with a false antecedent is true. So those which concluded that there were not three but four, or seventeen thousand, things which are either-F-or-G would be true too. It is obvious that there are more than two things in the world, but it is not obvious that there are more than 10^{79}. If in fact there are at least $10^{79} + 3$ things then on this analysis '$(10^{79} + 1) + 2 = 10^{79} + 3$' will be a truth of arithmetic and '$(10^{79} + 1) + 2 = 37$' will be false. But if there are fewer things then they will both be true, and we could adopt a system which included either. So despite the analysis of arithmetical statements into predicate-logical terms, on this account different arithmetics could be used in worlds of limited size with equal legitimacy and equal claim to truth.

It is possible, all the same, that some other reduction of arithmetic to logic can be found which does not make arithmetical truth depend on how many things there are in the world.[21] In that case presumably there could be no alternatives to our present arithmetic (except in so far as there may be alternatives to the fundamental laws of logic). But whether or not there are alternatives, at least arithmetical statements have nothing specially to do with time. It may, indeed, be held that the truths of arithmetic are known through a special faculty of a priori intuition which reveals to us the nature of the numbers (or which, perhaps, we somehow make use of in constructing them), and this view is possible even if they can be reduced to logical truths since we may need such a faculty to discover the laws of logic. But the intuition cannot be identified with Kant's pure intuition of time. And there is another respect too in which Kant's account must be wrong. For Kant held, with arithmetic as with geometry, that what we found synthetic a priori in the first instance was a set of truths about our intuition, and that there was then a further question of whether or how that intuition applied to the world. But since arithmetical truths, whatever their status, have to do with counting, no such problem can arise over their application. Because measurement is a physical operation, the application of geometry to physical objects requires co-ordinative definitions which incorporate assumptions about physical laws. But counting is not a physical operation; so that arithmetic remains true of the world no matter how the world works.

3   The transcendental expositions

It was only fairly late on that Kant came to think arithmetic bore the same relation to time as geometry did to space, and one must suspect that his reasons for doing so were principally architectonic – it would seem a very neat way for things to turn out. In the *Inaugural Dissertation* of 1770 arithmetic is said to be concerned with both space and time, apparently because the fingers or dots have to be thought of as spatially arrayed, and the branch of mathematics which has to do with time alone is said to be pure mechanics.[22] Surprisingly enough this still seems to be his position in the Transcendental Aesthetic when he wants to provide a temporal parallel to the argument from geometry. Instead of saying, as we should expect him to, that in arithmetic we possess a body of synthetic a priori truths about time and that therefore time must be an a priori intuition, he starts rather from pure mechanics and from such other principles as that different times are not simultaneous but succes-sive. Unfortunately it is by no means clear why he should think we have synthetic a priori knowledge about time in these areas, for he tells us nothing more about mechanics in the *Critique of Pure Reason*[23] and the other principles he cites look suspiciously analytic. And everywhere else in the *Critique*s, and in the *Prolegomena*, it is arithmetic and not mechanics which is treated as the analogue of geometry.

The argument from geometry is called by Kant the transcendental exposition of the concept of space, and the parallel argument for time is called the transcendental exposition of the concept of time. The separ-ation of these arguments from the metaphysical expositions was not made in A, but there is a significant distinction to be drawn. The tran-scendental expositions reach the same conclusions as the metaphysical expositions do (that space and time are pure intuitions), but the meta-physical expositions are simply pieces of conceptual analysis whereas the transcendental expositions are transcendental arguments. More exactly, the metaphysical exposition of a concept is an analysis of it which 'con-tains that which exhibits the concept *as given a priori*' (B 38); which presumably means that it makes clear the concept's a priori origin. Properly speaking the transcendental expositions should perhaps be called metaphysical as well, but the converse does not hold: a meta-physical exposition does not have to be transcendental and can dispense with premises about what our knowledge or experience is like.

The transcendental expositions do require such premises: they start from the claim that we have knowledge of a fairly specific kind, synthetic a priori knowledge about space and time, and go on to argue that it is only if space and time are pure intuitions that this is possible. This is not the sort of very general claim that every sceptic would be bound to concede, and as we have seen few people nowadays would be prepared to agree that either geometry or arithmetic gives us the a priori information about space or time that Kant thought they did. He himself did not expect to meet with serious disagreement on this point, but he recognized all the same that such disagreement was possible, and it is therefore important from his point of view that the transcendental expositions are strictly dispensable. The metaphysical expositions are intended to establish the same results, and the metaphysical expositions do not rest on any assumptions about synthetic a priori knowledge.

Assumptions about synthetic a priori knowledge are strictly out of place in the *Critique*, for it is the aim of that work to assess whether and to what extent synthetic a priori knowledge is possible at all; there will be a circularity in the argument if it is assumed to start with that we do possess knowledge of that very kind. Instead we must start from scratch, or as nearly from scratch as possible, and proceed in the manner Kant calls synthetic or progressive, 'by enquiring within pure reason itself, and trying to determine in this source itself, according to principles, both the elements and the laws of its pure employment.'[24] The transcendental expositions are presumably inserted for heuristic reasons; for heuristic purposes it is reasonable to take for granted what one expects the reader will grant, and one can then adopt the method of the transcendental expositions. Kant calls it the analytic or regressive method: it takes the reality of certain kinds of synthetic a priori knowledge as given, and 'ascends to the condition under which alone [they are] possible'.[25] The *Prolegomena*, which was written with heuristic aims very much in view, proceeds according to the analytic method.

The *Critique*, however, must take the harder path, and its transcendental arguments should not rely on premises which take synthetic a priori knowledge for granted. If they are to be successful against the sceptic their premises must be such as the sceptic can hardly deny. The most effective arguments of this kind rely only on the minimal premise that there is experience, and examine the conditions under which experience of any sort is possible; and these arguments are not transcendental expositions, but transcendental deductions.

VI

The Transcendental Deduction of the Categories

Kant borrows the word 'deduction' from legal usage, in which a deduction is a proof of the legitimacy of something. A transcendental deduction is a deduction which is carried out by a transcendental argument, and which is effective as a justification because the assumptions upon which it rests are so minimal that the sceptic cannot fail to concede them. There are deductions of other kinds too, of course; for example, we can show the legitimacy of applying a straightforward empirical concept like 'red' just by appealing to our experience of red things, and this is called an empirical deduction.[1] He also speaks once, though only once, of a metaphysical deduction, and he is there referring to the argument which derives the categories from the twelve forms of judgment;[2] this is supposed to constitute a justification for his own systematic table of categories, in contrast to Aristotle's disgracefully rhapsodic collection. Unlike empirical deductions, transcendental deductions are a priori arguments; unlike metaphysical deductions, they proceed by arguing that something must be the case if experience is to be possible.

He speaks of transcendental deductions for ideas and for types of judgment, as well as for concepts.[3] But his most important transcendental deduction is that of the pure concepts of the understanding, the categories. The deduction of a concept is designed to show that it can properly be applied within experience – unlike such 'usurpatory concepts' as those of fortune and fate, which cannot be. Empirical concepts like 'red' do not require a transcendental deduction, but with the categories there is no other way of showing that their application is justified. We cannot simply look and see that they apply, as Hume most effectively showed in the case of the category of causality; instead we must establish that without them experience would not be possible. 'The explanation of the manner in which concepts can thus relate a priori to objects I entitle their transcendental deduction.' (A 85/B 117.) p 121

Rather surprisingly, the first transcendental deduction which Kant claims to have provided is that of the concepts of space and time. 'We have already, by means of a transcendental deduction, traced the concepts of space and time to their sources, and have explained and determined their a priori objective validity.' (A 87/B 119.) He is apparently thinking of the metaphysical expositions, but the metaphysical expositions do not appear to be transcendental arguments at all and they make claims which are valid only for us as beings whose intuition happens to be spatio-temporal. But a little further on he sketches in a more helpful way how the deduction is supposed to have gone:

p 122

> For since only by means of such pure forms of sensibility can
> an object appear to us, and so be an object of empirical intuition,
> space and time are pure intuitions which contain a priori the
> condition of the possibility of objects as appearances, and the
> synthesis which takes place in them has objective validity.
> (A 89/B 121 f.)

p 123

This suggests that the real claim is that all sensible experience, whether like ours or not, requires 'such pure forms of sensibility', in which case the deduction is not strictly of space and time at all but rather of forms of intuition in general (though one may also wonder why Kant should think he has proved this). On this interpretation space and time come in only because for us they fill that bill.

At any rate, it is quite clear that the transcendental deduction of the categories, like the other transcendental deductions he talks about elsewhere, is supposed to hold not just for our sort of experience, but for any experience at all which involves sensible intuition. This is made explicit at B 145. The remaining restriction to what may be called sensible experience need not worry us greatly. He is only ruling out the experience of God, for whom to think an object is to create it and whose intuition is said to be purely intellectual; and this does not really seem to be experience at all.

The purpose, then, of the transcendental deduction of the categories is to show that these twelve concepts do find legitimate application in experience, and to do it by showing that unless they did no (sensible) experience would be possible. Actually Kant claims to show rather more than this: he claims to establish that 'everything that can come to empirical consciousness' must be subject to, ordered by, the categories.[4] But before we can have any hope of assessing the argument we must be clearer about the starting-point: we must understand what Kant means by 'experience'.

It would seem that this should not be difficult, as he is by no means reticent on the matter. Experience, he tells us often enough, is the self-conscious knowledge of the objects of the senses.[5] Unfortunately, however, the word 'object' is ambiguous in a way he seems never fully to have appreciated. In one sense, objects are entities in the external world – things like tables and tiepins, capable of existing independently of their perceivers. Understood in this way, the admission that we have experience builds in more than we might have expected or wished, for it builds in a commitment to a world of independent entities which we perceive. In a second sense 'the objects of the senses' can be taken rather to mean the intentional objects of our sensory awareness, including our own inner feelings and whatever we seem to perceive, veridically or not. If we take it like this there is no commitment to an external world, and Kant's definition of 'experience' pretty well captures the normal meaning of the word; we can now regard the fact that we have experience as an unquestionable starting-point. But he never clearly distinguishes the two senses, and this is one of the things that makes his argument difficult to follow. Sometimes he intends the latter sense, but at other times the former, as when he distinguishes between judgments of perception and judgments of experience in the *Prolegomena* – judgments of experience being those which purport to 'agree with' some independent object.[6] The confusion is compounded by a parallel ambiguity in the word 'objective'. In one sense only judgments which make claims about independent objects are objective; judgments of experience, that is to say. In another, all judgments can be called objective in so far as they have truth-values, for the claims that they make are either true or false regardless of what anyone may suppose; for example, the judgment of perception 'I feel warm' is true and hence objective in this second sense.

It is therefore quite wrong to suppose, as Strawson does, that the aim of the deduction is to establish that we must be aware of objects in the first or strong sense, items whose *esse* is distinct from their *percipi*.[7] On the contrary; the argument starts from the premise that we have (sensible) experience, and on the more dominant of the two interpretations between which Kant vacillates that premise already assumes Strawson's conclusion. This is not to deny that there are patches of argumentation which run more or less along the lines Strawson suggests; some are in the deduction, though the most important is the second-edition Refutation of Idealism. We shall have occasion to consider them – together with the sophisticated argument Strawson himself develops – later. The deduction equally contains an argument running the other way, to show that knowledge of objects (in the strong sense) must involve self-conscious experience on the grounds that it requires a necessary connection of past and present representations.[8] This is all very ancillary material; none of it represents the main thrust of the deduction, which is concerned to vindicate the categories by showing that they must apply throughout experience.

As time went on Kant got increasingly clear about how the argument ought to go. The version in B is a great improvement on that in A, but his subsequent statements of it are clearer still and very considerably shorter. It will be simplest, I think, to start with the latest version, which is that in the Prize Essay on the Advances of Metaphysics ('*Fortschritte*', 1794). It occupies only about a page – though he did indeed suggest in the *Metaphysical Foundations of Natural Science* (1786) that the argument could be presented even more economically, 'for,' he said, 'it can be carried out almost in a single step from the precisely specified definition of a *judgment* in general (as an action through which given representations first become knowledge of an object)'.[9]

As this indicates, in its late form the transcendental deduction turns entirely on the notion of a judgment. All experience – whether or not it is experience of objects in the strong sense – involves making judgments, for the data that are given to us in intuition must be classified and subsumed under concepts. And (as has been shown in the metaphysical deduction) there are only twelve fundamental forms of judgment. But the categories can be identified with these twelve forms of judgment, at least so far as they are employed in judging about what is empirically given; to make such a judgment is the same thing as to apply the relevant category. Hence all experience involves the categories.

This is a very simple argument, and one may wonder whether it is worth so much fuss. But it is not completely trivial. Kant is pointing out that experience is not a passive matter; the data of sensibility have to be ordered and classified, and this ordering is something we must do. The data themselves do not tell us how to do it, or even that we need to do it at all; as he puts it in the *Fortschritte*, the concept of ordering, or putting-together,

> is not derived from intuitions . . . but is a fundamental concept which must be a priori; in fact the one fundamental a priori concept which takes its origin in the understanding and lies at the foundation of all concepts of objects of the senses. (Ak. XX: 271.)

The mind can perform this synthesis in a number of different ways, so there must correspondingly be a number of a priori concepts which the mind can use for ordering its experience; because a concept just is a rule for ordering, a principle of classification.[10]

That the mind is active in judging is perhaps a fairly obvious point, but it is one that needs to be stressed all the same; that how it acts in classifying things is not dictated by the data, and is therefore in a sense a priori, is perhaps the most important insight of the deduction. Kant was by no means clear about its significance, and seems to have been uncertain how much it showed. Certainly it is not sufficient to establish that all of the twelve categories are required to order our experience, rather than just that some are; it might be that we could dispense with disjunctive or modal judgments, for example, and consequently do without the corresponding categories. And in those statements of the deduction which antedate the *Fortschritte* he himself appears to think the argument about judgment requires supplementation in another way. In the *Fortschritte* the elementary synthesis of the immediately given, the synthesis of hitherto unconceptualized data which he usually calls the synthesis of apprehension, is counted as a sort of judgment, for 'the understanding exhibits its capacities solely in judgments'[11] – and indeed in the *Prolegomena* too this is called judgment, for it is the only synthesis involved in judgments of perception. Elsewhere, however, and most importantly in B, 'judgment' is understood more narrowly to include only what the *Prolegomena* calls judgments of experience, i.e. judgments which make a claim about objects in the strong sense, independent particulars. Therefore in B there has to be a double argument. First it is argued in a manner which foreshadows the *Fortschritte* that experience of objects requires judgment, and hence application of the categories,[12] but this stage is complete by § 20, and in § 21 we find him saying that 'in the above proposition a beginning is made of a deduction of the pure concepts of the understanding'[13] – a beginning only. The second stage comes in § 26, where he tries to show that even that most elementary synthesis of apprehension which 'renders perception possible', and to which he is here refusing the name of judgment, is subject to the categories. So we get the conclusion that 'all possible perceptions, and therefore everything that can come to empirical consciousness, . . . must . . . be subject to the categories.' (B 164 f.)

The second stage, one feels, ought not to be very complicated; for although the synthesis of apprehension is not being called a sort of judgment, it must nevertheless be exactly like judgment except for being exercised on elements which have not yet had concepts applied to them. The synthesis of apprehension is a matter of classifying data together as similar, and this can hardly be sharply distinguished from judging objects similar. Not only did Kant recognize this in the *Fortschritte*, he stated it explicitly in the *Critique*: 'The same function which gives unity to the various representations *in a judgment* also gives unity to the mere synthesis of various representations *in an intuition*'; and he adds, 'and this unity, in its most general expression, we entitle the pure concept of the understanding.' (A 79/B 104 f.) In each case the mind is active, in the twelve ways we have learned about; so, by essentially the same argument as before, even the synthesis of apprehension involves the application of the categories.

Actually, however, the argument of § 26 is more complex than this; Kant considers that he needs to guard himself against the possibility that the synthesis of apprehension might be governed entirely by empirical concepts, concepts acquired from experience. Concepts are rules for synthesis; those classifications of the data which constitute the synthesis of apprehension might be altogether determined by concepts abstracted from experience, without the help of the categories. He thinks that in apprehension we certainly do use empirical concepts – he takes 'red' to be empirical, for instance – but he argues that we must use a priori concepts as well. For the data must be presented in space and time (or, presumably, in something analogous to them, to allow for the possibility of beings with a different mode of sensible intuition), and space and time themselves are a priori. So in becoming aware of the data, even at the most primitive level, we shall have to be aware of spatio-temporal relations, and for this we shall need a synthesis which is a priori, determined by a priori concepts. And so we shall require the categories.[14]

This is confused. The a priori concepts we need to express spatial relations are, of course, no more to be identified with the categories than is the concept of a triangle or any other pure sensible concept. It is perfectly true that applying them involves the categories, but applying empirical concepts involves the categories for exactly the same reason: the application of any concept either is, or closely resembles, judgment. And it is quite irrelevant whether, or to what extent, the judgment is itself empirical, since the twelve forms of judgment are forms of judgment in general and not just forms of a priori judgment.

We have here a clear case of failure adequately to carry through the consequences of his doctrine of synthesis. He is unable to cut himself altogether free from the Lockean view that empirical concepts are somehow given to us from outside and therefore do not need the category-governed activity of the mind. This is quite incompatible with his recognition that at every level classification is something we our-selves do. Whatever the world is like it cannot compel us to classify *a* together with *b* rather than with *c*; where we find similarities depends ineluctably on us, who do the classification. For this reason all synthesis, even the synthesis involved in seeing two red patches as red, is spontane-ous or self-active, as Kant often recognizes: it is an activity we carry out, not something which can be done for us by the way things are. The notion of a synthesis that could be determined for us by experience is an impossible hybrid, a hopeless attempt to graft an element of Lockean empiricism onto an entirely different theory. Because synthesis is active, we could never learn any kind of synthesis simply by contemplating the given, for in receiving the given we are passive. All that are given are particular cases; we could not learn the concept 'red' just by being shown particular cases, for the possession of the concept requires an ability to extrapolate to new instances – an ability to synthesize other cases together with those we have been shown. Of course it is important

79

to be able to point to examples in teaching a child what the word 'red' means, but no amount of examples will help unless the child itself can perform the relevant synthesis (and indeed perform it in the same way as the rest of us).[15]

There seems to have been a phase in which Kant held that mere 'perception' does not involve the categories: they are required for knowledge of objects, but not at the more elementary level of the synthesis of apprehension. This is the view of the *Prolegomena* (§ 18) and of occasional passages in the *Critique* which some commentators have regarded as pre-Critical, notably A 89 f./B 122. It is tempting to imagine a three-stage development in Kant's thought, starting with (1) the view of the *Inaugural Dissertation*, that spatio-temporal ordering is the only thing imposed by the mind on experience, and that otherwise things are in themselves just as they appear to be. Then (2) the intermediate view that the mind is active and contributes a priori elements in building the world of physical objects and physical laws out of the data given to us in sense, but that no further contribution from the mind is required for the mere apprehension of these data in perception. Finally (3) the view dominant in the *Critique*, though more clearly in the second edition than the first, that even apprehension requires synthesis in accordance with the categories. This three-stage picture is quite a useful one, though it can only be an idealization of Kant's development; his loose use of the words 'object' and 'objective' – never more careless than in the papers surviving from the 1770s – obscured for him the line between (2) and (3).[16]

The first stage of the deduction is also more complex in B than it is in the *Fortschritte*. He is not content simply to observe as he does there that the making of any judgment is a mental act and must accord with the table of judgments, though he comes rather close to this in §§ 19 and 20. He again thinks that something more is required in order to rule out the possibility that the synthesis involved is merely empirical, governed by empirical and not by a priori concepts; and to supply this extra something he brings on the transcendental unity of apperception, or self-consciousness.

The given by itself is multiplex and lacking in order. For me to be conscious of it at all I must introduce order, synthesize; and in particular I must synthesize all my representations together as mine, as belonging to one consciousness. Not that I must consciously lay claim to each experience, any more than I must consciously apply the word 'red' to everything that appears to me so; nevertheless I must in some sense recognize all the experiences I have as belonging to a single consciousness. Otherwise they are just not my experiences; an experience cannot be mine unless I am at least potentially aware of it as such. As Kant points out, this is analytic, but an important point none the less because it draws our attention to the need for synthesis: 'it reveals the necessity of a synthesis of the manifold given in intuition, without which the thoroughgoing identity of self-consciousness cannot be thought' (B 135). Moreover, of course, this synthetic unity of apperception is transcendental: it is 'an objective condition of all knowledge . . . a condition under which every intuition must stand in order *to become an object for me*' (B 138).

So far this seems relatively straightforward; and it would appear enough to guarantee the application of the categories without going any further. For the ascription of mental states to myself will be a sort of judgment, and hence subject to the table of judgments; moreover, since the synthesis involved in self-ascription is transcendentally necessary it could hardly be held to be governed by an empirical concept, learned by abstraction from experience. So even if empirical synthesis does not require categories, the synthesis required for self-consciousness must.

He does not leave it at this, because although he could reach his main conclusion in that way he would not have shown as much as he would like. He would like to show that we have to make use of the categories not only in thinking about how our experiences relate to us, but also in thinking about their interrelations and in constructing an objective world out of them. It is central to the Analytic of Principles and to the *Metaphysical Foundations of Natural Science* that the categories are constitutive of nature, and that the most general scientific laws are in a sense determined by them. He could have argued for this directly, as he does in the *Fortschritte*, by observing that what we say about nature must also take the form of judgments and so involve the categories; though it may reasonably be doubted whether the applicability of the categories, as virtually the equivalents of the judgment-forms, is enough to support the rather grandiose conclusions that he draws. But in the *Critique of Pure Reason* he takes a more roundabout route, because he feels he has to show that judgments about nature require some synthesis which is not merely empirical; that the concepts we use for interrelating our experiences amongst themselves are not all acquired by abstraction.

At this point the argument is a great deal clearer in A than in B, which in § 18 touches quite unwonted depths of obscurity. In fact there are two arguments, though one of them – the one Kant puts more weight on – hardly deserves to be called an argument at all. It is more a statement, to the effect that because I must think of myself as a unity, I must also think of my experiences as forming a unity amongst themselves.[17] I must be able to see them as representing a unified objective world. This objective interconnectedness must again be the product of our synthetic activity, and it must be transcendental: Kant christens it the 'transcendental affinity' of appearances.[18] It is transcendental, i.e. required for experience to be possible, because it is an immediate

81

consequence (according to Kant) of the requirement that I think of my-self as a unity, which is transcendental. But a synthesis which is transcen-dentally necessary cannot be determined solely by concepts acquired from experience, for we could have no experience in advance of the synthesis and hence no means of acquiring the concepts. So, we have the required proof that our judgments about the interrelations of appear-ances involve some non-empirical synthesis, and can conclude that the categories are at work. The trouble is that we do not have a proof at all, because Kant has made the crucial step, or rather leap, without offering any justification for it. It is very far from obvious that the unity of self-consciousness presupposes any sort of unity in the objective world. It is not an indefensible thesis, and we shall return to it later in another connection. But the merits of this present argument are easily assessed, for there is no argument.

The other line of thought is quite interesting, and concerns the con-cept of an object. It does not seek to show that all self-conscious aware-ness must be awareness of objects in any sense, but only that if we are aware of objects we must be synthesising our data with the aid of concepts that are not purely empirical (so that, once again, the categories must be in the offing). For the concept of an object itself is not empirical in Kant's sense. Only representations, or what we might call sense-data, are given empirically; objects are neither sense-data nor logical con-structions out of sense-data. The concept of an object takes us beyond what is or could be given, to the idea of something which is not itself a representation but a cause of ordered sets of representations. As Kant puts it, the representations given to us in sense 'in turn have their object – an object which cannot itself be intuited by us, and which may, therefore, be named the non-empirical, that is, transcendental object = x' (A 109). In talking about the concept of an object here Kant must mean that of a physical object, an independent particular in the external world; the theory of perception which is revealed is of considerable importance in understanding his conception of the world of appearances and consequently his transcendental idealism generally, so we shall return to it in chapter VIII.[19]

These arguments about self-consciousness and about objects are note-worthy for their own sakes, but they are quite inessential to the deduc-tion of the categories. They come in mainly because of Kant's confusion over empirical synthesis, and when this is recognized it is clear that the argument can indeed be 'carried out almost in a single step from the precisely specified definition of a *judgment* in general'.[20] It is therefore wrong to say that 'the principle of apperception is the highest principle in the whole sphere of human knowledge' (B 135) if this is meant to imply that it is upon it that the deduction turns. It is even more mis-guided to think that the deduction turns on a point about criteria for personal identity.[21] In discussing the unity of apperception Kant only says that I must be able to ascribe all my representations to myself as mine; he says nothing about how this can be done, and from what he says later it appears to be his view that criteria are not relevant. The self-ascription is not made on the basis of any criteria, and it is not even necessary that I have a grasp of any such criteria which I could appeal to if pressed. In discussing the Third Paralogism in A he makes it clear that my self-ascriptions are quite independent of any identity-criteria there may be.[22]

Those who write about the transcendental deduction customarily distinguish, as Kant did, between a subjective and an objective deduction, though they rarely agree on what the difference between them is. I think it is a mistake to look for two separate arguments, one of which can be called subjective and the other objective; rather we have two sides to the same argument. Kant says that the subjective deduction 'seeks to investigate the pure understanding itself, its possibility and the cognitive faculties upon which it rests; and so deals with it in its subjective aspect' (A xvi). So it is really that side of the argument which is concerned with making claims about the various faculties of the mind and how they must work in order to produce sensible experience, an aspect I have not emphasized so far because Kant himself rather plays it down in the second edition. Indeed even in the first he says it is dispensable.[23] Very roughly, it goes something like this. If experience is not to be haphazard and arbitrary, the manifold given in sensible intuition must be synthesized by the mind to introduce order. The synthesis must be carried on by that mental faculty the function of which is to bring together concepts and intuitions; this can be called imagination, but it is something more than the faculty for reproducing mental pictures.[24] But besides sensibility and imagination there must also be a third faculty. For we must think of ourselves as unitary subjects, and we must likewise think of objects (and perhaps the objective world) as unitary. This cannot be the work of the imagination, for the imagination has always to work on sensible intuitions, and cannot by itself take us beyond them in the way that these syntheses require. So we must have a faculty of pure thought, capable of being used (even though this use may not always be legitimate) beyond the limits of intuition.[25] This faculty of thought – which, when it is applied to intuition, is called understanding – provides the rules which govern these transcendental syntheses; and being supplied by the understanding, these rules must be pure concepts of the understanding, that is, categories.

Some people react violently to this talk of faculties. But before doing so it would be well to ask how seriously it is meant. Kant's terminology is very fluid; if he really placed great reliance on the distinction between the faculties of imagination and understanding we should not expect to find him ascribing the same role to them at different times without a word of explanation.[26] Because they take the claims about faculties to be important, and because these claims are manifestly inconsistent, Vaihinger and Kemp Smith are obliged to regard the subjective deduction as a patchwork of passages of different dates; so much so that they have to see Kant as (in Paton's rather memorable words) 'a pedantic old professor, armed with an external architectonic, incompetently tacking together old notes of what he used to think'.[27] It would be more reasonable to conclude that the faculty terminology is not intended seriously; Kant is succumbing to the temptation to be scientifically fashionable by accommodating Tetens' recent psychological distinctions.[28] Besides which, what more can really be meant by the talk of faculties than just that the mind performs these various operations which we have already met in the earlier statements of the argument? So that really the subjective deduction adds nothing to the objective deduction, which is the line of argument we have principally been discussing (experience requires synthesis, a synthesis which the mind must carry out on its own without learning from experience how to do it, and this in turn involves the categories.)

The doctrine of synthesis itself has sometimes been attacked as a piece of impossible a priori psychology. If it is, that undermines the whole deduction and not just its subjective side. Strawson's objections to what he calls Kant's transcendental psychology are largely objections to transcendental idealism,[29] but transcendental idealism plays a very subsidiary part in the deduction, even the subjective deduction, and in any case I shall argue that transcendental idealism is true. Admittedly Kant sometimes sounds as if he is engaged in an entirely unverifiable study of the *Ich an sich*, and some colour can be given to this idea by a misunderstanding of the word 'transcendental', which is taken to have a deep and profound significance. But he makes it perfectly clear that he is still using the word in the same way as before. The transcendental unity of apperception is so called because it is a condition of the possibility of experience; the same goes for transcendental synthesis, and for the other cases. For just this reason he cannot be accused of making gratuitous claims about how our minds operate. What he says about synthesis and the unity of apperception is backed up by transcendental arguments: these things must be so if experience is to be possible; and if transcendental arguments are ever legitimate, there is no general reason why they should not be available to establish how our minds must work. It is true and indeed incontestable that the mind must be active in judging and in applying concepts, though whether, or to what extent, this activity can be said to have anything to do with Kant's categories is no doubt a further question, and one to which we must now turn.

The obvious objection to my account of the transcendental deduction is that it assimilates the categories far too closely to the forms of judgment. It actually equates them with the forms of judgment, or at any rate with the forms of synthetic judgment. This is what makes the argument so nearly trivial; that the forms of judgment are involved in judging, or even perhaps in concept-application, is not great news. It enables Kant nevertheless to emphasize the extent to which experience depends upon the synthetic activity of the mind, an activity without which experience would not be possible. But are the categories not something more (and perhaps, something more problematic) than I have allowed? And how could a concept, a pure concept of the understanding, be identical with a form of judgment?

To start with, there is good textual evidence for the attribution I have made to Kant. At B 143 he says that 'the categories are nothing other than these very functions of judgment, in so far as they are employed in determination of the manifold of a given intuition', and he uses almost the same words in the *Fortschritte*.[30] Two reservations are admittedly required. If, as commonly in B, the synthesis of apprehension needed for the most basic concept-application is not counted as judgment, then the categories are not just forms of judgment but extend to the (parallel) kinds of synthesis here. And further Kant cannot really mean to restrict the categories to judgments about what is empirically given, since it is an important part of his later theory that transcendent metaphysics arises from a use of the categories which is independent of empirical conditions. It would have been better to say that the categories were the forms of synthetic judgment in general; or simply that they were the twelve forms of judgment, thought of as employed in making synthetic claims.

They are, of course, concepts. But Kant's view – neither an unreasonable nor an unusual one – is that in making a judgment I do not only employ those concepts which appear as the terms of the judgment. I also exercise the concepts which give the judgment its logical form – quantifiers, logical connectives, modal operators. He did not express this quite as we should, largely because he did not have quite our picture of which concepts are required as primitive. But his twelve fundamental logical concepts, considered as applied in synthetic judgments (or in the synthesis of apprehension), are the basic pure concepts of the understanding, or categories. It may be misleading to call them forms of judgment because the word 'form' has such a vague meaning, so that 'form of judgment' may mean 'kind of judgment'; no doubt one would not wish to identify the universal quantifier with the class of universally quantified judgments. But it is not very misleading, all the same.

It may be objected that Kant calls the categories 'concepts of objects in general', and that this suggests they should be first-order predicates of objects, or relations between objects: '. . . is a substance' and '. . . causes ——' instead of logical concepts of the highest generality. But in the first place we have seen that the categories are deeply involved in our knowledge of objects, sufficiently so for it to be understandable that Kant should call them concepts of objects even though they are not first-order predicates. And more importantly we must remember how loose his use of the word 'object' can be. At times he speaks of all concepts as 'of objects', just in virtue of their being concepts; 'of objects' is here a dummy expression. 'Concepts of objects in general' is simply a translation of the phrase '*praedicata entium generalia*', standard among the metaphysicians of the time; the word '*ens*' was specially designed to be as free as possible from any particular content. What Kant, like these metaphysicians, wanted to call attention to was the utter generality of these pure concepts.

Still the objection remains that the categories Kant wants to come out with include concepts like 'cause' and 'substance', which do not look much like logical concepts. But the answer to this is that he wants these as schematized categories, not as pure ones, and that between pure and schematized categories there is fixed at least a middle-sized gulf. It is to this gulf that we must turn now.

VII

Schematism and Principles

1   Schematism

To set out, as Kant did in the Deduction, to establish conditions for any sensible experience at all is an ambitious undertaking. After our examination of that argument it is natural to feel that if it can be said to have succeeded this is only because its aims turned out to be very much less considerable than one might have thought. Experience is indeed a matter of thinking and judging, so whatever logical concepts we have to make use of in thinking and judging must be employed if experience is to be possible. But that does seem a little unexciting, as a conclusion of so much argument, even though it no doubt gives us a transcendental deduction – a justification for the use of such non-empirical concepts as the quantifiers, the concept of a subject, the if . . . then relationship, and so on. An important point is being made, inasmuch as Kant is calling attention to the mind's spontaneous activity in synthesis, but the actual conclusion of the argument cannot be denied to be a little disappointing.

It is the task of the Analytic of Principles to convert this result into something much more remarkable: a set of synthetic a priori principles giving substantive information about our experience, including the principle that every event has a cause. Exactly how this transformation takes place is unfortunately a matter of some obscurity. But what Kant does in effect is to offer us a new set of transcendental arguments, starting from a different premise: they assume not just that our experience is sensible, but that it is spatio-temporal – or at any rate temporal.

The ambivalence between 'spatio-temporal' and just 'temporal' need not greatly concern us. In some places, notably the chapter on Schematism, he concerns himself with time because all of our experience, inner as well as outer, is in time; elsewhere, for example in discussing the Axioms of Intuition, he is equally interested in space. Either

87

way, it is perfectly reasonable for Kant to develop whatever transcendental arguments he can from this new starting-point. Since he has proved, at least to his own satisfaction, that space and time are a priori, the conditions of spatio-temporal experience can also be called a priori; the principles he is seeking to establish will be knowable independently of any particular experience. And his arguments should be of use against sceptics, for no interesting sceptic will deny that our experience seems spatio-temporally arrayed; though it is true that he might deny there are independently existing spatio-temporal objects, and Kant does sometimes (though not always) assume that there are such things. This is a further and natural consequence of his confusion over the word 'object', which we noticed in the last chapter.

The new transcendental arguments are set out in the second chapter of the Analytic of Principles, the chapter entitled 'System of all Principles of Pure Understanding'. Kant tells us at the start of the chapter that the table of categories is 'our natural and safe guide' in looking for principles to establish in this way, but it is not altogether obvious why it should be. Clearly the conditions for all sensible experience will equally be conditions for temporal experience, but one might have thought that the conditions required for temporal experience alone could well have turned out to be a quite unrelated set. Kant, however, is anxious to show that there is a close correspondence between them, and his attempt to do this is contained in the deeply obscure and infuriating chapter on Schematism. In broadest outline, the suggestion is that there must be certain empirical conditions under which we apply the categories to our temporal experience, and that the new principles are just propositions to the effect that these conditions obtain.

Kant distinguishes quite generally (not just in the case of the categories) between a concept and its schema. The schema is the rule for subsuming under the concept items that are empirically given; it is what we have to know if we are to understand how to apply the concept in our experience. Every concept must therefore have a schema if it is to be applicable to experience at all. In the case of empirical (and mathematical) concepts he says that the schema is a rule for producing images;[1] more generally, it is what one knows when one knows what an instance of the concept would look like, feel like, etc. The schema of the concept 'dog' is

> a rule according to which my imagination can delineate the figure of a four-footed animal in a general manner, without limitation to any single determinate figure such as experience, or any possible image that I can represent *in concreto*, actually presents.
> (A 141/B 180.)

It is only if I have grasped this schema, this rule, that I can recognize dogs when I meet them.

He comes close to seeing that images can be dispensed with, but so far as empirical concepts are concerned he never quite takes that step. Mental images have become redundant in the account of concept-application once it is recognized that what is needed is a rule. Berkeley made the first move in this direction when he attacked the Lockean theory that to recognize an instance of the concept 'dog' I must compare it with an abstract mental image that ingeniously combines the features of an Alsatian and a chihuahua. But Berkeley's own suggestion was that I somehow use the image of a quite specific dog as though it will do for all dogs, setting aside the features that make it special; and how I am supposed to manage this he leaves quite unclear. He just says that it 'all . . . seems very plain and not to include any difficulty in it'.[2] Kant's theory is rather like Berkeley's except that he appreciates the difficulty, and tries to meet it by saying that what is required is a schema. But then the images are no longer necessary; a rule for concept-application may make use of images, but it has no need to, and as has often been observed against Locke and Berkeley we are quite commonly able to apply concepts without summoning up the relevant images or even being capable of doing so. I should know a stormy petrel if I saw one, for example, but I cannot at present call up a mental picture of one.

In the case of the categories Kant does recognize that no image is either necessary or appropriate.[3] But he thinks there is a special problem over their schematism. He states it in a finely mysterious way by saying that in other cases the concept and what it applies to are 'homogeneous', but that the categories are 'quite heterogeneous from empirical intuitions' (A 137/B 176). This can only be remedied by finding some intermediate thing, homogeneous both with the category and with what is given in experience; and that turns out to be time, which is a priori like the categories but is also an intuition.[4]

I can do nothing to salvage this argument for bringing in time; it is hard to avoid suspecting that Kant adduces it chiefly because it gives him the right results. But it is easy to see what he is getting at in complaining about the lack of homogeneity between the categories and experience. Empirical concepts, he thinks, are learnt by abstraction from experience, but the categories are produced by the resources of the mind itself. So we learn an empirical concept through learning the empirical conditions under which it is applied, but a pure concept is not learnt in this way, and that brings out the point he wants to emphasize: there is a difference in principle between grasping one of the pure concepts of the understanding and knowing how to apply it in experience. So far we have only learnt what the categories are; how they are to be applied empirically remains to be investigated.

He does not of course wish to suggest that anyone might fail to know how to apply the categories in his experience. Such a person could not have any experience at all. But it is an important part of Kant's theory that creatures radically different from ourselves must share the categories with us, though applying them differently in their non-spatial and non-temporal intuition; and that we ourselves can think about things in themselves by using the categories in their unschematized form, independently of the spatio-temporal conditions which allow us to apply them to our intuition. This ability to think about things in themselves does not get us very far; it does not help us to gain any knowledge about them; but it does provide a large part of the explanation of metaphysical error.

It has been objected against Kant by Warnock that the separation between having a concept and being able to apply it is illegitimate.[5] But if by 'being able to apply it' one means being able to recognize instances of it when one comes across them, then there certainly is a distinction to be drawn. At least this is true for a priori concepts, and also for a great many of the concepts we should ordinarily call empirical. One may be able to use the concept of a molecule in a fairly wide range of contexts without being able to recognize a molecule as such; and with photons and black holes there could be strong theoretical reasons for supposing that no one could ever learn to recognize them as such. Perhaps we should therefore adopt a broader interpretation, and say that one can apply a concept empirically provided only that one can recognize the evidence that would confirm or disconfirm statements to the effect that it is instantiated; but it is still quite possible to have a concept without knowing even this. Most of those concepts of theoretical physics that I possess, I possess in this manner; I know a certain amount about conceptual interrelations within the theory, but little or nothing about what evidence is relevant to establishing what. Moreover, if physics were to develop in such a way that these intra-theoretical relationships remained largely unchanged, while people altered their views entirely on the way experimental evidence should bear upon the theory, there would be a good sense in which we could say that the concepts were still the same although views about their empirical application had altered. Of course one could rule this out by adopting tighter criteria for concept-identity, and insisting that the concepts had changed too, but nothing forces one to do that. It is only with those concepts that do no more than classify what is empirically given that we simply cannot distinguish between concept and schema; for it is only with them that to possess a concept is just the same as to be able to apply it in experience.

The pure, unschematized categories resemble the concepts of a scientific theory taken in isolation from whatever empirical content they may be given. We can understand these concepts because we can understand the theory and their interrelations within it; and the theory the pure categories belong to is logic. Kant says their meaning is 'purely logical', and takes the example of the category of substance, which, 'when the sensible determination of permanence is omitted, would mean simply a something which can be thought as subject (without being a predicate of anything else)' (A 147/B 186). It is this concept that we share with someone whose intuition is wholly different from ours, for we all share the same logic, but we apply it to what endures in space and time whereas he can hardly do this. Every being with sensible experience must employ the same logical concepts in formulating judgments about its experience. The question for us is what empirical criteria we use; what the general empirical criteria are, given our modes of intuition, for the truth of hypothetical judgments, subject-predicate categoricals, and so on. These will be the schemata. 'The schema is, properly, only the phenomenon, or sensible concept, of an object in agreement with the category' (A 146/B 186).

Kant lists these schemata for us, but even before looking at his list we must feel the gravest misgivings. Why should we suppose that there are any general criteria to be found? It is not immediately obvious that there is anything in common to all the empirical hypotheticals we make; they form rather a diverse collection, and the categoricals even more so. Given that we must make judgments of these types about our experience it does not follow that there can only be one single way of doing so for each type. And when one does look at the list one finds it a little surprising: not quite what we should have expected, given the table of judgments and the close relationship supposed to obtain between the pure categories and the judgment-forms. The transmogrification of the categories of quality, corresponding to affirmative, negative, and infinite judgments, is particularly remarkable: they emerge as concepts of degree. Nor is it clear why each schema should have to be an 'a priori determination of time' (A 145/B 184). Kant seems to be anticipating, somewhat over-confidently, the results he hopes to get in the remainder of the Analytic of Principles.

He apparently thinks his schemata emerge directly from the consideration that the pure categories are to be applied in temporal experience. This is excessively implausible, even with more promising (and more central) cases than the categories of quality. If we must make hypothetical judgments about our experience, then since our experience is temporal it follows that we must make hypothetical judgments about things that happen in time. But it is hard to see how Kant could have thought he could infer that all, or even some, of these hypotheticals must be causal hypotheticals, judgments concerning 'the real upon which, whenever posited, something else always follows' (A 144/B 183). Without an entirely new argument (which we do not get until the Second Analogy) it would seem quite possible that the only hypo-

SCHEMATISM AND PRINCIPLES

thetical judgments we made about our experience might have been non-causal, the events in their antecedents perhaps being simultaneous with or subsequent to those in their consequents.

It may be that we are interpreting him wrongly. It is possible (though his procedure suggests otherwise) that he does not think he can yet establish how the categories are to be schematized. On this alternative interpretation, it is a matter of far greater labour to determine the schemata, a labour which is not complete until all the principles of pure understanding have been separately derived. All we can be given at the moment, therefore, is a list that anticipates the conclusions that are to come. It is an added advantage of this interpretation that it leaves a proper job for the rest of the Analytic of Principles to do, for if the derivation of the schemata can be carried through in the chapter on Schematism the real work of the Transcendental Analytic comes to an end there (except for the drawing of a few consequences). Once we know how to schematize the categories we can easily work out the principles of pure understanding. The principles are just 'rules for the objective employment' of the categories (A 161/B 200); they are syn-thetic a priori propositions whose truth is guaranteed by the require-ment that we should apply the categories, thus schematized, throughout all our experience.[6]

I doubt if either of these interpretations can be called right; Kant seems to be confused between them. But if our original reading made redun-dant the bulk of the Analytic of Principles, the alternative proposal threatens to do the same with the metaphysical and transcendental deductions. For the synthetic a priori propositions which it is Kant's main objective to establish, like the principle of causality, are proved only in the chapter on the principles of pure understanding and by argu-ments apparently independent of the earlier deductions; so that on this interpretation the deductions make no real contribution to their defence. There is not even any reason to expect them to give us a particularly useful clue as to what principles we shall be able to establish. On the earlier interpretation, the correspondence between categories and principles was accounted for by effectively deriving the principles from the pure categories. The schemata are worked out first and shown to give rise to certain principles; independent arguments can then be provided for these principles as a sort of confirmation. But on the new interpretation we start by examining the conditions for temporal experience, and find by what can (or should) only be a coincidence that the principles we are able to prove correspond with the categories. It could perfectly well have turned out that we could establish far more such principles than there are categories, for there might be many more conditions special to temporal experience than there are conditions of sensible experience in general. And on the other hand there might well be pure categories with no unitary schemata in time, no general empirical criteria but only a variety of alternative criteria, giving rise therefore to no corresponding principles for temporal experience.

Before the notion of schematism can properly be used as a connecting link it should really be shown not only that a given category must be applied in a particular way, but that there is no other way in which we can apply it. Otherwise we may not have been given its schema – the rule for applying it empirically – but only a partial schema. Thus it is not enough to show that we must make use of the notion 'if . . . then' in the form of causal judgments about the events we experience, so long as there are other ways we can use it as well. To establish that the empirical conditions for recognizing causes provide us with the relevant schema Kant would have to prove that the only true empirical hypotheticals are causal ones. It is possible he might have thought he could manage this with hypotheticals – though it is stretching things to say that 'If Jones is now alive, he must have been born after 1650' is causal. But it is hard to see how he could seriously have supposed that the only way to apply negation was in talking about degrees of reality.[7]

The reason Kant is so anxious to set up a close correspondence between the principles and the categories is only partly to be found in his excessive enthusiasm for system. He considers it important also for his account of metaphysical error. The limits of what we can know are set at the limits of possible experience; the only synthetic a priori truths we can discover are those which can be validated in terms of possible experience, as the principles themselves are validated by means of transcendental arguments. But the claims of metaphysicians far outrun this limitation. It is natural and unavoidable for them to do so, because the pure concepts of the understanding have no built-in restriction to the spatial and temporal order. Hence we can (and Kant thinks inevitably must) find ourselves employing the pure categories in a way which can never give us knowledge, in order to think about things which are objects of no possible experience. We abstract from the temporal conditions of their application, and this leaves us with purely logical concepts, which we can use (as Leibniz and his successors did) to frame complex metaphysical systems; systems which are purely speculative and contain no synthetic propositions we can ever have reason to believe.

Actually, though, this is not a good reason for insisting on the correspondence. For however many alternative ways there may be of applying the categories in our spatio-temporal experience, and however little these may have to do with the general conditions transcendentally required for such experience, it will still be possible to abstract the pure categories from their conditions of application and use them to think metaphysical thoughts. And on the other hand whatever principles are found to be needed as conditions for (spatio-) temporal experience we can as metaphysicians illegitimately transmute them into conditions for things as they are in themselves, beyond the limits of space and time, and so nourish our empty speculations in another way as well. So it does not matter to Kant's campaign against the 'dogmatists' that the chapter on Schematism does not successfully bridge the gap between the categories and the principles.

2   Principles

The new transcendental arguments of the chapter on the principles of pure understanding proceed largely, if not entirely, without reliance on the transcendental deduction of the categories. The only one which appears to draw on it at all is the general argument for the Analogies (A 177–81/B 218–24), and even it bases nothing on the conclusion of the deduction but only on the thesis that the objects of experience must be synthetically united. The general argument for the Analogies is in any case dispensable in favour of the three arguments for the three particular Analogies, none of which appears to make any use of the deduction at all.

There is a lot to be said about these arguments which I shall omit, for they are generally invalid, and there is not usually much to be gained by examining in detail where they go wrong. But since the principles he is trying to establish are the ones he regards as constitutive of the world of appearances, it is worth briefly running over what they are.

The axioms of intuition

Kant tells us that axioms are to be found only in mathematics. They are synthetic a priori propositions which have that immediate self-evidence which comes from the construction of concepts in intuition.[8] So it is not surprising to find that under this heading he seeks to show that mathematics – arithmetic and geometry – applies in its full rigour to whatever we experience. We have already examined this argument in chapter V; we found that in the case of arithmetic no such proof was necessary, and that in the case of (Euclidean) geometry he makes a rather unobvious mistake. For the co-ordinative definitions we use in applying a geometry to the space of pure intuition are different from those we use in applying it to physical space. So the fact that the phenomenal space of pure intuition turns out to be Euclidean does not show, as Kant supposes it does, that physical space must be Euclidean too.

His concern with the geometry of physical space shows clearly that he is here interested in the conditions for spatio-temporal, not just temporal, experience, and also that it is being assumed to be experience of objects, independent entities. The present section is supposed to correspond to the three categories of quantity (unity, plurality, totality), but Kant is unable to think up three separate principles which could plausibly be supposed to match these. Instead he gives us just the one: 'All intuitions are extensive magnitudes.' The same applies in the case of

The anticipations of perception

Here the principle offered is: 'In all appearances, the real that is an object of sensation has intensive magnitude, that is, a degree.' This is supposed to match the categories of quality (reality, negation, limitation), but any connection with them seems crudely fudged up. It also has little to do with either space or time, and is completely unargued into the bargain. Kant's point is that the qualities we sense must come in degrees – heat and cold, light and dark, colour qualities, and so on. 'Every sensation . . . is capable of diminution, so that it can decrease and gradually vanish' (A 168/B 210), so the same is true of those qualities of objects which our sensations immediately represent.

It may be true that the qualities of which we are sensorily aware do come in degrees. Things feel more or less smooth, more or less heavy; they look more or less bright, more or less yellow. Kant considers it an important fact about these degrees that they are densely ordered – between every two there is another; and although our powers for noticing such differences are in practice limited, it is plausible to say that we feel them to be susceptible of improvement without limit and are quite confident that we should always find more distinctions to be drawn. But what we should have expected is an argument to show that beings with (spatio-)temporal intuition must perceive sensible qualities in this way, and Kant gives us no such argument. He merely invites us to inspect our sensations.[9] It seems possible to imagine an experience, rather unlike ours but still spatio-temporal, in which sensory qualities are not naturally thought of as coming in degrees. Things might feel either hot or cold, without gradations between them, every hot thing feeling equally hot and every cold thing equally cold. Red things might always look (and be) the very same shade of red, with the same brightness, saturation, and hue. There might be a limited number of possible shapes, such that each object fitted (and appeared to fit) one precisely, not more or less roughly. And so on.

In claiming that sensations, and therefore the sensible qualities they represent, must admit of degrees Kant is purporting to show that another sort of mathematics must apply to our experience: the mathematics of intensities (*mathesis intensorum*).[10] He is extremely vague about what this is, and unclear in his attempts to explain the difference between the intensive magnitudes it is concerned with and the extensive magnitudes with which geometry and arithmetic more familiarly deal. But on the basis of certain of his examples and remarks it is perhaps not too fanciful to suppose he is feeling his way to a distinction between cardinal and ordinal measurements. A cardinal scale is appropriate where we can sensibly speak of one thing's being twice as . . . as another, as we can do in the case of Kant's extensive magnitudes. 'Twice as long as', 'ten times as many as', 'four times as high as' make perfectly good sense. But 'twice as loud as' and 'twice as bright as' seem much more doubtful, for we have no very natural criteria for determining what is meant. For scientific purposes we may agree to take the doubling of the sound- or light-source as determining this, but it continues to feel rather artificial as a standard. And with other qualities, like temperature and colour-saturation, no attempt to introduce 'twice as . . . as' could avoid being arbitrary in the extreme. These can be measured ordinally, but not cardinally; and they are – roughly at least – Kant's intensive magnitudes.[11]

The analogies of experience

In this case – undoubtedly the one Kant was most interested in – we do have three principles corresponding to the three categories of relation, as well as a summary principle covering them all. In the next section I shall be discussing causality, the subject of the Second Analogy; and in the next chapter touching on substance, the subject of the First. The Third Analogy maintains that it is a necessary condition of our perceiving objects as coexistent that they should be in thoroughgoing inter-action with one another. But since this unlikely conclusion is reached by essentially the same device as is used for the Second Analogy – namely, the idea that the time-relations of objective phenomena can be deter-mined only if they are in all respects governed by causal law – I shall not discuss it specially.

All three principles are concerned with conditions for temporal experience. The third talks about space as well, but that is really inessential; it is simply concerned with the co-existence of objects in time.[12] The second and third both clearly have to do with conditions for experiencing an objective temporal world; the first is more ambivalent on this, but appears to argue simply from the fact that I am aware of changes, whether objective or not.

It is perhaps worth stressing that Kant is not here trying to establish the principles of Newtonian physics. It is perfectly true that he does think he has philosophical proofs for the law of conservation of matter, the law of inertia, and the law of the equality of action and reaction. It is also true that he makes use of the Analogies in these proofs. But the proofs do not come in the *Critique*; they come in the *Metaphysical Foundations of Natural Science*, and require two further elements which that work supplies. One of these is the general assumption from which it starts, that there is such a thing as movable matter which occupies space and possesses moving force. The other is a lot of staggeringly dreadful argument.[13]

The postulates of empirical thought in general

In this case Kant presents us with a series of definitions, which at first sight do not look much like synthetic a priori principles. But they are intended to be what he calls real definitions. A real definition, in contrast to a nominal definition, does not merely fix the meanings of words, but carries a guarantee that the concept defined does have application; it 'makes clear not only the concept but also its *objective reality*'.[14] It is indeed clear without further argument that the three concepts he defines can be applied in our experience.

In fact it appears that on the definitions Kant offers the three terms defined, 'possible', 'actual', and 'necessary', are coextensive; certainly 'actual' and 'necessary' are. Something is actual if it 'connects with the material conditions of experience (sensation)' (A 218/B 266); he elucidates this as requiring 'the connection of the object with some actual perception, in accordance with the analogies of experience' (A 225/B 272). By the Second and Third Analogies everything that ever exists in space is related by law to my perception, and so can be called actual. And likewise necessary; for something is necessary if 'its connection with the actual is determined in accordance with universal conditions of experience' (A 218/B 266), and as Kant points out this comes to the same thing because the only relevant 'universal conditions' are the Analogies. To be possible is to 'agree with the formal conditions of experience, that is, with the conditions of intuition and of concepts' (*ibid.*), and this would seem to allow different worlds from our own to be admitted as possible; but Kant is reluctant to countenance that, and confusedly argues that nothing can be possible unless it is *'in all respects* possible', i.e. unless it satisfies every relevant condition – in which case it will be actual.[15]

We can think of Kant's 'necessary' as 'causally necessary given *a*', where *a* is something actual; and of his 'possible' as 'causally possible', or if he insists on the 'in-all-respects' rider then 'causally possible given *a*'. These modalities would not be coextensive, of course, if the universe were not deterministically interconnected in a very thoroughgoing way, but Kant thinks the Analogies have shown that it is.[16]

Incidentally, the schemata he offers for the modal categories do not entirely match the three Postulates. Those for possibility and actuality can perhaps be brought into line, but for necessity the schema is said to be 'existence of an object at all times' (A 145/B 184). This would give us an entirely different sort of necessity, more like that of Diodorus; Kant must have changed his mind about it while writing the *Critique*.

3 The Second Analogy

The most important section of the chapter on the principles, and the one that has received most attention, is the Second Analogy. Here Kant tries to show that 'all alterations take place in conformity with the law of the connection of cause and effect' (B 232). If he is successful he will have given a transcendental justification for our ordinary, non-Humean conception of cause as implying a necessary connection between events. He will have shown that this concept must apply in our experience, because without it no temporal experience would be possible – or at any rate no experience of objective change. And he will have shown more than this: he will have shown that every event must have a cause.

This contention still finds defenders today, chiefly among those who think it scientific. There are even some scientists who would subscribe to it, despite the indeterministic character of quantum theory. But their reluctance to accept that there can be fundamental laws which are not causal but statistical in character is a little reminiscent of the prevailing attitude to gravity in Newton's time. Almost without exception Newton's contemporaries assumed that forces acting at a distance could not appear as primitive in the fundamental laws of nature; Newton himself took this for granted, and spent considerable effort trying to produce more ultimate mechanistical explanations for gravity. With the passage of time and a growing familiarity with the idea of action at a distance such a further explanation came to seem unnecessary, until by the time of Boscovich and of Kant's *Monadologia Physica* it had become possible to argue that action by contact required explanation in terms of action at a distance rather than the other way about.[17]

L. W. Beck accepts quantum indeterminacy, but argues that something rather like Kant's strong thesis can still be defended: in order to determine objective time-relations among the macroscopic events we can observe we must suppose that each of them has a cause, and only by doing this can we get the sort of evidence we require for theories which concern unobservables, like quantum mechanics. In other words 'there are good epistemological grounds for regarding our knowledge of indeterminacy as parasitic upon our knowledge of causal determinacy'.[18] But even if the causal principle is restricted to the realm of the familiar and middle-sized, it is difficult to see why every such event must be taken to have a cause. It is plausible to hold that some causal connections are required in order to set up an objective time-series, though in due course I shall be arguing that this is in fact not so. But granting a reasonable amount of causality, why should it have to be universal? We could concede that an event can be placed in the time-series only through its causal relations with other events, without conceding that every event must have a cause. An uncaused event could still have effects which allowed us to date it – a point Beck can hardly deny, for it is in just this way that he thinks we can date the uncaused occurrences at the subatomic level.[19]

W. H. Walsh says that once we admit the possibility of uncaused events occurring at all we can have no assurance that they will not happen too frequently for coherent experience to be possible.[20] But does that matter? We can have no such assurance in any case. If we could not experience objective events unless each of them had a cause, there still might come a time when this condition was not met and objective experience was no longer possible. Nothing guarantees our immortality as spectators of an objective world, or assures that world's indefinite continuance. Kant regards the causal principle as a priori, because he takes its truth to be a precondition for temporal experience; the same claim may be made, with more plausibility, for the weakened version that Beck and Walsh consider inadequate.

Walsh also asks how we could distinguish an uncaused event from a complete illusion, and so indeed does Kant.[21] But this does not seem very difficult to answer. If witnesses were all agreed that the event had occurred, if it could be photographed and its effects measured, our grounds for regarding it as objective would be about as good as they ever are, cause or no cause. Walsh, Beck and Kant all seem to be confusing the thesis that every event must have a cause with the thesis that every event must stand in some causal relation, i.e. have either a cause or an effect; though actually this is still false. Setting aside the possibility that there might be events about which no one could know anything – for these could not be in any sense objects of experience – we might on the basis of non-causal regularities have strong grounds for believing in the existence of events with neither causes nor effects. Suppose, for instance, that it were quite a common thing for books to spring into existence causelessly on the shelves of the Bodleian Library overnight.[22] Suppose moreover that one night every tenth book along the shelves were to vanish, again causelessly. Except in one case, where we have a row of eighteen books exactly as they were on the previous day; and arranged in such a way that there would have been room for another book between the ninth and tenth. Would it not be reasonable to suppose that during the night a book had come and gone again, leaving no trace of its presence? It would certainly be the most economical hypothesis.

Kant argues that to think the event B follows the event A in an objective time-series is tantamount to supposing there is a necessary connection between A and B.[23] But he does not make clear what this has to do with causal relationships. Certainly he does not think that each event at the earlier time causes each event at the later; he is clear that A causes B only if some law relates A-type events in general with B-type events, and that such laws can only be discovered empirically.[24] Still, although A need not cause B, he considers that the necessary connection between them must hold in virtue of causal laws. In his example of the ship moving downstream (A 192/B 237) we do not have to say that the ship's being upriver at t_1 is the cause of its being further down at t_2, but only that the two events are connected in the fuller picture of a physical world in which the governing laws are causal (the important ones here being to do with the action of wind on sails). But why do they have to be causal? Kant assumes without argument that if an earlier and a later event are 'necessarily connected' this must somehow be due to causal laws.[25] And that is not obvious, for the work might be done by laws we should not wish to call causal, and there might even be direct necessary connections between individual events, unmediated by any law.

He cannot be said to have made out the earlier part of his claim either: the contention that A and B must be necessarily connected. His idea appears to be that to think of their succession as objective requires an a priori contribution from the mind, for objectivity is never simply given in perception but has to be read in by the mind interpreting its data.[26] We connect A and B in thought by using our a priori conception of objectivity. Kant now seems gratuitously to equate 'a priori', in the present sense, with 'necessary', and to move from saying that this connection is made a priori in thinking of the sequence as objective, to the conclusion that we must think of A and B as necessarily connected.

Recognizing perhaps that this is unconvincing he tries to bolster it up by inserting an intermediate step, concerned with perceptions. He suggests that if I have two perceptions one after the other, then to regard them as perceptions of an objective sequence of events requires me to regard the perceptions themselves as necessarily connected. From there he gets to his conclusion by supposing that if the perceptions are necessarily connected the events of which they are perceptions must be necessarily connected too;[27] a move which looks fishy, but which one cannot assess without being clear what kind of necessity connects the perceptions. As to this, his reason for thinking there is any such necessity is the same as before, namely that the mind must be connecting the perceptions in accordance with the a priori conception of objectivity; but although the argument is no better the contention does look more acceptable this time. He contrasts watching the ship move downstream, which is an objective process, with perceiving the different parts of a house, which are all simultaneously there though I perceive them one after another. And it is quite true that there seems to be a sense in which my perceptions of the house are order-indifferent, and could easily have occurred the other way about, whereas those of the objective process are not and could not have done.

On closer examination, however, it turns out that there is nothing in this to assist Kant. It would have been perfectly possible for me to perceive the ship lower down the river before I perceived it higher up; that could happen in several ways. If it was a very fast ship, and I was standing at the river mouth, then I might see it travelling down towards me before I heard it cast off up river; for light travels faster than sound. And if it actually went faster than the speed of light I should even see it pass me before I could see it cast off, since the light would take longer than the ship to reach me. (That this is far fetched is not relevant; we are considering whether Kant's argument is valid, and it can be so only if it caters for all the logical possibilities.) A more commonplace possibility is that my perceptions could have come in the reverse order if the ship itself had been going upstream backwards.

As this last example brings out, our only reason for not regarding our perceptions of the ship as order-indifferent was that we knew them to be perceptions of an objective sequence: the ship was upstream and then downstream, and just because of that I could not have seen it downstream before I saw it upstream. And as the other examples help to show, even this requires qualification; further stipulations must be built in to ensure that the perceptions occur in the same order as the events. So our feeling that they were not order-indifferent was entirely due to the logical truth that if A precedes B, and if the perceptions occur in the same order as the events, the perception of A precedes the perception of B. This does not in the least support Kant's contention that there is a necessary connection between the perceptions. To suppose it did would be to move from 'Logically necessarily: if p then q' to 'Non-logically necessarily: q' (where 'q' is 'the perception of A precedes the perception of B'). This would combine an illicit move from one kind of necessity to another with a modal fallacy – the conversion of a conditional into an absolute necessity.[28]

However, it may perhaps seem that none of this fuddled argument of Kant's is necessary at all if we are interested only in the weakened thesis that to apply concepts of objective sequence we must make use of the notion of cause. For is it not fairly obvious that we can date events objectively only by fitting them into some picture of an external world which is at least very largely governed by causal law? In fact I think this is by no means obvious; so far as I can see it is false. The arguments that are adduced for it show at best that we must think of our experience as governed by lawlike regularities, and not that these must be causal.

In order to set up a public dating system we need to find events which recur in a fairly constant fashion: the change of the seasons, the rising and setting of the sun, the movements of a pendulum. But there is no need to suppose that anything causes these regularities, and for vast periods of time people have managed to avoid speculation on the subject; it is enough that they occur. To date some other event we need only look and see how it relates to the members of the regularly recurrent series; this is a matter of direct observation, not causal hypothesis. Even if there were no such recurrences we could still place events in an objective time-order, through observing them and reaching general agreement with other people; we should not be able to measure intervals of time in that case, but we might get on quite happily without that. The opinions of others would help us to correct our own false impressions and the objective time-series would be a very straightforward construction out of the order in which events seemed to each of us to happen.[29]

It is true that if we are to set up an objective time-series without using the notion of causation we must abjure the causal theory of perception. But this is not overwhelmingly difficult to do. One alternative would be to replace it with a theory of perception based not on causation but on a relation which is rather similar; I shall go into that possibility in a moment. But it is enough if we just think of ourselves as directly aware of events, without supposing that the event out there causes traces in us which permits us to infer its existence; and this is a highly natural position to adopt. It is not necessary either, or even appropriate, to construe the event as a cause of the remarks I make about it, when I compare notes with other people; my awareness of it may provide me with a reason for saying what I do, but that is another matter.

All the same, must there not be a network of causal relations in the world for us to be able to apply the concept of an object to it at all? Strawson argues that the reidentification of objects is possible only in a relatively stable, causally-ordered world, and it is plausible to maintain that to recognize something as an object at all I must have some causally-based idea of what I would perceive, or how it would react, if this or that took place.[30] According to Strawson

> our concepts of objects are linked with sets of conditional
> expectations about the things which we perceive as falling under
> them . . . concepts of *objects* are always and necessarily compendia
> of causal law or law-likeness, carry implications of causal power
> or dependence. (*Bounds of Sense*, pp. 145 f.)

So the concept of an object itself, and not just that of objective sequence, occasions the need for causality.

There is an important point here, but it is not being very exactly stated. An object can be perceived by more than one person, and it can go on existing while no one is perceiving it. If it continues to exist while unperceived then no doubt there is some set of conditions under which it would be perceived, and if I alone am perceiving it there will be conditions under which others would do so too (such as their being in the neighbourhood). I do not have to know precisely what the conditions are, but if I am to recognize it as an object I must have a rough idea, or I could have no conception of what kind of a thing it was. Similarly I must have some idea how the conditions of perception can affect its appearance; and since the object persists, retaining its identity through a variety of circumstances, I must know approximately what sorts of change it can undergo while remaining the same object. It is true, therefore, that if my experience were completely chaotic I should be able neither to reidentify an object when I came across it again, nor even to recognize it as an object in the first place. But there is nothing in this which requires the orderliness to be secured by causal law.

It is part of my conception of a persisting object, e.g. a chair, that it can undergo certain changes and not others without ceasing to be a chair. But I might have no explanation to offer, and there might be no explanation to find, of why it changes as it does within these limits. I do in fact have various causally-based expectations about it, but these are not essential. If I were wrong about them – if it changed colour mysteriously, or spontaneously sank through the floor, or survived an atomic explosion – I should be none the less able to identify it as the same chair. It does not seem necessary that these changes should be regular and predictable, but they could be so without the regularity being a causal one: the chair might just always sink through the floor at noon on Tuesdays. In much the same way I can know how the object looks from various angles, sounds from various positions, and so on, without there being causal laws which determine how it looks and sounds. It is enough that there are regularities.

They must be the sort of regularities that will support counterfactual conditionals, for example to the effect that if I were in a certain position I should see the object in a particular way. But not all regularities which support counterfactual conditionals are causal. They may involve any sort of lawlike relationship between phenomena, and one thing may depend upon another in a variety of ways. The dependence need not even be absolute; our regularities might be statistical in character and still license counterfactuals to the effect that if it were the case that p, then with an n per cent probability it would be the case that q. But statistical laws are not causal. It would also be possible for us to rely entirely upon regularity-generalizations which were like causal laws in all but one far from trivial respect: they might be confined to the present and the past. This is important, for it means that there is nothing here to help us with the traditional problem of induction. Kant was never much concerned about induction, but many people have seen the Second

Analogy and the more recent arguments about causality as making a contribution to that problem.

Causal generalizations are unrestricted as to time; they say that whenever the causal conditions obtain, the effect follows. The generalizations we require in order to apply the concept of an object do not have to be unrestricted in this way; it is enough if they are considered to hold only at certain times, and they do not therefore have to extend to the future. If on independent grounds one considers it reasonable to suppose the future will be like the past, then one will no doubt consider it reasonable that they should cover the future as well, but we are not concerned here with what might be thought reasonable. The point is that it is not a necessary condition for having experience of objects in time that we should make generalizations which cover future instances. Or at least, the argument does not show that it is.

Of course if the objects around us are to go on existing in future the generalizations we make about them must continue to apply. But we have no guarantee that they will, and do not need to pretend that we do in order to recognize them as being objects now. They are objects in virtue of their present condition, and nothing that happens or fails to happen in future can alter that; I am not the less able to see them as objects now if all the laws of nature are about to break down, though in that case every one of the predictions I believe warranted on the basis of past evidence may be falsified. So I could get by with a form of regularity-generalization which was not causal, in that it did not attempt to license predictions.

Thus we are not entitled to conclude that the notion of cause is essential for experience of objects in time. But it has emerged that we must commit ourselves to the truth of a variety of counterfactual-supporting regularity-generalizations; and in fact it is not just temporal experience that requires this. As we saw when we discussed life in a timeless world, with atemporal experience it is equally true that the percipient can recognize objects only if there are lawlike truths which entail counterfactuals. We can find evidence for these generalizations only if we can find regularities in our experience to generalize over, and that seems to show that not only the objective world but also the data given to us in experience – the manifold of intuition – must be in a measure orderly. But two notes of caution must be sounded regarding this conclusion. First, it imposes no real limitation on what the content of experience may be like, for orderliness and chaos are in the eye of the beholder: what I see as orderly depends on my propensities for classifying things together as similar. A set of experiences which seemed to me completely chaotic might seem monotonously regular to a being who classified in a radically different way, and what seemed orderly to me might be ungraspably chaotic to him.[31] So no set of data can be said to be inherently orderly or disorderly, though of course given that I see similarities and differences in the way I do there are severe restrictions on what my experience can be like if I am to find the appropriate regularities in it. And in the second place we must remember that this orderliness is required only if we are to have *grounds* for applying the concept of an object. Whatever my experience was like nothing could stop me quite arbitrarily picking out items as objects, as reappearances of the same object again, and so on. I might even be right. We have seen already that it is irrelevant to raise the genetic question how I could have acquired the concept of an object if my experience were not orderly; the concept can hardly be acquired from experience in any case. Without having any grounds I could apply the concept, and might (by accident) do so correctly, though I would be able to see no point in introducing it.

All the same, we can draw from Strawson's argument the conclusion that if I am to have grounds for applying the concept of an object then I must be able to recognize in my experience regularities, over which I can generalize in such a way as to support counterfactuals. This is important; it shows that I must go beyond the evidence, and it suggests a transcendental justification for doing so: unless I did I should have no reason for applying the concept of an object. How effective this is as a transcendental argument must obviously depend on how essential it is that any experience should include an awareness of objects. And it is to this that we must turn in the next chapter.

VIII

The Transcendental Object

It is frequently said that Kant is a phenomenalist. But this is untrue. The mistake is due to a regrettable tendency to depreciate the transcendental object $= x$, which has in fact been one of the most unfortunate casualties of Kantian scholarship. Kemp Smith and many others have condemned it as a disreputable survival from the days of the *Inaugural Dissertation* or even before,[1] and it is not really surprising that it should have met this fate. The term is mysterious and obscure, and it is certainly sometimes used to refer to things as they are in themselves, independent of the categories and the conditions of sensibility. So when we find passages in which the transcendental object is given a crucial part in explaining our perception of ordinary physical things, it is understandable that they should be regarded as left over from a time when Kant regarded the objects of perception as being things in themselves.

But he does not quite say that we perceive transcendental objects. He says that the objects of perception 'must be thought only as something in general $= x$' (A 104); that the relevant representations are 'referred' to a 'something' which is the transcendental object (A 250). It is not wholly obvious what this means, but perhaps we should not dismiss it as pre-Critical until we are more confident. Kemp Smith does, it is true, have an independent reason for regarding these passages as early in date: there is less mention of the transcendental object in B than in A, and he claims to have discovered 'its absence from all [Kant's] later utterances'.[2] Since, however, it plays a considerable part in the *Opus Postumum*, which was written fifteen to twenty years after the *Critique*, this cannot be entirely correct.

Kant introduces his theory about perception in the course of the first-edition deduction. He there tries to argue that when I interpret my sense-data as representing an object I must be reading something in which is not empirically given. It is not simply that I must connect the

106

data together, though that is true, nor just that I must add in the ideas of other past or possible sense-data, though that is true too. What enables me to unite these actual and possible perceptions together is the non-empirical conception of an object, as something which underlies the perceptions and provides a focus around which they can be united. The conception is non-empirical in the same way that the concept of cause is: it is not to be acquired by abstraction from experience, and we cannot verify that it applies just by an appeal to the empirically given. It is simply the idea of a thing which exists independently of me and of all other perceivers. But like the concept of cause it can be called transcendental, for we cannot (Kant thinks) dispense with it if experience is to be possible. We may naturally ask why in that case he did not consider it a category; but it turns out that at one time he did, for in the *Duisburg'sche Nachlass* (c. 1775), where we can see the doctrine of the transcendental object developing, it is quite clearly this that Kant means by 'substance'.[3] The idea that substances are individual particular things, and do not have to be absolutely permanent, is present in a number of places in the *Critique* as well, but presumably the official doctrine of that work would be that the concept of an individual object is a 'predicable', a pure concept which is somehow derivative from a category.[4]

Kant is not saying that in talking about objects we commit ourselves to the existence of things in themselves, which cause our perceptions. He does believe in things in themselves, but not for this reason. The independent entities we commit ourselves to are in space and time, subject to causal law, and so on; there is nothing deeply mysterious about them, any more than there is about the objects postulated by a modern causal theory of perception. They cause sensations in us; on the basis of these we can infer large amounts of information regarding them and their interrelations. What Kant calls noumena, things in themselves, are entirely different from this: they are outside space and time, and altogether independent of the forms of thought which human minds impose upon the world and employ in constructing nature as we know it.

It is perfectly true that in other places he applies the term 'transcendental object' to what are unequivocally noumena. But now that we have seen we are dealing with something like a category this double usage ceases to be so problematic. It is a familiar point that we can make use of the categories to think about matters which transcend the limits of possible experience; that is how metaphysical mistakes arise. We can make use of them in their pure, unschematized form, leaving out whatever conditions tie them down to spatio-temporal experience; and if we do this with the concept of an object we are left with the idea of a thing in general, an independent entity, free of any limitation to space, time, and causal law – in other words, the idea of a noumenon. So we have here the contrast between a pure category and its schematized version, except that we are dealing not strictly with a category but with a predicable.

It is a pity that Kant does not explain his reasons for rejecting phenomenalism in favour of this causal theory. He may not have been very clear about them, or able precisely to formulate where the disagreement came. Indeed sometimes we find him saying things which sound very phenomenalistic. But on his view our experience of objects involves a form of synthesis which the phenomenalist cannot allow. We must at least think of objects as genuinely independent things and not as logical constructions out of sense-data. The phenomenalist holds that statements about objects are reducible to sets of statements about sense-data; that they can be analysed into descriptions of sense-data, connected by logical devices and nothing more. But Kant thinks this proposed reduction cannot be carried through; and in this he is right. Phenomenalistic analyses of material-object statements reduce them to sets of statements about what people would perceive, if such-and-such were the case. But there is no satisfactory way to fill out the conditionals without drawing on notions which the phenomenalist is not entitled to use; they all rely, directly or indirectly, on the concept of an object.

The easiest way to see this is to ask what the percipients themselves must be like. On the phenomenalist account, to say that there is a pink elephant sitting in my armchair must be to say that if A, B, C, etc., were in my room, with suitable lighting conditions and so on, they would have the sense-data appropriate to seeing a pink elephant in an armchair; and also that under certain further conditions they would have the relevant tactual, auditory, and perhaps olfactory sense-data. Now let us grant (for the sake of argument only) that these various sense-data can be characterized in a manner satisfactory to the phenomenalist, and that the conditions regarding lighting, observers' positions, and the like can also be spelt out without presupposing the notion of an object. There remains a further difficulty over A, B, and C, for what if they were suffering from delirium tremens and were systematically hallucinated? No doubt it is not very likely that they would all have the same hallucination; and perhaps not likely that even one of them would have a hallucination sufficiently systematic and coherent to extend to all the relevant senses, and all the different positions from which the putative objects might be perceived. But it is logically possible, and that is enough to cause trouble: the phenomenalist is offering us an analysis, an account of what we mean when we talk about objects, and he is therefore obliged to cope with all the logical possibilities.

The natural thing for him to suggest is that in such a case we should count heads: by definition, to be right is to be on the side of the big battalions and hallucinations are suffered only by the few. It is true of the majority of people that if introduced into my room they would have no pink elephant-like sense-data, and that decides the matter. Unfortunately, however, this view has strongly counterintuitive consequences. What if the majority is a very narrow one? If the world's population is $2n+1$, of whom n would have pink-elephant-like sense-data and $n+1$ would not, the proposed solution looks arbitrary in the extreme. If one of the majority now dies, does the matter become indeterminate? If two die, we shall have to say there now is a pink elephant there (though there was not before), and that it is the other party who are now suffering the delusions. One will be able to turn one's (systematic) hallucinations into reality by a bit of judicious murder: if I alone perceive the elephant, I can bring it about that there really is an elephant there by the simple expedient of wiping out everybody else.

It is no remedy to say that the truth of the matter is determined by what the majority of other people would say if there were any other people. For (waiving any difficulties there may be over talking about possible people in the first place) there is a denumerable infinity of possible people who would perceive the pink elephant, just as there is a denumerable infinity who would not. There are no majorities among possible people. The only way out is to stop taking votes, and to say that there is a real elephant there if and only if it would be perceived under the relevant conditions by those (actual or possible) people who perceive what is there. But this would be circular as an analysis; it assumes the notion of what is really there, i.e. the notion of an object.

Kant does regard the ordinary world as being a construction of a kind, but as constructed not simply out of what the senses give us but (roughly) out of our beliefs. It is a construction we effect by reading in a priori concepts like those of objectivity and causality, and accordingly the world contains objects and causes which instantiate those concepts. When he is contrasting it with the noumenal world, the world of things in themselves, he naturally stresses its mind-dependent character, but although it is dependent on our minds in the sense of being synthetically built up by us in this way, it contains objects whose existence does not depend on our having the appropriate sense-data and which can there-fore, in another and more ordinary sense, be said to be independent of us. It contains such objects just because that is the way we construct it. He does say that to suggest there are inhabitants of the moon 'only means that in the possible advance of experience we may encounter them' (A 493/B 521), but this is not intended to convey that the claim requires a phenomenalistic analysis; he is only making the point that if an object is real it must be possible to perceive it. He also has a habit of saying that objects are only representations (thus A 378, A 492/B 520), but this is again to emphasize that in a sense they are dependent on us; it would be hard to read in any more precise significance, for his word 'representation' ('*Vorstellung*') is used even more vaguely than Locke's 'idea'. The same goes for those passages in which he says that an object is a sum (*Inbegriff*) of representations: even if the representations are here supposed to be sense-data the word '*Inbegriff*' is itself too vague to imply a definite commitment on how much else is required for their synthesis.[5]

He sounds at his most phenomenalistic in his discussion of the Fourth Paralogism in A, which at first sight seems to be directed explicitly against a causal theory of perception. It also seems to embrace in a very short compass three mutually incompatible views: phenomenalism, a sort of direct realism, and the causal theory he started out by repudiating. More careful reading, however, reveals that these initial impressions were misleading, and that Kant's theory is the same here as elsewhere. The object of the section is to refute the suggestion that we cannot be certain of the existence of the external world, a suggestion backed up by the argument that the external world can only be inferred as a cause of our perceptions. What Kant says is that if the external world were a world of things in themselves we should indeed have no right to infer its existence by means of any causal argument – the principle of causality holds only within the world of appearances. But since external objects are only 'a species of representations' (A 370) no such problem arises with them; within the world of appearances causal inferences are perfectly legitimate. He does rather overstate his case by saying that material objects are immediately perceived and not inferred,[6] but he makes clear that this marks no real change of view by reiterating that we must rely on causal considerations to discriminate between veridical and illusory perceptions.[7]

He concludes that 'empirical realism is beyond question; that is, there corresponds to our outer intuitions something real in space' (A 375). Given that we have the intuitions we do this seems an entirely proper conclusion, but we have not been given a transcendental argument to show that all experience, or all temporal experience, requires the application of the concept of an object in order to count as experience at all. And one would seem to be needed, for although the concept of an object may have been demoted from its status as a category it still remains an a priori concept, and an important one whose everyday use as much requires a vindication as does that of the categories. But it is not evident where such an argument should be fitted into Kant's neat architectonic scheme. In the first edition the need for it is not clearly recognized, though some rather gnomic utterances in the Deduction and the First Analogy may be intended to do the job. In the second, the Refutation of Idealism is interpolated for this purpose.

In the Refutation of Idealism Kant claims to prove that there must be objects, or more exactly that one must apply the concept of an object within one's experience. He says they must be 'in space outside me'

(B 275), but 'in space' should not be taken too seriously; he does not think he can prove that all temporal experience must be experience of a spatial world. Rather he is taking it for granted that space is the form of our outer sense and arguing 'that inner experience in general is possible only through outer experience in general' (B 278 f.). He is arguing against the possibility of what Strawson calls a purely sense-datum experience[8] – an experience in which the subject can do no more than assign to himself sense-data without being aware of any objects, things capable of existing independent of his perceptions. Independent, that is, in the ordinary sense in which we take physical objects to be independent of us: not in the other, transcendental, sense in which only things in themselves are properly independent of the minds whose synthesis creates the world of appearances. Things in themselves are not at issue at present; for the remainder of the chapter I shall continue to use the word 'independent' in the ordinary way.

The argument starts, as always in the Analytic of Principles, from the assumption that the experience we are considering is at least temporally ordered. It really consists of two stages, of which only the second appears under the heading 'Refutation of Idealism'; this rests upon and is a continuation of the argument of the First Analogy, which we must therefore look at to begin with. The First Analogy maintains that in all temporal experience one must be aware of something permanent, and the Refutation of Idealism adds that this permanent thing cannot be within me but must be an external object. So Kant reaches his conclusion that there must be independent objects by way of the much stronger contention that there must be some permanent objective thing – a 'substance' in the technical sense of the *Critique of Pure Reason*.

The other two Analogies were concerned with conditions for the experience of an objective temporal world. It is not quite clear whether the First Analogy is meant to be taken in the same way, but if it is there is an element of circularity in the Refutation of Idealism. For since it rests on the First Analogy the argument will now show that if we are to have objective experience (of a temporal kind) we must have experience of independent objects. This is not perhaps entirely trivial, but it escapes triviality only in so far as it excludes the possibility of an objective world which does not contain objects – persisting particulars – but only, for example, events. Such a possibility is hardly likely to have occurred to Kant, seeing how muddled he was over the notion of objectivity.

Whichever way one takes it the argument of the First Analogy is quite remarkably unpersuasive. The main argument in A says that something permanent is required in order to determine objective time-relations; in B an argument is added which is similar except that it appears to say the permanent is needed in order to have any time-relations at all, objective or not. So far as any grounds are offered for this remarkable allegation, they consist in the thought that unless something were permanent time could not be measured,[9] to which there are two obvious replies. One is that to measure time all we require is regularity, not permanence; a regular series of flashes would do as well as a clock. The other is that experience of temporal order would be quite possible even if we could not measure time; we could still relate events as contemporary or successive.

He does also say that if there were only relatively permanent things we could not have a single unitary time-order.[10] But (leaving aside the question whether we need such a thing) for that we do not even require that the same regularities should continue. If we have been used to measuring time by the sun, and the sun stops rising and setting, we shall need some new regularity to measure time by; but provided that the two have worked side by side for a period we shall be able to carry the old measurements over. And even if there is no overlap – even if, at an instant, the entire world of physical objects with all its regularities changes completely – this does not destroy the unity of the temporal ordering of events, for this is sufficiently established by the general agreement of observers.

He adds another argument, to the effect that the only changes we can perceive are changes in the state of something that persists throughout the change; 'a coming to be or ceasing to be that is not simply a determination of the permanent but is absolute, can never be a possible perception' (A 188/B 231). For to perceive something coming into or going out of existence we should have to perceive the 'empty time' before the thing was there or after it had gone. This is again unconvincing; we should not have to perceive an empty world at all but only a world which did not have that particular thing in it, which is entirely possible and quite commonplace. Kant's reply is that such a change can be no more than an alteration in the qualities of the stuff that underlies all material objects, and that the continued existence of this stuff throughout is attested by the fact that both before and after the change there do exist material objects. But this is mere juggling with words. Of course you can say that something permanent exists (so long as anything exists at all) if you stipulate that whatever changes occur are alterations in the continuing world-whole, or that all physical changes are alterations in the underlying matter. Kant has given us no reason for regarding this stipulation as less than arbitrary; he has not shown why we must think of matter as a single thing, and take the highly unnatural course of construing bottles and bookcases as modifications of it. And he has given us no shadow of a reason for supposing that its quantity can neither be increased nor diminished, though he apparently thinks this follows. Objects might be created or annihilated, without compensating adjustments elsewhere to keep the quantity of matter constant; our only reasons for thinking this does not happen are derived from physics. One can easily imagine watching the Great Pyramid being annihilated, and if Kant insisted on describing such changes as alterations in matter we should just have to say that matter could change in quantity (grow larger or smaller).

Even if the arguments of the First Analogy were valid, they would not show that the permanent substance must be an object of outer sense. So far as human experience is concerned we may feel that matter in space is a reasonable candidate, but Kant has not yet produced an argument to prove that temporal experience necessarily requires the existence of something permanent which is external to the percipient himself. This is what the Refutation of Idealism is supposed to do. The argument is obscurely stated, but its point is that in inner sense I can intuit nothing that is permanent, only the flux of my representations. It is true that I must think of myself as a unitary subject, but I do not intuit any such persisting unity. Hence the permanent must be sought elsewhere than in inner sense. It must nevertheless be something I can be aware of, and if not in inner then in outer sense: it must be something objective, external to me.[11]

If we concede the need for something permanent in experience, there seem to be four ways in which I might find it without having recourse to external objects. (1) I might have non-veridical perceptions as of some permanent external object. (2) I might have some feeling, like a headache, to which I ascribed permanence even though I was not always conscious of it, e.g. because asleep or otherwise absorbed. (3) I might be continuously aware throughout my existence of some permanent inner representation, like a steady hum. (4) I might be simply aware of myself, as the permanent subject of all my experience.

Against (1) Kant can say that it does not fulfil the condition conceded to be necessary. For in this case there is nothing really permanent; there are only my misleading perceptions, and these are not permanent themselves. But he cannot so easily dismiss (2), (3), and (4). There are some who might question the coherence of (2), holding it analytic that feelings can exist only so long as they are felt, but this is an unpromising line which draws too heavily on ordinary language. Whatever the common usage of the term, it would be possible to use 'headache' to apply to something which went on while the percipient was unaware of it. If sometimes I woke with a headache which felt just like the one I had when I went to sleep, and if I had reason to believe that I should have felt something similar at any intervening time had I woken then, this would be enough to give point to a use of the word which allowed me to speak of numerically the same headache continuing. And it might, perhaps, last throughout all my life, and thus be (so far as I am concerned) permanent.

Even more clearly (3) I might be uninterruptedly conscious through-out my life, and uninterruptedly aware of a headache or a continuous hum. It is no defence to say that one would never notice such a thing if it were there, for if this is a fact at all it is only a psychological fact; to refute Kant it is enough that there should be logically possible counter-instances to his claim. He says nothing to show these are not logical possibilities, and seems to rely on the contingent fact that we do not have such representations; which he is hardly entitled to do in an a priori argument.

The most natural suggestion is (4): why should not I myself be that permanent substance which continues throughout all my experience? Kant does at least see that this needs an answer, and his answer is that my self is not an object of possible experience. He holds this because he thinks that as an agent I am free and spontaneous in a way which would be inconsistent with my belonging to the world of appearances and being subject to the law of causality. My active self is therefore noumenal and unknowable. But at the same time he does not want to deny that there is a sense in which I can know a great deal about myself through experience, and particularly through introspection. The difference is that what I can know through experience is myself as appearance; the corresponding noumenon, myself as I am in myself, can never be known. Swallowing, for the moment, this doctrine, why should I not regard my various representations as all modifications of one permanent phenomenal self, not unknowable but known through them? It is hard to see what objection Kant could have to this, since he favours the closely parallel proposal of regarding all physical changes as modifi-cations of one permanent substance in space. His discussion of the Paralogisms offers nothing against it, for what he is objecting to there is the claim to knowledge about my noumenal, active self.[12]

For all the worthlessness of Kant's arguments, though, it may be felt that he does have a point to make against the idea that someone might have experience without being aware of an objective world. Perhaps nothing permanent is required for the setting up of a temporal ordering, but all the same a fairly high degree of order and stability is necessary. And if this order and stability were purely internal to me I could at best set up a private time-order, which I could not share with anyone else. But is that really coherent? A private time-order would rely heavily on my memory, but my memory is not self-authenticating, and even to understand what a memory-claim amounts to I must admit the possi-bility that my claim might be mistaken. I must recognize that my present memory-belief does not decide the matter. But in that case surely it must be possible at least in principle to appeal to further evidence, to check whether my memory is reliable. It would be no good just to call on other memories of my own, for they would only give me more evidence of the same kind. So it must in principle be possible for other people to correct me; and this in turn requires a public, objective world with a shared time-order.

This argument, which is essentially a modification of Wittgenstein's objection to a private language, is criticized by Bennett on the grounds that it is unnecessary to bring in other people. 'What people say is just a special case of what objects do';[13] to interpret what someone else says, even to recognize him as a person at all, I must rely on my theory of how the world works, built up on the basis of the order and regularity in my experience. It is enough, in Bennett's view, if this order and regularity enables me to recognize an objective world, whether or not we allow that other people might inhabit it. For in that case I can supplement my original memory-claim with a whole variety of data that bear on it in complex ways, and so give content to the distinction between my claim and how things actually were. An objective world is governed by laws, and these laws enable me to use present evidence to confirm memories, as when my memory of a fire is confirmed by seeing ash; and to use memories of different things to support one another, as when a recollection of the sun shining confirms a memory of feeling warm.[14]

Bennett's criticism is a good one; the regularities I have observed amongst my experiences do provide me with ways to test the reliability of particular memory-judgments. But do these regularities have to be as elaborate as Bennett supposes? He thinks they must have that specially thoroughgoing character which entitles me to say that my experience is of objects; so he agrees with Wittgenstein and Kant about the necessity for objects, though not entirely assenting to their arguments. But he does not show why the regularities should have to take this form, and on reflection it is clear that if their role is just to enable memories to be brought to bear on one another they do not have to. If I had no conception of an object, and my experience was entirely inner or private, I might still notice regularities within it: for example, that whenever I felt a stab of pain I immediately felt a tickle. I could then use my memory of a pain to confirm my recollection of a tickle, or my memory of being pain-free at the relevant time to disconfirm it. Where there was a straight conflict between two apparent memories, as in this last case, I should not know which to trust, but other regularities might provide further collateral evidence: tickles might always be accompanied by a buzzing sound, perhaps. There might be quite a network of regularities, all of them holding simply amongst the actual data of experience and none of them taken to warrant claims about unperceived existents, or about experiences that would have occurred had things been a little different. The network would be a less elaborate one than that which is required for the experience of an objective world; it would not have the same rich complexity. But the difference is of degree, and I could still find occasion to distinguish between veridical and apparent memories.

Actually I could do so even without such regularities. The regularities provide a device for making some of my memories corroborate or disconfirm others, but the device is dispensable. For as Ayer pointed out long ago I may be able to check my memory of the stab of pain by means of other memories of mine concerning the very same event.[15] My initial tentative recollection of the pain may be quite defeated by the subsequent strong conviction that I certainly had no pain then: I can remember all my experiences at the relevant time in the greatest detail, and pains were not among them. The Wittgensteinian objection that this only gives me more evidence of the same kind as my original memory-belief (like taking in several copies of the same newspaper)[16] is quite beside the point, which is that it provides me with a way of distinguishing genuine from apparent memories. Of course it is not a completely reliable way of doing it; my initial impression may have been right after all, and the later conviction misplaced; and this may be what the Wittgensteinians have in mind. But no method of testing memories is completely reliable, not even one which invokes complex general laws and the memory-claims of millions of other people; there is always the possibility that the event in question is an exception to what we took for laws (a miracle perhaps), and similarly everyone may be wrong about it (Stalin did not invent the steam-engine). It may be asked why I should accept the strong, detailed, subsequent memory-claim instead of the weak, earlier one, but to this I can only reply that this is how conviction works: I can no more justify it than I can justify a preference for simple hypotheses. But no defence more ultimate than this can be offered for preferring the testimony of others to my own apparent memory, when they conflict; or for rejecting a memory-claim because it runs counter to what are thought to be natural laws.

A somewhat analogous argument to those of Wittgenstein and Bennett is developed by Strawson; this time to the effect that without experience of an objective world we could not be self-conscious. Strawson considers it to be the central argument of the transcendental deduction of the categories, a view we have found reason to doubt. He also considers a version of it to be present in the Refutation of Idealism. But whether or not the argument traces back to Kant, the mistake it makes is quite Kantian in character, for it rests on a confusion over the word 'objective'; and it is an interesting and important argument on its own account.

I have said that it starts from the requirement that experience be self-conscious, but 'self-conscious' is a vague term. As Strawson makes clear it is not necessary for the argument that the subject have any very full-blooded conception of himself; all that is needed is that 'experience must be such as to provide room for the thought of experience itself',[17] by which is meant that he must be able to find a use for the distinction between how things are and how things seem to him to be – the contrast between reality and his experience of it. This is a distinction we are familiar with by now, and we can agree that it is indeed essential that the subject should understand it; though as we have also noticed there is a difference between understanding it and finding in one's experience grounds which make it rational to apply it. Still, Strawson assumes that the subject's experience must provide him with such grounds, so for the sake of argument let us concede this to him. It now follows immediately, he thinks, that our experience is of an objective world, for to find a use for the is/seems distinction just is to distinguish between what is objective and what is subjective.[18] But this does not follow, for the distinctions are not identical; not if 'objective' is taken in the way Strawson intends. Mental states of my own may be objective in the sense that I can be right or wrong about them, but they do not belong to an independent objective world.

Strawson is attacking the idea that someone could have what he calls a purely sense-datum experience, lacking contact with an objective world. It is sometimes held that one is incorrigibly aware of one's sense-data, and we can grant that if that is the case an experience which consisted entirely of sense-data would provide no grounds for the distinction between how things are and how they seem to be. But to give the distinction a grip it is not necessary to go to the extremity of admitting an objective world of independently existing things. One's own mental states can give plenty of opportunity to exercise the is/seems distinction, just as long as there are some of which one is not incorrigibly aware; and clearly I can wrongly assess my own desires and moods, and correct the assessment by a more careful introspection. Even one's sense-data will do, if mistakes can be made about sense-data; and as soon as memory is introduced it brings with it the possibility of misremembering, a possibility which as we have seen can be recognized without appeal to a world of independent objects. We saw in chapter VI that Kant tended to confuse two senses of the word 'object', and that his use of 'objective' carried a like ambiguity; sometimes his objects are the intentional objects of our awareness, at other times they are independently existing things. Strawson seems to be making a rather similar conflation: his argument shows the need for something that is objective in the sense that one can make mistakes about it, but not for something non-mental that exists independently in an external world.

He sometimes puts his point by saying that the world must allow a diversity of possible 'experiential routes' through it.[19] This, I think, is just a way of saying that without things actually being different my experiences of them could have been. But one can also read it as claiming that it must be possible for other people to share my world with me, and this is a claim Strawson is not entitled to make, for the 'objective' features of my mental life may be altogether private to me. By bringing in other people it sounds a little reminiscent of his earlier argument in *Individuals*, to the effect that the ability to ascribe states of consciousness to oneself cannot be separated from the ability to ascribe them to others. There he observed that expressions like 'is a person' and 'is in pain' are predicates, and that predicates can always in principle be applied to more than one entity; so that to understand them I must know how to apply them not only to myself but also to others.[20] If an argument along these lines could show that I must actually come across other people, it would suffice for the conclusion that I must have experience of independently existing objects, for as far as I am concerned other people are a kind of external object. But of course it does not show this, and does not purport to; it claims only that I must be able to recognize other people as people, and to ascribe states of consciousness to them, if I do happen to meet any. Mastery of a predicate does not require the existence of instances to which it applies. In fact mastery of a predicate does not even require an ability to recognize instances of it, as we saw when discussing schemata.[21] I know perfectly well what is meant by saying that an element has a radioactive isotope with a half-life of a million years, but I have no idea how to discover which do. So that the argument is again invalid. I might understand what was meant by the suggestion that someone else was in pain, or had a feeling just like this one, without knowing how to find out whether or not it was true (not, one may think, a wholly unrealistic possibility).

The argument can also be faulted at an earlier stage. For one might be able to understand an expression which did the work of 'is in pain' in effecting a classification within one's own experience, without being at all prepared to admit that it could be used to describe the states of some other subject. It might, as it were, be defined for the one case only. If it be held that it is therefore not a predicate, there is no need to quarrel about terminology; it does have a classificatory function, as predicates do, only one confined to the events of a single person's experience. It is true that if all the predicates or quasi-predicates I could apply to myself were of this kind I should not be able properly to think of myself as a person; and it is certainly possible to argue that I cannot be called self-conscious unless I have a sufficiently full-blooded concept of myself to be able to see myself as at least potentially one among others. But it is not clear that the capacity to distinguish how things seem from how they are, and hence to perform a rather limited kind of self-ascription, does require me to be self-conscious in this sense.

However that may be, the arguments designed to take the place of the Refutation of Idealism in showing that we must have experience of independent objects have failed. *A fortiori* we have no proof of the need for independent objects which persist, whether permanently or only for a time. It is true that unless experience exhibits a measure of stability it will be difficult to correct one's mistaken judgments, difficult to distinguish what is from what seems to be, though I have suggested that, in the case of memory judgments, strength of memory might serve us adequately as a test. But experience can exhibit considerable stability without giving us occasion to apply the concept of an object or an unperceived existent; the regularity may be entirely within what is experienced, as in the example of the felt tickle following upon the stab of pain, and thus need not provide a foothold for any beliefs about independently existing things. It will not do to argue, as Ross Harrison does, that once any degree of regularity has been conceded it always might be that it developed in such a way as to provide occasion for these beliefs,[22] for though it might, it also might not. The question at issue is not whether we might find room to apply the concept of an object, but whether it is a condition of all possible (or all temporal) experience that the concept be applied.

But perhaps we should change the question, and see whether we can salvage at least something by asking a different one. Given that we have experience of an independent, objective world, does it have to include experience of objects – relatively long-lasting reidentifiable particulars? I have been tending to write as though an objective world and a world of objects were the same thing, but it is by no means evident that one could not have experience of an objective world in which there were no things that endured, even in the non-permanent way characteristic of tables and coffee-spoons. In fact when we consider the matter it again seems that the transcendental arguments fail us; objects are dispensable, for regular patterns of events could take their place equally well. Strawson thinks that persisting objects are required, but his ground for this is just that otherwise we could have no picture of an enduring objective world independent of our perceptions.

> But there is only one way in which perceived things or processes
> can supply a system of temporal relations independent of the order
> of the subject's perceptions of them – viz. by *lasting* and being
> *re*-encounterable in temporally different perceptual experiences.
> (*Bounds of Sense*, p 127.)

This overlooks the possibility that the same job might be done by a sufficiently regular ordering of events. He also argues that persisting objects are needed to set up an enduring spatial framework,[23] but again their place could be taken by patterns of events. If all I could perceive were tiny flashes of coloured light, which I could locate at different places within my visual field and which came in regular and predictable sequences (rather as lighthouse signals do), I might perfectly well be able to find room for the idea of a flash or a series of flashes going on unperceived. If I could change my field of vision at will, moving gradually from one display to another and then back again, I could have grounds, closely comparable to those I do in fact have, for thinking things had gone on in the usual way during my absence. We can suppose that the patterns of flashes have the same sort of stability that in our world objects have, and then they will be able to play just the same part in establishing a system of objective spatio-temporal relations that objects do for us. It may be said that in that case the patterns of flashes can themselves be considered as enduring objects, and in a way this is true; but there is no reason why the percipient should be obliged to think of them as objects – as substances -- rather than as collections of events. He does not have to employ the concept of an object at all.

Certainly Strawson argues in *Individuals*, and argues persuasively, that for us the identification of events depends in general upon the identification of particular things.[24] But this argument is only meant to be about us and our way of looking at the world, whereas our present concerns are more abstract and cover the possible experience of beings very different from ourselves. He points out that for the most part when we refer to events we do so by relating them to objects in some way – as when we refer to a birth as the birth of Shakespeare, or to a bang as the sound of my tyre bursting. It is only in those rare cases where we have a sequence of events of which one member can be picked out by direct demonstration, and the others can be referred to as 'the nth member before/after this one', that we make event-identifications which are genuinely unmediated by our identifications of objects. This may strike one as too restrictive, even as an account of our practice, for after all the Declaration of Independence was an event; but Strawson would say we can identify it as that specific event only through the time and place of its occurrence, which means that we implicitly rely on the identification of objects since it is through them that our system of dates and places is set up. And that is no doubt true; we do work in that way. But the percipient we have been talking about sets up his spatio-temporal framework in a different way, relying on the stability of his flash-patterns as we rely on the stability of material objects.

We have to conclude, therefore, that not only Kant's arguments, but also the more hopeful-looking reconstructions of them, are unsuccessful. Experience does not have to be of objects, although ours is; it would seem that some being of a different sort could perfectly well have experience without applying to it the concept of an object, or even without thinking of himself as in contact with an independently existing objective world. He could still distinguish between what is the case and what only seems so; he could think of himself as a person, potentially one among many, though nothing in his experience indicated the actual existence of others. So Kant's attempt to provide a transcendental justification for the use of the a priori concept of an object, as necessary for any temporal experience, has broken down, as did his analogous attempt at a transcendental defence of the use of the concept of cause. That is not of course to say that transcendental arguments cannot be found which will perform these tasks; one can never be certain that what one thinks one can imagine really is a genuine possibility, and experience without objects may be incoherent after all. But there is no special reason to think it is. And we must ask ourselves how much this matters. An important part of Kant's enterprise has collapsed, that part which initially looked most promising: transcendental arguments have not achieved what was required of them. Can anything perhaps be rescued from that side of his thought which at first looked strange and rather repellent – his transcendental idealism?

IX

Transcendental Idealism

Strawson and others like him start out with the expectation that transcendental arguments can be used to establish something about what the world must be like, and not just about what we must take it to be like, if we are to have experience of it. Strawson criticizes Kant for thinking they show that our minds impose certain things upon our experiences, thereby constructing a 'world of appearances': he regards this as a quite unwarranted extra step, enmeshing Kant in 'the imaginary subject of transcendental psychology'.[1] The conditions are not read in by us, it is just that unless the world were of a certain kind – unless, for example, there were objects enduring in time and located in something akin to space – self-conscious experience would not be possible. In fact, however, the arguments we have been considering (Strawson's as well as Kant's) generally do not seem directed towards conclusions about the world, but only towards showing that we must apply certain concepts, like the concept of an object, in our experience. To say we must apply the concept of an object in our experience is to say we must think there are objects; but it would take a further move to show that there actually are.

Despite our lack of success with transcendental arguments it is worth going into this a little, for it raises the question how much such arguments can reasonably be expected to prove. Stroud has maintained that as a rule it is only with the help of the Verification Principle that they can reach conclusions about the world,[2] and I think an examination of the matter will show that Stroud is broadly right. It will also show that it is Strawson, not Kant, who is taking an unwarranted extra step.

There is certainly no impossibility in someone's producing a transcendental argument which does show how the world must be, not just how we must think it to be. Some such arguments are very plausible;

one, to which we shall return, is that experience requires a subject to have the experience, and many people find equally persuasive the argument that experience requires a world of events ordered in time. It may be that similar arguments can be found which will directly establish stronger conclusions about the world; either starting from the minimal premise that we have experience (or knowledge), or else taking some stronger assumption about what our experience is like. But it cannot be said that this looks likely to get us far. The mere fact that we have certain experiences does not seem likely to entail many conclusions about how the world must be.

We can do better if we are prepared to accept something less than entailment. Normally, of course, we think that the fact we have the experiences we do is explained by the way the world is, and we can look upon such ordinary beliefs as the belief in reidentifiable, persisting objects as part of a theory based upon our sense-experience and satisfactorily accounting for it. But in the present context this is not good enough. The argument is not transcendental: it does not offer conditions logically necessary for the experience we have, but only conditions empirically required to explain it. And we cannot take on trust the principles we ordinarily rely on in constructing explanations and theories. Our theory goes beyond the evidence, in claiming for example that objects continue to exist unperceived; to do this it relies on the principle that the simplest theory is likely to be correct – only so can we decide against the alternative hypothesis that objects spring into existence whenever a percipient comes near. It is such principles that the sceptic doubts, and they therefore need to be justified. And they cannot be justified by appeal to experience, for it is these very principles that we have to use to assess the legitimacy of any appeal to experience. If we could find some transcendental argument which showed that they would – always or usually – yield the right results, that would serve our turn, but it would be optimistic to suppose that any such transcendental argument can be provided. For it would have to show not simply that these principles are natural or convenient, or that they conform to our standards of rationality, but that they lead us to the truth about how things really are.

An alternative suggestion is that our experiences may provide us not just with evidence on which to base a theory, but with 'criteria' for the truth of our beliefs about the world – in something like Wittgenstein's sense.[3] Sometimes people who make this suggestion seem to be claiming only that to doubt these beliefs in the circumstances would be irrational by our standards of rationality, without attempting any defence of these standards. In that case all we need say is that a defence is clearly required. More usually, however, they mean that the experiences offer some sort of quasi-logical guarantee of the truth of the relevant beliefs, though a guarantee of a less than watertight kind – one that holds 'most of the time' or 'other things being equal'. But this also requires defence, and again a transcendental argument would seem to be called for; again without great prospect of its being provided. The situation is much as before, except that the principles needing justification are not general principles of scientific reasoning but specific principles about how evidence supports particular types of belief. The problem cannot of course be avoided by contending that these principles are 'built into the concepts' that we ordinarily use, for that only transfers the issue to whether these concepts are appropriate. No serious epistemological (or zoological) issue is resolved by introducing the concept of a runicorn, designed to be just like our concept of a unicorn except for incorporating the stipulation that under normal circumstances the sighting of a red patch constitutes adequate grounds for believing that there is a runicorn – and therefore, indeed, a unicorn – in the neighbourhood. It may be that we do use concepts which have such evidential principles built in. But even if it could be shown that it was transcendentally necessary for us to use them this would not guarantee that the evidential principles were any more correct than the one built into 'runicorn' is. It would show only that we had to treat them as correct. The theory that forces itself upon us is still our theory; it may not be the right one, but just how we have to think if we are to make sense of our experience.

It does seem reasonable to suppose it may be easier to show that we must have certain concepts or beliefs than to establish what the world is really like – in spite of our failure to establish very much on either count. But anyone who subscribes to the Verification Principle will regard this separation between what we believe and what is really the case as highly artificial, for as Stroud points out the Verification Principle would allow us to bridge the gap. According to it no one can have a belief without knowing how he could, in principle, verify or falsify that belief; i.e. discover whether it is really true or false, and not simply whether it passes certain tests we happen to approve of. Similarly no one can have a concept without knowing how he could, in principle, determine whether or not that concept is genuinely instantiated. This disposes of the problem at a stroke; in effect it guarantees that our ordinary methods of verification are adequate, for they are the only ones we know how to use, and without reliable methods of verification we could have no concepts and no intelligible thought. The only question is why we should accept the Verification Principle. It would be convenient to be able to bring it on like this, as a *deus ex machina*, but the very fact that it solves the problem so neatly shows how much we are assuming if we do accept it. Why should it be thought that to understand a sentence I must know how to find its real truth-value, instead of simply knowing what place it has within the web of my belief?

Various weaker forms of verification may be devised, but as long as they are powerful enough to bridge the gap between what we believe and how things are the same difficulty will arise with them. The most plausible forms, I think, are those which do not bridge the gap at all. It is reasonable to hold that to understand many words and sentences I must know what empirical conditions are normally taken to justify asserting the sentence or making some use of the word. But this is not a matter of discovering how the world is, but only of seeing how certain elements fit into our general theory about the world.

Some people would hold that there is a large class of concepts which are learned through paradigm cases, in at least the majority of which – just because they are paradigms – the application of the concept cannot but be correct. This may be true of concepts which simply describe the content of our experience, but for concepts which go beyond that it is not true at all. It would be logically possible for a child to learn English even though all his experience was a systematic hallucination, produced by a clever neurophysiologist who manipulated his brain. He could be taught to use the word 'chair' when he had the visual and tactual sensations we associate with coming across a chair, and in general he would learn to apply his words within the make-believe world the neurophysiologist was creating for him. But if the electrodes were removed, and he were released into the everyday world, he would be able to apply them there without further teaching; even though the 'paradigms' by which he learned them were one and all illusions. In learning the word 'chair' he learned not just to associate that word with certain visual and tactual impressions, he also learned an element of theory: chairs are objects which persist independently of our perceiving them. He learned the word under circumstances which were from his point of view indistinguishable from those under which we learn it, only in his case the theory (however reasonable) is false, for he never does perceive a genuinely independent object. And it may be the same with us.[4]

I am not trying to recommend a particularly futile kind of scepticism, but merely to point out, following Stroud, that the conclusions most transcendental arguments can be expected to establish are about ourselves and our beliefs, not about the world. To see this as a reason for distress at our alienation from reality would of course be absurd, and it is an absurdity Kant is anxious to expose. For when he contrasts the world of appearances – the world as we believe it to be on the basis of our canons of scientific procedure and theory-construction – with the world of things as they are in themselves, it is to make the point that speculation about things in themselves is empty and without purpose. What we can determine empirically about the world belongs to the world of appearances, for the world of appearances is just the world as we take it to be when we make the best use of our scientific principles. And for all ordinary purposes this is good enough. Our theory works; the fact that with different principles different theories could be constructed which would work equally well, like the theory that objects spring into being at the approach of an observer, need not disturb us.

We can conclude from this that Strawson is over-optimistic in what he expects from transcendental arguments. His supposedly austere re-interpretation of Kant turns out to be far less moderate than a more truly Kantian position, which only expects these arguments to provide conclusions about our concepts and beliefs – about the world of appearances and not about things in themselves. Though at the same time Strawson is right to this extent, that there is nothing in the character of transcendental arguments themselves that restricts them to conclusions of this sort; it just seems most improbable that many will turn up which establish stronger results, and those put forward by Strawson himself could only hope to do so by relying on something like the Verification Principle. It may be objected that there is a lot more to Kant's distinction between the two worlds, and the transcendental idealism to which that distinction belongs, than there is to the comparatively harmless distinction between our theory about the world and how the world really is. Actually I do not think there is as much to Kant's distinction as there appears to be, but we shall return to that shortly. It may also be suggested, however, that since we have not been very successful in our search for valid transcendental arguments of any kind, the fact that it is Strawson and not Kant who expects unreasonably much from them is of comparatively little importance. But at the least something a little like transcendental idealism has turned out to be more plausible than is often supposed, and this may encourage us to have a closer look at the thesis of transcendental idealism itself. There may be more of value in it than the recent contemptuous dismissals would lead us to believe.

It will be remembered that Kant's solution to the problem of synthetic a priori judgments is a double one, though he fails to separate the two strands. Originally his idea was that synthetic a priori knowledge is possible because the mind reads certain things into the world of appearances in constructing it. When he came to extend this idea beyond the limits of the *Inaugural Dissertation*, and to hold that certain a priori concepts were read in by the mind as well as the forms of intuition, he saw a need to distinguish those concepts which genuinely belonged to the construction from other non-empirical concepts which – like the concepts of fate and destiny – find no proper application even within the world of appearances. So he introduced transcendental arguments, and in particular the transcendental deduction of the categories, as a means of showing that those pure concepts are objectively valid in the world of appearances. Now as Strawson and others have insisted one can jettison the mind-imposition thesis and still regard transcendental arguments as capable of providing important conclusions. But one can also return to Kant's earlier position, and stress the transcendental idealism while setting no great store on transcendental arguments. One must then tackle in some other way the problem of why some non-empirical concepts should be objectively valid and others not, but as we shall see this is less of a difficulty than it appears.

Setting transcendental arguments aside, then, it still seems evident that our beliefs about the world form a theory which goes beyond the evidence. This evidence must come through the senses; for the moment let us suppose it comes in the form of sense-data, more or less as Locke and Hume thought. The theory is constructed on the basis of the evidence, but sense-data can hardly supply the principles we use in theory-construction – our canons of inductive evidence and the grounds we adduce for preferring one theory to another when neither is contradicted by the facts. These principles can therefore be called a priori, and we must supply them ourselves; it is in the nature of the human mind to react to the evidence in this particular way. By their help we build up our scientific picture of the world of neutrinos, photons, and gravitational force; by their help likewise we build up from the sense-data our everyday picture of the world of rocks and trees and waterfalls. To speak of ourselves as the creators of the world as we know it may be a misleading way of putting this, but it is not entirely wrong. It might be taken to suggest that we had some choice in how to effect the construction; and that there was no more to the world than the picture we make of it. But Kant takes care to repudiate both these misleading suggestions. The second is taken care of by his insistence upon things in themselves; the first by his contention that these principles force themselves on us through the very forms of judgment in which our thought must be expressed.

For these principles of theory-construction are, in Kant's eyes, the categories; or more precisely the principles of pure understanding to which the categories give rise when schematized in space and time. Much work has been done on scientific method since Kant's day, and the character of theories has become clearer. Looked at in this light his list of principles will not do; he imposes too specific restrictions on the shape the theory must take, insisting from the outset that it must yield a world of substances in thoroughgoing interaction with one another and governed by causal laws; ordered, moreover, in Euclidean space and with qualities susceptible of ordinal measurement. It would be better to look for more general principles applicable to theories of all kinds, which in connection with the sensory data give us a picture of the world more or less as Kant describes it. Not that finding them is an altogether straightforward or uncontroversial affair: simplicity and convenience are obvious desiderata, but it is no easy matter to say in what they consist or what other principles are needed to supplement them. Fortunately it is not necessary for our purposes to provide a list of the principles that should replace Kant's, and I shall make no attempt to do so.

Indeed, the fact that Kant's own list is inadequate is essentially a detail, now that we have rejected his method of deriving categories from the fundamental conditions for thought and experience, and the transcendental argument that was designed to show we cannot avoid using them. On what really matters Kant is perfectly right: 'the understanding is the origin of the universal order of nature, by virtue of which everything that is only to be known through experience is necessarily submitted to its laws.'[5] One can agree with him on this without committing oneself to the details of his semi-psychological account of how the mind works, with its systematic investigation of the various faculties. As I said in chapter VI, I cannot believe that Kant himself assigned great significance to much of this talk of faculties; its very inconsistency shows that it was only a vehicle (perhaps rather a fashionable, up-to-date vehicle) for his main point about the activity of the mind. We must actively interpret the sense-data we receive, finding in them new connections which were not obvious at first glance, such as the connection between the various different representations of a single changing object. So our activity can be called a kind of synthesis. On the basis of the sensory data, the mind synthesizes that ordinary view of the world which all of us share.

But this is only part of Kant's theory. It is the part he emphasizes in the *Prolegomena*, where the categories are said to be required for judgments about objects ('judgments of experience') but not for descriptions of one's own sense-experiences. It is the part which, I suggested earlier, marks the second stage of Kant's development, when having recognized the categories as a priori concepts he did not yet see they were needed even for the most elementary experience – even for that synthesis of apprehension which 'renders perception possible' (B 161). But Kant shares the reservations many people feel about the idea that sense-data provide us with the evidence on which to build our theory; he would agree with those who point out that there is no kind of experience, however primitive, which is not coloured by interpretation. There can be no awareness of what we passively receive from outside, without some synthetic activity by the mind. One does not naturally talk or think in sense-datum language, and how we perceive things depends to a surprisingly large extent on what we think we are perceiving. Even if that were not so, the qualities we perceive need us to classify them. Perceptions are, as Hume says, distinct existences; if we classify together a whole range of them as green, there is nothing in the perception that compels us to make this classification rather than some other. Instead we might have classified together the green ones experienced before midnight tonight and the blue ones afterwards: these are just the things Goodman calls 'grue', and in this case 'grue' would have been a primitive concept for us, and we might have seen no similarity between what is green (and therefore grue) today and what is green (and not grue) tomorrow. Or again we might have failed to see any similarity amongst the things we call green even at one time, and classified together the visual appearance of one particular blade of grass, the coffee in my cup, this page, and the planet Mars. Such radically different forms of classification seem to us highly unnatural, and if the differences were great enough we might find it difficult to communicate with someone who saw similarities in so strange a way. But there would be nothing logically wrong with his alternative classifications, though they might make it harder for him to make sense of the world. One can put things into sets in endless ways; any arbitrary set could be classified together by someone, and they would then be similar for him. He would be synthesizing the manifold differently from us. So unavoidable do our own classifications seem that we tend to think the similarities we see are objective and independent of us, but 'combination does not lie in the objects, and cannot be borrowed from them' (B 134). If God had decided to mark out certain similarities as 'right' this would still have placed no logical constraint on the making of classifications which cut across them, nor would it have made it more likely that the similarities we find so natural are the same as these 'right' ones.[6]

So the synthetic activity of the mind is required at all levels of experience. But the fact that we cannot be aware of what is empirically given without classifying it and applying concepts to it does not, of course, mean that we create experience for ourselves entirely and that nothing is empirically given at all. That would be absurd. What we do is introduce the principles whereby the data are classified together under concepts and used to support or confute theories. But as Kant would say our minds must be receptive as well as spontaneous; the data themselves must come from some other source.

On the basis of our experience, then, we build for ourselves a picture of the everyday world which is satisfactory for ordinary purposes and which can therefore be taken as true. Alternative theories might serve just as well, but that does not matter so long as our one works and gives the right results. The construction is not phenomenalistic, first because the theory makes claims, e.g. about objects, which are not to be analysed into sense-datum statements, and secondly because sense-data themselves involve synthesis and are therefore part of the construction. But perhaps we can call it a *quasi*-phenomenalistic construction without being too misleading.

Although Kant calls it the world of appearances he does not of course mean to identify it with the set of all the things that seem to us true. We often make mistakes; we misdescribe our experiences and we put forward badly chosen theories. But it is by means of our own principles that they are shown to be so. What is true in the world of appearances is not what seems at first sight to be so, but what is yielded by the most thorough application of our principles to the data.[7] So we are far from the full truth about the world of appearances; that is what we should have if science were completed – completed in accordance with the principles that govern human thought.

We can now see why it was not necessary to find a transcendental argument in order to show that the categories are objectively valid. They genuinely apply within the world of appearances, as the concepts of fate and destiny do not, because within that world it is our principles themselves that determine the standards: they are the yardstick of objectivity. If in practice we can use the general agreement of observers as a mark of objectivity, this is because our principles lay it down that most people are likely to be right and discount the possibility of collective delusions. If we ask whether these principles are themselves objectively valid the question is self-answering; as Kant says, they are constitutive of the world of appearances, and so are bound to hold within it. But they are constitutive of it not because no experience, or no experience of an objective world, would be possible with different principles, but just because they are the ones we use in our construction.

How does this differ from Kant's transcendental idealism? There is one important respect in which it does differ from the position Kant clearly holds, though not from the position he ought to hold. For it is certainly his opinion that the world of things in themselves is quite unlike the world of appearances, not even being in space and time. Nothing in what I have said offers the slightest reason for thinking the real world will be in any way different from the world of appearances, let alone so radically different as that. On the contrary, the world of appearances represents the best guess that can be made, using the resources of the human mind, as to the nature of the real world, and though we have no guarantee that it is an accurate guess we have certainly no reason to suppose it is not. But this ought to be admitted by Kant. For his official position is that we can know nothing at all about things in themselves, because they lie beyond the limits of possible experience; which certainly precludes our knowing that they are not just as we take them to be.

Beyond the limits of possible experience we can know nothing, we can only speculate: that is Kant's case against the dogmatic metaphysicians. What we can discover empirically belongs to the world of appearances, and synthetic a priori propositions can be recognized as true only if we read them into the world of appearances; they must either be statements of the principles we use in constructing it, or true in consequence of such principles. It is important to remember, though, that Kant does not think the speculations of the dogmatic metaphysicians are unintelligible. If he did his entire account of dialectical illusion would founder, for it depends on our being able to think about things in themselves and to form beliefs about them which can neither be supported nor confuted. It is true that he occasionally says that talk about things in themselves is 'meaningless', but he makes clear that he does not regard it as nonsense but only as futile and lacking in empirical application.[8] And before the rise of the Vienna Circle people did not automatically interpret 'meaning-less' as equivalent to 'unintelligible', even if we find it natural to nowadays. Strawson has furthered the confusion here by speaking of 'Kant's principle of significance':[9] Kant has no principle of significance. He places limits on the extent of human knowledge, but does not accuse his opponents of talking nonsense.

But we cannot remain satisfied with the world of appearances, and this is where many of Kant's difficulties and confusions arise. Where material objects are concerned it is perhaps all we need worry about; if teapots and cricket bats are only our quasi-phenomenalist construc-tions it does not greatly matter as long as they behave as we expect. But with minds it is different. We can hardly be content to regard them as quasi-phenomenalist constructions, for it is important to us that people (both ourselves and others) really exist in their own right. In Kantian terminology we cannot regard people as mere appearances, but only as things in themselves. Yet we think we have good reason to believe in their existence.

Kant says extraordinarily little about other minds. The only one he discusses at any length is a very special case: God. His discussion con-sists largely in a refutation of the classical arguments for the existence of God – the ontological argument, the cosmological argument, the argument from design; arguments he considers doomed from the start because God is not an object of possible experience. It is not just the fact that no man has seen God at any time that leads Kant to say he is not an object of possible experience, nor is it simply that he is the supreme being, but that he is conceived as having a mind like ourselves. We could not therefore be satisfied with a proof which showed a need for God within the world of appearances. We want to know whether he exists in the noumenal reality, as we believe our friends and our enemies do.

All he says about other minds in general is that one must conceive them by analogy with one's own.[10] But with one's own mind the problem is acute. It must be more than a quasi-phenomenalist construc-tion: it must exist to carry the construction out. I am conscious of my own states through inner intuition and can construct out of them an object which I call myself, rather as Hume builds the self out of a bundle of perceptions,[11] but this object belongs to the world of appearances and is constructed according to its rules. It is 'myself as I appear to myself'. There must be more to me than this appearance or there would be nothing to appear to; though in conformity with Kant's general position 'I have no *knowledge* of myself *as I am* but merely as I appear to myself' (B 158). And therefore he says 'I cannot know as an object that which I must presuppose in order to know any object' (A 402). But how can I presuppose it without knowing something about it, namely that it exists?

Incidentally, he is not making Ryle's peculiar point that the 'I' is systematically elusive: that I can never catch my present self, though I can be fully aware of the 'I' of a moment ago. According to Ryle,[12] 'My commentary on my performances must always be silent about one performance, namely itself, and this performance can be the target only of another commentary'. This is unargued, and supported only by wit and rhetoric; it seems quite untrue. In this sentence I am commenting on my present performance, namely the writing of this sentence itself. Kant's point is rather that although I can know myself (including my present self) as an object of experience I must also be more than just an item in the phenomenal world, or there would be no subject for experiences and therefore no experience.

It is clear enough what his position ought to be if his views on the limitations of human knowledge are to be taken seriously. I must think of myself as a genuinely existing substance, but I am not entitled to affirm that I am one – this is the mistake made by the dogmatic metaphysicians who are attacked in the chapter on the paralogisms. The paralogisms are fallacious syllogisms by which these metaphysicians (whom Kant calls rational or transcendental psychologists) attempt to establish conclusions about the self: that it is a substance, that it is simple and unitary, that it retains its identity through time, that it is independent of outer things. According to Kant it is a requirement of the unity of apperception that I should think of myself like this, but from the fact that one must think something we cannot infer that it must be the case, unless we limit ourselves to the world of appearances. Within that world the inference can hold, for the world of appearances is our construction. But the rational psychologist wants conclusions about the self as it really is, and these he has no right to draw. Putting his argument in syllogistic form, as Kant does, what happens is this. He takes as a first premise something which is true within the world of appearances: in the case of the first paralogism, 'That which cannot be thought of except as substance is substance', or in the slightly expanded version Kant gives 'That which cannot be thought otherwise than as subject does not exist otherwise than as subject, and is therefore substance'. He then takes a second premise which Kant also accepts as true: 'As a thinking being I cannot think of myself otherwise than as subject'. But when I think about myself as subject it is not my observable, phenomenal self that I am interested in, but the real or noumenal self which does the constructing. So the rational psychologist is not entitled to put the two premises together and draw his conclusion, that I 'exist also only as a subject, that is, as substance' (B 411).[13] The second and third paralogisms follow this model as well, and the fourth is also said to, though (as so often with the fourth of Kant's tetrads) it does not quite fit – and moreover has radically different versions in the two editions of the *Critique*.

So far so good. For what we have here is an elaborate and careful criticism of the consequences Descartes draws from '*cogito*'. It is nowadays a commonplace to point out that Descartes ought not to infer that he is a unitary thinking substance, independent of other substances and persisting through time so as to be the subject of many thoughts. At best he can claim that his present thought has a subject; nothing follows about its identity with subjects of other thoughts, or about its capacity for independent existence as a substance, though equally clearly I can hardly avoid regarding myself as a continuing and self-subsistent thing. On the other hand, however unjustified Descartes is, Kant's views about the limits of human knowledge commit him not only to denying that these conclusions could ever be justified by any means, but also to denying he can properly claim that he exists even simply as the subject of '*cogito*', whatever else he may or may not be.

And this is an uncomfortable position. Uncomfortable for anyone, but especially so for Kant. For the existence of the self, as subject if not as enduring and independent substance, is a condition of the possibility of experience. In the transcendental deduction appeal is frequently made to the part the self must play in synthesis; and this could not be simply the phenomenal self, even if Kant did not repeatedly make it clear that synthesis is the spontaneous activity of the self as it is in itself. The construction of the phenomenal world must be effected somehow; it could not be that the agent of the construction, and the act of constructing, belonged only to the world of appearances and were themselves constructions. One's bootstraps have only finite strength.

How he resolves this is swathed in an obscurity indicative of confusion. So far as an answer does emerge it is that although I have no intuition of myself as subject, I am nevertheless *conscious* of myself as subject in the awareness of the 'I think' that accompanies all my representations. My real existence is somehow 'given' not through sensibility but to consciousness directly.[14]

In the transcendental synthesis of the manifold of representations in general, and therefore in the synthetic original unity of apperception, I am conscious of myself, not as I appear to myself, nor as I am in myself, but only that I am. This *representation* is a *thought*, not an *intuition*. (B 157.)

He stresses that the only thing I am conscious of is my existence; I do not have an intellectual apprehension of myself as noumenon which would enable me to know what my real self is like. But why could I not have? The flood-gates are opened; the principle that I can have no knowledge regarding things in themselves has been breached. It is not surprising that Kant is reluctant to admit this, and that a certain lack of lucidity results.

But in fact the damage is not irreparable. It appears so only if, like Kant, we fail to distinguish the two solutions to the problem of synthetic a priori judgments, by transcendental idealism and by transcendental arguments. Transcendental idealism is no use here, but as we have seen there is nothing to prevent transcendental arguments from establishing conclusions about how things really are in themselves – although valid arguments to such conclusions are unlikely to be common. That is what we have in the present case. There is no need to invoke a special and unexplained consciousness of the existence of the self, for without the self as the active subject of synthesis neither knowledge nor experience could be possible at all. By not distinguishing the two solutions Kant is prevented from recognizing his own commitment to this simple and straightforward argument, and from seeing how in this instance he can give a perfectly satisfactory account of how one can know something about the real world.

This is not the only transcendental argument to a conclusion about things in themselves which we can find in the *Critique of Pure Reason*. For he considers that besides myself other things must exist in their own right to affect me. Only so can I receive the sense-manifold as something given, and indeed 'it follows, of course, from the concept of an appearance in general that something must correspond to it which in itself is not appearance' (A 251, cf. B xxvi f.). As an argument one may not find this as convincing as the last; some of Kant's successors were bold enough to reject its conclusions, and to regard even the sense-manifold as entirely the creation of the knowing mind. But such radical idealism is a singularly unattractive theory, rather in the way that solipsism of the present moment is unattractive. Most of the time Kant seems to have thought it too silly to be worth bothering about. In the *Prolegomena* he just says that it 'has never entered his mind to doubt' the reality of things in themselves, and when his disciple Fichte moved in that direction he reacted with unusual (and irrational) impatience.[15] It is hard not to sympathize with him. It may well be that there is no way satisfactorily to refute the theory that everything is created by the knowing mind, but there can be little positive reason to hold it if transcendental idealism remains a viable alternative. And transcendental idealism, which admits the existence of things in themselves while recognizing that our theory about the world is our theory and may not be the right one, does have the support of reflective common sense.

X

Postulates, Ideas and Aesthetic Judgments

1 The moral world

Kant is thus obliged to admit that his noumenal, active self exists even though it does not belong to the world of appearances: it must exist in order to carry the quasi-phenomenalistic construction out. He also has another reason, which we have not so far touched on, for at least *believing* in its existence. The Second Analogy supposedly showed that within the phenomenal world every event has a cause. But in Kant's view – not an uncommon or an unreasonable one – it is a condition of being morally accountable that one's will be free, in a sense incompatible with its being determined by antecedent causes. If I belonged only to the phenomenal world I could not therefore be free, or morally responsible. For the moral law to apply to me I must be something more: a noumenon, existing in its own right and determining its choices independently of phenomenal conditions. I cannot take morality seriously unless I assume I have this noumenal freedom, even though the matter may not be susceptible of any theoretical proof.

And I have to make the same assumption where other people are concerned. I can happily regard teapots as mere quasi-phenomenalistic constructions to which no noumenal reality corresponds, but I cannot take this view of other human beings. If I did I could not ascribe to them the freedom required for accountability, and I should be failing to treat them as subjects of experience co-ordinate with myself and possessing the same moral rights and the same intrinsic moral worth as I do.

This assumption that I and others are free noumenal agents Kant calls a postulate of pure practical reason. Altogether there are three such postulates, suppositions which morality requires us to make but which cannot be established theoretically. The other two are, that the soul is immortal, and that God exists. Unfortunately Kant's argument for regarding these as being equally necessary assumptions is abnormally tenuous, as he sometimes seems to be aware.

It starts from the idea that serious moral action would be impossible unless one could regard one's act as helping to promote the Highest Good, a state of affairs in which virtue and happiness are jointly maximized. It is an important tenet of Kant's that the only thing inherently valuable in its own right is virtue, but that is not to deny that a totality containing virtue and happiness is better than one containing virtue alone – provided that the happiness comes as the reward of virtue, and not out of all connection with it.[1] For the value of happiness, though real, is derivative and secondary: in conjunction with virtue it is a good, but without it it is entirely lacking in worth.

> A rational and impartial spectator can never feel approval in contemplating the uninterrupted prosperity of a being graced by no touch of a pure and good will, and . . . consequently a good will seems to constitute the indispensable condition of our very worthiness to be happy. (*Grundlegung* p. 2, Ak. IV: 393.)

Now it is unfortunately obvious that in the world as we know it there is no prospect of bringing about the Highest Good, and one may despair of even making significant advances towards it. Virtue is usually not rewarded, and nothing in the laws of nature gives us any reason to think it ever will be rewarded in a systematic way. On the other hand, we have to think of the Highest Good as a possibility, and one which we can help to bring about through moral action. This demands that we postulate something beyond the sensible world: there must be a supreme and benevolent being who so arranges things that our virtuous acts do lead towards the Highest Good, and who has it in his power to set up that state of affairs in which virtue is automatically rewarded.[2] Moreover it is not enough that these things should come about only for the benefit of our distant descendants; we each have a direct and personal interest in the Highest Good. We can never get close to it in this life, but all the same we must regard it as a goal to which we ourselves can approximate more and more nearly without limit; which we shall only be able to do if our souls are immortal.[3]

Evidently there are a number of things wrong with this argument. But since it turns on the idea of the Highest Good it is enough to observe that one can perfectly well be a serious moral agent while remaining altogether pessimistic about whether virtuous acts achieve anything or will ever be rewarded. Kant attempts to deny this, in a particularly unsatisfactory passage on Spinoza. Spinoza is put forward as the example of a righteous man who thinks himself an atheist. As he sees things,

Deceit, violence and envy will always be rife around him, although he himself is honest, peaceable, and benevolent; and the other righteous men that he meets in the world, no matter how deserving they may be of happiness, will be subjected by nature, which takes no heed of such deserts, to all the evils of want, disease, and untimely death, just as are the other animals on the earth. And so it will continue to be until one wide grave engulfs them all – just and unjust, there is no distinction in the grave – and hurls them back into the abyss of the aimless chaos of matter from which they were taken – they that were able to believe themselves the final end of creation. (*Critique of Judgment* § 87, Ak. V: 452.)

If his atheism is sincere this gloomy picture must lead him to abandon the futile pursuit of the Highest Good and so to give up morality. On the other hand,

perhaps he resolves to remain faithful to the call of his inner moral vocation. . . . If so he must assume the existence of a *moral* author of the world, that is, of a God. (*Ibid.*)

This is obviously wrong. If the atheist can adhere to the moral law despite his depressing beliefs so much the better for him, and there is no reason why he should not be able to. Kant himself stresses that an action has moral worth only if it is done out of respect for the moral law, not for the sake of achieving any end; an end can have value only if the moral law requires us to promote it. (So the obligation to strive towards the Highest Good is derived from the moral law, and not *vice versa*.[4]) There is therefore – as he is aware – an actual danger in the belief in God and immortality, for the believer may allow himself to be guided by the thought of heavenly rewards and punishments, and that would for Kant be an entire abandonment of morality. Whereas the atheist who does not regard the Highest Good as attainable may still recognize his obligation to promote virtue and happiness to the modest extent he can.

However, inadequate though his argument is, Kant does hold that we must all believe in the immortality of the soul and the existence of God, as well as in the freedom of ourselves and of others, if we are to take morality seriously. 'These postulates are not theoretical dogmas, but suppositions practically necessary'.[5] We can have no speculative knowledge about such things, because they transcend the limits of possible experience, but he says rather puzzlingly that the postulates do amount to knowledge 'from a practical point of view'.[6] It is unclear what justifies this claim, or what it is supposed to amount to. Is there a difference between believing something because we must if we are to behave morally, and 'knowing it from a practical point of view'? And if not why introduce this perverse and misleading reformulation?

In fact there is no difference, and I think we can understand why Kant finds the reformulation natural if we recall what he said about the world of appearances. We can have a good deal of knowledge about the objects which make up the world of appearances, but that world and those objects are constructions from the sensory evidence, effected by the mind's synthetic activity. For a claim to be true within the world of appearances is for it to fit in the appropriate way with the sensory data and with the principles we have adopted for their interpretation. The principles of pure understanding are laid down by us as standards constitutive of the world of appearances, and it is to this that they owe their status as synthetic a priori truths. Now the postulates of pure practical reason are likewise synthetic a priori, though they do not belong to the world of appearances.[7] They have a similar part to play: they are constitutive not of the phenomenal world but of what we might call the moral world. The moral world is a construction not out of sensory evidence but out of those beliefs which morality, or pure practical reason, requires in us. Because they are beliefs which we must all share we can call them objective in a sense, just as we were able to find room for a kind of objectivity within the world of appearances. It is this objectivity which makes Kant think of it as a world, about which we can know things; though no doubt we can agree that in this case, even more than with the phenomenal world, it is a highly misleading and dangerous way of talking.

Since the moral world is constructed not from phenomena but from beliefs which practical *reason* requires it can perhaps be called a noumenal world, but if we call it such we must be careful to distinguish noumena in this sense from things as they really are in themselves. The real nature of things remains, of course, as unknown as ever; all we have done is to observe the need for a certain system of beliefs and decide to regard them as constitutive of a derivative objectivity. This idea of a moral world, contrasted with the ordinary world of appearances, goes back to the *Dreams of a Spirit-Seer*, where it is conceived of as a spiritual realm governed and united by the 'rule of the general will';[8] while in the *Fortschritte* Kant actually speaks of God, freedom and immortality as creations of our own minds, in a manner reminiscent of his talk of the mind as making nature: 'From a practical point of view we make these objects for ourselves, so far as we consider the idea of them to be helpful for the purpose of our pure reason.'[9] But of course we could never be content to regard them as being only that. In the case of the world of appearances we can reconcile ourselves to viewing material things as quasi-phenomenalistic constructions; but what matters to us here is that these beliefs should really be true, and not that they should meet some derived standard of truth and objectivity which is a function of what we ourselves believe.

These synthetic a priori principles which we can be said in one sense or another to know are constitutive of the 'worlds' they describe. Besides them Kant recognizes also principles of another class, regulative principles, which force themselves upon us in a somewhat similar way but which play no part in determining the objective character either of the world of appearances or of any other world. Regulative principles are not to be understood as true or false but rather as setting out rules for the understanding to follow. It is natural to state them in a propositional form, but that leads us into the mistake of thinking they express synthetic a priori truths about the world of appearances; properly we must recognize that the claims they make could never be established by any possible experience, and that all we are entitled to do is to act as if they were true.[10]

This tendency to take as true principles we ought only to treat as regulative is the fundamental error denounced in the Transcendental Dialectic. We have come across it already in connection with the Paralogisms. I must think of myself as a unitary, persisting, simple substance, and I must act accordingly, but I cannot legitimately claim to know such things about myself. In a similar way, Kant thinks, we have a need to employ regulatively the ideas of the world as a totality and of God as its creator, and we are perfectly entitled to do so; but we cannot claim knowledge about such things, for they are not objects of possible experience. (We cannot claim practical knowledge of them either; pure practical reason does not require belief in a creator, but only in a God who helps to bring about the Highest Good.) When we try to argue seriously about the world as a completed whole we get into contradictions – the Antinomies. And the failure to realize the limitations of our knowledge leads us into specious attempts to prove the existence of God.

In general one can understand Kant's refusal to treat these principles as a further class of synthetic a priori truths constitutive of the world of appearances.[11] But why does he not do with them as he did with the postulates of pure practical reason, and call them constitutive of some other 'world', the factitious objectivity of which is a reflection of our general agreement about them? Not only, I think, because it would be confusing to do so, even more here than in the moral case. More importantly because the practical postulates must actually be believed by all rational moral agents, whereas it is by no means necessary for us to suppose that the regulative principles express truths. There is a continual temptation to do so, but like all good temptations it can be overcome. What we cannot get rid of is an illusion, which may no longer deceive us any more than the standard optical illusions do once we have understood them; an illusion which can no more be prevented than we can prevent the sea appearing higher at the horizon than at the shore, since we see it through higher light rays; or to cite a still better example, than the astronomer can prevent the moon from appearing larger at its rising, although he is not deceived by this illusion. (A 297/B 353 f.)

2   More transcendental deductions

That the illusion is unavoidable he tries to show by providing a 'transcendental deduction' of the ideas of speculative reason. An 'idea' is a non-empirical concept which can find no application within the world of appearances, and the three principal ideas of speculative reason are those of the self (as a unitary substance), the world (as a completed totality), and God. The transcendental deduction of the categories was intended as a proof that the categories did have application; clearly no parallel claim can be made out for these ideas.[12] What Kant hopes to do is to provide a transcendental proof of the legitimacy of employing them

> not as *constitutive* principles for the extension of our knowledge to more objects than experience can give, but as *regulative* principles of the systematic unity of the manifold of empirical knowledge in general (A 671/B 699);

and to do this by showing we have no alternative but to use them in this way.

His argument is that reason continually drives us to seek for more and more adequate explanations, and to see the world more and more as a systematically united whole. Reason is essentially the same faculty as the understanding, which subsumes the given manifold under concepts and finds order and unity in experience; except that the understanding is conceived of as remaining within the limits of what can be determined empirically, while reason goes beyond these limits in searching for a degree of completeness and unity in explanation which no experience can ever show to be well-founded.[13]

We have seen before how the need to think of all my experiences as systematically united (in the transcendental unity of apperception) leads to the idea of myself as a simple substance. Reason's demand for completeness also leads to the idea of the world as a totality, pressing us to follow up any series of conditions as far as we can go and to treat it as though it were endless.[14] We cannot know that the world is infinite either in time or in space, but we must act as if it is, never being satisfied that we have reached its outer limit or that our researches have taken us back to the earliest moment. Analogously we must treat matter as if it were infinitely divisible, not regarding any division as ultimate, for otherwise we should be leaving something unexplained. And we must think of the chain of determining causes as if it stretched back indefinitely (though in view of the Second Analogy Kant might have been expected to allow that we can actually know that it does). 'If the conditioned is given, a regress in the series of all its conditions is *set* us *as a task*.' (A 497 f./B 526.)

In a similar, if slightly more complex, way we are led to the idea of God; as a demand now of speculative, not of practical, reason. Firstly, everything in the phenomenal world is contingent – it has to be explained by reference to some other thing that causes it – so that our need for a complete explanation can be satisfied only by going outside the world to a being which is self-explanatory and on which all things depend.[15] Secondly, it is only if we think of nature as designed by a single wise being that we can expect to find any overall systematic unity amongst its laws; especially since (according to Kant) the most satisfactory kind of explanation for reason to discover is purposive in form, so that the demand for systematic unity is in part a demand for a teleological order in things which can naturally be viewed as the outcome of a wise creator's choice.[16] These may seem rather slender arguments. But thirdly, and (as I shall argue in chapter XII) more interestingly, the working assumption we all make that the laws governing nature are such as to render its systematic unity comprehensible to us must lead to the idea of the world as designed to fit our cognitive faculties, and hence to the idea of a designer. The second and third of these arguments both invoke teleology, but for the second it is the phenomena within nature that call for teleological explanation whereas for the third it is rather that the system of natural laws must be thought of as designed to suit our capacities.

Of course the Analogies are supposed to have established that nature must be a unity in the sense of being bound together by thoroughgoing causal laws. It is a transcendental requirement that there should be such laws, in Kant's opinion. But what the laws are – what actually causes what – is a contingent matter which we can learn only from experience (of constant conjunctions), and some causal laws might be so overwhelmingly complex as to make them quite ungraspable to us. Moreover, the empirical laws we did discover might be so radically diverse that we could never attain to the more general laws underlying them, and so could never come to understand nature as a systematic totality held together by common laws.

> For the variety and diversity of the empirical laws might be so great that, while it would be in part possible to unify perceptions into an experience by particular laws which we happen in fact to have discovered, it would never be possible to unify these empirical laws themselves under a common principle. (*First Introduction to the Critique of Judgment*, Ak. XX: 209.)

So there is no transcendental guarantee that nature will be comprehensible to us to the extent that we regularly expect, and indeed very commonly find it to be.[17]

Still, whatever one may think about the later steps of the argument, this supposed transcendental deduction of the ideas of speculative reason fails right at the start. For it rests on the claim that reason inevitably pushes us to look for more and more adequate explanations. But if this claim is to play a significant role in a transcendental argument it must be more than an observation about how our minds work; Kant must think our minds have to work in this way if they are to be capable of experience at all. And indeed he does think this; but his argument for it is very weak. He points out that unless we could find some degree of uniformity amongst appearances we could not apply concepts to them at all, so that it is a requirement for experience that we should look for uniformities. Now only a rather limited amount of uniformity has to be detected for experience to be possible, as we have just seen, but Kant feels that the mind has no reason to abandon the search once that limited amount has been discovered. And because it has no reason to abandon the search, it must go on searching; even when the search leads it beyond the limits of possible experience.[18]

> The law of reason which requires us to seek for this unity is a necessary law, since without it we should have no reason at all, and without reason no coherent employment of the understanding, and in the absence of this no sufficient criterion of empirical truth. (A 651/B 679.)

But as a transcendental claim this is entirely unjustifiable, though as empirical psychology it may have some appeal. It is not transcendentally necessary that we continue the search beyond the minimum; experience would be perfectly possible for a being who rested there content, and sought for no further unity amongst appearances than is required to subsume them under concepts and make judgments about them in accordance with the categories. And in fact there would seem to be quite a few such incurious beings in the world.

In the *Critique of Judgment* the deduction of the ideas is carried a stage further with the aim of yielding something yet more ambitious: a transcendental deduction of judgments of taste, or in other words a transcendental proof of their legitimacy. Their legitimacy is in doubt because they lay claim to a certain sort of objectivity; though they are not objective in the same way as factual judgments, for they do not make assertions about any state of affairs but express the pleasure or displeasure that the speaker feels. Nevertheless when I judge that something is beautiful I am not merely expressing my own pleasure in it; I am also claiming that everyone else can be expected to feel a similar pleasure. How can I be entitled to do this?

Kant's answer is that we all feel an automatic pleasure whenever we come to understand anything better, or more adequately to grasp the workings of nature. This is because reason inevitably seeks for better and better explanations, and according to Kant the attainment of any objective is coupled with a feeling of pleasure.[19] Indeed, this pleasure will result merely from the realization that things are in some respect comprehensible to us, even before we actually comprehend them; and the awareness that things are comprehensible to us is in effect the awareness of them as being as though designed to suit our cognitive capacities. Kant calls this 'the consciousness of a formal purposiveness' in the object, and at one point (Ak. V: 222) goes so far as to identify it with the pleasure itself, though he can hardly mean this literally. Such pleasure, though subjective in the obvious sense that each person's pleasure is his own, is yet in a sense also objective. For on the assumption that everyone else sees the world as I do and has cognitive faculties similar to mine, they can be expected to feel a like pleasure in similar circumstances. This assumption is one we are entitled to make, 'as otherwise men would be incapable of communicating their representations or even their knowledge'.[20] Anyone who fails to feel pleasure in the appropriate circumstances has failed to appreciate the formal purposiveness in the object; he has failed to detect its suitability for our common cognitive capacities.

We may notice in passing that this argument is unique among Kant's transcendental arguments in taking as an explicit premise not simply that there is experience, or knowledge, but that our experience or knowledge can be communicated to others; so that in effect we have here a recognition, and at the same time a dismissal, of that problem about other minds which the *Critique of Pure Reason* simply neglected.

Aesthetic judgments are not of course to be equated with scientific discoveries; Kant's aesthetics can be called overly intellectual, but not quite as overly intellectual as that. The aesthetic judgment abstracts from any gain in knowledge or understanding which may accrue, and is concerned only with the pleasure or displeasure which we take in the object as a result of its seeming well or ill designed for our cognitive powers. Indeed quite standardly when we call something beautiful we are unable to make any illuminating cognitive judgment about it, and we call it so only because it appeals to our cognitive faculties as being, as it were, designed to suit them. Without giving us any new knowledge it gives us only the indeterminate idea of nature as comprehensible to us, and does not exhibit it as falling under any specific law. But this is enough to occasion pleasure in all beings constituted as we are, and the pleasure thus occasioned is specifically aesthetic.[21]

The alleged transcendental deduction can clearly be criticized at a number of points. It rests on the claim that we must want to find nature thoroughly comprehensible, which we have already discussed. Also on the claim that we must feel pleasure whenever we achieve (or partly achieve) an objective; which again may have some psychological plausibility, but is not an obvious a priori truth. Not, at least, if by 'pleasure' we mean a recognizable and identifiable feeling, as is required in this context; Kant's position would be uninteresting if he were to define 'pleasure' so as to make it analytically true, and he would not have accounted for our introspectible aesthetic feelings, for such 'pleasure' need never be consciously felt. At times he does come close to defining it in this trivializing way, and he is forced to admit explicitly that we often have pleasures that we do not notice: the pleasure is really there but is so familiar that it has become 'fused with simple cognition, and no longer arrests particular attention'.[22] This is an awkward consequence; who is to say what hidden pleasures and pains we may be undergoing, quite unknown to ourselves?

Still, the theory is an interesting attempt to salvage a kind of objectivity for aesthetics. Previously Kant had not believed this could be done; his 1764 essay *Observations on the Feeling of the Beautiful and Sublime* treats aesthetic feeling as a form of subjective sentiment which can only be empirically observed, and the *Critique of Pure Reason* (at least in the first edition) firmly repudiates the attempt 'to bring the critical treatment of the beautiful under rational principles' (A 21 n.).[23] But the attempt, though interesting, is hardly altogether satisfactory, even when one sets aside the inadequate transcendental deduction. Kant's theory is commonly criticized for being excessively formalistic, and with some justice, since he holds that to see something as beautiful is to see it as exhibiting an order which makes it readily comprehensible to us. It is, indeed, hard to see how nature could strike us as readily comprehensible without appearing orderly. Kant does not actually suppose that all aesthetic appreciation is appreciation of order, because he also gives a quite separate account of our feelings for the sublime, where what moves us is an awareness of nature as lacking in order. But normally we would think that there are many instances in which aesthetic appreciation has little to do with an awareness either of form or of formlessness. Pure colours can be beautiful, as can pure sounds, and it is hard to accept Kant's suggestion that what is beautiful is not the colour but the purity – allegedly a formal feature.[24] A beautiful picture or a landscape might well not be equally beautiful if every colour were replaced by its complement, although the form would be the same.

A defender of Kant's general position might try to argue that it is not simply through its orderliness that something can appear as though designed to suit our cognitive capacities. But we should still have to object that the theory intellectualizes aesthetic feeling far too much. Aesthetic appreciation is not a sort of failed cognition, nor is the enjoyment of beauty a side-effect in the process of finding things out. If what pleases us about a rose is its appropriateness for our cognitive faculties, a cockroach or a dead cow should please us as much; they are no less readily comprehensible. And an empty expanse of flat sand should be far more pleasing than a Sussex landscape, being much more regular and more easily reduced to rule by reason.

It is a further objection to the theory – and more illuminating, perhaps, for the understanding of Kant as a man – that it is primarily an account of natural beauty, and makes art altogether secondary to nature.[25] He recognizes the value of art, and of literature (especially poetry) and music as well; but 'art can only be termed beautiful, where we are conscious of its being art, while yet it has the appearance of nature'.[26] The objects of art can exhibit the same conformity to our cognitive powers that the objects of nature can, but they are not of so much direct value to reason in its attempt to understand nature better. His view seems to be that the value of a work of art must consist in its ability to convey to the mind something which at least indirectly helps us to feel at home in the world, and encourages us to think of nature as though designed to suit our cognitive capacities.[27]

It is interesting that although Kant thought he could give a transcendental deduction for the (limited) objectivity of aesthetic judgments, he did not think he could do the same in morals. It is true that he does offer some 'transcendental deductions' in the *Critique of Practical Reason* – they are the arguments we have already met for the indispensability of the postulates of pure practical reason. But they do not start from the premise that we have experience, or even that we can communicate with one another; they start instead from the 'fact of pure reason', that the moral law is binding upon us. This 'fact' is fundamental and cannot be argued for further; it 'stands fast by itself' and is not susceptible of any further deduction.[28] Kant thinks that every rational being is 'a priori conscious' of being bound by the moral law, but he cannot argue the point. He seems to take it as constitutive of rationality: just as in the theoretical sphere one cannot be rational without recognizing the laws of logic, so in the practical sphere rationality requires recognition of the moral law.[29] Of course, not even such widespread recognition proves that we really are subject to the moral law, or as Kant puts it that pure reason can really be practical: however rational the law may be, we can be subject to it only if it is possible for us to act upon it, and that requires the sort of freedom that cannot be found within the world of appearances. For practical purposes we can and must postulate that we are noumenally free agents, but there is no way of proving that we actually are, for that would require us to go beyond the limits of possible experience. The best we can do is to show that there is no contradiction in supposing both that (as noumenal agents) we are free and independent of causal determination, and also that (as inhabitants of the phenomenal world) all our behaviour is determined by causal law. Further than that we cannot go.

> Reason would overstep all its limits if it took upon itself to *explain how* pure reason can be practical. This would be identical with the task of explaining *how freedom is possible*. (*Grundlegung* p. 120, Ak. IV: 458 f.)

3 Freedom

The argument-structure in the *Grundlegung* (1785) is not quite the same as that in the *Critique of Practical Reason* (1788). In the latter Kant starts from our a priori consciousness of the moral law, and derives from that the need to postulate freedom. In the *Grundlegung*, on the contrary, he derives our consciousness of the moral law from the claim that we have to think of ourselves as free agents, and defends this in turn by arguing that only if we regard ourselves as free and as 'independent of alien influences'30 can we be rational. Here he is attempting to avoid having to take the 'fact of pure reason' as simply given, and to provide something more in the way of a proof that we cannot be rational unless we regard ourselves as bound by the moral law. The attempt fails, and it is not surprising that it is not repeated in the *Critique of Practical Reason*.

We can grant for the sake of argument that every rational agent must think of himself as free. As Kant says, he must take himself to be the author of his own decisions; though there is much to be said for the 'soft' determinist's reply, that the decisions are no less his if they are determined by elements in his character which are themselves in turn determined by his upbringing and environment. But conceding that he must think of himself as free in Kant's strong sense, why should it follow that he must recognize the moral law as binding on him? Could he not be entirely free without ever acknowledging any moral obligations at all?

It is a pity that the *Grundlegung* is such a convenient work and so standardly taken as the definitive account of Kant's view on these matters. For at this point it is radically confused in a way Kant generally was not, either before or afterwards. At the beginning of chapter III of the *Grundlegung* he actually equates freedom with following the moral law,31 and once the equation is made it is obvious that anyone who thinks he can act freely, and understands what this involves, must recognize that the moral law applies to him. But the equation is absurd, for it has the consequence that no free act can ever be wrong. Kant always took the view that one is morally responsible only for acts that are freely performed, so we get the result that the only acts one is responsible for are in accordance with the law and one can never properly be blamed for anything. And this was certainly not a result Kant wanted. 'Freedom is the greatest good and the greatest evil', he wrote in a note of uncertain date,[32] and in his later works on ethics he straightens matters out by drawing an important distinction that was not made in the *Grundlegung*: the distinction between *Wille* and *Willkür*.

The equation between freedom and obedience to the moral law is made with the help of the idea of autonomy. In the second chapter of the *Grundlegung* he argues that the autonomous will is the will which lays down the moral law for itself and makes its decisions accordingly, and in chapter III he asks 'What else then can freedom of will be but autonomy – that is, the property which will has of being a law to itself?'[33] But if 'autonomy' is understood in the same way as in the previous chapter this question is easily answered: freedom of will consists in the completely unfettered ability to decide whether to take the morally right course (i.e. to be 'autonomous') or whether to adopt instead some different line of action. This is what he later calls freedom of the *Willkür*, and it is freedom of the *Willkür* that is the source of moral responsibility. The *Willkür* is the will as we ordinarily think of it, able to choose one course or another; it is sometimes translated 'arbitrary will'. The *Wille*, on the other hand, is the good will, the will acting in accordance with the moral law which it prescribes for itself. Autonomy in Kant's somewhat technical sense is called freedom of the *Wille*, though it is rather redundant to call it such: a *Wille* which was not autonomous, not free, would be a contradiction in terms.[34]

Since every event in the phenomenal world is causally determined, genuine freedom of the *Willkür* is a luxury reserved for noumenal agents. To the question why I (as my noumenal self) choose the evil course rather than the good one, no answer can be given.[35] If I choose the evil course, I freely decide to let my sensuous inclinations have their way; it is not that they are too strong for me and determine my decision, for then I should not be properly free and accountable for my choice. Sensuous inclinations belong in any case to the phenomenal world, and cannot therefore influence the *Willkür* of the noumenal self.

Unfortunately Kant's attempt to reconcile noumenal freedom with the thoroughgoing determinism of the phenomenal world is a hopeless failure, as has often been pointed out. From a purely formal point of view he succeeds in showing that the two ideas are consistent, but at the cost of detaching freedom utterly from the context in which it was originally required: that of everyday life and ordinary moral appraisal. According to Kant the noumenal world is outside space and time; the particular decisions I am aware of making from day to day belong in the phenomenal series and must be causally determined by the previous events within that series. He wants to say that despite that I am entirely responsible for these decisions, 'for through no cause in the world can [I] cease to be a freely acting being'.[36] How can this be? It is only possible, as he occasionally admits, if my noumenal self is responsible not just for the particular decision I made on Thursday afternoon, but for the entire series of causes which constitute my empirical character and which led up to that decision.[37] And we can hardly stop here. Since it belongs to the phenomenal world my empirical character must also be causally determined – by heredity, upbringing, and the effects other people have had on me; if my responsibility is to be salvaged these also must have been freely decided upon by my noumenal self. Indeed, in view of the thoroughgoing causal interaction that the Third Analogy requires, my noumenal self must have freely chosen the entire causal series that makes up the phenomenal world. Perhaps it did so by itself, perhaps in collusion with other noumenal subjects who all happened to agree. Either way my responsibility extends far beyond my own character: I can be blamed for the First World War, and for the Lisbon earthquake that so appalled Voltaire. Gandhi is no less guilty than Amin of the atrocities of the Ugandan dictator.

The unavoidable result of taking this seriously is the complete collapse of our ordinary system of moral evaluations; and of Kant's own moral theory, which is intended to be a refined and clarified formulation of what lies behind our ordinary views.[38] In his *Lectures on Ethics* (the most popular and down-to-earth of his moral works) he recognizes a gradation of different degrees of responsibility, saying for example that if a starving man steals food he is less responsible for his theft than a well-fed man would be, because he is less free;[39] but this is incompatible with his official theory of freedom, whereby in each case the phenomenal choice is determined and the noumenal agents are equally free all the same. At all times he writes as though an action in accordance with the moral law was the sort of thing I could freely decide, on a given occasion, to perform, and not as though free choices could only be made in an atemporal realm. And it is central to his own thinking about moral and political matters that freedom is a value to be promoted. The function of the state is to guarantee

> everyone his freedom within the law, so that each remains free
> to seek his happiness in whatever way he thinks best, so long as he
> does not violate the lawful freedom and rights of his fellow
> subjects at large. (*Theorie und Praxis*, Reiss p. 80, Ak. VIII: 298.)

If 'freedom' is understood in some relatively ordinary way, as civil liberty or as the absence of certain sorts of constraint, this makes good sense, but not if freedom is the inalienable property of every noumenal will.

Kant himself thought that the most important question a moral philosopher had to face was: how can pure reason be practical? Or in other words, how can the moral law, which is a purely rational law, motivate someone to act? His answer was that it can if, but only if, the agent is free in his strong sense of the world, and that the question whether we really are free in that sense is one which can never be answered from the sources available to speculative reason. We have seen that his account of freedom is not a success. If we abandon it, and think instead of a more ordinary sort of freedom which can make its appearance within the phenomenal word – as the absence, perhaps, of external constraint – then the problem of how moral action is possible becomes quite different (the moral motive will then just be one phenomenal motive among many). But at the same time the main body of Kant's moral and political theory can be taken seriously again, and is not to be dismissed out of hand.

XI

The Moral Law

1 The categorical imperative

Considering its importance in the history of moral thought Kant's moral philosophy is surprisingly underdeveloped. It contains some major insights, but not all of them are sufficiently analysed for it to be clear exactly what they amount to. Certain claims are left so vague that one suspects him of using them as devices to get the concrete moral results he wants. His most valuable contributions are (not surprisingly) at the most abstract level, and have to do with the character and the form of the moral law; what he tells us about the content of that law, and about its applications in politics and private life, is less satisfactory and less adequately worked out.

For Kant the fundamental fact about morality is that its commands are direct and not optional. Morality is not to be pursued for the sake of anything else; it does not owe its value to anything outside itself. It is not a skill that is worth cultivating only if one happens to want the end that it subserves. Imperatives which tell us how to achieve some goal that we can take or leave Kant calls hypothetical imperatives: if we are not interested in the goal we can disregard them. Morality leaves us no such latitude and commands us unconditionally; its commands are categorical and may never be disregarded. He is thus entirely opposed to the conception of morality as just a set of recipes for achieving some external objective like happiness, for even though we all do seek for happiness there is nothing that obliges us to. The moral law can itself command us to pursue certain ends, and as we shall see it does; but it is then the law that makes the ends worth pursuing, not any independent value in the ends that makes the law worth while.

It is not of course the verbal form of an imperative which decides whether it is categorical or hypothetical. A hypothetical imperative can be expressed unconditionally – 'Put sixpence in the slot' – if the agent's goal is assumed, and it is none the less hypothetical for that. And a categorical imperative may appear in hypothetical form: 'If you see someone drowning, leap in and save them.' The point is that the categorical imperative is obligatory regardless of what desires or inclinations one may have; the hypothetical imperative depends on one's having an independent interest in some goal.

His defence of this claim about the independent and categorical character of the moral law rests ultimately on an analysis of what is involved in our ordinary, everyday thinking about morality. The first two chapters of the *Grundlegung* analyse and progressively refine what is presupposed by 'the common rational knowledge of morality', in order to show that the categorical imperative as Kant conceives it underlies our ordinary moral beliefs; it is only in the third chapter that he turns to the question whether we are really bound by such a categorical imperative at all, or whether perhaps morality is a 'mere phantom of the brain'.[1]

That the commands of morality are taken to be categorical in this sense is indeed a feature of our ordinary moral thinking. In support of his claim Kant adduces two other contentions, which can themselves also be plausibly defended by an appeal to our common understanding of morality. They are, that the moral law must bind all rational beings as such, regardless of their preferences and inclinations; and that the only thing good without qualification is a good will. (In which case, since a good will is one which acts out of respect for the moral law, there can be nothing independent of morality from which morality gets its value.) The first of these contentions is clearly acceptable; the moral law is generally felt to be the same for everyone, everywhere and always. Of course different circumstances need to be handled in different ways, but that will be taken for granted in the formulation of the moral law itself.[2] The second is not so obviously part of what we normally think, but nevertheless there is something very attractive in the suggestion that the only thing unqualifiedly good is a good will. Kant is not denying that things like happiness have value as well, but their value is not an independent one: unless a good will somehow comes into the picture they are worthless. It may be natural to aim for happiness, success, or money, but when one gets them does it not become clear that one has missed the point and that they are not, after all, what is really worth while? And if we find that wicked people have attained such goals, we definitely do not consider it a good that they should have done so. Happiness and the like are goods only when rightly distributed; we would not think so highly of a god who sent bad people to Heaven and good people to Hell as of one who pursued the more traditional policy.[3]

From the fact that the moral imperative must be categorical Kant argues that it must also be universal in form. Because we must obey the law for its own sake and not for any external inducement,

> nothing is left but the conformity of actions to universal law as such, and this alone must serve the will as its principle. That is to say, I ought never to act except in such a way *that I can also will that my maxim should become a universal law.* (*Grundlegung* p. 17, Ak. IV: 402.)

It is not immediately clear what he means by 'universal' here, but in any case the conclusion does not follow. It is compatible with the independent character of morality that the moral law should take any form whatever so long as it is obligatory in its own right. In the *Critique of Practical Reason*, however, the requirement of universality is instead derived directly from the reflection that the moral law must bind all rational beings as such;[4] and this is a more promising line to take. For to say that the law binds all rational beings just is to say that it is universal – in the sense of applying to everyone whoever they may be. The law is not different for different people.

But it soon becomes clear that Kant means more than this by calling it universal. In the sense he intends, a universal principle cannot make exceptions in favour of particular individuals, or give a special status to them. 'Do whatever R. C. S. Walker wants' could perfectly well be a principle binding on everyone, but it is not universal in this further sense, because it gives a special status to me. His argument is not adequate to show that the moral law must be universal in this sense, but only that it must bind everyone. In itself the absence of argument does not greatly matter, for the requirement is a plausible one, and could be defended by a direct appeal to the common rational knowledge of morality. What is more serious is that he never gives a precise formulation of what he means by 'universal'. It is apparently because he fails to distinguish these two senses of the word that he takes himself to have shown more than he has.

Hare, who also holds that moral principles are universal in something like this sense, gives an account of it which is much more satisfactory and precise. In his view moral principles can always be expressed in a form in which no singular terms occur; 'Do whatever R.C.S.W. wants' cannot, because it essentially contains a proper name. Of course particular moral judgments like 'Cain did wrong to kill Abel' do contain singular terms, but they must be derivable from principles which can be stated without any. This (he says) is because it is a feature of moral words that if they apply to one case, they must apply in the same way to all other cases that are relevantly similar; and this similarity can at least in principle be stated without using singular terms. So that moral principles apply not just to isolated instances but to whole classes of similar cases. Cain's action was wrong because it is in general wrong to kill your brother unless strongly provoked.[5]

Now it seems untrue that similarities can always be specified without using singular terms. One can perfectly well describe a whole class of actions as 'doing what R.C.S.W. wants' – or 'doing what Jesus says' – and here the singular terms are essential in defining the similarities. So while Hare's argument may exclude isolated particular judgments from counting as moral, it seems inadequate to rule out '(Let everyone, always) do whatever R.C.S.W. wants'. Still, argument or no argument, his conclusion is a plausible one; it is reasonable to hold that judgments not based on purely universal principles, principles statable without using singular terms, cannot count as moral judgments at all.

Hare suggests that his test can be put graphically by asking someone who says 'It is right for me to treat X in such-and-such a way' whether he would be prepared to be treated like that himself, if he were in X's circumstances. If he says 'no', that shows that he does not subscribe to an underlying universal principle that covers all the relevantly similar cases. Of course it is not always easy to put oneself in someone else's shoes; one has to imagine that one shares both his physical and his mental circumstances, so far as they are relevant to the case. This may mean taking over his past experience, his desires, his inclinations; the only thing one must not take over is his moral views, for it is one's own moral assessment of the situation that is at issue.[6] The criminal no doubt thinks he did right to steal; but the judge can imaginatively put himself into his shoes in every other way and still assent to the proposition that he did wrongly and should be punished.[7]

How easy it is will vary from case to case, and will depend very much on the strength of one's imagination. Often, indeed, one is asked to imagine something that is logically impossible: I simply would not be myself if I had as many of the characteristics of the other as the case requires, especially if he is vastly different from me – a Japanese noble-man or an Eskimo child. Fortunately our imaginations view the logical constraints on personal identity with a certain easy tolerance; one may be able to imagine the situation even if it is impossible. Nevertheless there comes a point beyond which the imagination will not stretch, and that is where Hare's question ceases to be a useful one to ask. And there are other cases too in which it will not help us – those in which there is no one at the receiving end whose shoes I can try on, as with duties which are not owed to anyone (if there are such) and duties to oneself.[8] Not that this is any objection to Hare's thesis; it just means that in these cases it is more difficult for me to find out whether the principle I subscribe to is properly universal.

Kant also offers a practical test for universalizability which appeals to the imagination; it consists in asking: would you find acceptable a state of affairs in which the principle ('maxim') on which you propose to act was regularly acted upon, as a matter of natural law, by everyone in your position? In effect this question makes the same point as Hare's, though where one of them fails to strike the imagination the other still may. For what you show by answering 'no' is that you cannot back up your maxim with a principle covering all relevantly similar cases. Morality requires you to 'act as if the maxim of your action were to become through your will a *universal law of nature*'.[9]

But this requirement, at least as Hare formulates it, still admits principles which discriminate arbitrarily between people. 'Always treat black people like animals' contains no singular terms, and someone – a 'fanatic' – might accept that if he were black he should be treated as an animal too.[10] (And he would be happy with a state of affairs in which everyone treated black people so.) One would like to say that moral principles must enjoin what we may call equality of respect; they must allow no exceptions in favour of any individual or group, however specified. Yet obviously morality does require us to act differently towards people in different categories – children, for instance, or murderers; and we feel that this does not violate the intuitive require-ments of equality of respect (unless, perhaps, we are avid proponents of Children's Lib). But what distinguishes these categories from categories like 'black people'? Hare might argue that he has come as close as one can to formulating the idea of equality of respect; he does not capture it fully, but what remains may be inherently unclear. Kant seems to intend that the moral law observe equality of respect in some fuller sense, and he would not consider it to be properly universal unless it did, but he does not recognize the difficulty involved in making the notion precise.

Even if he could clarify it he would still only have given a necessary condition that moral principles must satisfy. Principles can meet the requirement of equality of respect without being morally right. 'Always make everyone as miserable as possible' is universal not only in Hare's sense but also in Kant's: it does the fullest justice to equality of respect. So if this were where he left things he would be liable to an accusation commonly made against him: that he does not provide an adequate test for discriminating right from wrong actions. And he does often sound as though he is leaving things here.

But fortunately this is not quite all there is to the categorical impera-tive. For he points out that universality constitutes only the form of the moral law, and that besides its form it must also have a matter. This matter consists in the ends that the moral law requires us to pursue.[11] His remarks on form and matter are unnecessarily confusing, for in a different sense the moral law is said to be purely formal and to abstract from all ends; but that only means that we must obey it for its own sake, and not for the sake of any further purpose.[12] This is quite compatible with holding that it may itself require us to pursue certain aims, 'objective ends'. I adopt these ends because the law tells me to; I do not adopt the law for the sake of them.

The ends the moral law lays down must be intrinsically valuable, 'ends in themselves'. We saw that only a good will could be called good without qualification, but Kant now says that all rational beings have an intrinsic value because their wills are *capable* of becoming good. 'Rational nature exists as an end in itself.'[13] This is not properly argued, but (as so often) it does seem to correspond at least to one element in what we ordinarily think. For we do think people have rights in a way animals do not; and that what gives them these rights is not the shape of their bodies, nor their ability to argue deductively, but their capacity for moral behaviour. We would not ascribe the rights of a person to a computer or even to a chimpanzee which could do sums, unless we considered them also to be capable of recognizing moral obligations and taking part in a moral community.[14]

But what does Kant mean by calling people ends? In his later works he largely abandons this peculiar way of talking, and says that we are obliged to promote people's virtue and happiness. In the *Metaphysics of Morals* he says there are two ends which the categorical imperative prescribes: my own perfection and the happiness of others.[15] (The perfection of others is not my concern, for Kant thinks – rather oddly – that there is nothing I can do to promote it; the pursuit of my own happiness cannot be morally obligatory, since I want it in any case.[16]) Elsewhere he says we must strive for that 'Highest Good' which we have already encountered – the condition in which human perfection is maximized and happiness is maximized in proportion to it.[17] And it is clear enough from the four examples in the *Grundlegung* that his idea here is essentially the same. By committing suicide I actively prevent my own development towards perfection; by allowing my talents to rot I fail to promote that development; and in either case I am said to be treating myself merely as a means. By making a false promise I actively subordinate someone else's interest, his happiness, to my own; by failing to help others I fail to promote their happiness; and in either case I am said to be treating other people as means, not as ends in themselves.[18]

He does not say enough about this, though; there will be situations in which whatever we do one person's interests must be subordinated to another's, and he does not tell us how to handle these. More generally it might be objected that a respect for human worth need not necessarily involve a concern for happiness. As ascetic might even hold that it requires us to trample on happiness, to achieve self-realization through the mortification of desire. On this point we can again defend Kant by saying that the ordinary moral consciousness does regard happiness as worth promoting. His own line of thought is something like this. Every rational being necessarily desires his own happiness, though happiness may consist in different things for different people. But rational beings are intrinsically valuable; so how can happiness fail to be (in general) worthy of pursuit?[19]

In Kant's view, then, the moral law has a content, as well as its universal form; and this content is provided by the conception of rational nature as an end in itself. But does this mean that those versions of the categorical imperative which do not mention ends are inadequate? He gives no sign that they are; indeed, he says that the various formulations are equivalent.[20] In fact they too build in (rather quietly) something beyond the formal requirement of universality, as we can see by looking at his first discussion of the four examples.[21] 'Let everyone neglect his talents' and 'Let no one ever help anyone else' are perfectly universal; what is wrong with them is that it would not be *rational* to will them universally. No one can rationally will the neglect of talents, since 'as a rational being he necessarily wills that all his powers should be developed'. No one can rationally will that those in need should never be helped, since as a rational being he necessarily wills his own happiness, and to achieve this he will sometimes require the help of others.

The other two examples similarly turn on what one can rationally will. 'Let everyone commit suicide when life threatens more pain than pleasure' is universal, but there is something actually inconsistent about willing it (according to Kant), since one would thus commit oneself both to the pursuit of pleasure and to steps which would render the pursuit of further pleasure impossible. This may sound rather thin, and in fact elsewhere Kant tries other arguments against suicide instead.[22] The analogous argument against false promising has rather more force. 'Make lying promises when it suits you' is again formally universalizable, but to will that it should be universally followed would be to get oneself into a contradiction: for one would have to will both that there be promises, and that they be generally broken when convenient – in which case promising would lose its point. One could not rationally will both of these things. It is worth noticing that Kant is not just saying that if everyone made false promises the institution of promising would collapse; he would hardly want to forbid refusing bribes on the parallel grounds that if everyone refused bribes the institution of bribery would collapse. The point is rather that if you were to will that everyone make false promises you would be both committing yourself to support for the idea of promising, and so for the principle that promises should in general be kept, and at the same time also willing that they should not be kept; you want to exploit the institution, and you can only do that so long as it continues in being. Whereas in refusing a bribe you are not trying to exploit the institution of bribery, and are in no way committed to its support.[23]

For Kant 'rationally to will' is pleonastic: he so defines 'will' that one wills something only if one chooses it rationally.[24] So the requirement of rationality is encapsulated in such formulations as 'Act only on that maxim through which you can at the same time will that it should become a universal law'.[25] The exception is in the first chapter of the *Grundlegung*, where the moral law is introduced as requiring only 'the conformity of actions to universal law as such'. But even this, as we saw, is immediately expanded to 'I ought never to act except in such a way that I *can also will* that my maxim should become a universal law'.[26] We can now see that this reformulation is quietly introducing the crucial requirement of rationality.

The justification for introducing it lies in a point we have already met: that the moral law binds all rational beings, as such. The law must itself be rational, and can hardly therefore involve self-contradiction, or conflict with those objectives which every rational being must, in virtue of his rationality, have. Unfortunately it is far from clear what these are. Kant says they involve happiness; but what does happiness consist in? What he actually does is tacitly to build into the conception of rationality all his substantive moral views. Self-abuse, for example, is just said to be 'contrary to the ends of humanity', i.e. to what one must rationally will.[27] For the same reason it is wrong for a woman to sell her hair for wig-making, though Kant admits that this (unlike masturbation) is a less vicious crime than self-murder.[28] One would have expected a more careful analysis of rationality, especially since Hume had held that one objective cannot be called more rational than another.

Kant says that the alternative formulations of the categorical imperative in terms of ends in themselves and in terms of what one can rationally will come to the same thing.[29] No doubt he can so manipulate the notion of rationality as to make this so. He gives two other main formulations, but they are also essentially equivalent. The formula of Autonomy – 'Act in such a way that your will can regard itself at the same time as making universal law through its maxims' – adds nothing new, except by emphasizing that you must obey the moral law for its own sake and not for fear of punishment or respect for authority; the decision to obey the moral law is your own, and it cannot be forced upon you from any outside source. The other formula says 'Act as if you were through your maxims a legislating member of a Kingdom of Ends'. A Kingdom of Ends would be a morally perfect community, where everyone governed himself by the moral law and treated everybody else as ends in themselves. So we have a combination of the idea of people as ends with that of imagining one's maxim as a law of nature governing everyone's behaviour, which gives us another imaginative test to which we can submit maxims: would this be the sort of principle one could act on in a morally perfect community?[30]

The various formulations do therefore seem essentially equivalent. Some, it is true, tell one to act in such-and-such a way, others to act *only* in that way – never to act in any other way. But Kant did not think this a significant difference. If the moral law binds me simply as a rational being, and if its form and content are what we have taken them to be, I can have no holidays from morality: for the law's command is not restricted to any particular occasion, but applies to me always. I must always make sure I can rationally will my maxim as a universal law; to fail in this, ever, is to act wrongly.

Thus Kant would maintain that his categorical imperative does give us an adequate test for distinguishing right from wrong actions. In some ways it appears to do so not badly, and to come reasonably close to capturing the common conception of morality. But this may be partly because of the regrettable vagueness in his account of the content of the moral law. No real explanation is offered of what rational beings must necessarily will, or why they must; and it is not enough to talk of furthering my own perfection and the happiness of others, without making clear in what these ends consist, or how to reconcile the cases where ends conflict. Nor can we say that Kant is entirely free from confusion on what his formal requirement of universality involves. We saw that his actual argument shows only that the moral law binds all rational beings, not that it must be free of reference to particulars or call for equality of respect. And one must admit that at times he talks as if he thought this formal requirement sufficient to yield the concrete prescriptions of morality – forgetting the need for content as well as form. Such occasional confusion does afford some excuse for those who accuse him of an empty formalism in ethics. But only some excuse. A closer examination shows that beneath his sometimes careless statements there lies a much more plausible theory, even if it is inadequately developed at a number of critical points.

2 Duty and the state

One of Kant's more memorable sayings is that an action can have moral worth only if it is performed out of a sense of duty. Respect for the moral law must be the agent's motive; if he acts honestly or kindly just because he feels like it, and not because he recognizes it to be his duty, then his action, 'however right and however amiable it may be, has still no genuinely moral worth'.[31]

Strictly, however, Kant's criticism in such cases is not of the action but of the agent: it is really the agent who lacks moral worth. The action can still be called right, or in accordance with duty (*pflichtmässig*), because it conforms to the moral law, even though it is not done for the law's sake. This distinction between the morality of acts and the morality of agents is in line with our ordinary moral thinking, and Kant's insistence that the righteous man is one who acts from duty and not from inclination finds an echo there as well. One does have a tendency to feel that the person whose desires are right deserves no credit for his actions, which can only be right accidentally if it is his desires and not the moral law which guide his choice. Though we are not altogether consistent on this matter, for one also has some inclination to think such a person good just because he has those desires, and to give him credit even if he never gives a thought to the moral law.

In line with the distinction just drawn Kant divides moral theory into two parts, the Theory of Right (*Rechtslehre*) and the Theory of Virtue (*Tugendlehre*). The Theory of Right is concerned with the rightness or wrongness of acts, setting aside questions of motivation. The Theory of Virtue has to do with the moral worth of agents, and it therefore takes motivation very much into account.[32]

As always in Kant this requires to be a little qualified, and unnecessary complications are caused by his differentiating between them in several different ways. The morality of acts has to be tested by reference to the Categorical Imperative, and the Categorical Imperative does not apply directly to actions but to maxims. The maxim is the 'subjective principle' on which the agent acts, so that it looks as though the Theory of Right must consider motivation after all. But this is not so. An act can be variously described, and it is not intentional under every description. Kant's point is that in determining the rightness of actions it is the descriptions by which they are intentional that we must take when we ask, 'can acts of this kind rationally be willed as a universal law?'[33] If unknown to me the bottle from which I give wine to my guests has been laced with poison, my act is not wrong, in Kant's view; for one can will universally that wine be given to guests, and under the description 'poisoning people' the act is not intentional. Now, two agents who perform the same act intentionally may yet do so from very different motives, and this is where the Theory of Virtue comes in. If my ultimate reason for giving them wine is that this is what the moral law requires then I act virtuously; if my ultimate reason is that I want some favour out of them then my act is still right but there is nothing virtuous about it.

The Theory of Right concerns what we can be compelled to do. Nobody can be compelled to act out of a sense of duty (though they may be encouraged to), but they can be compelled to keep promises, pay debts, and in general to perform right actions.[34] Kant also says that the Theory of Virtue has to do with ends in a way that the Theory of Right does not, because no one else can compel me to adopt an end,[35] but here he seems to be confused. I can certainly be compelled to work for a certain objective, and either to achieve it or to approximate to it as closely as I can; all I cannot be forced to do is to pursue it for its own sake, or from any other particular motive. He goes on to infer that the Theory of Right should specify precisely the acts that are required of us, while the Theory of Virtue instead prescribes ends without saying exactly how we must pursue them – except that we must further them 'as much as is possible for us in the given conditions'.[36] This cannot be quite right; one can be properly compelled, and compelled by law, to bring up one's children as good citizens, though it may not be laid down exactly how one should do this.

The Theory of Right is closely connected with legality, as the German word *Rechtslehre* implies. But Kant assimilates it too closely to the legal systems of his time by stipulating (albeit not quite consistently) that it has to do only with relationships between different people.[37] For I can be compelled to look after my own interests (and Kant himself allows for precisely specified duties towards oneself); indeed, in certain cases it is very arguable that this is an appropriate field for governmental legislation. Many people would hold that to debilitate oneself through heroin should be illegal. Kant, however, has a 'liberal' conception of the proper sphere of positive law, in that he regards the state as essentially a nightwatchman functioning to prevent people interfering with the freedom of others; the basic imperative being 'act externally in such a way that the free use of your will (*Willkür*) is compatible with the freedom of everyone according to a universal law'.[38] He never provides any justification for such a restricted view of the role of governments, and never seems to appreciate that there is a need to do so. Nor does he clearly define what constitutes an infringement of the freedom of others.

He does think it right for the state to support those in need by means of taxation; but only in order to secure its own stability.[39] He clearly regards the stability of the state as an end which the Theory of Right requires us to pursue (though he does not put this in so many words, so that the contradiction with his other remarks about ends does not become obvious). It is by reference to this end that the raising of armies and police forces can be justified.[40] The establishment and continuance of states is required by the moral law, and is of such importance that however bad a government may be it is always wrong to revolt against it.

It thus follows that all resistance against the supreme legislative power, all incitement of the subjects to violent expressions of discontent, all defiance which breaks out into rebellion, is the greatest and most punishable crime in a commonwealth, for it destroys its very foundations. This prohibition is *absolute*.
(*Theorie und Praxis*, Reiss p. 81, Ak. VIII: 299.)

Kant was sympathetic to the French Revolution, and is often accused of inconsistency in this respect; but he regarded its earlier and more attractive stages not as an overthrow of the existing state, but as a voluntary transfer of power from the king to the people.[41] It is hard to resist a certain nostalgia for the time when reasonable men could think that no government could be evil enough to destroy utterly its own moral foundation; when the depths of bad government appeared to have been reached by Nero and Elagabalus, and Hitler and Amin had never been thought of.

The state is morally required, in order to safeguard the rights of every individual. It is principally property rights which Kant thinks need safeguarding, but all such rights are derived from the one fundamental right which every individual has – the right to freedom.[42] In a state of nature no man would be free to pursue his own courses without the danger of arbitrary incursions by others, and therefore the rights he has may be said to be 'provisional'; it is only in a civil society, with a system of public laws, that they are secured to him and become 'peremptory'.[43] We may say that the state rests upon a decree of the General Will, but that is only a graphic way of saying that it is morally required: it is what everyone would agree to if they decided things rationally. The General Will is *Wille*, not *Willkür*; Kant does not think of it as actually embodied in a consensus of the people, but as an 'idea', only imperfectly realized in practice.[44] In the same way he speaks of the state as founded by an 'original contract', without supposing that any such contract was historically agreed to or even that it would be agreed to by ordinary, less than rational citizens if they were asked.[45]

In an ideal state every act of government would be in accordance with the General Will – which is another way of saying it would be morally right. Real governments are less than perfect, because human nature is imperfect: 'from such crooked wood as man is made of, nothing perfectly straight can be built'.[46] Like many of his contemporaries, Kant thinks that a part of the key to good government is the separation of powers, though he never says much in defence of this claim. The three powers in the state are the legislative, the executive, and the judiciary; failure to keep them apart leads, he tells us, to 'despotic government' – government which fails to protect the freedom of its subjects and deprives them of their rights.[47] States which observe the principle of the separation of powers he calls republican,[48] and these, he believes, will generally be governed well. To be republican in this sense a state need not be in any way democratic; indeed, he recognizes that democracies are liable to become despotic, as in Cleon's Athens, since the demos will take over the executive power as well as the legislative and use it to oppress individuals and minorities.[49] Nevertheless Kant himself thinks that the wisest form of constitution to have is one in which the legislature is elected by all the citizens. Not everyone is properly a citizen, though:

> The only qualification required by a citizen (apart, of course, from being an adult male) is that he must be his *own master* (*sui iuris*), and must have some *property* (which can include any skill, trade, fine art or science) to support himself. (*Theorie und Praxis*, Reiss p. 78, Ak. VIII: 295.)

This is not as unreasonable as it may sound; he wants to ensure that his electorate will come as close as possible to expressing the ideal General Will, and thinks that it cannot be expected to do so if it includes children, or people who are dependent on others in such a way that they will not make their minds up rationally.[50]

In a well-governed state the rights and needs of individuals will be looked after, so there will be little temptation for such a state to wage war except in self-defence. But so long as wars continue states are themselves in that condition of insecurity which individuals occupied in the state of nature. Just as there is a moral need for individuals to unite in a civil society which enforces public laws, so there is a moral need for states themselves to unite under a world government, which can institute perpetual peace and guarantee them freedom from interference by their neighbours. Only thus can their own rights be secured, and only thus can they properly protect the rights of their citizens. But Kant is not so sanguine as to think this will ever actually be achieved; it is an 'idea' only, though one that we are morally obliged to work towards. (It is, in fact, another *end* prescribed to us by the Theory of Right.) What prevents its realization in practice is the size of the earth and the disparateness of its peoples, together with the unwillingness of nation states to give up their sovereignty.[51] But we can move in the right direction by encouraging states to band together in voluntary international federations, and to submit their disputes to international law. It is gradual steps of this kind 'which alone can lead, by a continuous approximation, towards the highest political good – perpetual peace'.[52]

Although this goal will never be attained Kant does think – surprisingly perhaps – that we are making progress towards it. Reason, constantly seeking for explanations, looks for a general theory of history and finds that it can be seen as an advance (though not without interruptions and setbacks) towards greater freedom and enlightenment; it can be understood only as a development, guided by the hand of Providence, towards the ultimately perfect society.[53] As a piece of evidence for this he cites the French Revolution, and the widespread sympathy and enthusiasm aroused by it.[54] We are entitled to conclude that 'The human race has always been in progress towards the better and will continue to be so henceforth.'[55]

It has lately become fashionable to describe Kant's political philosophy as unjustly neglected. It is worth noticing, but from a purely philosophical point of view – leaving aside, that is, its influence on his contemporaries – its neglect is largely justified. It is not the most original part of his work, and it suffers from the basic defect of all his concrete moral theory: its central conceptions are inadequately worked out and defended. The absence of argument at the critical points is more noticeable here than anywhere else. For this one should not blame him too much. He did not write a systematic work on the subject until very late in his life, and by the time of the *Metaphysics of Morals* (1797) he was no longer at the top of his intellectual form. Many of his ideas are interesting and suggestive, all the same; and not least so his interpretation of history as directed towards the greatest human freedom and the greatest human good. This does not only point ahead to Hegel; it forms an important part of Kant's teleological conception of nature, a view of the world which leads the mind naturally – if deceptively – to a belief in God.

XII

God

Of all the arguments for the existence of God, it is the argument from design which has the deepest appeal and most closely reflects the tendency of unanalysed religious thought. Hume said that in contemplating nature 'A purpose, an intention, a design strikes everywhere the most careless, the most stupid thinker',[1] and Kant says of the argument (which he calls the physico-theological argument) that it 'always deserves to be mentioned with respect' as 'the oldest, the clearest, and the most accordant with the common reason of mankind' (A 623/B 651).

Still, regarded as a sober proof it is weak, and Kant considers it effective only in justifying the regulative assumption of the idea of a wise designer of the world. The analogy between the world and an artefact is not very close, but it is close enough for Reason to have to think of nature as though it were designed. This does not yet give us the traditional conception of God, however, even as an idea of Reason, for God is usually conceived as creating his material *ex nihilo* whereas a craftsman can work with the material he finds to hand. To get to the idea of God as a genuine creator, who does not simply shape what is already there, we accordingly require another argument: the cosmological argument.

By 'the cosmological argument' Kant understands the argument that because everything in the world is contingent, there must be a supreme being which exists necessarily. By saying it exists necessarily he means that its existence is self-explanatory, and that it provides an ultimately satisfactory explanation of why everything else is as it is.[2] The argument actually consists of two stages, the first of which receives its proper discussion under the heading of the Fourth Antinomy. Here the existence of a necessary being (not yet asserted to be God) is inferred from that of contingent things; a move which is liable to some familiar objections. If it belongs within the world of appearances it cannot be absolutely necessary, for it must in turn have a cause; if it does not, we are not entitled to claim any knowledge of it, since it lies beyond the limits of possible experience. Besides which, nothing entitles us to postulate a self-explanatory being in any case, for no reason can be given why the chain of causes or explanations should ever come to an end. The idea of such a being does again have a regulative use, according to Kant; but no more than that.

The second stage of the argument is designed to show that the self-explanatory being must be the supremely real being, i.e. God as conceived by the theologians. It claims that the only way something can be self-explanatory is by existing as a matter of logical necessity. But the concept of a being that exists as a matter of logical necessity is just what Descartes used for his ontological argument: the idea of a supreme being who unites all the perfections, including existence. So the self-explanatory being must unite all the perfections, and this is just how the theologians think of God.[3]

There is an objection to this which Kant does not make. If the only way something can be self-explanatory is for it to exist by logical necessity, it does not actually follow that the only self-explanatory being must be one which unites the perfections. For if existence could be construed as a defining predicate at all it could equally well be built into the conception of the devil (as the worst possible being) or that of a gragon (gragons have three essential properties: they are dragons, they are green, and they exist). And these would then also exist by logical necessity. Kant's own objection, of course, is that to speak of anything existing by logical necessity is incoherent. Existence is not a 'real predicate';[4] it is not a characteristic co-ordinate with others, to be included in the definition of a thing. This is his reply to the ontological argument, and he considers it fatal also to the present argument because it falls into the same incoherence. The ontological argument sets out from the concept of a supremely perfect being to prove that such a being must necessarily exist; the present argument maintains that a necessarily existing being must be supremely perfect in Descartes' sense.[5] So the arguments are different (despite what Kant sometimes says[6]), but they make the same mistake.

The physico-theological argument differs from the others in that it draws its support from how things are in the world. For nature appears to afford considerable evidence of design. It is much more highly ordered than there is any transcendental necessity for it to be, and ordered in ways we are readily able to grasp; as we saw, the Analogies are supposed to have shown that there must be a thoroughgoing interconnection of things by means of causal laws, but not that these laws must be reducible to some system or that they should be easy for us to understand. Moreover, Kant considers that we find in nature things we can only explain teleologically, by reference to purposes within nature. We can make this comprehensible to ourselves only by supposing that nature has been arranged by a wise designer. Which does not prove that such a designer exists, but shows that the idea is one for which Reason has a regulative employment.[7]

The things in nature which most clearly seem to need teleological explanation are organisms. We say that an acorn develops as it does in order to grow into an oak tree; we say that fish have gills in order to breathe. As we have seen, human history is also in Kant's view to be understood as a gradual progress towards an ultimate objective, which he thinks of as nature's highest end:[8] the ideal cosmopolitan state which secures to each individual the maximum freedom compatible with a like liberty for others. He did not, of course, wish to deny that all that happens must be subject to causal law; nor did he even wish to assert that the teleological explanations we like to give for these things are strictly speaking true – only that they work, and enable us to unify and subordinate to a rule phenomena that would otherwise seem radically diverse, so that we must think of nature as if it were operating purposively. He says we can never hope for a Newton who will reduce even the simplest organism, like a blade of grass, to purely mechanical principles, for the matter is entirely beyond our reach; but this does not preclude a superhuman understanding from being able to effect the reduction.[9] Yet even if we could carry the reduction out, the appearance of design is so great that we should have to regard the mechanical laws as taking the form they do in order to produce these effects. We should have to regard the mechanical explanation as subordinate to the teleological.[10]

The discoveries of Darwin have made Kant's remarks about organisms less convincing; political developments since his day have made his optimistic view of history untenable. The theory of evolution enables us to explain the development of organisms and the function of their various parts in a perfectly satisfactory way by principles Kant would have called mechanical. Kant thinks mechanical laws would always seem to leave something unaccounted for – the acorn's development is governed by the laws of matter in motion, but unless its growth into a tree is also explained in another way it must be due to blind chance, and blind chance explains nothing. He himself suggests a crude evolutionary theory, and considers it inadequate for this reason.[11] But Darwinian explanation leaves nothing over for chance. Whatever the teleological account explains can equally be explained along Darwinian lines, the appearance of purpose being provided by the working of natural selection upon randomly generated mutations. One can say that the teleological explanation is not replaced but spelt out further, in such a way as to show that there is nothing irreducibly teleological about it at all – any more than there is anything irreducibly teleological in the behaviour of a thermostat, or of a guided missile.

The thermostat and the guided missile are products of human design, and it is quite possible to accept Darwin but to argue that the whole system of nature which works by natural selection must analogously be the work of a designer. But the argument is weak. The analogy is unconvincing, and it is not clear why the system in its entirety should require explanation at all. There is not even any special reason to think of it as if it were the product of design. One can just accept that this is how things are.

If anything is to be made of the physico-theological argument it will not be by adducing such supposed evidences of design as sea shells and baboons. It will rather be by returning to an earlier point: to the consideration that the world turns out comprehensible to us a surprisingly large amount of the time, and substantially more than it need do simply to be an object of possible experience for us. It is not transcendentally necessary that causal laws should be so readily discoverable as many of them are, nor that we should be able to unify particular laws under more general ones in the way we find we can. To put it another way, we have adopted certain standards for judging how things are on the basis of empirical evidence, and it is transcendentally necessary that we should have done, but it is not transcendentally necessary that these standards should have been so spectacularly successful in enabling us to understand the world – or that they should continue to work so well as time goes on. This alone, Kant would say, is enough to lead us to the 'idea' of a wise author of the universe who has our interests at heart.[12]

It may be objected that Kant, at least, has no right to argue in this way. For does not his transcendental idealism altogether remove any grounds for surprise about the orderliness of nature? 'The order and regularity in the appearances, which we entitle nature, we ourselves introduce' (A 125); of course nature will conform to the human understanding, if the human understanding has constructed nature in the first place. Kant makes it quite clear that he considers particular natural laws to be empirical,[13] but if one thinks along these lines it becomes puzzling how he can adopt such a position. The principle that every event has a cause is allegedly imposed by the mind; how can the mind impose a general principle like that except by so ordering particular appearances as to provide causal connections in each individual case? And if they are read in by the mind it ought to be possible – at least in principle – to know each specific law a priori.

But we must remember the status Kant gave to the principle of the Second Analogy. It is not an Axiom of Intuition: it does not say that all intuitions whatever must be subject to causal law, only that objective events must be. He is thus able to follow Wolff in using the principle as a criterion of objectivity, or, as he calls it, a criterion of empirical truth.[14] It sets a standard that must be met by any phenomenon we can call objective; whatever fails to meet the test is not objective, but only an illusion or a dream. We impose the standard, and we use it in constructing the world of appearances from the data we receive in intuition. But we do not create the data – on the contrary, they are given to us – and it is therefore an empirical question which of them exhibit the orderliness we require in order to construe them as perceptions of objects, and in what way they exhibit it. And it is an empirical question whether they will continue to exhibit this orderliness in future. Certainly we are responsible for the initial classification of the data as well as for their subsequent interpretation, but once we have settled on a classification it is an empirical matter what regularities occur and in no way for us to determine.

Thus we do not have a free hand to construct the world of appearances just as we like. We cannot build in natural laws as we please; the laws of nature cannot, in general, be discovered from an armchair. It is true that Kant does leave a place for what he calls a priori natural science, and claims that such very general laws as the inverse square law and the law of inertia belong to it.[15] But he also says that this pure natural science rests upon an empirical concept, the concept of matter.[16] By 'matter' he does not simply mean whatever is the object of outer experience, for arguably that concept could not be empirical at all – it must be instantiated for experience to be possible, if the Refutation of Idealism is successful. Instead he defines matter as the movable in space, and in the first part of the *Metaphysical Foundations of Natural Science* uses this concept to establish a law for the composition of motions.[17] Each subsequent part of the work extends the definition by building more into it in order to get more interesting conclusions out: matter is the movable in so far as it fills space, in so far as it possesses moving force, and in so far as it is an object of possible experience.[18] It cannot be decided a priori whether matter, as thus conceived, exists at all: it is not a condition for the possibility of experience that it should. Someone might conceivably inhabit a world, even a spatial world, in which he was conscious of objects external to himself, but in which nothing ever moved or was thought of as movable. Things might change in regular and systematic ways without moving: they could change in colour and in brightness, for example, and these changes might sometimes occur in such a way as to afford a basis for thinking of objects as continuing to exist when unperceived (temporarily obscured, perhaps, by the unusual brightness of a nearby light source). It is true, no doubt, that as our sense-organs are constituted we could not perceive anything in a purely static world, but that is only a contingent fact about us.[19]

So the concept of matter must be acquired from experience, and only through experience can we discover that it has application in the world.

But having once acquired it we can work out, without need for experiment, certain principles which must hold of any matter there may be. Not unexpectedly Kant uses the table of categories as his guide in this, deriving (for example) the law that action and reaction are equal and opposite with the help of the category of community.[20] The standard of argumentation in the *Metaphysical Foundations of Natural Science* is remarkably low, but he uses it to develop an interestingly advanced picture of the physical world as a system not of Newtonian corpuscles but of point centres of force attracting and repelling one another. What is established can only be strictly hypothetical, however: if there is such a thing as matter, then these laws will be true of it. Or, to put it another way, if the data we receive in outer sense are of a certain kind, then given our general method of constructing the world of appearances we shall find that these laws hold within nature.

Since an empirical concept is involved it is perhaps surprising to find Kant calling this a priori natural science; or pure natural science, as he also does. Some confusion is caused by his using the word 'pure' in two senses. In one of these, distinguished at B 3, a priori natural science is not pure, just because it involves an empirical concept. It remains a priori in that it can be known without further appeal to experience than is required to provide the concepts – just as an analytic proposition like 'All bachelors are unmarried' can be a priori though its concepts are empirical. In the other sense, however, 'pure' just means the same as 'a priori', so that in this sense it is pure. He admits that in the *Critique of Pure Reason* he uses 'pure' in these two distinct ways without explanation and in the space of two pages, and petulantly asks 'But who can think of every possible source of misunderstanding?' (Ak. VIII: 184).

It is therefore misleading to speak of the mind as 'prescribing laws to appearances' (B 163), for 'empirical laws, as such, can never derive their origin from pure understanding' (A 127).[21] The phenomenal world is a construction which our minds effect by working on the data they receive and interpreting these data in accordance with the principles that govern their thinking. Even those highly general laws which Kant ascribes to pure natural science in the *Metaphysical Foundations of Natural Science* will hold only if our experience takes a form which there is no transcendental need for it to take. They are a priori only in that we can tell in advance that if our experience is of that kind – if there is 'matter', in Kant's sense – then they are bound to hold. The more specific laws which govern the details of the natural world can only be discovered empirically, though again to discover them, or indeed to find out anything at all about the world, we must rely on these same principles of human thinking: which for Kant include both the principles of pure understanding, constitutive of the world of appearances, and the regulative principles, which we do not have to regard as expressing truths but which guide our search for the greatest systematic unity in nature.

What is remarkable is that it should be so easy for us to discover laws – not just simple causal laws, but more sophisticated higher order laws that enable us to find unity within widely diverse natural phenomena. Kant himself cites the division of things into species and genera;[22] other examples are to be found from all the branches of science and observation. We prefer simple hypotheses, and mathematically simple ones in particular; how providential, then, that so many fundamental laws of physics and chemistry are expressible as elementary arithmetical relationships. How convenient for us that the periodic table should turn out so neatly, and that gravitational attraction should require no more complex function than the inverse square! There was no transcendental necessity that things should be so readily comprehensible.

Of course the immediate reply is that there is nothing remarkable or providential about it at all. The principles that we use in thinking and in constructing theories are themselves adopted because they give results; if they did not work, or if they worked less successfully, then we should jettison them, just as we should jettison theories which do not prove fruitful. But this entails that it is open to us to do this, a suggestion Kant would rightly have disputed. We could hardly abandon the preference for simple explanations, for example. If the world did not permit us to find these we should be disappointed and frustrated, but we would not be led to adopt an alternative preference for explanations of a rococo complexity. Nor would adverse evidence lead us to give up the principle of induction, according to which it is reasonable to assume that unobserved instances will resemble observed ones, and more specifically that the future will (in general) resemble what we have observed of the past. Alternative counter-inductive procedures are conceivable, whereby the future is expected to be different from the past; but no experience of the failure of induction would make us adopt counter-induction instead. For the counter-inductivist's reaction to the observation that past futures have not resembled past pasts is to expect that this will now cease, and that in future things will turn out as his inductivist rival would anticipate.

Fortunately induction has proved pretty reliable so far; and it may be argued that despite our inability to give it up this provides a reason why we should find nothing remarkable in its continuing success from moment to moment. If that were so we still ought to be grateful for finding ourselves in a world in which induction does work so effectively, since it might well not have done, in which case life would have been a great deal more difficult for us. But the argument suffers from the disadvantage of being circular, since one can infer the principle's continuing reliability from its past successes only by relying on induction.

And unlike the circularity in the defence of deduction this circularity matters. It is perfectly conceivable that induction should not work, or should not work so effectively, whereas if deduction failed us there would be no possibility of significant thought.[23]

Even if we regarded the inductive principle as sufficiently justified, so that nature's continued conformity to it need no longer seem remarkable, we should still have to face the fundamental difficulty pointed out by Goodman.[24] We could expect the future to 'resemble' the past; but in what will this resemblance consist? Whether two things are to be accounted similar depends upon the concepts we are working with; they can be said to resemble one another only if we classify them together under a common concept. Taking some arbitrary time T – say, midnight tonight – we normally regard today's green grass as being still the same colour after T if it is still green. But, as Goodman points out, we might have worked instead with an alternative colour concept, 'grue', such that something is grue at t if, and only if, either t is before T and it is green, or else t is at or after T and it is blue. In that case we should say that tomorrow's grass was the same colour as today's only if it were still grue – i.e. only if it were blue, for tomorrow is after T. This has the devastating consequence that by itself the inductive principle is quite useless for guiding our expectations about the future. If 'green' is the colour concept we work with it tells us to expect grass to be green tomorrow; but if we use 'grue' instead it tells us to expect it to be blue. And of course the problem arises in exactly the same way for concepts of all kinds, not just for colour concepts. So which predictions are licensed by the principle depends entirely on what concepts we happen to use. And here, surely, we have evidence of design much more striking than before. Nature keeps on working in such a way as to meet our expectations: yet our expectations are based on nothing more secure than the accident that we normally classify in one way rather than another – that we use the concept 'green' rather than the concept 'grue'.

That it is up to us how we classify things is not a point original with Goodman; Kant made it (though not quite consistently) when he defended the spontaneity of the synthesis that is involved in concept-application, including the synthesis of apprehension. But it took Goodman to state it so incisively and to appreciate its bearing on induction. And Goodman has not lacked critics who have argued that his 'new riddle of induction' is not a genuine problem. They object that 'grue' is a more complex concept than 'green', and suggest we need only say that the resemblances which permit of inductive extrapolation are the simple ones. If this were correct it would bring us back to the question why the world should show this convenient preference for simplicity, but in fact these critics miss the point.[25] Of course from our point of view 'grue' is a more complex predicate than 'green'; it is introduced by means of the concepts 'green' and 'blue'. But what matters is not that it is possible to introduce the new word 'grue' among people like ourselves, but that there could perfectly well be people for whom 'grue' is as primitive a concept as 'green' is for us. They would not just use a different word from us, they would classify the data differently. They could tell that something was grue just by looking at it; to them grue things would look alike regardless of the time, and green grass tomorrow would look a different colour from green grass today. They would look upon 'green' as a complex predicate, to be defined in terms of 'grue' and its complement 'bleen' – where 'bleen' applies to blue things up to T, and to green things at T and after. And they would be disposed to say of us, as Blackburn says of 'grue'-users, that we could not tell what colour an object was just by looking at it without also knowing the time.[26] For (other things being equal) an object that looks grue will be green if it is earlier than T, blue if it is T or later; by looking at it without a watch, they would be inclined to say, you can tell only that it is grue, and not whether it is green or blue. These people would evidently be very different from us, and if it were not only their classification of colours that was strange but their classification of shapes, sizes and so on as well they would be very different indeed. But there is nothing wrong with their ways of classifying things – except in so far as they may encourage them to make the wrong inductions. At least, we hope that those inductions will turn out to be the wrong ones to make.

When we make predictions we expect our concepts, not theirs, to lead us to the right results; and in the past such expectations have been repeatedly justified. For there are endless analogues of 'grue' which take as the value for T not midnight tonight but some past time, and for every one of these – so far as our knowledge reaches – the expectations which might have been based on them have been falsified by events. This leads Quine to suggest that in this area also the theory of evolution can be used to explain away the apparent indications of design. Those animals which relied upon 'grue'-type predicates would have been sorely deceived by their expectations when T came along, and would have died out in consequence. 'Creatures inveterately wrong in their inductions have a pathetic but praiseworthy tendency to die before reproducing their kind.'[27] Natural selection has favoured us because our predictions have been based on concepts which are not of the 'grue' variety and which therefore have not (broadly and in general) played us false. We have survived because our concepts match the articulations by which nature itself works; and no doubt also because we have been flexible enough to alter them when we found a scientific advantage in doing so.

But the Darwinian explanation is quite useless here. It might explain the non-survival of people using 'grue'-type predicates for which T is in the remote past. It can hardly explain the preference for 'green' over 'grue' where *T* is midnight tonight. 'Grue'-users and 'green'-users have always had the same expectations about times earlier than midnight tonight, so that nothing has yet happened to promote the survival of one group rather than the other. By this time tomorrow things may be different, but it is little consolation to know that one of the groups is going to be discriminated against by events, unless we have reason to suppose we shall be among the winners. And we have no reason, evolutionary or otherwise; we can only put our faith in the idea of nature as designed to meet our needs and to fit our cognitive capacities.

When he asked himself how we might know anything about the world Kant replied that there were three possible theories.[28] Knowledge might be read off from the world; the empiricists would explain all our knowledge in this way. It might be read into the world by us; this is Kant's own view about the limited synthetic a priori knowledge we possess. Or there might be a pre-established harmony between the world and our cognitive faculties; and this was the view of Descartes and Crusius, who held that what seems to us self-evident is guaranteed as true by a God who is no deceiver. The empiricist solution neglects the fact that in constructing its picture of the world the mind has to go far beyond what is given to it (though it rightly emphasizes the importance of the given element). Kant's own account is promising; at least in a slightly modified form – he has no right to deny that the picture we construct may coincide with the real nature of the world in itself, and his list of the principles of human thinking requires amendment. But it will not cover all the ground. As we saw earlier, constraints internal to his theory require him to admit the existence of things in themselves, with his own mind amongst them as an active subject of synthesis. It would be difficult to reject the hypothesis that other minds exist as well, in their own right and not just as quasi-phenomenalistic constructions, though this can only be a hypothesis, not something that must be true for experience to be possible at all. And finally we have now seen that Kant's solution leaves it unexplained why the world should be so readily comprehensible to us, and that it affords no ground for our confidence that the future will continue to follow those relatively simple laws which we make the basis for our inductive extrapolations. These are not things that can be read into the world, in the construction of the world of appearances; they depend on how the world itself turns out, and therefore on the character of the data we receive in sensory experience.

The ready comprehensibility of the world in the past and in the present is something we can discover empirically, though it must lend support to the view that things are designed to suit our cognitive powers. But we cannot discover empirically that the future will fit our expectations; not, that is, until the future arrives. The faith that we place in these expectations, and on which we constantly depend, amounts to a trust in the continuing conformity of the world to our own faculties. The trust may be innate and unreflective, but unless the two have some-how been arranged in harmony our faith is groundless and our trust misplaced. The words 'pre-established harmony' have a derogatory overtone, perhaps from their association with the 'magic world' of Leibniz's monads;[29] but the only other alternative is that the continued success of our predictions, determined as they are by the concepts we happen to employ, is a sustained and massive accident – the chance long run of heads in the endless tossings of the cosmic coin.

It is not only for predicting the future that we rely on the conformity of the world to our capacities. The same faith is required whenever we talk about other people or make claims about the world as it is in itself. The existence of other minds is not presented to us amongst the data of experience; our belief in them rests on the same principles of thought and of theory construction that we use in forming our beliefs about the physical world. In the case of the physical world we can resolve the question of their validity by making them constitutive of the world of appearances, which then becomes a quasi-phenomenalistic construction; but since other minds are not to be regarded as mere constructions, in this area the problem of validity is less easily dismissed. We can only have faith in a pre-established harmony between the world and our cognitive powers.

'Pre-established harmony' may seem unnecessarily objectionable. What is required is that there be a harmony; the inference to its having been established, set up by a designer, is no doubt less compelling. One could say that the harmony had been arranged by nature itself; though if this is not to mean just that it is accidental it ascribes to nature the benevolent purposiveness of a pantheistic God. The alternative view that it has come about through the operation of causal laws in the evolutionary process proves untenable, as we have seen. Under these circumstances the most reasonable hypothesis – the hypothesis to which our usual canons of scientific method lead us – is to ascribe it to a God who has so designed the world and us as to ensure that we will generally get things right: a God who is no deceiver. Like all hypotheses, this can be advanced as a tentative explanation only, but unless we are to demand higher standards of cautiousness here than in any other area it would seem to be the one to advance.

As Kant pointed out, arguments from design do not entitle us to postulate a God who created the world from nothing, but only one who has designed it, perhaps finding the materials already there in advance. As Hume also saw,[30] they give us no right to ascribe to him the tra-ditional and troublesome attributes of omnipotence, omniscience, and moral perfection. A certain general concern for human beings is indicated by his having arranged things to suit us as well; but no more than that. Of course it may be that the God who has so arranged the world possesses these other properties too, but such arguments do not warrant us in saying so.

Kant is wrong to think that the belief in a designer must only be a regulative assumption for the purposes of speculative reason. The hypothesis is as well grounded as one can reasonably expect, and what makes Kant treat it as merely regulative is his overriding reluctance to admit that our knowledge can extend beyond the limits of possible experience. We have seen that he is unable to sustain this position. Transcendental arguments, which he himself subscribes to in a furtive way, require him to admit the existence of the active noumenal subject and of a world of things in themselves. What we have here is a hypothesis, put forward on reasonable though not absolutely conclusive grounds; just like the hypothesis of other minds. We are surely therefore entitled to take it as true. It would be awkward to have to say that we are only justified in behaving *as if* there were minds other than our own.

It must certainly be granted that in calling these hypotheses reasonable one must rely upon our ordinary standards for reasonableness – those standards and principles that govern all our scientific thought. And these standards lack an external guarantee unless a benevolent designer provides it. The argument does therefore in a certain sense rest upon itself; and circularity was Kant's principal objection to Crusius and Descartes. But this is unavoidable and not a vice. It would indeed be viciously circular if it were proposed as an apodeictic proof that there is a God who guarantees these things. Our standards may not be correct after all. Induction may break down at any moment; it is not impossible that our success hitherto was entirely a matter of chance. And my belief in other minds may be a sad mistake. But these are not the things we normally think. We normally think our standards are the right ones, and give us access to the truth. By applying those standards themselves we conclude that we can trust them only if the universe is adapted to our comprehension, presumably by a designer who makes our interests his concern. The hypothesis of a benevolent designer is thus what our system of thought requires to secure its own coherence. We cannot ask for more than this, since the standards we possess are our only way of determining what is reasonable and what is not.

In chapter IX we found that Kant's transcendental idealism, in a slightly modified form, was a very appealing theory, and much more promising than the alternative approach through transcendental arguments with which he supplemented it and which has sometimes been alleged to be all that is worth saving. It is indeed satisfactory, even compelling, if one limits one's concern to the material world as it is now and as it has been in the past. Within this range it enables us to avoid the serious sceptical questions; the principles on which we customarily rely cannot but be the right ones, for the objective world as we know it is a construction effected by means of them. We are thus entitled to claim knowledge, and indeed a priori knowledge, about the world, though admittedly it is knowledge of appearances only and not of things in themselves. But transcendental idealism is powerless to validate our confidence in induction and in the existence of other minds. On these matters transcendental arguments will not help us either; it is not a condition of the possibility of experience that there should be others besides myself, or that experience should continue into the future at all – much less that it should continue to accord with the concepts we find natural. We must accept that here we can never have the assuredness which transcendental idealism gives us concerning the world of appearances. We must be content with rational conjecture, with a faith that is wholly unfounded unless the principles of our thought and the concepts we happen to find natural do actually correspond to the nature of things. And that faith can be vindicated in its own eyes only if this correspondence is no accident but the product of benevolent design; a design which manifests itself to us both in the continued conformity of the world to our expectations, and also in the simplicity and aesthetic neatness of those laws by which we find nature to be governed.

> One great foundation of the COPERNICAN system is the maxim, *that nature acts by the simplest methods, and chooses the most proper means to any end*; and astronomers often, without thinking of it, lay this strong foundation of piety and religion. The same thing is observable in other parts of philosophy: And thus all the sciences almost lead us insensibly to acknowledge a first intelligent Author; and their authority is often so much the greater, as they do not directly profess that intention. (Hume, *Dialogues*, p. 265.)

Notes

Where bibliographical details are not fully given they may be found in the Bibliography.
For abbreviated forms of reference see above, p. xii.

I How is synthetic a priori knowledge possible?

1 To J. H. Lambert, 31 December 1765, Ak. X: 56 (53).
2 B. Russell, *A Critical Exposition of the Philosophy of Leibniz*, Cambridge University Press, 1900; L. Couturat, *La Logique de Leibniz*, Félix Alcan, Paris, 1901.
3 Leibniz, *Nouveaux Essais sur l'entendement humain*, book iv ch. 2, Gerhardt V: 343 ff.; *Generales Inquisitiones de Analysi Notionum et Veritatum*, in L. Couturat, ed., *Opuscules et fragments inédits de Leibniz*, Félix Alcan, Paris, 1903, pp. 371, 388.
4 C. Wolff, *Ontologia*, § 28.
5 C. A. Crusius, *Entwurf der nothwendigen Vernunft-Wahrheiten*, § 85.
6 *Ibid.*, § 31.
7 Wolff, *op. cit.*, § 27; Crusius, *Weg zur Gewissheit*, § 256.
8 Crusius, *Entwurf der nothwendigen Vernunft-Wahrheiten*, § 287.
9 Goerwitz p. 74, Ak. II: 342.
10 Goerwitz p. 117 (translation amended), Ak. II: 370.
11 Goerwitz p. 121, Ak. II: 373.
12 Goerwitz pp. 107 f., Ak. II: 363 f.
13 Lucas p. 9, Ak. IV: 260.
14 Goerwitz p. 112, Ak. II: 367; To Moses Mendelssohn, 8 April 1766, Ak. X: 70 (67).
15 *Untersuchung über die Deutlichkeit der Grundsätze der natürlichen Theologie und der Moral*, Ak. II: 273–301. For a different view of it see L. W. Beck, *Early German Philosophy: Kant and his Predecessors*, p. 448.
16 Ak. II: 383. In their translation (p. 43) Kerferd and Walford misread the German text: *Erfahrung* for *Erkenntniss*.
17 Refl. 5037. Though the view is manfully resisted by G. Tonelli, 'Die Umwälzung von 1769 bei Kant', *Kant-Studien* 54 (1963), pp. 369–75.

18 Goerwitz p. 119, Ak. II: 372; cf. A 820 f./B 848 f.
19 *Inaugural Dissertation,* § 11.
20 To J. H. Lambert, 2 September 1770, Ak. X: 98 (94). Cf. *Inaugural Dissertation,* §§ 14.6, Ak. II: 401 f., and 15.E, Ak. II: 404 f.
21 Ak. XX: 274; B 161; B 218 f. See further below, pp. 14–18 and 75–6.
22 A 11/B 25; A 56/B 80; A 85/B 117; To J. W. A. Kosmann, September 1789, Ak. XI: 81 f. (79).
23 A 146/B 185; A 221 f./B 269. Cf. C. Wolff, *Vernünfftige Gedancken von Gott, der Welt, und der Seele des Menschen,* § 144; *Ontologia,* § 498. Admittedly more needs to be said about this; for a somewhat different view cf. N. Hinske, *Kants Begriff des Transzendentalen,* Bd. 1, W. Kohlhammer, Stuttgart, 1970. It may or may not be a disadvantage of my suggestion that it requires a different account to be given of Kant's use of the term 'transcendent', which he distinguishes from 'transcendental' (A 296/B 352 f.) though he does often confuse the two. A concept or a principle is transcendent if it attempts to go beyond the limits of possible experience and to treat what is unknowable as though it could be known.
24 P. F. Strawson, *The Bounds of Sense,* part I and *passim.*

II   Transcendental arguments

1 P. F. Strawson, *Individuals,* p. 35.
2 *Prolegomena,* § 4; § 5, Lucas p. 31 n., Ak. IV: 276 n.
3 Cf. A 56/B 80; *Prolegomena,* Lucas p. 144 n., Ak. IV: 373 n.; KdU, Introduction, § V, Ak. V: 181.
4 It would be a mistake to read B 23 as implying that it is synthetic. The paragraph is about the analytic propositions made by the dogmatists within their metaphysical systems, which of course do not include those used in transcendental arguments. Cf. *Prolegomena,* Lucas pp. 23 f., Ak. IV: 273 f. The metaphysics which here and elsewhere (A 10/B 13, etc.) is said to be synthetic a priori is that speculative knowledge out of pure reason which the transcendental arguments of the *Critique* are supposed to make possible.
5 A 155 ff./B 194 ff.; A 718 ff./B 746 ff. Kant also (and equivalently) speaks of possible experience as the third thing, e.g. at A 737/B 765.
6 A 721 ff./B 749 ff.; A 736 f./B.764 f.; A 782 f./B 810 f.
7 B 135; B 138.
8 *Logik,* § 106, Ak. IX: 143; cf. L. W. Beck, 'Kant's Theory of Definition', *Philosophical Review* 65 (1956), pp. 179–91.
9 In his note at Ak. XVIII: 699.
10 T. E. Wilkerson, *Kant's Critique of Pure Reason,* ch. 10 esp. § 3; 'Transcendental Arguments', *Philosophical Quarterly* 20 (1970), pp. 200–12.
11 Wilkerson, 'Transcendental Arguments', p. 211.
12 *Logik,* § 36, Ak. IX: 111.
13 Cf. G. Frege, *The Foundations of Arithmetic,* 2nd ed., tr. by J. L. Austin, Blackwell, Oxford, 1959, § 3.
14 On this see W. V. Quine, 'Two Dogmas of Empiricism', in *From a Logical Point of View,* Harvard University Press, 1953.

15 A. N. Prior, 'The Runabout Inference-Ticket', *Analysis* 21 (1960–1), pp. 38–9; also in P. F. Strawson, ed., *Philosophical Logic*, Oxford University Press, 1967.

16 D. Mitchell, *An Introduction to Logic*, 2nd ed., Hutchinson, London, 1964, p. 136.

17 E.g. in *Word and Object*, M.I.T. Press, Cambridge (Mass.), 1960, § 13.

18 K. Reich, *Die Vollständigkeit der kantischen Urteilstafel*, Berlin, Richard Schoetz, 1932; 2nd ed., 1948. Reich's argument is summarized in English by J. Ellington, in the essay accompanying his translation of the *Metaphysical Foundations of Natural Science* (MAdN).

19 Mitchell, *op. cit.*, ch. 7.

20 A 75 f./B 100 f.

21 Cf. D. Wiggins, 'The *De Re* "Must" ', in G. Evans and J. McDowell, eds., *Truth and Meaning*, Oxford University Press, 1976, pp. 295–301.

22 A 55 ff./B 79 ff.

III Space and time as a priori

1 § 14.1, Ak. II: 398 f.; § 15.A, Ak. II: 402.

2 Ak. XX: 280; cf. A 271 f./B 327 f.

3 A 27/B 43; B 72; Ak. XX: 267.

4 B 72; B 139; B 145. But he does also say that we cannot ascribe an understanding to God 'in the proper sense of the word': KdU, § 90, Ak. V: 465, and cf. *Prolegomena*, § 57, Lucas pp. 122 f., Ak. IV: 355 f.

5 *Bounds of Sense*, p. 128.

6 *Individuals*, p. 71.

7 *Ibid.*, ch. 2.

8 J. F. Bennett, *Kant's Analytic*, p. 37.

9 Cf. Bennett, *op. cit.*, ch. 3. J. R. Lucas (*A Treatise on Time and Space*, p. 123) argues that it must be continuous because change is continuous, and because our criteria for object-identity incorporate continuity of position. But in such a world change would not have to be continuous, and our criteria for identity could be different and perhaps less rigid.

10 Bennett, *op. cit.*, p. 48.

11 Because it is not essential that the ordering be in space I should not consider it a powerful objection if someone were to say that a static world cannot be spatial, on the grounds that the concept of space essentially involves the possibility of moving around. I do not think this is in fact true, since the phenomenological character of our percipient's experience seems close enough to our own to justify calling it spatial, but even if it were true it is not the spatiality of his experience that matters but the fact that it is ordered along a dimension on which appropriate regularities occur.

12 Cf. D. Williams, 'The Myth of Passage', *Journal of Philosophy* 48 (1951), pp. 457–72.

IV Space and time as intuitions

1 At least in the exoteric Correspondence with Clarke. Elsewhere he tries to reduce them to monadic predicates applicable to minds. Cf. below, note 13.

2 Refl. 2392; cf. Ak. XXIV: 257 f.; *Logik*, § 21, Ak. IX: 102; A 69/B 94.

3 B 41; cf. A 19/B 33; A 50/B 74; A 92/B 125; *Prolegomena*, § 8, Lucas pp. 37 f., Ak. IV: 281; *Fortschritte*, Ak. XX: 266; Ak. XXVIII: 546; To J. S. Beck, 3 July 1792, Ak. XI: 347 (334); Refl. 5643. For the suggestion that an intuition is simply any representation of a particular cf. J. Hintikka, 'On Kant's Notion of Intuition', in Penelhum and MacIntosh, eds., *The First Critique*.

4 In fact the entries under '*Anschauung*' and '*Begriff*' in the *Philosophisches Wörterbuch* of Kant's disciple G. S. A. Mellin (6 vols., F. Frommann, Züllichau and Leipzig, 1797–1804) read in parts almost like an exposition of Russell.

5 Thus e.g. B 307; *Prolegomena*, § 45; B 157.

6 Thus Introduction, § V, Ak. IX: 36.

7 § 14.2, Ak. II: 399; § 15.B, Ak. II: 402.

8 Ak. IV: 481, 559.

9 Strawson, *Individuals*, p. 37.

10 Leibniz to Clarke IV: 4, Gerhardt VII: 372; Leibniz to the Electress Sophia, 31 October 1705, Gerhardt VII: 563.

11 *Von dem ersten Grunde des Unterschiedes der Gegenden im Raume*, Ak. II: 382 f.

12 P. Remnant, 'Incongruent Counterparts and Absolute Space', *Mind* N.S. 72 (1963), p. 399.

13 Ultimately relations are unreal, for Leibniz; a relation would be 'an accident in two subjects, with one leg in one, and the other in the other; which is contrary to the notion of accidents' (Leibniz to Clarke V: 47, Gerhardt VII: 401; the translation is Clarke's, p. 71 in H. G. Alexander's edition). Hence it must be possible to analyse all true statements into non-relational form. Statements about spatial relationships are to be analysed into statements ascribing to individual substances (monads) various different degrees of clarity and distinctness in perception; and although it is difficult at the best of times to see how this analysis can be adequate, it would be especially unpromising to attempt such a treatment of 'x is to the left of y as seen from z'.

14 G. Nerlich, *The Shape of Space*, pp. 33–44. The suggestion that they should be so treated was made by J. Earman, 'Kant, Incongruous Counterparts, and the Nature of Space and Space-Time', *Ratio* 13 (1971), pp. 1–18 esp. p. 9.

15 Nerlich, *op. cit.*, pp. 35–7.

16 Ak. II: 378.

17 Nerlich, *op. cit.*, p. 43.

18 *Ibid.*, pp. 44–9. Cf. the article by L. Sklar to which Nerlich is replying: 'Incongruous Counterparts, Intrinsic Features, and the Substantiviality of Space', *Journal of Philosophy* 71 (1974), pp. 277–90.

19 MAdN, Ak. IV: 481, 559.

20 Newton, *Principia*, scholium to df. VIII: pp. 10–2 in vol. 1 of F. Cajori's edition.

21 MAdN, Ak. IV: 561.

22 A. Quinton, 'Spaces and Times', *Philosophy* 37 (1962), pp. 138–47.

23 R. Swinburne, *Space and Time*, pp. 44 f.

24 R. Swinburne, 'Times', *Analysis* 25 (1964–5), pp. 185–91; *Space and Time*, ch. 10.

25 R. Swinburne, 'Conditions for Bitemporality', *Analysis* 26 (1965–6), pp. 47–50.

26 R. Swinburne, *Space and Time*, pp. 205–6.

27 *Ibid.*, p. 206.

28 See further D. Lewis, 'The Paradoxes of Time Travel', *American Philosophical Quarterly* 13 (1976), pp. 145–52. Cf. also M. Hollis, 'Times and Spaces', *Mind* N.S. 76 (1967), pp. 524–36.

29 *Summa Theologica* Ia q. 14 art. 13 *ad* 4. Cf. also Boethius, *De Consolatione Philosophiae*, book V ch. 6; p. 426 in the Loeb edition translated by S. J. Tester, Heinemann, London, 1973.

V   Geometry and arithmetic

1 B 40 f.; cf. A 24; A 716/B 744.

2 H. J. de Vleeschauwer, *La Déduction Transcendentale*, vol. III, pp. 467–70; *The Development of Kantian Thought*, pp. 157–9. De Vleeschauwer relies on such passages as Ak. XX: 276 and 332, which do not seem by any means decisive.

3 H. Reichenbach, *The Philosophy of Space and Time*, pp. 14 ff.

4 See G. Nerlich, *The Shape of Space*, ch. 4, for a detailed description of life in several such worlds.

5 Strawson, *Bounds of Sense*, p. 284; cf. also E. Nagel, *The Structure of Science*, Routledge & Kegan Paul, London, 1961, p. 225.

6 Cf. A 24. But see G. J. Hopkins, 'Visual Geometry', *Philosophical Review* 82 (1973), pp. 3–34, for a careful defence of the view that the matter is contingent.

7 Hume, *Enquiry Concerning the Human Understanding*, § II, pp. 20 f. in Selby-Bigge's edition; and also his *Treatise of Human Nature*, book I part I § I, p. 6 in Selby-Bigge.

8 M. C. Escher, *The Graphic Work of M. C. Escher*, Pan/Ballantine, London, 1972, esp. § X; R. L. Gregory, 'Perceptual Illusions and Brain Models', *Proceedings of the Royal Society* Series B, vol. 171 (1968), pp. 279–96 esp. pp. 284 ff., reprinted in R. L. Gregory, *Concepts and Mechanisms of Perception*, Duckworth, London, 1974; L. S. and R. Penrose, 'Impossible Objects: a Special Type of Visual Illusion', *British Journal of Psychology* 49 (1958) pp. 31–3. See also Berkeley, *An Essay Towards a New Theory of Vision*, Dublin, 1709; J. L. Mackie, *Problems from Locke*, Oxford University Press, 1976, pp. 31 f.; and on the other hand E. J. Craig, 'Phenomenal Geometry', *British Journal for the Philosophy of Science* 20 (1969), pp. 121–34.

9 *Bounds of Sense*, p. 285.

10 Cf. Refl. 10. On the relation between pure intuition and the imagination see *Entdeckung*, Ak. VIII: 192 n. and 240; *Prolegomena*, § 10; A 713/B 741; To Marcus Herz, 26 May 1789, Ak. XI: 53 (53).

11 A 33/B 50; B 154. On fingers and dots see B 15 f., A 140/B 179.

12 A 140/B 179.

13 A 734/B 762. A 717/B 745 may seem to support the alternative view, but it does not require it, and is too brief and vague to necessitate so awkward an interpretation.

14 To J. Schultz, 25 November 1788, Ak. X: 557 (530). Cf. *Prolegomena*, § 10; A 142 f./B 182.

15 L. E. J. Brouwer, 'Intuitionism and Formalism', *Bulletin of the American Mathematical Society* 20 (1913), pp. 81–96; 'Consciousness, Philosophy, and Mathematics', *Proceedings of the Tenth International Congress of Philosophy*, North Holland, Amsterdam, 1948, vol. I, pp. 1243–9; 'Historical Background, Principles and Methods of Intuitionism', *South African Journal of Science* 49 (1952), pp. 139–46. The first two of these are reprinted in P. Benacerraf and H. Putnam, eds., *Philosophy of Mathematics*, Blackwell, Oxford, 1964.

16 Arithmetic may be used for other purposes besides counting, and the alternative systems might be less satisfactory for these. But equally they might not; and the matter is of secondary importance, since these applications are not essential to arithmetic in the way that its connection with counting is.

17 J. S. Mill, *A System of Logic*, Longman, London, 1843; 9th ed., 1875; book II ch. 6.

18 *Ibid.*, (9th ed.) vol. 1, p. 269.

19 D. A. T. Gasking, 'Mathematics and the World', *Australasian Journal of Philosophy* 18 (1940), pp. 97–116; reprinted in Benacerraf and Putnam, *op. cit.*

20 H. N. Castañeda, 'Arithmetic and Reality', *Australasian Journal of Philosophy* 37 (1959), pp. 92–107; also reprinted in Benacerraf and Putnam, *op. cit.*

21 On this see D. Bostock, *Logic and Arithmetic: Natural Numbers*, Oxford University Press, 1974, esp. ch. 1.

22 § 12, Ak. II: 397.

23 He does discuss it in the third part of MAdN. Here, however, it emerges that it is a priori only in rather a weak sense, in that it relies upon the empirical concept of motion (Ak. IV: 482, A 81/B 107, cf. below pp. 169–70), and there is no argument against the suggestion that the intuition of time might be empirical too.

24 *Prolegomena*, § 4, Lucas p. 29, Ak. IV: 274.

25 *Prolegomena*, § 5, Lucas p. 31 n., Ak. IV: 276 n.

VI   The transcendental deduction of the categories

1 A 85/B 117; cf. To J. W. A. Kosmann, September 1789, Ak. XI: 81 f. (79).

2 B 159.

3 Thus A 671/B 699; KdU, § 31, Ak. V: 280.

4 B 164 f.

5 Cf. Ak. XX: 274; B 161; B 218 f.

6 *Prolegomena*, § 18. The examples in the *Prolegomena* are carelessly chosen, and obscure the distinction he is trying to draw. Judgments like 'The room is warm' are said to be judgments of perception (§ 19, Lucas p. 57, Ak. IV: 299), though they make a claim to general assent and go beyond

the description of what is immediately given to me. Kant must really have meant judgments of perception to be judgments like 'It seems to me now that the room is warm'; indeed, he explains in the *Logik* that this is so, and there says explicitly that 'The stone is warm' is a judgment of experience. (*Logik*, § 40, cf. also Refl. 3146.)

7 Strawson, *Bounds of Sense*, pp. 85–117.

8 A 100 ff.; A 107; A 123; B 138.

9 Ak. IV: 475 n. The deduction in the *Fortschritte* is at Ak. XX: 271 f. See also his summary statement of the key point of the argument in a letter to J. S. Beck, 16 (17) October 1792, Ak. XI: 376 (361 f.); and the earlier but very illuminating versions in the *Nachlass*, Refl. 5923 and Refl. 5934.

10 A 106; cf. A 68/B 93; *Anthropologie* I § 7, Ak. VII: 141.

11 Ak. XX: 271; cf. *Prolegomena*, § 39, Lucas p. 86, Ak. IV: 323.

12 Cf. also *Prolegomena*, § 21a, Lucas p. 63, Ak. IV: 304; Refl. 5923; Refl. 5934.

13 B 144. Kant italicizes 'deduction'.

14 Cf. also B 150; A 99.

15 B 129 f.; B 134; A 120; Ak. XX: 275 f.

16 Though surprisingly enough in *Loses Blatt* 13 of the *Duisburg'sche Nachlass*, which dates from this period, he seems to be fairly clear that the categories do govern the synthesis of apprehension. (Haering p. 120, Ak. XVII: 664.)

17 A 108; A 121 ff.

18 A 113 f.; cf. A 122.

19 The argument in B seems to follow the same lines in considerably more obscure terminology, except that he now appears ambivalent as to whether heis discussing this notion of an object or rather that of objectivity in some broader sense. The obscurity is mainly occasioned by his deciding to call the synthesis employed in using concepts of objects – or of the objective – the 'objective unity of self-consciousness'. Cf. Refl. 5923 and Refl. 5934.

20 Ak. IV: 475 n.

21 Cf. Bennett, *Kant's Analytic*, ch. 8.

22 A 362 f. Cf. Bennett, *op. cit.*, pp. 113 ff., and Strawson, *Bounds of Sense*, pp. 162–9.

23 A xvii.

24 A 120; A 124; B 151 f.; B 164.

25 A 106 ff.; A 119; A 123 f.; B 137; etc.

26 B 130 vs A 124 or B 151 f. Cf. also (for example) the question whether reproductive synthesis can be pure – A 101 vs A 118 – which Vaihinger and Kemp Smith puzzle over.

27 H. J. Paton, *Kant's Metaphysic of Experience*, Allen & Unwin, London, 1936, vol. 1, p. 56. See H. Vaihinger, 'The Transcendental Deduction of the Categories in the First Edition of the *Critique of Pure Reason*', in M. S. Gram, *Kant: Disputed Questions*; and N. Kemp Smith, *A Commentary to Kant's 'Critique of Pure Reason'*, pp. 202–34. For a more recent, and more sober, version of the patchwork theory see R. P. Wolff, *Kant's Theory of Mental Activity*, pp. 78 ff.

28 J. N. Tetens, *Philosophische Versuche über die menschliche Natur und ihre Entwicklung*, Leipzig, 1777–8; vol. 1 was reprinted by the *Kantgesellschaft*, Reuther & Reichard, Berlin, 1913.

29 Strawson, *Bounds of Sense*, pp. 31–2, 93–7. It should be noticed that Kant also uses the expression 'transcendental psychology', but not to describe what he himself practises: transcendental psychology is that branch of rationalist metaphysics which has to do with the nature of the soul. Because it oversteps the limits of possible experience it would be better to call it transcendent psychology, not transcendental.

30 Ak. XX: 272. Cf. also B 128; *Prolegomena*, §§ 21, 28 and 39, Lucas pp. 61, 72 and 87, Ak. IV: 302, 311 and 324; MAdN, Ak. IV: 474 n.; Refl. 5933; Refl. 5555.

VII *Schematism and principles*

1 A 140–2/B 179–81.
2 *A Treatise Concerning the Principles of Human Knowledge*, Dublin, 1710, Introduction § 15. On the dispensability of images see Bennett, *Kant's Analytic*, pp. 141–8.
3 A 142/B 181.
4 A 138 f./B 177 f.
5 G. J. Warnock, 'Concepts and Schematism', *Analysis* 9 (1948–9), pp. 77–82. There is an excellent reply to Warnock, with which I am much in agreement, in L. Chipman, 'Kant's Categories and their Schematism', *Kant-Studien* 63 (1972), pp. 36–50.
6 See also *Prolegomena*, § 23; A 148/B 187.
7 A 143/B 182 f.
8 A 732 f./B 760 f. The principle is therefore not itself an axiom, but has to do with the application of axioms to our experience.
9 A 168/B 209 f.
10 *Prolegomena*, § 24, Lucas p. 67, Ak. IV: 307. He takes the term from Wolff and from Wolff's pupil A. G. Baumgarten, whose *Metaphysica* he used as a textbook for lectures.
11 This interpretation fits Kant's use of the intensive/extensive distinction at Ak. XXVIII: 637, Refl. 6399, and in the MAdN at Ak. IV: 539 f., as well. On the other hand he also calls weight an intensive magnitude (A 168 f./B 210 f.; *Prolegomena*, § 24), and at A 179/B 221 says one can 'construct the degree of sensations of sunlight by combining some 200,000 illuminations of the moon'. I am here following a suggestion made by Mr D. Bostock.
12 Despite B 291 ff.
13 See further below, pp. 169–70.
14 A 242 n.; cf. *Logik*, § 106, Ak. IX: 143.
15 A 231 f./B 284; cf. A 234 n./B 287 n.
16 So much so that every event is linked by causal law to every other.
17 R. J. Boscovich, *Theoria Philosophiae Naturalis*, Vienna, 1758; Kant, *Metaphysicae cum Geometria iunctae Usus in Philosophia Naturali, cuius Specimen I. continet Monadologiam Physicam*, 1756, Ak. I: 473–87.
18 L. W. Beck, 'The Second Analogy and the Principle of Indeterminacy', in Penelhum and MacIntosh, eds., *The First Critique*, p. 95; reprinted from *Kant-Studien* 57 (1966), pp. 199–205.
19 *Ibid.*, Penelhum and MacIntosh, pp. 93–5.

20 W. H. Walsh, 'Kant on the Perception of Time', in Penelhum and MacIntosh, *op. cit.*, p. 85; also in L. W. Beck, *Kant Studies Today*, p. 176; reprinted from *Monist* 51 (1967), pp. 376–96. Also W. H. Walsh, *Kant's Criticism of Metaphysics*, Edinburgh University Press, 1975, p. 140.

21 A 194 f./B 239 f.; A 201 f./B 247 (though cf. A 451/B 479, which surprisingly appears to concede that the 'criterion of empirical truth' would not collapse completely if there were a few uncaused events, provided they remained extremely rare). Walsh, 'Kant on the Perception of Time', Penelhum and MacIntosh, *op. cit.* p. 85; Beck, *Kant Studies Today,* p.176.

22 How we could know there was no cause for this does not greatly matter; it might be the reasonable thing to conclude after we had repeatedly failed to find a causal explanation.

23 B 234; A 194 f./B 239 f.; A 198/B 243; A 200/B 245.

24 A 127; B 165; A 766/B 794; KdU, Introduction, Ak. V: 180, 183 ff.; *Prolegomena,* § 36, Lucas p. 80, Ak. IV: 318.

25 B 234; A 202/B 247.

26 B 219; B 234; A 195 f./B 240 f.; A 199 f./B 244 f.

27 A 193 f./B 238 f.

28 See further Strawson, *Bounds of Sense*, pp. 133–40; as will be obvious, my account of the Second Analogy owes a great deal to Strawson's.

29 It is not in fact necessary that one should be able to consult other people, though it is convenient. See below, pp. 114–16.

30 *Bounds of Sense*, pp. 143–6.

31 See above, pp. 79 f.; also below, pp. 128 f. and 172–4.

VIII   The transcendental object

1 N. Kemp Smith, *A Commentary to Kant's 'Critique of Pure Reason'*, pp. 204–19.

2 *Ibid.*, p. 205.

3 Most unequivocally in *Loses Blatt* 13, Haering pp. 115–18, Ak. XVII: 663 f.; see also Haering's notes *ad loc.* and p. 141.

4 A 81 f./B 107 f.; *Prolegomena,* § 39, Lucas, p. 86, Ak. IV: 324.

5 A 191/B 236; A 494/B 522; To J. S. Beck, 20 January 1792, Ak. XI: 314 (301). The translations by Zweig and by Kerferd and Walford both make nonsense of this last passage by mistranslating '*Inbegriff*'.

6 A 371; A 375.

7 A 376.

8 *Bounds of Sense*, p. 101.

9 A 183/B 226.

10 A 186/B 229; A 188/B 231 f.

11 B 275 f.; B 277 f.; B xxxix ff. n.

12 See further below, pp. 132–4 and 140.

13 Bennett, *Kant's Analytic*, p. 213.

14 *Ibid.*, p. 208.

15 A. J. Ayer, 'Can There Be a Private Language?' *Proceedings of the Aristotelian Society* Supplement 28 (1954), pp. 63–76.

16 L. Wittgenstein, *Philosophical Investigations*, Blackwell, Oxford, 1953, § 265.

NOTES TO PAGES 117-34

17 *Bounds of Sense*, p. 107.
18 *Ibid.*, pp. 101, 110 f.
19 *Ibid.*, pp. 104, 128.
20 *Individuals*, pp. 99 f.
21 Above, p. 90.
22 Ross Harrison, *On What There Must Be*, pp. 151 ff.
23 *Bounds of Sense*, p. 129.
24 *Individuals*, pp. 46–9.

IX   *Transcendental idealism*

1 Strawson, *Bounds of Sense*, p. 32.
2 B. Stroud, 'Transcendental Arguments', *Journal of Philosophy* 65 (1968), pp. 241–56; also in Penelhum and MacIntosh, eds., *The First Critique*.
3 Cf. P. Hacker, 'Are Transcendental Arguments a Version of Verificationism?' *American Philosophical Quarterly* 9 (1972), pp. 78–85, esp. p. 83.
4 Cf. A. J. Ayer, 'The Concept of a Person' in *The Concept of a Person and Other Essays*, Macmillan, London, 1963, pp. 106 ff., for an analogous example.
5 *Prolegomena*, § 38, Lucas p. 84, Ak. IV: 322.
6 See further below, pp. 172 ff.; and cf. N. Goodman, *Fact, Fiction, and Forecast*, pp. 72–81.
7 Strictly it is only those principles Kant calls constitutive which determine what is true in the world of appearances, the fundamental constitutive principles being the principles of pure understanding. In Kant's view we are guided also by regulative principles like the principle that we should view the world as if it were the creation of an intelligent designer. But regulative principles only exist to guide us and may or may not be believed; constitutive principles are integral to the world of appearances, and must be accepted as true by anyone who can regard that world as objective. See below, pp. 140 ff.
8 Thus A 239/B 298; A 696/B 724.
9 *Bounds of Sense*, p. 16.
10 A 353 f. Though see also below, pp. 136 and 144.
11 Hume, *Treatise of Human Nature*, book I part IV § VI, known to Kant through the German translation of Beattie's *Essay on the Nature and Immutability of Truth*. On this see R. P. Wolff, 'Kant's Debt to Hume via Beattie', *Journal of the History of Ideas* 21 (1960), pp. 117–23.
12 G. Ryle, *The Concept of Mind*, Hutchinson, London, 1949, p. 195.
13 Actually Kant seems a little confused as to how the mistake arises; he diagnoses it better in B than in A. Contrast B 411 with A 402 f.
14 Cf. B 422 f. n.; and esp. B 428 ff.
15 *Erklärung in Beziehung auf Fichtes Wissenschaftslehre*, 7 August 1799, Ak. XII: 370 f. (396 f.); cf. also, for instance, his much earlier remarks about Schulze in a letter to J. S. Beck, 4 December 1792, Ak. XI: 395 (381). The quotation from the *Prolegomena* is from § 13 Note III, Lucas p. 50, Ak. IV: 293; the context makes clear that it is things in themselves he is speaking of.

X Postulates, ideas and aesthetic judgments

1 *Religion*, Preface, Greene and Hudson pp. 4 ff., Ak. VI: 4 ff.; KdpV, Abbott pp. 206 ff., Ak. V: 110 ff.

2 KdpV, Abbott pp. 220 ff., Ak. V: 124 ff.; KdU, § 87, Ak. V: 450; *Fortschritte*, Ak. XX: 295, 297; Ak. VIII: 139.

3 KdpV, Abbott pp. 218 ff., Ak. V: 122 ff.; *Fortschritte*, Ak. XX: 309.

4 *Religion*, Preface, Greene and Hudson, p. 5, Ak. VI: 5.

5 KdpV, Abbott p. 229, Ak. V: 132.

6 KdpV, Abbott pp. 231, 233, Ak. V: 133, 135.

7 And cannot, or there would be an antinomy between free will and the causal determinism of the Second Analogy.

8 Goerwitz p. 64, Ak. II: 335. On the role of the General Will in Kant's political philosophy see below, pp. 162 f.

9 Ak. XX: 299.

10 A 508 ff./B 536 ff.; Appendix to the Transcendental Dialectic, *passim*; *Prolegomena*, § 56.

11 Though more, perhaps, in some cases than in others. If our minds supply space, time, and the categories to the world of appearances, could they not also contribute such principles as the Antithesis of the First Antimony, that the world is infinite in extent?

12 A 336/B 393; A 663 f./B 691 f. But he speaks of 'the transcendental deduction of all ideas of speculative reason' at A 671/B 699.

13 A 650 ff./B 678 ff.; A 326 ff./B 382 ff.; *Prolegomena*, § 45.

14 A 685/B 713.

15 A 615 ff./B 643 ff.; Ak. VIII: 137 f.

16 A 686/B 714; cf. KdU, § 67, Ak. V: 379.

17 KdU, Introduction § V, Ak. V: 185; KdU, First Introduction § II, Ak. XX: 203.

18 A 651/B 679; A 653 f./B 681 f. On this see further G. Buchdahl, 'The Relation between "Understanding" and "Reason" in the Architectonic of Kant's Philosophy', *Proceedings of the Aristotelian Society* 67 (1966–7), pp. 209–26, esp. pp. 221–5.

19 KdU, Introduction § VI, Ak. V: 187.

20 KdU, § 38 n., Ak. V: 290 n. Cf. KdU, §§ 8, 21, 39.

21 KdU, § 9, Ak. V: 217; KdU, §§ 14, 15. Cf. D. W. Crawford, *Kant's Aesthetic Theory*, pp. 90–1.

22 KdU, Introduction § VI, Ak. V: 187. Cf. KdU, § 12, Ak. V: 222.

23 Cf. Crawford, *op. cit.*, pp. 8–13.

24 KdU, § 14, Ak. V: 224. Cf. his uncertainty about how to handle music in § 51, Ak. V: 324 f., which is due to a doubt as to where the formal elements come in.

25 Cf. KdU, § 42, Ak. V: 299 ff.

26 KdU, § 45, Ak. V: 306.

27 KdU, § 49, Ak. V: 314 ff. Kant's theory of art is complex, and it deserves a more extended discussion than it can be given here. His account of the aesthetic ideas which art is supposed to communicate is suggestive, if rather obscure; but the general character of his aesthetics prevents

him from giving art more than a secondary place and a derivative importance.

28 KdpV, Abbott p. 136, Ak. V: 46 f.
29 KdpV, Abbott p. 118, Ak. V: 30.
30 *Grundlegung* p. 101, Ak. IV: 448.
31 *Grundlegung* p. 98, Ak. IV: 446 f.
32 Refl. 7217.
33 *Grundlegung* p. 98, Ak. IV: 446 f.
34 MdS, Introduction § I, Ak. VI: 213, and § IV, Ak. VI: 226; cf. *Religion*, book I, Greene and Hudson pp. 19 ff., Ak. VI: 23 ff.
35 *Religion,* book I, Greene and Hudson pp. 20 f. and 38, Ak. VI: 25 and 43.
36 *Religion,* book I, Greene and Hudson p. 36, Ak. VI: 41.
37 A 551 ff./B 579 ff.; KdpV, Abbott pp. 191 ff., Ak. V: 97 ff.
38 *Grundlegung* pp. xiv and 95, Ak. IV: 392 and 445.
39 *Vorlesung über Ethik*, Infield p. 63, Menzer pp. 75 f.

XI The moral law

1 *Grundlegung* p. 96, Ak. IV: 445.
2 Cf. MdS T, Introduction § VII, Ak. VI: 390; *Vorlesung über Ethik*, Infield p. 21, Menzer p. 26. Kant is thus by no means liable to the accusation of inflexible rigorism, which used commonly to be made against him; except in the late and rather senile paper *Über ein vermeintes Recht aus Menschenliebe zu lügen* (Ak. VIII: 423–30), where he does commit himself to the principle that one should never tell a lie under any circumstances. On this see H. J. Paton, 'An Alleged Right to Lie: a Problem in Kantian Ethics', *Kant-Studien* 45 (1953–4), pp. 190–203.
3 Cf. *Grundlegung*, pp. 1 ff., Ak. IV: 393 f.
4 See the argument leading up to § VII of ch. I, Abbott pp. 119 ff., Ak. V: 30 ff.
5 R. M. Hare, 'Universalisability', *Proceedings of the Aristotelian Society* 55 (1954–5), pp. 295–312; reprinted in his *Essays on the Moral Concepts*, Macmillan, London, 1972. See also Hare, *The Language of Morals*, Oxford University Press, 1952, ch. 11 § 5; and Hare, *Freedom and Reason*, Oxford University Press, 1963, ch. 2.
6 Hare, *Freedom and Reason*, p. 113.
7 *Grundlegung* p. 68 n., Ak. IV: 430 n.
8 *Ibid.*; and cf. Hare, *Freedom and Reason*, ch. 8.
9 *Grundlegung* p. 52, Ak. IV: 421; and see the section on the Typic of Pure Practical Judgment in KdpV, Abbott p. 161, Ak. V: 69.
10 Hare, *Freedom and Reason*, pp. 105 f.; ch. 9 § 1.
11 *Grundlegung* p. 80, Ak. IV: 436; cf. pp. 63 f. and 70, Ak. IV: 427 and 431. Also MdS T, Introduction § I, Ak. VI: 380; KdpV, Abbott p. 123, Ak. V: 34.
12 *Grundlegung* pp. 14 and 64, Ak. IV: 400 and 427; KdpV, Abbott pp. 107 ff. and 114 f., Ak. V: 21 f. and 27.
13 *Grundlegung* p. 66, Ak. IV: 429; cf. pp. 77 ff. and 82 f., Ak. IV: 435 f. and 437 f.

14 At any rate most of us would not. There are exceptions: see S. R. L. Clark, *The Moral Status of Animals*, Oxford University Press, 1977.

15 MdS T, Introduction § IV.

16 Though contrast *Grundlegung* p. 11 f., Ak. IV: 399, where he says that I do have a duty to assure my own happiness.

17 Thus KdpV, Abbott pp. 206 ff., Ak. V: 110 ff.

18 *Grundlegung* pp. 67 ff., Ak. IV: 429 f.

19 *Grundlegung* pp. 42 and 69, Ak. IV: 415 and 430; MdS T, Introduction §§ VIII and IX.

20 *Grundlegung* pp. 79 and 82, Ak. IV: 436 and 437.

21 *Grundlegung* pp. 53 ff., Ak. IV: 421 ff.

22 *Vorlesung über Ethik*, Infield pp. 120, 147–54, Menzer pp. 149 f., 185–93; MdS T, § 6.

23 Cf. M. G. Singer, *Generalization in Ethics*, p. 293.

24 *Grundlegung* p. 36, Ak. IV: 412.

25 *Grundlegung* p. 52, Ak. IV: 421.

26 *Grundlegung* p. 17, Ak. IV: 402; italics altered.

27 *Vorlesung über Ethik*, Infield pp. 124, 170, Menzer pp. 154 f., 213 f.; MdS T, § 7. M. J. Gregor (*Laws of Freedom*, pp. 130, 139) thinks that Kant has an argument to the effect that self-abuse weakens one physically and mentally, thereby destroying one's capacity for the rational exercise of freedom. But these comments about its likely consequences appear only in the *Pädagogik* (Ak. IX: 497), where they are presented less to establish Kant's case than as points worth making to children to discourage them from the practice, which is inherently wrong on other grounds. And no parallel argument seems possible for the wig-making example.

28 MdS T, § 6, Ak. VI: 423.

29 *Grundlegung* pp. 82 f., Ak. IV: 437 f.

30 *Grundlegung* p. 84, Ak. IV: 438.

31 *Grundlegung* p. 10, Ak. IV: 398.

32 MdS, Introduction § III; MdS T, Introduction § VI.

33 On this see Onora Nell, *Acting on Principle*, chs. 3 and 7.

34 MdS R, Introduction §§ D, E; MdS T, Introduction § II.

35 MdS T, Introduction § I, Ak. VI: 381.

36 Ak. XXIII: 394; cf. MdS T, Introduction § VII, Ak. VI: 390.

37 MdS R, Introduction § B, Reiss pp. 132 f., Ak. VI: 230; *Vorlesung über Ethik*, Infield pp. 48 and 117, Menzer pp. 58 and 145 f. He does not maintain this consistently, though; cf. Ak. XXIII: 395; MdS R, Introduction, Ak. VI: 236 f. See the useful discussion by M. J. Gregor, *Laws of Freedom*, chs. 7 and 8.

38 MdS R, Introduction § C, Reiss p. 133, Ak. VI: 231 (translation by Ladd).

39 *Theorie und Praxis*, Reiss p. 80, Ak. VIII: 298; cf. MdS R, § 49, General Remark C, Reiss pp. 149 f., Ak. VI: 325 f.

40 *Ibid.*, cf. MdS R, § 49, General Remark B, Reiss p. 149, Ak. VI: 325.

41 MdS R, § 52, Reiss p. 164, Ak. VI: 341 f.

42 MdS R, Introduction, Ak. VI: 237.

43 MdS R, §§ 8, 9, 44.

44 Ak. XXIII: 351; MdS R, § 41, Ak. VI: 306; MdS R, § 46, Reiss p. 139, Ak. VI: 313 f.

45 *Theorie und Praxis*, Reiss p. 79, Ak. VIII: 297; MdS R, §§ 47 and 52, Reiss pp. 140 and 162, Ak. VI: 315 and 339.

46 *Idee zu einer allgemeinen Geschichte in weltbürgerlicher Absicht*, Beck pp. 17 f., Reiss p. 46, Ak. VIII: 23 (translation by Beck).

47 *Theorie und Praxis*, Reiss p. 74, Ak. VIII: 291; MdS R, § 49, Reiss p. 141, Ak. VI: 316 f.

48 *Zum ewigen Frieden*, Reiss p. 101, Ak. VIII: 352.

49 *Ibid.*, *loc. cit.* and also Reiss p. 118, Beck p. 120, Ak. VIII: 372; *Streit der Facultäten*, Reiss p. 184, Beck p. 147, Ak. VII: 88.

50 Cf. also MdS R, § 46, Reiss pp. 139 f., Ak. VI: 314 f.

51 MdS R, § 61; *Zum ewigen Frieden*, Reiss pp. 103 and 105, Beck pp. 98 f. and 101 f., Ak. VIII: 354 f. and 357.

52 MdS R, § 62, Reiss p. 175, Ak. VI: 355.

53 *Idee zu einer allgemeinen Geschichte*, esp. Ninth Thesis; *Theorie und Praxis*, Reiss pp. 90 f., Ak. VIII: 311 f.; KdU § 83, Ak. V: 432 f.

54 *Streit der Facultäten*, Reiss p. 182, Beck p. 144, Ak. VII: 85.

55 *Streit der Facultäten*, Reiss p. 185, Beck pp. 147 f., Ak. VII: 88 (translation from Beck).

XII God

1 Hume, *Dialogues concerning Natural Religion*, part XII, p. 264 in Kemp Smith's edition.

2 Cf. A 559/B 587; A 562/B 590.

3 A 605 ff./B 633 ff.; Descartes, *Meditation* V.

4 A 598/B 626.

5 Refl. 6214, Ak. XVIII: 503; Refl. 6247, Ak. XVIII: 526; cf. KdU, General Remark on Teleology, Ak. V: 475 f.

6 Thus A 607/B 635.

7 KdU, § 75.

8 KdU, § 83, Ak. V: 432 f.

9 KdU, § 75, Ak. V: 400; KdU, § 77, Ak. V: 405 f. and 409 f.

10 KdU, § 78, Ak. V: 414.

11 KdU, § 80, Ak. V: 419 f.; cf. KdU, § 73, Ak. V: 393.

12 A 686 ff./B 714 ff.

13 A 127; B 165; A 766/B 794; KdU, Introduction § IV, Ak. V: 180, and § V, Ak. V: 183 ff.; *Prolegomena*, § 36, Lucas p. 80, Ak. IV: 318.

14 A 451/B 479; cf. C. Wolff, *Ontologia*, §§ 77 and 498.

15 MAdN, Preface, also Ak. IV: 519 and 543; Ak. XXI: 311. Though he also occasionally uses the phrase 'a priori natural science' and its equivalent 'pure natural science' to refer to something more general still: that set of unequivocally a priori truths which are constitutive of the world of appearances and which we do contribute to it, viz. the principles of pure understanding and whatever consequences they directly entail. Thus *Prolegomena*, § 15, Ak. IV: 294 f.

16 MAdN, Preface, Ak. IV: 470; A 848/B 876.

17 Ak. IV: 490 ff.
18 It appears to have been the intention of his projected late work *The Transition from the Metaphysical Foundations of Natural Science to Physics* to carry this on through a similar but more extended examination of the concept of force. See Ak. XXI–XXII.
19 On this see further my article 'The Status of Kant's Theory of Matter', *Synthese* 23 (1971), pp. 121–6. Cf. also above, pp. 34–7.
20 Ak. IV: 544 f.
21 And cf. KdU, Introduction § IV, Ak. V: 180.
22 A 652 ff./B 680 ff.; KdU, Introduction § V, Ak. V: 185.
23 See above, pp. 25 f.
24 N. Goodman, *Fact, Fiction, and Forecast*, pp. 72–81.
25 Sometimes they miss it, or avoid it, by defining 'grue' in such a way that the problem disappears. This is true, for example, of Barker and Achinstein, 'On the New Riddle of Induction', *Philosophical Review* 69 (1960), pp. 511–22 esp. p. 514; reprinted in P. H. Nidditch, *The Philosophy of Science*, Oxford University Press, 1968, esp. p. 152. On this matter generally, cf. S. W. Blackburn, 'Goodman's Paradox', *American Philosophical Quarterly* Monograph 3 (1969), pp. 128–42, esp. pp. 137 ff.
26 S. W. Blackburn, *op. cit.*, and also his *Reason and Prediction*, Cambridge University Press, 1973, ch. 4.
27 W. V. Quine, *Ontological Relativity and Other Essays*, Columbia University Press, New York, 1969, p. 126.
28 To Marcus Herz, 21 February 1772, Ak. X: 130 ff. (124 ff.); B 166 f.
29 Kant's phrase: Ak. XX: 285.
30 Hume, *Dialogues concerning Natural Religion*, part V, part X; *Enquiry concerning the Human Understanding*, § XI.

Bibliography

I Works by Kant

Kant's gesammelte Schriften, ed. by the *Königlich Preussische Akademie der Wissenschaften* and its successors. Georg Reimer (subsequently W. de Gruyter), Berlin, 1902– .

Der Duisburg'sche Nachlass und Kants Kritizismus um 1775, ed. by T. Haering, Mohr, Tübingen, 1910.

Eine Vorlesung Kants über Ethik, ed. by P. Menzer, Pan, Berlin, 1924.

The following books contain several of Kant's works in translation; they are referred to below and in the notes simply by the name of the editor:

Abbott, T. K., *Kant's Critique of Practical Reason and Other Works on the Theory of Ethics*, Longmans, London, 1873; 6th ed., 1909.

Beck, L. W., *et al.*, *Kant: on History*, Bobbs-Merrill, Indianapolis, 1963.

Kerferd, G. B., & Walford, D. E., *Kant: Selected Pre-Critical Writings*, Manchester University Press, 1968.

Reiss, H. B., *Kant's Political Writings*, tr. by H. B. Nisbet, Cambridge University Press, 1971.

Those works of Kant's which are mentioned in the text or notes and which are available in English translation are:

Principiorum primorum cognitionis metaphysicae Nova Dilucidatio (1755)
  in F. E. England, *Kant's Conception of God*, Allen & Unwin, London, 1929.

Beobachtungen über das Gefühl des Schönen und Erhabenen (1763)
  tr. by J. T. Goldthwait, as *Observations on the Feeling of the Beautiful and Sublime*, University of California Press, Berkeley, 1965.

Untersuchung über die Deutlichkeit der Grundsätze der natürlichen Theologie und der Moral (1764)
  in Kerferd & Walford, as *Enquiry concerning the Clarity of the Principles of Natural Theology and Ethics*.
  in L. W. Beck, *Kant's Critique of Practical Reason and Other Writings in Moral Philosophy*, University of Chicago Press, 1949, as *An Inquiry into the Distinctness of the Fundamental Principles of Natural Theology and Morals*.

Träume eines Geistersehers, erläutert durch Träume der Metaphysik (1766)
tr. by E. F. Goerwitz as *Dreams of a Spirit-Seer*, Swan Sonnenschein, London, 1900.
Von dem ersten Grunde des Unterschiedes der Gegenden im Raume (1768)
in Kerferd & Walford, as *Concerning the Ultimate Foundation of the Differentiation of Regions in Space.*
De mundi sensibilis atque intelligibilis forma et principiis (1770)
in Kerferd & Walford, as *The Inaugural Dissertation.*
Eine Vorlesung über Ethik (c. 1780)
tr. by L. Infield as *Lectures on Ethics*, Methuen, London, 1930.
Kritik der reinen Vernunft (1781 and 1787)
tr. by N. Kemp Smith as *Immanuel Kant's Critique of Pure Reason*, Macmillan, London, 1929.
Prolegomena (1783)
tr. by P. G. Lucas, Manchester University Press, 1953.
tr. by L. W. Beck, Liberal Arts, New York, 1950.
Idee zu einer allgemeinen Geschichte in weltbürgerlicher Absicht (1784)
in Beck, as *Idea for a Universal History.*
in Reiss.
Grundlegung zur Metaphysik der Sitten (1785)
tr. by H. J. Paton as *The Moral Law*, Hutchinson, London, 1948.
tr. by L. W. Beck as *Foundations of the Metaphysics of Morals*, Liberal Arts, New York, 1959; also in his *Kant's Critique of Practical Reason and Other Writings in Moral Philosophy.*
in Abbott, as *Fundamental Principles of the Metaphysic of Morals.*
Metaphysische Anfangsgründe der Naturwissenschaft (1786)
tr. by J. Ellington as *Metaphysical Foundations of Natural Science*, Liberal Arts, Indianapolis, 1970.
Kritik der praktischen Vernunft (1788)
in Abbott.
tr. by L. W. Beck in his *Kant's Critique of Practical Reason and Other Writings in Moral Philosophy*, Chicago University Press, 1949.
Erste Einleitung in die Kritik der Urteilskraft (1790)
tr. by J. Haden as *First Introduction to the Critique of Judgment*, Liberal Arts, Indianapolis, 1965.
Kritik der Urtheilskraft (1790)
tr. by J. C. Meredith, Oxford University Press, 1928.
tr. by J. H. Bernard, 2nd ed., Macmillan, London, 1914.
Über eine Entdeckung (1790)
tr. by H. E. Allison, in *The Kant-Eberhard Controversy*, Johns Hopkins, Baltimore, 1973.
Die Religion innerhalb der Grenzen der blossen Vernunft (1793)
tr. by T. M. Greene and H. H. Hudson as *Religion within the Limits of Reason Alone*, Open Court, Chicago, 1934.
Über den Gemeinspruch: Das mag in der Theorie richtig sein, taugt aber nicht für die Praxis (1793) (for short, *Theorie und Praxis*)
in Reiss, as *On the Common Saying* etc.
Zum ewigen Frieden (1795)

in Reiss, as *Perpetual Peace.*

in Beck; also in Beck's *Kant's Critique of Practical Reason* etc.

Die Metaphysik der Sitten (1797)

much of the first part, the *Rechtslehre*, is tr. by J. Ladd as *The Metaphysical Elements of Justice*, Liberal Arts, Indianapolis, 1965.

the second part, the *Tugendlehre,* is tr. by M. J. Gregor as *The Doctrine of Virtue*, Harper, New York, 1964.

excerpts from the *Rechtslehre* in Reiss.

Über ein vermeintes Recht aus Menschenliebe zu lügen (1797)

in Abbott, as *On a Supposed Right* etc.

in Beck's *Kant's Critique of Practical Reason* etc.

Der Streit der Facultäten (1798)

part in Reiss, as *The Contest of Faculties.*

part in Beck.

Anthropologie in pragmatischer Hinsicht (1798)

tr. by M. J. Gregor as *Anthropology from a Pragmatic Point of View*, Nijhoff, The Hague, 1974.

Logik (compiled 1800)

tr. by R. S. Hartman and W. Schwartz, as *Kant's Logic*, Liberal Arts, Indianapolis, 1974.

Correspondence

selections in Kerferd & Walford.

more extensive selections tr. by A. Zweig in *Kant: Philosophical Correspondence 1759–99*, University of Chicago Press, 1967.

II General bibliography

Adickes, Erich, *Kant und das Ding an sich,* Pan, Berlin, 1924.

Adickes, Erich, *Kant als Naturforscher*, 2 vols., de Gruyter, Berlin, 1924–5.

Beck, Lewis White, *A Commentary on Kant's Critique of Practical Reason,* University of Chicago Press, 1960.

Beck, Lewis White, 'The Second Analogy and the Principle of Indeterminacy', *Kant-Studien* 57 (1966), pp. 199–205; also in Penelhum and MacIntosh (eds), *The First Critique* (see below).

Beck, Lewis White, (ed.) *Kant Studies Today,* Open Court, La Salle, 1969.

Beck, Lewis White, *Early German Philosophy*: *Kant and his Predecessors,* Belknap, Cambridge, Mass., 1969.

Bennett, J. F., *Kant's Analytic,* Cambridge University Press, 1966.

Bennett, J. F., 'Strawson on Kant', Philosophical Review 77 (1968), pp. 340–9.

Bennett, J. F., 'The Difference between Right and Left', *American Philosophical Quarterly* 7 (1970), pp. 175–91.

Bennett, J. F., *Kant's Dialectic,* Cambridge University Press, 1974.

Bird, G., *Kant's Theory of Knowledge,* Routledge & Kegan Paul, London, 1962.

Broad, C. D., *Five Types of Ethical Theory,* Kegan Paul, London, 1930, ch. 5.

Buchdahl, G., 'The Relation between "Understanding" and "Reason" in the Architectonic of Kant's Philosophy', *Proceedings of the Aristotelian Society* 67 (1966–7), pp. 209–26.

Buchdahl, G., *Metaphysics and the Philosophy of Science,* Blackwell, Oxford, 1969, ch. 8.

Chipman, L., 'Kant's Categories and their Schematism', *Kant-Studien* 63 (1972), pp. 36–50.

Chipman, L., 'Things in Themselves', *Philosophy and Phenomenological Research* 33 (1972–3), pp. 489–502.

Craig, E. J., 'Phenomenal Geometry', *British Journal for the Philosophy of Science* 20 (1969), pp. 121–34.

Crawford, D. W., *Kant's Aesthetic Theory,* University of Wisconsin Press, Madison, 1974.

Crusius, Christian August, *Entwurf der nothwendigen Vernunft-Wahrheiten,* Leipzig, 1745.

Crusius, Christian August, *Weg zur Gewissheit und Zuverlässigkeit der menschlichen Erkenntnis,* Leipzig, 1747.

Delekat, Friedrich, *Immanuel Kant,* 2nd ed., Quelle & Meyer, Heidelberg, 1966.

Descartes, René, *Meditationes de Prima Philosophia,* Paris, 1641.

Duncan, A. R. C., *Practical Reason and Morality,* Nelson, London, 1957.

Earman, J., 'Kant, Incongruous Counterparts, and the Nature of Space and Space-Time', *Ratio* 13 (1971), pp. 1–18.

Ewing, A. C., *A Short Commentary on Kant's Critique of Pure Reason,* Methuen, London, 1938.

Goodman, Nelson, *Fact, Fiction, and Forecast,* 2nd ed., Bobbs-Merrill, Indianapolis, 1965.

Gram, M. S., *Kant: Disputed Questions,* Quadrangle, Chicago, 1967.

Gregor, M. J., *Laws of Freedom,* Blackwell, Oxford, 1963.

Hacker, P. M. S., 'Are Transcendental Arguments a Version of Verificationism?' *American Philosophical Quarterly* 9 (1972), pp. 78–85.

Hare, R. M., *Freedom and Reason,* Oxford University Press, 1963.

Harrison, Ross, *On What There Must Be,* Oxford University Press, 1974.

Henrich, Dieter, *Identität und Objektivität*, Carl Winter, Heidelberg, 1976.

Hintikka, Jaakko, 'On Kant's Notion of Intuition', in Penelhum and MacIntosh, (eds.), *The First Critique* (see below).

Hopkins, G. J., 'Visual Geometry', *Philosophical Review* 82 (1973), pp. 3–34.

Hume, David, *A Treatise of Human Nature,* London, 1739–40; ed. by L. A. Selby-Bigge, Oxford University Press, 1888.

Hume, David, *Enquiry concerning the Human Understanding,* London, 1748; ed. by L. A. Selby-Bigge, 2nd ed., Oxford University Press, 1902.

Hume, David, *Dialogues concerning Natural Religion,* London, 1779; ed. by N. Kemp Smith, Oxford University Press, 1935.

Kemp, J., 'Kant's Examples of the Categorical Imperative, *Philosophical Quarterly* 8 (1958), pp. 63–71; also in R. P. Wolff, *Kant* (see below).

Kemp, J., *The Philosophy of Kant,* Oxford University Press, 1968.

Körner, S., *Kant,* Penguin, Harmondsworth, 1955.

Körner, S., 'Kant's Conception of Freedom', *Proceedings of the British Academy* 53 (1967), pp. 193–217.

Körner, S., 'The Impossibility of Transcendental Deductions', *Monist* 51 (1967), pp. 317–31; also in Beck, *Kant Studies Today* (see above).

Leibniz, Gottfried Wilhelm, Freiherr von, *Die philosophischen Schriften,* ed. by C. J. Gerhardt, 7 vols., Weidmann, Berlin, 1875–90.

Leibniz, Gottfried Wilhelm, Freiherr von, *A Collection of Papers which passed between the late Learned Mr Leibnitz and Dr Clarke,* London, 1717; ed. by H. G. Alexander, Manchester University Press, 1956.

Lucas, J. R., *A Treatise on Time and Space,* Methuen, London, 1973.

McFarland, J. D., *Kant's Concept of Teleology,* Edinburgh University Press, 1970.

Mackie, J. L., *The Cement of the Universe,* Oxford University Press, 1974, ch. 4.

Matthews, H. E., 'Strawson on Transcendental Idealism', *Philosophical Quarterly* 19 (1969), pp. 204–20.

Nell, Onora, *Acting on Principle,* Columbia University Press, New York, 1975.

Nerlich, Graham, *The Shape of Space,* Cambridge University Press, 1976.

Newton, Sir Isaac, *Mathematical Principles of Natural Philosophy,* tr. by A. Motte, London, 1727; revised by F. Cajori, 2 vols., University of California Press, Berkeley, 1934.

Parsons, C., 'Kant's Philosophy of Arithmetic', in Morgenbesser, Suppes and White, (eds.), *Philosophy, Science and Method,* Macmillan, London, 1971.

Paton, H. J., 'The Key to Kant's Deduction of the Categories', *Mind* N. S. 40 (1931), pp. 310–29; also in Gram, *Kant: Disputed Questions* (see above).

Paton, H. J., *The Categorical Imperative,* Hutchinson, London, 1946.

Penelhum, T. and MacIntosh, J. J. (eds.) *The First Critique,* Wadsworth, Belmont, 1969.

Quinton, A., 'Spaces and Times', *Philosophy* 37 (1962), pp. 130–47.

Reichenbach, Hans, *The Philosophy of Space and Time,* tr. by M. Reichenbach and J. Freund, Dover, New York, 1957.

Remnant, P., 'Incongruent Counterparts and Absolute Space', *Mind* N.S. 72 (1963), pp. 393–9.

Silber, J. R., 'The Importance of the Highest Good in Kant's Ethics', *Ethics* 73 (1962), pp. 179–97.

Singer, M. G., *Generalization in Ethics,* Eyre & Spottiswoode, London, 1963.

Smith, Norman Kemp, *A Commentary to Kant's 'Critique of Pure Reason',* 2nd ed., Macmillan, London, 1923.

Strawson, Sir P. F., *Individuals,* Methuen, London, 1959.

Strawson, Sir P. F., *The Bounds of Sense,* Methuen, London, 1966.

Strawson, Sir P. F., 'Bennett on Kant's Analytic', *Philosophical Review* 77 (1968), pp. 332–9.

Strawson, Sir P. F., 'Imagination and Perception', in Foster and Swanson, eds., *Experience and Theory,* Duckworth, London, 1970; also in Strawson, *Freedom and Resentment,* Methuen, London, 1974.

Stroud, Barry, 'Transcendental Arguments', *Journal of Philosophy* 65 (1968), pp. 241–56; also in Penelhum and MacIntosh, (eds.), *The First Critique* (see above).

Swinburne, R., 'Times', *Analysis* 25 (1964–5), pp. 185–91.

Swinburne, R., 'Conditions for Bitemporality', *Analysis* 26 (1965–6), pp. 47–50.

Swinburne, R., *Space and Time,* Macmillan, London, 1968.

Thompson, M., 'Singular Terms and Intuitions in Kant's Epistemology', *Review of Metaphysics* 26 (1972–3), pp. 314–43.

Vaihinger, Hans, *Kommentar zu Kants Kritik der reinen Vernunft*, 2nd ed., Union Deutsche Verlagsgesellschaft, Stuttgart, Berlin and Leipzig, 2 vols., 1922.

Vaihinger, Hans, 'The Transcendental Deduction of the Categories in the First Edition of the *Critique of Pure Reason*', in Gram, *Kant: Disputed Questions* (see above), tr. by Gram from an essay first published in 1902.

de Vleeschauwer, H. J., *La Déduction transcendentale dans l'oeuvre de Kant*, Leroux, De Sikkel and Nijhoff, Paris, Antwerp and The Hague, 3 vols., 1934–7.

de Vleeschauwer, H. J., *The Development of Kantian Thought*, tr. by A. R. C. Duncan, Nelson, Edinburgh, 1962.

de Vleeschauwer, H. J., 'Wie ich jetzt die Kritik der reinen Vernunft entwicklungsgeschichtlich lese', *Kant-Studien* 54 (1962–3), pp. 351–68.

Walsh, W. H., 'Philosophy and Psychology in Kant's *Critique*', *Kant-Studien* 57 (1966), pp. 186–98.

Walsh, W. H., 'Kant on the Perception of Time', *Monist* 51 (1967), pp. 376–96; also in Beck, *Kant Studies Today*, and Penelhum and MacIntosh, (eds.), *The First Critique* (see above).

Walsh, W. H., *Kant's Criticism of Metaphysics*, Edinburgh University Press, 1975.

Ward, K., *The Development of Kant's View of Ethics*, Blackwell, Oxford, 1972.

Warnock, G. J., 'Concepts and Schematism', *Analysis* 9 (1948–9), pp. 77–82.

Weldon, T. D., *Kant's Critique of Pure Reason*, 2nd ed., Oxford University Press, 1958.

Wilkerson, T. E., 'Transcendental Arguments', *Philosophical Quarterly* 20 (1970), pp. 200–12.

Wilkerson, T. E., *Kant's Critique of Pure Reason*, Oxford University Press, 1976.

Williams, T. C., *The Concept of the Categorical Imperative*, Oxford University Press, 1968.

Wolff, Christian, Freiherr von, *Philosophia Prima sive Ontologia*, new ed., Renger, Frankfurt and Leipzig, 1736.

Wolff, Christian, Freiherr von, *Vernünfftige Gedancken von Gott, der Welt, und der Seele des Menschen*, new ed., Renger, Halle, 1751.

Wolff, Robert Paul, *Kant's Theory of Mental Activity*, Harvard University Press, 1963.

Wolff, Robert Paul, (ed.) *Kant*, Doubleday Anchor, New York, 1967.

Wolff, Robert Paul, *The Autonomy of Reason*, Harper, New York, 1973.

Index